In a Madhouse's Din

In a Madhouse's Din

Civil Rights Coverage by Mississippi's Daily Press, 1948–1968

SUSAN WEILL

Foreword by Ira Harkey

PRAEGER

Westport, Connecticut
London

Library of Congress Cataloging-in-Publication Data

Weill, Susan, 1953–
In a madhouse's din : civil rights coverage by Mississippi's daily press, 1948–1968 / Susan Weill ; foreword by Ira Harkey.
p. cm.
Includes bibliographical references (p.) and index.
ISBN 0–275–96960–6 (alk. paper)
1. African Americans—Civil rights—Mississippi—History—20th century. 2. African Americans—Press coverage—Mississippi—History—20th century. 3. Civil rights movements—Mississippi—History—20th century. 4. Editorials—Mississippi—History—20th century. 5. American newspapers—Mississippi—History—20th century. 6. Journalism—Mississippi—History—20th century. 7. Mississippi—Race relations. I. Title.
E185.93.M6W35 2002
323.1'1960730762'09045—dc21 2001036710

British Library Cataloguing in Publication Data is available.

Library of Congress Catalog Card Number: 2001036710
ISBN: 0–275–96960–6

First published in 2002

Praeger Publishers, 88 Post Road West, Westport, CT 06881
An imprint of Greenwood Publishing Group, Inc.
www.praeger.com

Printed in the United States of America

The paper used in this book complies with the Permanent Paper Standard issued by the National Information Standards Organization (Z39.48–1984).

10 9 8 7 6 5 4 3 2 1

This book is dedicated to the people in Mississippi who have learned to see beyond race.

Contents

Foreword

2 Men Escape in Car Crash, Negro Killed
—from a headline in a Mississippi newspaper in the 1960s

Younger non-Southerners may be baffled by the headline's implication that the unfortunate Negro was not also a "man."

The news item that followed gave full identification of the "men," who were not hurt, including their names, addresses and occupations. The dead Negro was identified only as a "yard boy" employed by one of the "men." Readers assumed the "men" were white because they were called men, not Negroes or "colored." In the conventional parlance of the time and place, the dead person was "just a nigger," worth no more space.

There are few bald examples, in this book by Susan Weill, of the age-old anti-Negro journalism of the kind in the headline mentioned above. The most virulent newspaper "racial haters" are examined and analyzed without rancor. James Ward, Fred Sullins, Tom Etheridge, the Hedermans and others are here, but they are not discussed in detail as the un-American disgraces their writing revealed them to be. Their racist legacy is recorded in their own words because Weill is a journalist who believes the readers should be given the facts and allowed to decide for themselves.

Daily newspapers were the most powerful force fostering retention of Jim Crow laws, which excluded the Negro from almost every good in public life. Using the newspapers, and being used by them, were the politicians, school leaders, lawyers and, incredibly, many churches. So closely did those four emulate the malevolent lead of the daily newspapers that it seems impossible to consider the five apart. Constant degradation of the Negro by these pervasive groups kept alive the public scorn for blacks, leading to unreasoned hatred.

Politicians seemed to run *against* Negroes instead of *for* office, and campaigners who expressed the deepest hate often gained election. Throughout the din of "nigger, nigger, nigger," the state's Negroes said little to nothing—until one day a wearier-than-usual Rosa Parks boarded a streetcar in neighboring Alabama.

White preachers discovered divine authority to treat Negroes chiefly as "drawers of water" and "hewers of wood." I could never understand what biblical commandment they used to prevent a black person's entry into a white "house of worship." During a few peaceful tests, blacks went to white churches and were invariably stopped there by sanctified bouncers often wielding baseball bats.

In 1962, an ignorant Mississippi Southern College (now the University of Southern Mississippi) faculty member spoke at Pascagoula High School and told the students there was a Communist in Mississippi and that he worked at their hometown newspaper, the *Chronicle*. I got so tired of being called Communist by purebred numskulls that I wrote in an editorial, "A Communist in Mississippi is anyone who advocates a Christian principle outside church." Very few of my readers then understood the ironic truth of that statement.

White Mississippians prided themselves on being Christians. They went to church every Sunday, Wednesdays for choir practice, and other days for various meetings. They didn't realize it, but because they barred some people—all Negroes—from any session, their churches in reality were only social clubs. The truly Christian minister who tried to open his door to a Negro was soon preaching to mules in the cotton fields, or worse.

In 1962, twenty-eight Methodist ministers in Mississippi issued a proclamation favoring racial integration. A year later, I received a letter from one of them. It was from California, the closest to home that he could find a pastorship. He wrote that all the men had been forced to leave the state to find appointments. Interestingly, the Methodist-supported Millsaps College in Jackson was one of the first white colleges in the state to accept Negro students. There were Christians out there, and they were beginning to speak.

Among Catholics there was little hysterical turmoil. I had expected Catholic churches to lead the way in reconciliation of the races as they had done in San Antonio and elsewhere in the South. At behest of the bishop of Natchez, the leader of Mississippi Catholics, the Negro Catholics maintained a quiet dignity. The bishop pointed out that the church was still on a missionary status in the state and should remain calm. Priests were told not to take part in the public frenzy that occupied so many Protestant churchmen. Without a word of opposition, my younger daughter's old Negro nurse came from New Orleans for her first communion and sat in the Pascagoula church with the "white folks."

Ridicule and scorn of the Negro were explicit and implicit in most white Mississippi schools through the 1960s. Cheers, whoops and whistles rang out in Pascagoula High School when the murder of President John Kennedy, "the great niggerlover," was announced on the loudspeaker on Monday after the deadly weekend. A Mississippi editor opposed to integration wrote that the Negro did not need better schools because "he was already getting all the education he could handle." During their shortened five- or six-month school term, black students tried to cope with tattered textbooks made almost unreadable by years of abuse in white, and then in black, schools.

Negroes in Mississippi outnumbered whites for years. Black faces were everywhere—everywhere, that is, except in white-owned newspapers, where they garnered coverage only for adversity. Few of the state's newspapers published announcements of black babies born or black marriages, but they published announcements for white babies born and white marriages. No Negro school honor rolls appeared, no cast members of the black school play, no king and queen of the black prom. But a Negro in trouble got space. A captured black fugitive even got his picture in the paper—standing in cuffs and leg irons between two grinning deputies, with a bored bloodhound lolling at his feet. A Negro would get a paragraph or two for almost any kind of infraction. If a story was about a Negro in trouble, the editors said so.

In the 1950s, my talk at the annual Mississippi Press Association convention caused a panic. They did not know what was coming when they invited me. I told them that I was going to drop the habitual "colored" tag that had followed the name of every Negro and that I would use "Negro" only when a story required a physical description. I also began using "Mrs." to designate married Negro women, instead of the usual Hattie Lewis or Minnie Jones. Few other Mississippi newspapers followed in my footsteps for nearly twenty years. I also began to seek and publish favorable stories from the Negro schools, clubs and fraternities. Dropping the Negro tag and using courtesy titles for blacks were most incendiary. In mock innocence, I explained to objecting white hordes that "Mrs." indicated only that a woman was married; it did not threaten the status quo. I told them that journalists are taught to write tight copy, not to use unnecessary words. I explained that in an ordinary story I would not use racial descriptions unless crucial to the facts, just as I would not use other physical characteristics such as fat or ugly. My lawyer, for instance, had feet that were eighteen inches long, but I never wrote a story about him that required mention of his champion underpinnings. He stormed into my office one day. "Harkey, put nigger back into the *Chronicle*," he shouted. "I want to know if I'm reading about a nigger so I can throw the paper down."

By alluding to my attorney, I feel I must also mention the other "champions of justice" in Mississippi during the years under discussion. They were busy cursing the U.S. Supreme Court. With few exceptions, they offered to defend school boards and other educational entities from the integration orders of the federal government. Rebellious words issued from judges in opening addresses at new court terms. "There is no place for moderation in the matter of segregation," said Judge O.H. Barnett in Scott County. "Segregation is right, it is Christian, and it should be taught from every pulpit in Mississippi."

Thomas P. Brady of Brookhaven, who became a member of the Mississippi Supreme Court, had written a shrill book in 1955, *Black Monday*, referring to the day in 1954 when "separate but equal" was struck down in the public schools. This morally deficient jurist was called the "elder hatesman" in my book, *The Smell of Burning Crosses: An Autobiography of a Mississippi Newspaperman* (1967). Brady's voice was an important voice on the wrong side.

Today in Mississippi, the newspapers are not recognizable from those of the 1940s, 1950s and 1960s. Most of the old, cruel sheets have been sold and are staffed by young men and women not raised during the festering days. Any old haters around know to keep their jaws locked. Northern civil rights officials now praise the once despised Mississippi for having more black elected officials than any other Southern state. Today, there are black police, sheriffs, highway patrol officers, legislators, county supervisors, mayors, superintendents of desegregated schools and, glory be, a Supreme Court justice.

This book by Susan Weill is a valuable study of the Mississippi daily newspapers' loathsome performance during the civil rights struggles of the bitter years 1948 through 1968. Her work is one of prodigious research and is presented in a fluid, readable style seldom found among academic works. She is to be both congratulated and thanked for producing this fine work on the messengers of hate who tried so long and pitilessly to keep the Negro a nigger.

Ira Harkey
Editor-Publisher
Pascagoula (Mississippi) Chronicle, 1948–1963
Winner, 1963 Pulitzer Prize for Editorial Writing

Preface

I became interested in the Southern news media as a transplanted Yankee child in rural Mississippi during the civil rights struggles of the 1960s. My parents, although from Michigan, were just as conservative about maintaining the segregated "closed society" as our Mississippi neighbors. Because we were originally from north of the Mason-Dixon Line, and teased in that regard, I decided to find out what all the commotion was about. Many Saturday mornings I walked the couple of miles into town to tag around with Paul Pittman, the editor of *The Tylertown Times*, our weekly newspaper. Mr. Paul was a fine journalist and one of my childhood heroes. He did not always agree with the social reformation being forced on the South, nor did he always think it was handled in an auspicious manner. But he thought that everyone was entitled to equal rights under the law, no matter what race they were labeled. In 1970, Tylertown High School finally desegregated. I was a member of the senior class that year, the first group of students to graduate from the desegregated Walthall County public schools. I am proud to have been part of that historic event, one marked by new friendships and greater understanding.

My interest in how equal rights and race issues are portrayed in the media led me to find no comprehensive analysis of the Mississippi daily press. What resulted, nearly a decade after a serious effort began, is this book. "In a madhouse's din" is a quote from an editorial written during the desegregation of Ole Miss by Pulitzer Prize–winning Mississippi editor Ira Harkey ("Confusing Times, Dangerous Times," Pascagoula *Chronicle*, 18 September 1962, 2). Of the thousands of editorials I perused, his four words best summarized, to my way of thinking, the three decades of civil rights struggles in Mississippi from 1948 through 1968. When I contacted

Mr. Harkey at his home in Texas and asked if he would do me the honor of writing the foreword to this book, he could not refuse. He had already written the title.

A goal of *In a Madhouse's Din* is to provide historians and media researchers access to primary information from newspapers in one of the most conservative Southern states during five critical times in the civil rights struggle: the Dixiecrat protest of the Democratic National Convention in 1948; the *Brown v. Board of Education* Supreme Court decision, which mandated desegregation of public schools in 1954; the court-ordered desegregation of Ole Miss in 1962; Freedom Summer in 1964; and the assassination of civil rights activist Martin Luther King, Jr., in 1968. Included are thousands of excerpts from news articles, syndicated columnists and editorials from the Mississippi daily press. Complete and detailed notes are offered at the conclusion of every chapter.

Each time period offered the newspapers a different type of challenge. The Dixiecrat protest was a regional confrontation between the South and North that rekindled memories of a Civil War only eighty years earlier. The *Brown v. Board of Education* decree was seen as just another Supreme Court decision that would be ignored, as *Plessy v. Ferguson* had been for half a century. The desegregation of Ole Miss was different, however, because federal officials arrived in the state to carry out the court order. Freedom Summer brought passage of the Civil Rights Act of 1964 and an "invasion" of "civil rights workers." The murder of King provided the editors an opportunity to explore the concerns and demands of a growing Black Power movement, but many of them thought King was a false prophet, an advocate of non-violence who instigated violence wherever he went.

To most editors of the Mississippi daily press during these time periods, blacks and whites were not ready for the reality of the integrated society proposed by King in 1968, the civil rights workers in 1964, James Meredith in 1962, the Supreme Court in 1954 or President Harry Truman in 1948. The editors thought national civil rights laws unjustly usurped states' and individual rights and had become a way to "court" black votes. According to the vast majority of the Mississippi daily press editorials examined for this study from 1948 through 1968, the notion that blacks and whites were equal as races of people was a concept that remained unacceptable and inconceivable. The traditional South lived on in most editors of the Mississippi daily press between 1948 and 1968.

In a Madhouse's Din is the result of much perseverance on the part of many people and institutions. I would like to recognize my supportive colleagues at the University of Alabama at Birmingham, particularly Mark Hickson, and my University of Southern Mississippi teachers and cronies: Arthur Kaul, David Davies, Mahzahrul Haque, Gene Wiggins and the late Barbara Shoemake. I would like to thank Marian Huttenstine of Mississippi State University for her solid advice and friendship, and I would like to offer special thanks to the staffs at the Mississippi Department of Archives and History and the Mississippi Press Association. I would like to express my gratitude to Bob McElvaine, Charles Sallis and the late Ross Moore at Millsaps College, who stimulated my interest in the past, and to Robert List and Doris Saunders at Jackson State University, who encouraged my pursuit of media research. Certainly, I must thank my patient and understanding family: my children, Tao and Maya Weilundemo; my friend and husband, Gary Durr; my other support on the home front, Luke and Charlotte Lundemo; and my refuge providers, Steve Germany and Michael Burns.

I hope this book will prove useful to students of history and media studies, and I hope it will stimulate further research on equal rights and race in the media. I also hope it will help everyone who reads it to understand how powerful and corrupting the media can be when the agenda is focused on a narrow view of society.

In a Madhouse's Din

Chapter 1

Civil Rights and the Mississippi Daily Press: An Introduction

"Negroes might be national Democrats," the chairman of the Mississippi Democratic Committee said in 1954, "but they are not Mississippi Democrats. We don't intend to have them voting in this primary."[1]

A decade later, not much had changed. When a federal civil rights law was enacted by Congress in 1964, Mississippi Governor Paul Johnson, Jr., voiced his defiance in the state's daily press. "They can pass all the laws they like," Johnson said. "But they can't make us take it or like it."[2]

Black Mississippians were not considered equal citizens by their governor or by the majority of white Mississippians in 1964, although their percentage of the state's population was substantial for more than a century. Mississippi was inhabited by nearly half a million black slaves who represented more than half the populace in 1860, prior to the Civil War. In 1900, three decades after the Thirteenth Amendment to the U.S. Constitution terminated the South's "peculiar institution," blacks constituted nearly sixty percent of Mississippi's people. They began to migrate northward in hope of a better life, however, and by 1960, only forty percent of Mississippi's 2 million people were of recognized African descent.[3]

Into the 1960s, Mississippi was a farming economy permeated with a conservative white power structure and a large black underclass. Jackson, the capital, was one of the few urban areas in the state that could be called a city,[4] and the racial composition was unique to the country. In no other state did blacks constitute such a large percentage of the population as they did in Mississippi. The repression and discrimination faced by Mississippi blacks were not written into the state's laws. This was not necessary, as noted by Mississippi historian Neil McMillen. "Wherever the two races came together, the forces of social habit and white opinion were in themselves usually sufficient to ensure that the races knew their places and occupied them with neither statute nor a 'white' or a 'colored' sign to direct the way," he wrote.[5]

The black flight out of Mississippi in search of a better life was a quest for civil rights—the right to equal legal, social and economic opportunity. Civil rights were slow in coming to people of color in the South. Black men were granted suffrage by Congress with passage of the 1867 Reconstruction Acts, and that year more than 60,000 emancipated slaves registered to vote in Mississippi.[6] By 1954, however, because of intimidation, restrictive poll taxes and violence by groups such as the Ku Klux Klan, the number of Mississippi blacks registered to vote had dropped to 20,000. "Most blacks were afraid to try to register, or to vote, and with reason," wrote historian John Dittmer. "Moreover, with all the state and local candidates for office pledged to maintain white supremacy, there was simply no one to vote for. No candidate dared to seek the black vote."[7] Also in 1954, the U.S. Supreme Court ruled against the legality of segregation in public schools. *Brown v. Board of Education* was greeted with outrage and contempt by most white Mississippians, including Governor Hugh White, who remarked, "We shall resist by every legal means at our command."[8]

Eight years later, in 1962, a ruling by the Fifth Circuit Court in New Orleans ordered the University of Mississippi to accept its first black student of record. Mississippi Governor Ross Barnett continued a long tradition of gubernatorial defiance toward segregation when he responded to the court order, "I'll go to jail before mixing schools."[9] Barnett was praised by the Jackson *Clarion-Ledger* as "courageous,"[10] and "fearless."[11]

Two years later, Freedom Summer blasted across the state, changing the fabric of Mississippi society and raising national and international awareness of the plight of the state's blacks. Mississippi Governor Paul B. Johnson, Jr., responded negatively to Freedom Summer projects, labeled the Civil Rights Act of 1964 "unconstitutional,"[12] and advocated "noncompliance."[13] Two years later, when Martin Luther King, Jr., was assassinated in Memphis, the Mississippi daily press had little sympathy for him. During Freedom Summer, King had been branded "the Rev. Dr. Extremist Agitator Martin Luther King junior" by the Jackson *Daily News*."[14]

How the Mississippi daily press documented King's murder, as well as the Dixiecrat protest of President Harry Truman's civil rights platform in 1948, the *Brown v. Board of Education* decision in 1954, the desegregation of Ole Miss in 1962, and Freedom Summer in 1964, has been evaluated to some extent from the perspective of several of the state's newspapers, but never from a complete analysis of the Mississippi daily press. A comprehensive investigation of that nature is the purpose of this book.

CIVIL RIGHTS AND AMERICAN LAW

The first federal statutes to mandate equal rights for blacks were instituted following the Civil War in 1865. The burning question then, which remained a century later, was, "Can racial equality really be achieved through the legislative process?" The Civil Rights Act of 1875 stated: "That all persons within the jurisdiction of the United States shall be entitled to the full and equal enjoyment of the accommodations, advantages, facilities and privileges of inns, public conveyances on land or water, theaters and other places of public amusement, subject only to the conditions and limitations established by law, and applicable alike to all citizens of every race and color, regardless of any previous condition of servitude."[15]

The Civil Rights Act of 1875 was the result of a decade of hard work by the Radical Republicans, and it has been called "the historical bridge between the Fourteenth Amendment [citizenship rights not to be abridged] and the Civil Rights Act of 1964,"[16] because it was the last legislation of its kind until 1957. Public opposition in 1875 eliminated the possibility of desegregation in schools and cemeteries, and what was left to the act was quickly castrated by not only Congress but the Supreme Court, as well.

The Voting Rights Act of 1957 created a Civil Rights Division in the Justice Department, which was to assist in federal enforcement of the Fifteenth Amendment [the right to vote not denied or abridged on account of race], but the act was so convoluted as to be considered a Southern victory. The Civil Rights Act of 1964, however, was another story. It is considered "the most significant civil rights legislation since the post–Civil War period,"[17] particularly because of the change in the national social climate into which it was introduced. The Civil Rights Act of 1968 furthered legal equality, and was signed into law shortly after the assassination of Martin Luther King, Jr.

CIVIL RIGHTS AND AMERICAN PRESS COVERAGE: AN OVERVIEW

Civil rights controversies were among the ongoing media sagas of the 1940s, 1950s and 1960s.[18] The Southern press in general and the Mississippi press in particular took a national beating during those years. "There are, of course, editors and reporters in Mississippi who are a credit to their profession," *Nation* magazine reported, "but, by and large, the press, confronted with a unique opportunity to exhibit the prime editorial virtues of courage, good sense and leadership, has turned in an ignoble performance."[19] The newspapers referenced in *Nation* are the Jackson *Clarion-Ledger* and the Jackson *Daily News*, the two most widely circulated daily newspapers in the state.

During the years of civil rights struggles, some media observers condemned Southern newspapers for their erratic reporting and inflammatory interpretation.[20] Journalist Ted Poston thought the Southern press should be castigated for the manner in which it covered the black fight for equality. "The majority of Southern editors and publishers have been cynically defending a myth they know to be untrue," he wrote in 1967, "white superiority, Negro indolence, and a baseless contention that the region's magnolia-scented values would triumph over the moral and legal might of the federal government."[21]

Southern newspapers often ignored civil rights activity. The editors' reasoning, according to media analyst John Hulteng, was that to give attention to the sit-ins, the picketing and the racial clashes would only make an unstable and potentially dangerous situation worse. The result of this censorship, Hulteng noted, was a deliberate altering of the picture of the world so far as the readers of these newspapers were permitted to perceive it. "The people in those communities, uninformed for years about the deep-seated troubles brewing in their midst, were taken by surprise when the lid could no longer be kept on," he wrote. "They were unprepared for the violent and bitter passages that followed as the civil rights movement gathered momentum in the South and throughout the nation."[22]

A civil rights activist in Mississippi agreed. "A close look at Mississippi reporting shows that the greatest fault lies in what is left out," Charles Butts wrote in 1964. "The state's press lacks any interest in exposing and dealing with serious social, economic and political problems which are constantly corroding the well-being of the people."[23]

Eugene Methvin, a senior editor of *Reader's Digest*, thought Southern journalists viewed themselves as protectors of their community's state of mind,[24] but journalist Ben Bagdikian does not agree. "Those of us who covered the early days of the civil rights movement well remember being scolded by authorities for giving voice to 'radicals' Thurgood Marshall and Martin Luther King because they did not represent the Negro community," he wrote. "We were urged to listen only to the 'real' leaders, who were saying that 'their' Negroes were happy with things as they were."[25]

Poston thought the problem was primarily with the editors and publishers of the Southern press, not with the working journalists. "I sometimes feel apologetic when I glance at the awards I won for coverage of racial developments in the South, for the facts in the cited series were not always a result of my reportorial brilliance," he wrote. "They were usually given to me by frustrated young reporters on the scene who knew what was going on, but whose editors would never let them print it."[26]

Other observers have determined that the Southern press "did an adequate job."[27] They maintain that while most Southern newspapers were averse to desegregation, as espoused in their editorials, and while they failed to offer much interpretive evaluation, they generally did a competent job of reporting the facts regarding the struggle for civil rights.

Although the Southern press has often found itself the target of scorn regarding coverage of civil rights issues, the Mississippi press is usually viewed with particular disdain.[28] Most of the state's newspapers, according to historian James Silver, stood "vigilant guard over the racial, economic, political, and religious orthodoxy" of the state.[29] Hodding Carter III, of the Greenville *Delta Democrat-Times*, agreed with this analysis and conceded, "None of us began to meet our responsibilities in the media and most of us still don't."[30]

Aaron Henry, Mississippi National Association for the Advancement of Colored People (NAACP) president from 1960 to 1994, thought the state's newspapers failed miserably in covering issues of relevance to the black community.[31] Henry had an arguable position, for the Mississippi daily press between 1948 and 1968 presented a clear illustration of what the 1968 President's National Advisory Commission on Civil Disorders, the Kerner Commission, called "the 'white press,' a press that repeatedly, if unconsciously, reflects the biases, the paternalism and the indifference of white America."[32]

The Southern press has been criticized for segregating news of the black community or ignoring it altogether. Looking back on his years as editor of his father's newspaper, the McComb *Enterprise-Journal*, John Emmerich said, "The only real news of blacks was when black activities or black interests somehow affected the white society and then probably we'd cover it."[33] This lack of coverage of the black community has been blamed for fanning the flames of a situation described by the Kerner Commission. "The absence of Negro faces and activities from the media has an effect on white audiences as well as black," the commission reported. "If what the white American reads in the newspapers or sees on television conditions his expectation of what is ordinary and normal in the larger society, he will neither understand nor accept the black American."[34]

Another criticism of the Mississippi daily press regarding coverage of the civil rights struggle was its failure to provide an understanding of race relations.[35] Because the story of black Mississippians had been disregarded for so long, the press was unprepared and uncertain how to deal with it.[36] By the time the state's newspapers began reporting adequately on the civil rights struggle, the movement had basically dissolved.[37]

There is another reason for what appears to have been a failure by the Mississippi daily press between 1948 and 1968 to better serve its black readers. Mississippi is primarily a rural state, and the editors and publishers of the Mississippi daily press between 1948 and 1968 were influenced by the conservative social values affiliated with the traditions of the rural South.[38] Besides being concerned about the reputation that they maintained in their communities, the editors and publishers were businesspeople out to sell a product. They were susceptible to the opinions and pressures directed at them by their advertisers and their subscribers.[39] "The press does not often have to be nudged to mind its manners," wrote media critic V.O.

Key, Jr. "In the long run, when the chips are down on the basic issues, the press has to be on the side of its advertisers as a class."[40]

THE MISSISSIPPI DAILY PRESS, 1948–1968

During the 1940s, 1950s and 1960s, there were nineteen or twenty daily newspapers in Mississippi, depending on the year, and Jackson was home of the two most widely circulated. The Jackson *Daily News* was established in 1892 in the back room of a bank building, and the newspaper gained the vociferous editorial voice of Frederick Sullens in 1904. Three years later Sullens was the publisher, and for the next half century, the Jackson *Daily News* was his mouthpiece. In his editorials and front-page column, "The Lowdown on Higher-Ups," politicians and federal laws were often the objects of his contempt. One local legend holds that Sullens, not a writer to hide behind his words, confronted Mississippi Governor Paul Johnson, Sr. (1940–1943), in the lobby of a Jackson hotel and broke a walking cane across the governor's back.[41] Other than political venom, the concept of desegregation on any level brought Sullens' poison pen to its most potent. His view was that integration would lead to "social equality in all its uglier forms."[42]

Across town, the equally conservative Hederman family owned and edited the Jackson *Clarion-Ledger*, a paper founded in 1837 in Jasper County and moved to the capital in 1865.[43] The Hedermans were despised by Sullens, and not long after the Dixiecrat walkout in 1948, they began secretly acquiring Jackson *Daily News* stock. When the plan was discovered by Sullens, he took the Hedermans to court and won the case, but he also went broke because of accrued legal debts. In August 1954, an elderly and ailing Sullens finally sold the Jackson *Daily News* to the Hedermans. He announced the decision to his flabbergasted staff. "You may think I prostituted myself," he said. "If so, I'm the highest paid he-whore in Mississippi."[44]

East of Jackson, almost to the Alabama line in Meridian, James H. Skewes, a Wisconsin newspaperman, bought the *Meridian Star* in 1922.[45] Skewes was firmly at the helm until 1958, and he had no qualms about making his editorial opinions known. Although his prose was sometimes difficult to comprehend because of his erratic writing style, Skewes' ideas came across loud and clear. There was no uncertainty that strides toward civil rights were viewed in an almost paranoid manner by Skewes, as stated in his editorial banner, "We Rise to Defend our Anglo-Saxon Way of Life."[46]

South from Meridian into the Piney Woods region of the state is Laurel, where the *Laurel Leader-Call* was first published as a weekly in 1896 known as *The Hustler*. The newspaper went through several hands and several name changes. In 1911, Edgar Harris, the future owner of the West

Point *Times-Leader*, acquired it, and in 1926, Skewes of the *Meridian Star* purchased what had become the *Laurel Daily Argus*. In partnership with Skewes, Thomas and Harriet Gibbons became the publishers and editors, positions they held for the next thirty years. In 1930, the *Laurel Leader-Call* was born, and Harriet Gibbons was the only woman editor of a Mississippi daily newspaper from 1948 through 1968. In her own subtle and sometimes condescending way, Gibbons advocated equal rights for her black neighbors. "Most certainly our colored citizens are developing a conception of what their citizenship means and they are supported in this by their white friends," she wrote.[47]

Edgar Harris, the onetime owner of the Laurel newspaper and the publisher and editor of the West Point *Times-Leader* from 1928 to 1953,[48] was a busy man in the Mississippi newspaper world. In 1907, he co-founded the Hattiesburg Printing and Publishing Company and the weekly newspaper, *The Hattiesburg News*.[49] In 1917, during World War I, the paper was re-named the *Hattiesburg American* when the publisher, F.D. Ladner, accused of being a German sympathizer, sold the paper to Howard Williams, who made sure the new name left no question regarding national patriotism.[50] The *Hattiesburg American* advocated Southern traditions and segregation.

West from Hattiesburg into the Loess Hills region of the state, in a town that came to be known for cross burnings and firebombed churches, J.O. "Oliver" Emmerich of the McComb *Enterprise-Journal* was attacked in the street twice and had shots fired into his office for reporting local incidents of racial violence.[51] Emmerich was a former agricultural county agent and an award-winning editorial writer who published and edited the McComb *Enterprise-Journal* from 1924 until his death in 1978. A traditional states' rights Southerner, Emmerich was sometimes thought to hold moderate views on issues of racial equality.[52]

Further west in the lowlands of the Mississippi River, the *Natchez Democrat* was founded in 1865 by two soldiers returning home from the Civil War. Paul Botto and James Lambert were colleagues and friends, and Lambert's family continued to own and operate the newspaper for the next century,[53] maintaining a "South shall rise again" editorial stance.

North along the Mississippi River from Natchez in the southern region of the Mississippi Delta is Vicksburg, where the *Vicksburg Evening Post* and the *Vicksburg Herald* were owned by the Cashman family for five generations since 1883. The policy of the Vicksburg newspapers in regard to civil rights from 1948 through 1968 was to support the traditional South, though editorial silence was often a response.

North from Vicksburg into the heart of the Mississippi Delta is Greenville, where Hodding Carter, Jr., and his *Delta Democrat-Times* gained a reputation for being "sensible and moderate" on the issue of race and race relations.[54] Before coming to Greenville in 1936 from the *Daily Courier* in

Hammond, Louisiana, Carter was fired by the Associated Press, where he was told he would never be a journalist. The Greenville *Delta Democrat-Times* was born in 1938 with Carter as a publisher and editor who attracted the wrath of everyone from Mississippi political icon Theodore Bilbo to the Mississippi legislature.[55] Carter was no integrationist, but he made a name for himself as a champion of justice for all people regardless of race,[56] a reputation he maintained for three decades in Mississippi. He was awarded a Pulitzer Prize for editorial writing in 1946, and his glory was dampened by gubernatorial sour grapes. "The late Theodore Bilbo, then running for re-election to the United States Senate, told his listeners that 'no self-respecting Southern white man would accept a prize given by a bunch of nigger-loving, Yankeefied Communists for editorials advocating the mongrelization of the race,' " Carter wrote.[57] Carter's son, Hodding III, took the helm as editor of the Greenville *Delta Democrat-Times* in 1962 and followed in his father's footsteps. Carter III went on to become assistant secretary of state for President Jimmy Carter from 1977 to 1981.

East of Greenville, where the Delta and the Loess Hills regions blend, the *Greenwood Commonwealth* and the Greenwood *Morning Star* served a small Delta town that would become the site of the national office of the Student Nonviolent Coordinating Committee during Freedom Summer in 1964. Just prior to the Dixiecrat controversy in 1948, however, the most newsworthy local event was the 1946 founding of the Greenwood *Morning Star* in competition with the *Greenwood Commonwealth*. Edited by James Alsop, the Greenwood *Morning Star* supported the states' rights campaign.

The Greenwood *Morning Star*'s rival publication across town, the *Greenwood Commonwealth*, was founded in 1896 by James K. Vardaman, who became a governor of Mississippi and a U.S. senator known as the "White Chief" for his supremacist views. As publisher and editor of the *Greenwood Commonwealth*, Vardaman worked diligently for the legal prohibition of liquor and so irritated a local saloon owner that he was called out into the street to settle the dispute in a gunfight. Vardaman shot the man dead.[58] Twice defeated in races for the governor's seat, Vardaman traveled around the state during his third and successful 1903 campaign, spouting racist rhetoric, advocating lynching to support his belief in the black man's desire for white women, and arguing against educational opportunities for blacks. He won the election by a wide margin.[59] Interestingly, Vardaman was considered a progressive governor during his tenure, 1904–1908. He ended convict leasing, increased school funding for both white and black schools, and tried but failed to get child-labor legislation passed.[60] Vardaman sold the *Greenwood Commonwealth* to James L. Gillespie in 1905, and the paper remained in the Gillespie family for the next fifty years. Sumpter Gillespie, the son of James, was the publisher and sometimes the editor from 1923 to 1958. He was remembered by a former staff member as a "kind of big daddy,"[61] and the *Greenwood Commonwealth* held the line on Southern conservatism.

Farther north into the Mississippi Delta, the newspaper that eventually became the *Clarksdale Press Register* was founded in 1865 as *The Coahomian*. Purchased in 1907 by Edgar Harris of West Point, who stayed in Clarksdale less than a year, the paper was renamed the *Clarksdale Daily Register* and became a daily in 1908 under the ownership of Guy P. Clark, the son of the founder of the town. In 1932, another daily, the *Clarksdale Daily News*, created competition with the *Clarksdale Daily Register* that lasted until 1936, when Clark purchased it and merged the two. Clark's son, Guy P. Clark, Jr., became involved with the newspaper after returning home from World War II. In 1948, Clark, Jr., asked Joseph F. Ellis, Jr., a fellow U.S. Army veteran, to edit what became the *Clarksdale Press Register*. Ellis agreed and served as editor and publisher of the paper for the next forty years.[62] He often published guest editorials rather than his own opinions on issues of civil rights. The guest editorials were not supportive of civil rights for blacks.

Northeast from Clarksdale on the Mississippi–Tennessee border, where the Black Prairie and the Tennessee Hills regions merge, the Corinth *Daily Corinthian* was first published in 1895. From 1948 through 1968, the newspaper supported the white power structure and often ridiculed the black struggle for equal rights.

South of Corinth on the Black Prairie is Tupelo, where the *Tupelo Journal* was founded in 1870. The paper became a daily in 1936, and the first motto of the Tupelo *Daily Journal* remained the same as the one established in 1870, "Be just, fear not."[63] In 1934, George McLean became publisher of the newspaper, a position he maintained until his death in 1983. McLean was no social reformer bent on altering the traditional Southern way of life, but he believed in equal justice for all people.

South of Tupelo in Columbus, where the first celebration of Memorial Day was observed in 1866, where the state capital was once located and where a great deal of Ku Klux Klan activity occurred just after the Civil War,[64] the Columbus *Commercial Dispatch* was founded in 1879. Edited by Birney Imes, Jr., from 1948 through 1968, the *Commercial Dispatch* was a cornerstone of the Old South.

Northwest of Columbus in West Point, Edgar and Buelah Harris founded the *Daily Times-Leader* in 1928 after excursions into newspaper publishing in Laurel, Hattiesburg and Clarksdale. When they arrived in West Point, they purchased the weekly *West Point Leader* from L.T. Carlisle, who had owned the newspaper since 1881. The Harrises also acquired the weekly *Times Herald* and combined the two newspapers into a semi-weekly publication. Edgar Harris "didn't like the idea of waiting 'til Friday to print Wednesday happenings,"[65] so in 1931, the *Daily Times-Leader* made its appearance. In his front-page "March of Events" column, Harris allied himself with states' rights, white supremacy and Southern conservatism on all levels.

Due west of West Point in Grenada, the last school desegregation riot of record in Mississippi took place in 1966, when 400 whites attacked more than 100 black students at John Rundle High School.[66] Two decades earlier, the stage was being set by Frank Jones, Sr., the prohibitionist and segregationist editor of the Grenada *Sentinel-Star*, which was founded in 1854. Jones' front-page column, "Briefed by Editor," took aim at bootleggers and any ideology originating north of the Mason-Dixon Line.

Two hundred miles south of Grenada on the Mississippi Gulf Coast, the Gulfport *Daily Herald* was founded in 1884 by George Washington Wilkes, whose son, Eugene, published and edited the paper from 1954 through 1968. The Mississippi Gulf Coast was settled by immigrants from many countries, including Lebanon, Yugoslavia and Italy, and because of the diversity of its population, the coast has long held a reputation as the most politically tolerant area of the state. As early as 1950, convention centers on the coast were integrated, more than a decade before this would be the case in the rest of the state.[67] The Gulfport *Daily Herald* had a moderate editorial tone regarding race issues but never openly supported civil rights.

THE MISSISSIPPI PRESS AND STUDIES OF CIVIL RIGHTS COVERAGE

The daily newspapers in Mississippi during the 1940s, 1950s and 1960s were written, edited and published in an ultraconservative and intolerant place. Mississippi editors who failed to conform did not face just verbal disapproval. Boycotts, bombs and bullets were used. Hazel Brannon Smith, the publisher of several weekly newspapers in Mississippi, was a segregationist, but one who believed in legal justice for all people regardless of race. She won a Pulitzer Prize for editorial writing in 1964, the first woman to ever be presented the coveted award.[68] Shortly afterward, her *Northside Reporter* in Jackson was bombed.[69] *Greenwood Commonwealth* editor Thatcher Walt, who was considered a staunch conservator of the Southern way of life, also found himself the target of threats in 1964 after writing a mild editorial condemning cross-burnings by the Ku Klux Klan.[70]

To date, no comprehensive evaluation of civil rights coverage by the Mississippi daily press from 1948, when the Dixiecrats stormed out of the Democratic National Convention in protest of the party's "middle-of-the-road stance on civil rights,"[71] through 1968, when Martin Luther King, Jr., was assassinated, has been undertaken. The only Mississippi daily newspapers evaluated to any extent have been the Jackson *Clarion-Ledger* and the Jackson *Daily News*, both found guilty of "distorting news that involves race,"[72] the Greenville *Delta Democrat-Times*, proclaimed "fair,"[73] and the McComb *Enterprise-Journal*, described as a newspaper that "slowly changed" to a more liberal stance in its view of the race issue.[74] Since twenty Mississippi daily newspapers were published between 1948 and 1968, information gained from a complete analysis is a significant contribution to mass communication historical studies. The findings will settle, once and for all, whether the prevalent belief that the Mississippi daily press provoked violence to maintain white supremacy[75] is true.

Published studies of Mississippi press involvement with the civil rights movement are few, although several have addressed the issue. A 1965 dissertation examined the writings of editor Sullens of the Jackson *Daily News*,[76] and a 1971 thesis combined a study of the black community Jackson *Advocate*, the McComb *Enterprise-Journal*, the Greenville *Delta Democrat-Times*, the Jackson *Daily News*, the *Meridian Star* and Jackson television station WLBT during the racially explosive years 1962 through 1964.[77] A 1981 dissertation assessed a Mississippi editor considered liberal for his day, P.D. East of the *Petal Paper*,[78] and a 1991 thesis examined the role of the McComb *Enterprise-Journal* in the civil rights events of the early 1960s.[79] Many articles have been written regarding Emmerich of the McComb *Enterprise-Journal*, a man who wanted, above all, he said, "to maintain peace and justice in his community."[80] A 1992 dissertation documented the *State Times*, whose brief existence was funded by prominent businesspeople from late 1954 to early 1961. The *State Times* offered alternative, but not radical, points of view.[81] A 1993 content analysis of ten white-owned Mississippi newspapers found that a "white resistance to integration" editorial stance was in concert with failure to cover civil rights issues in an unbiased or thorough manner and that the percentage of black-related stories in newspapers studied was not equal to the percentage of blacks in the communities served by the newspapers.[82]

A conference was held at the University of Mississippi in 1987 to discuss the role and involvement of the news media in the struggle for civil rights. "Covering the South" was the theme of the National Symposium on the Media and the Civil Rights Movement held at the Center for the Study of Southern Culture in April that year. No publication has resulted from the event, although audiovisual recordings and transcripts are available.

OTHER AMERICAN MEDIA AND STUDIES OF RACE AND CIVIL RIGHTS

News media studies from around the country began a half century ago that dealt with race and the treatment of blacks in the press, but not necessarily civil rights. A 1932 study of black news as it was printed in seventeen metropolitan newspapers discovered that nearly half the black news reported was devoted to anti-social activities, compared to twelve percent for whites.[83] A 1957 study of the desegregation-related content in North

Carolina dailies in 1955 found that pressure-group spokespeople and black attorneys in desegregation suits accounted for the majority of black news sources.[84] A 1967 textual analysis of several major newspapers concluded that while most journalists were doing a responsible job of covering racial matters, editorial bias and unethical editing often slanted the final published reports,[85] and a 1968 investigation of the image of blacks in films found that out of 100 films produced through 1944 with black actors or characters, the majority were "anti-Negro."[86] Also in 1968, a former newspaper and television reporter conducted a survey and found that news about blacks lacked analysis and interpretation,[87] and a 1969 examination of the coverage of civil disorders in North Carolina concluded that the *Winston-Salem Journal* opted to simply ignore many events leading up to a race riot and was at least partially responsible for the ensuing violence.[88] A 1971 study of *Time, Look, Newsweek, Life* and *U.S. News and World Report* compared news photos and discovered that readers of the magazines saw twenty pictures showing blacks and whites separate for every picture they saw showing blacks and whites together, perpetuating a tradition of segregation.[89] In another analysis of *Life* magazine, including issues from 1937 through 1972, it was found that coverage of blacks failed to show a substantial increase over time, which led the author to conclude that coverage of blacks in *Life* was closely related to the reality of blacks within American society. Another conclusion was that *Life* failed to provide a thorough overview of blacks during the years that it was published.[90] A content analysis of issues of the *New York Times*, the *Atlanta Constitution*, the *Boston Globe* and the *Chicago Tribune* from the 1950s, 1960s and 1970s concluded that the four newspapers provided little coverage of any type regarding blacks in the 1950s, but civil rights-related activities of blacks were consistently covered in the press from 1956 to 1970.[91] Another study of civil rights coverage comparing Northern and Southern newspapers "did not support the literature-driven assumption that Southern newspaper performance was less socially responsible, in terms of balance and fairness, than Northern newspaper performance."[92] An analysis of the photographs of blacks in the *New York Times*, the *Chicago Tribune*, the New Orleans *Times-Picayune* and the *San Francisco Chronicle* from 1937 through 1990 found that although photo coverage of blacks had increased dramatically over the years, stereotypical images, such as crime, entertainment and sports, had remained high.[93]

METHOD OF RESEARCH AND QUESTIONS EXPLORED

Two decades before the Dixiecrat walkout from the Democratic National Convention in 1948, Walter Lippmann, who is referred to as "one of the most powerful opinion makers of his time,"[94] expressed concern that editors often controlled public access to the news as it suited their purpose.[95]

Around that same time, social responsibility as a notion of the press was incorporated into the 1923 Canons of Journalism of the American Society of Newspaper Editors. A list of actual "press requirements" pertaining to social responsibility, however, was not drawn up and formally stated until the years following World War II, by a group of scholars who came to be known as the Hutchins Commission. Just prior to the onset of the civil rights protests of the mid-1940s, Henry Luce of Time, Inc., contracted with Robert Hutchins, chancellor at the University of Chicago, to conduct an extensive study on the freedom and responsibility of the press. The ensuing Commission on Freedom of the Press, also known as the Hutchins Commission, was composed of notables Archibald MacLeish, a former secretary of state; Arthur Schlesinger, a professor of history at Harvard; and Beardsley Ruml, chair of the Federal Reserve Bank of New York. After a five-year intensive study of American mass communication, they released *A Free and Responsible Press*, a publication that recommended social responsibility to the news media in five ways: "providing a truthful, comprehensive, and intelligent account of the day's events in a context which gives them meaning; providing a forum for the exchange of comment and criticism; projecting a representative picture of the constituent groups in society; presenting and clarifying the goals and values of the society; and providing a full access to the day's intelligence."[96]

Evaluated from the perspective of the Hutchins Commission recommendations, five questions were addressed in this examination of Mississippi daily press coverage of civil rights from 1948 through 1968. What were the major issues of concern raised by editors of the Mississippi daily press during the civil rights struggle? What was the editorial propensity toward coverage of civil rights activities in the Mississippi daily press? Did the Mississippi daily press advocate violence or rejection of civil rights during the civil rights struggle? Were the two most widely circulated daily newspapers, the Jackson *Clarion-Ledger* and the Jackson *Daily News*, representative of the other daily Mississippi newspapers in their coverage of the civil rights movement? Did the Mississippi daily press localize the civil rights struggle or focus on the issue as a concern for other areas of the state and nation?

The time sequence selected in which to answer these questions focused on five historic events for Mississippi: the Dixiecrat protest at the Democratic National Convention in 1948; the *Brown v. Board of Education* Supreme Court decision, which mandated desegregation in public schools in 1954; James Meredith's admission to the University of Mississippi in 1962 as the first black student of record; Freedom Summer in 1964; and the assassination of Martin Luther King, Jr., in 1968.

Every issue of every daily Mississippi newspaper published during the following time periods was examined: July 1948, the month of the Democratic National Convention; May 1954 and August 1954, the month of the *Brown v. Board* of Education decision and the month before school was to begin that year; September 1962, when Meredith enrolled at the University of Mississippi; June through August 1964, Freedom Summer; and April 1968, the month when King was assassinated.

Approximately 5,000 issues of Mississippi daily newspapers were examined. From those papers, nearly 1,000 editorials and 7,000 news articles and headlines were recorded and evaluated. This information was placed into historical perspective utilizing archival materials, government documents, memoirs, historical manuscripts and oral testimony. All issues of the newspapers in the previously mentioned months of 1948, 1954, 1962, 1964 and 1968, except for one month of the Corinth *Daily Corinthian*, were available on microfilm at the Mississippi Department of Archives and History. The copies of the *Daily Corinthian* missing from the state archives were located at the Corinth Public Library.

The Mississippi daily newspapers included are *Clarksdale Press Register*, Columbus *Commercial Dispatch*, Corinth *Daily Corinthian*, Greenville *Delta Democrat-Times, Greenwood Commonwealth*, Greenwood *Morning Star*, Grenada *Sentinel-Star*, Gulfport *Daily Herald, Hattiesburg American*, Jackson *Clarion-Ledger*, Jackson *Daily News*, *Laurel Leader-Call*, McComb *Enterprise-Journal, Meridian Star, Natchez Democrat, Natchez Times*, Pascagoula *Chronicle*, Pascagoula *Mississippi Press, Starkville Daily News*, Tupelo *Daily Journal*, *Vicksburg Herald, Vicksburg Evening Post* and the West Point *Times Leader*. Except for 1954, when there were twenty daily newspapers published in Mississippi, the other time periods each had nineteen. Circulation figures of the newspapers ranged from 2,000 to over 50,000. Unless otherwise noted, editorials from each newspaper are attributed to the editor.

NOTES

1. James Loewen and Charles Sallis, eds., *Mississippi: Conflict and Change* (New York: Pantheon Books, 1974), 256.
2. "Gov. Johnson Pledges New CR Law to Be Challenged," AP, Jackson *Clarion-Ledger*, 5 July 1964, 1.
3. U.S. Department of Commerce, Bureau of the Census, *U.S. Census of Population: 1960*. Vol. 1, *Characteristics of the Population*, Part 26, *Mississippi* (Washington, D.C.: Government Printing Office, 1963), 9.
4. Mississippi Power and Light Company Economic Research Department, *Mississippi Statistical Summary of Population, 1800–1980* (Jackson: Mississippi Power and Light Company, 1983), 10.
5. Neil R. McMillen, *Dark Journey: Black Mississippians in the Age of Jim Crow* (Chicago: University of Illinois Press, 1990), 10.
6. Loewen and Sallis, *Mississippi*, 149.
7. John Dittmer, *Local People: The Struggle for Civil Rights in Mississippi* (Chicago: University of Illinois Press, 1994), 28.
8. Loewen and Sallis, *Mississippi*, 256.

9. "Barnett in Open Defiance of Integration Order," UP, Corinth *Daily Corinthian*, 14 September 1962, 1.

10. Tom Etheridge, "Courageous Speech," Jackson *Clarion-Ledger*, 15 September 1962, 1.

11. Gene Wirth, "Place Assured in History for Fearless Ross Barnett," Jackson *Clarion-Ledger*, 15 September 1962, 1.

12. "Civil Rights Bill Passes as Southern Leaders Stand Pat," AP, *Natchez Democrat*, 3 July 1964, 1; "Civil Rights Measure Becomes Law," AP, *Starkville Daily News*, 3 July 1964, 1; "Govs. Wallace and Johnson Rap Passage of 'Unconstitutional' Civil Rights Bill," UPI, Corinth *Daily Corinthian*, 3 July 1964, 1; "Johnson Signs Civil Rights Bill in Historic Ceremony," AP, Jackson *Clarion-Ledger*, 3 July 1964, 1; "LBJ Signs Civil Rights Bill," UPI, Grenada *Sentinel-Star*, 3 July 1964, 1; "Let Courts Rule on Civil Rights, Says Paul," AP, *Greenwood Commonwealth*, 3 July 1964, 1; "President Signs Bill, Urges Compliance by All," UPI, Tupelo *Daily Journal*, 3 July 1964, 1; "President Urges Justice for All in Signing Civil Rights Bill," AP, *Vicksburg Evening Post*, 3 July 1964, 1; "Two Johnsons, Two Different Views on Civil Rights," UPI, Grenada *Sentinel-Star*, 3 July 1964, 1; "Wallace Won't Obey New Law," AP, *Laurel Leader-Call*, 4 July 1964, 1.

13. "Don't Comply Is Advice of Gov. Johnson," AP, Jackson *Daily News*, 3 July 1964, 1; "Don't Comply Until Law Is Tested, PBJ Advises," AP, McComb *Enterprise-Journal*, 3 July 1964, 1; "Gov. Advises Citizens Not to Comply with Law until Tested," AP, *Hattiesburg American*, 3 July 1964, 1; "Gov. Johnson Pledges New Civil Rights Law to Be Challenged," AP, Jackson *Clarion-Ledger*, 5 July 1964, 1; "Gov. Johnson Pledges New Civil Rights Law to Be Challenged," AP, Jackson *Daily News*, 5 July 1964, 1; "Governor Deplores Civil Rights Timing," AP, *Starkville Daily News*, 3 July 1964, 1; "Governor Says Strife to Come from Civil Rights Law," UPI, Pascagoula *Chronicle*, 3 July 1964, 1; "Governor Sees Chaos in Civil Rights Bill," UPI, Tupelo *Daily Journal*, 3 July 1964, 1; "House Backs Paul on Noncompliance Stand," AP, *Starkville Daily News*, 9 July 1964, 1; "Paul Predicts Real Trouble under Civil Rights Bill," AP, *Natchez Democrat*, 3 July 1964, 1; "PBJ Expects 'Civil Strife and Disorder,' " UPI, West Point *Times-Leader*, 3 July 1964, 1; "PBJ Tells State Not to Comply, Advises Wait for Court Test," AP, *Laurel Leader-Call*, 3 July 1964, 1; "Should Refuse, Pending Tests, PBJ Says," UPI, *Meridian Star*, 3 July 1964, 1; "State Businessmen 'on Their Own' in Dealing with Civil Rights Act," Jackson *Daily News*, 3 July 1964, 1.

14. Jackson *Daily News*, unsigned editorial, 22 July 1964.

15. Bernard Schwartz, ed., *Statutory History of the United States: Civil Rights Part I* (New York: McGraw-Hill, 1970), 657.

16. Ibid.

17. Ibid., 1017.

18. Roy E. Carter, Jr., "Segregation and the News: A Regional Content Study," *Journalism Quarterly* 34 (Winter 1957): 9; Thomas Clark, *The Emerging South*, 2nd ed. (New York: Oxford University Press, 1968), 199; Carolyn Martindale, *The White Press and Black America* (Westport, Conn.: Greenwood Press, 1986), introduction.

19. "Belting One Down for the Road," *Nation*, 6 October 1962, 190.

20. Ibid.; Charles Butts, "Mississippi: The Vacuum and the System," in *Black, White and Gray: 21 Points of View on the Race Question*, ed. Bradford Daniel

(New York: Sheed and Ward, 1964), 104; "Dilemma in Dixie," *Time*, 20 February 1956, 76; "Dixie Flamethrowers," *Time*, 4 March 1966, 64; "Moderation in Dixie," *Time*, 19 March 1965, 71; Ted Poston, "The American Negro and Newspaper Myths," in *Race and the News Media*, ed. Paul Fisher and Ralph Lowenstein (New York: Praeger, 1967), 63; Pat Watters and Reese Cleghorn, *Climbing Jacob's Ladder: The Arrival of Negroes in Southern Politics* (New York: Harcourt, Brace and World, 1967), 73; Simeon Booker, *Black Man's America* (Englewood Cliffs, N.J.: Prentice-Hall, 1964), 15; Roger Williams, "Newspapers in the South," *Columbia Journalism Review* 6 (Summer 1967): 27; James Boylan, "Birmingham Newspapers in Crisis," *Columbia Journalism Review* 2 (Summer 1963): 30.

21. Poston, "The American Negro and Newspaper Myths," 63.

22. John Hulteng, *The Messenger's Motive: Ethical Problems of the News Media* (Englewood Cliffs, N.J.: Prentice-Hall, 1976), 176.

23. Butts, "Mississippi: The Vacuum and the System," 105.

24. Eugene H. Methvin, "Objectivity and the Tactic of Terrorists," in *Ethics and the Press*, ed. John Merrill and Ralph Barney (New York: Hastings House, 1975), 200.

25. Ben H. Bagdikian, "Editorial Responsibility in Times of Urban Disorder," in *The Media and the Cities*, ed. Charles Daly (Chicago: University of Chicago Press, 1968), 21.

26. Poston, "The American Negro and Newspaper Myths," 66.

27. Roy E. Carter, "Racial Identification Effects upon the News Story Writer," *Journalism Quarterly* 36 (Summer 1959): 284–290, and "Segregation and the News: A Regional Content Study," 3–18; William Peters, *The Southern Temper* (Garden City, N.Y.: Doubleday and Company, 1959), 115; Robert Hooker, "Race and the News Media in Mississippi, 1962–1964" (Master's thesis, Vanderbilt University, 1971), 240–241; Hodding Carter III, "The Wave beneath the Froth," in *Race and the News Media*, ed. Paul Fisher and Ralph Lowenstein (New York: Praeger, 1967), 6; Buford Boone, "Southern Newsmen and Local Pressure," in *Race and the News Media*, ed. Paul Fisher and Ralph Lowenstein (New York: Praeger, 1967), 53.

28. "Belting One Down for the Road"; Hugh Davis Graham, *Crisis in Print: Desegregation and the Press in Tennessee* (Nashville: Vanderbilt University Press, 1967), 314–316.

29. James W. Silver, *Mississippi: The Closed Society* (New York: Harcourt, Brace and World, 1966), 30.

30. Quoted in Hooker, "Race and the News Media in Mississippi," 241.

31. Ibid., 242.

32. Kerner Commission, *Report of the National Advisory Commission on Civil Disorders* (New York: Bantam, 1968), 203.

33. Quoted in William Lance Conn, "Crisis in Black and White: The McComb *Enterprise-Journal*'s Coverage of Racial News, 1961–1964" (Master's thesis, University of Mississippi, 1991), 9.

34. Kerner Commission, *Report of the National Advisory Commission*, 210–211.

35. William Lang Baradell, "An Analysis of the Coverage Given by Five North Carolina Newspapers of Three Events in the Civil Rights Movement in the State" (Master's thesis, University of North Carolina at Chapel Hill, 1990), 154–155;

Sharon A. Bramlett, "Southern vs. Northern Newspaper Coverage of a Race Crisis—The Lunch Counter Sit-In Movement, 1960–1964:" An Assessment of Press Social Responsibility (Ph.D. diss., Indiana University, 1987), 103; Martindale, *The White Press and Black America*, 79.

36. Jack Lyle, ed., *The Black American and the Press* (Los Angeles: W. Ritchie Press, 1968), xii.

37. Watters and Cleghorn, *Climbing Jacob's Ladder*, 55–56.

38. Carter, "Wave beneath the Froth," 54, and "Comment on the Coverage in the Domestic Press," in *The Black American and the Press*, ed. Jack Lyle (Los Angeles: W. Ritchie Press, 1968), 39–40.

39. Gene Gilmore and Robert Root, "Ethics for Newsmen," in *Ethics and the Press*, ed. John Merrill and Ralph Barney (New York: Hastings House, 1975), 29; Loren Ghiglione, "Small-Town Journalism Has Some Big Ethical Headaches," in *Questioning Media Ethics*, ed. Bernard Rubin (New York: Praeger, 1978), 172.

40. V.O. Key, Jr., *Public Opinion and American Democracy* (New York: Alfred A. Knopf, 1961), 381–382.

41. Frank E. Smith, *Congressman from Mississippi* (New York: Pantheon Books, 1964), 41.

42. Reed Sarratt, *The Ordeal of Desegregation: The First Decade* (New York: Harper and Row, 1966), 253.

43. Dan Davis, "State-wide Newspaper's Historic Commitment Spans 154 years," in *Mississippi Press Association 125th Anniversary Report* (Jackson, 1991), 47.

44. "Revolt in Mississippi," *Time*, 8 November 1954, 60.

45. "The *Meridian Star*," in *Mississippi Press Association 125th Anniversary Report*, 58.

46. James H. Skewes, "We Rise to Defend Our Anglo-Saxon Way of Life," *Meridian Star*, 18 July 1948, p. 4.

47. Harriet Gibbons, *Laurel Leader-Call*, 27 July 1948, 4.

48. "Edgar Harris Founded *Times-Leader* in 1928," in *Mississippi Press Association 125th Anniversary Report*, 81.

49. Janet Braswell, "*American* Dates Back to 1800s," in *Mississippi Press Association 125th Anniversary Report*, 41.

50. Tim Doherty, "Red, White and Blue since 1917," in *Mississippi Press Association 125th Anniversary Report*, 41.

51. Hooker, "Race and News Media in Mississippi," 44.

52. David R. Davies, "J. Oliver Emmerich and the McComb *Enterprise-Journal*: Slow Change in McComb, 1964," *Journal of Mississippi History* (February 1995): 2; Conn, "Crisis in Black and White," 7.

53. Joan Gandy, "Democrat Reports Natchez History 126 Years," in *Mississippi Press Association 125th Anniversary Report*, 61.

54. Hooker, "Race and the News Media in Mississippi," 49.

55. Ibid., 81–93; Hodding Carter, Jr., *Southern Legacy* (Baton Rouge: Louisiana State University Press, 1950), 5–7; Hodding Carter, Jr., *First Person Rural* (Garden City, N.Y.: Doubleday and Company, 1963), 210; see also Harry D. Marsh, "Hodding Carter's Newspaper on School Desegregation, 1954–1955," *Journalism Monographs* 92 (May 1985).

56. Hodding Carter, Jr., *Where Main Street Meets the River* (New York: Rinehart, 1953), 3–66.

57. Carter, *First Person Rural*, 211.

58. Susan Montgomery, "The *Commonwealth*: A 95-Year View," in *Mississippi Press Association 125th Anniversary Report*, 40.

59. Loewen and Sallis, *Mississippi*, 192–193.

60. Ibid., 194.

61. Montgomery, "The *Commonwealth*: A 95-Year View," 40.

62. "The *Clarksdale Press Register*," in *Mississippi Press Association 125th Anniversary Report*, 30.

63. "A History of Growth and Progress," in *Mississippi Press Association 125th Anniversary Report*, 75.

64. Loewen and Sallis, *Mississippi*, 2, 133, 162.

65. "Edgar Harris Founded *Times-Leader* in 1928," in *Mississippi Press Association 125th Anniversary Report*, 81.

66. Loewen and Sallis, *Mississippi*, 282.

67. Ibid., 25.

68. Arthur J. Kaul, "Hazel Brannon Smith," *Dictionary of Literary Biography*, vol. 127, ed. Perry Ashley (Detroit: Gale Research, 1993), 299–300.

69. Ibid.; "Appreciation Day," *Newsweek*, 13 December 1965, 70; Smith, *Congressman from Mississippi*, 266.

70. John Herbers, "Communique from Mississippi," *New York Times Magazine*, 8 November 1964, 126.

71. Loewen and Sallis, *Mississippi*, 245.

72. Butts, "Mississippi: The Vacuum and the System," 104.

73. Susan Weill, "African Americans and the White-Owned Mississippi Press: An Analysis of Coverage from 1944 to 1984" (Master's thesis, Jackson State University, 1993), 80; Hooker, "Race and the News Media in Mississippi, 1962–1964," 49.

74. Davies, "J. Oliver Emmerich and the McComb *Enterprise-Journal*: Slow Change in McComb, 1964," 2.

75. "Dilemma in Dixie," 76; "Dixie Flamethrowers," 64; "Moderation in Dixie," 71; Edwin W. Williams, "Dimout in Jackson," *Columbia Journalism Review* 9 (Summer 1970): 56.

76. John Ray Skates, Jr., "A Southern Editor Views the National Scene: Frederick Sullens and the Jackson, Mississippi, *Daily News*" (Ph.D. diss., Mississippi State University, 1965).

77. Hooker, "Race and the News Media in Mississippi, 1962–1964."

78. Gary Lynn Huey, "P.D. East: Southern Liberalism and the Civil Rights Movement, 1953–1971" (Ph.D. diss., Washington State University, 1981).

79. Conn, "Crisis in Black and White: The McComb *Enterprise-Journal*'s Coverage of Racial News, 1962–1964."

80. Davies, "J. Oliver Emmerich and the McComb *Enterprise-Journal*: Slow Change in McComb, 1964," 23.

81. James T. Sellers, "A History of the Jackson *State Times*: An Agent of Change in a Closed Society" (Ph.D. diss., University of Southern Mississippi, 1992).

82. Weill, "African Americans and the White-Owned Mississippi Press: An Analysis of Coverage from 1944 to 1984."

83. Noel P. Gist, "The Negro in the Daily Press," *Social Forces* 10 (March 1932): 405–411.

84. Roy E. Carter, "Segregation and the News: A Regional Content Study," 3–18.

85. Poston, "The American Negro and Newspaper Myths," 63–72.

86. Royal D. Colle, "Negro Image in the Mass Media: A Case Study in Social Change," *Journalism Quarterly* 45 (Spring 1968): 55–60.

87. Woody Klein, "News Media and Race Relations: A Self-Portrait," *Columbia Journalism Review* 7 (Fall 1968): 42–49.

88. David Paletz and Robert Dunn, "Press Coverage of Civil Disorders: A Case Study of Winston-Salem, 1967," *Public Opinion Quarterly* 33 (Fall 1969): 328–335.

89. Guido H. Stempel III, "Visibility of Blacks in News and News-Picture Magazines," *Journalism Quarterly* 48 (Summer 1971): 337–339.

90. Mary Alice Sentman, "Black and White: Disparity in Coverage by *Life Magazine* from 1937 to 1972," *Journalism Quarterly* 60 (Fall 1983): 501–508.

91. Martindale, *The White Press and Black America.*

92. Bramlett, "Southern vs. Northern Newspaper Coverage of a Race Crisis—The Lunch Counter Sit-In Movement, 1960–1964: An Assessment of Press Social Responsibility."

93. Paul Martin Lester, "African-American Photo Coverage in Four U.S. Newspapers, 1937–1990," *Journalism Quarterly* 71 (Summer 1994): 380–394.

94. Stanley J. Baran and Dennis K. Davis, *Mass Communication Theory: Foundations, Ferment and Future* (Belmont, Calif.: Wadsworth, 1995), 69.

95. Walter Lippmann, *Public Opinion* (New York: Harcourt, Brace, 1922), 42.

96. Commission on Freedom of the Press, *A Free and Responsible Press—A General Report on Mass Communication: Newspapers, Radio, Motion Pictures, Magazines and Books* (Chicago: University of Chicago Press, 1947), xi.

Chapter 2

1948: The Dixiecrats and the Mississippi Daily Press

Eighty years after the Civil War and just prior to the organization of the States' Rights "Dixiecrat" Democrat Party in 1948, the changes wrought by World War II altered Southern society forever. Black Mississippians had constituted nearly sixty percent of Mississippi soldiers inducted during the war,[1] a larger percentage than their representation in the state's population. Mississippi historian Neil McMillen concluded that it was love of country. "For the most part, the state's black majority seemed to agree with Du Bois when he argued that during an emergency the higher aspirations of the race should be temporarily submerged in a singleness of national purpose," McMillen wrote.[2] Considering the Jim Crow mentality rampant in the South at the time, however, it seems just as likely that many blacks saw the military simply as an available job that got them out of Mississippi with a chance to see the world.

Coming home from their wartime experience, black veterans in Mississippi and the rest of the country would never be the same. "The war brought changes to Mississippi," historian John Dittmer wrote. "Yet it remained to be seen whether, in the critical area of race relations, the state would move forward with the times or continue to cling to the vestiges of Jim Crow society that had for so long retarded the advancement of the majority of its citizens, black and white."[3]

Not long after World War II and the transformation that the experience manifested in the minds and hearts of many black Mississippians, the presidency of Harry Truman began to challenge the state's conservative society. The increasingly supportive mood of Truman, the U.S. Congress, and the nation in general toward civil rights for all people was a primary motivation for the creation of the States' Rights Democrats in 1948 and the party's presidential ballot that year of Senator J. Strom Thurmond of South Carolina and Mississippi Governor Fielding Wright. The Dixiecrats were formally organized in 1948, when a group of Southern Democrats stormed out of the Democratic National Convention in protest of the adopted Democratic platform,[4] which included a civil rights plank.

The Dixiecrats were dedicated to the preservation of the established Southern society. They believed in each state's right to govern itself without federal interference—which in the Mississippi of 1948 meant the segregation of the races, the maintenance of white supremacy and the denial of equality to the state's blacks. According to McMillen, the States' Rights Party was "the child of dissent, sired by tradition-minded white men in reaction to advancing civil rights for Negroes."[5]

PRESIDENT TRUMAN'S CIVIL RIGHTS PLATFORM

The states' rights controversy and the justification to sweep aside civil rights under that umbrella was one of the ongoing issues raging in the Mississippi daily press in 1948. Every newspaper published at least one article a day pertaining to the upcoming presidential election and the threat of Truman's presidency to states' rights. None of the editors of the Mississippi daily press openly supported Truman's re-election, for a number of reasons. The outside perspective by syndicated opinion columnist James Marlow was that "Southerners are burned up by Mr. Truman's civil rights platform."[6] The editors of the Mississippi press agreed to various degrees. Hodding Carter, Jr., of the Greenville *Delta Democrat-Times* observed less dramatically, "Southern conservatives don't like Mr. Truman's civil rights program,"[7] while J.O. "Oliver" Emmerich of the McComb *Enterprise-Journal*, who was a delegate-at-large to the 1948 Democratic National Convention and a member of the executive committee of the Mississippi States' Rights Party in 1948, went a bit further with his denunciation. "Truman has become a disease," he wrote.[8] J.H. Skewes of the *Meridian Star* proclaimed, "Truman has already defeated his own self,"[9] and Fred Sullens of the Jackson *Daily News* referred to Truman as a "renegade."[10] Frank Jones, Sr., of the Grenada *Sentinel-Star* wrote that Truman had forsaken "true American principles"[11] and included Truman in a list of those "unfaithful to the cause of America including FDR, Henry Wallace and Benedict Arnold."[12] Elliott Trimble of the *Natchez Democrat* noted Truman's record of "Southern disservice,"[13] and a letter to the editor of the Jackson *Daily News* complained in moral indignation, "President Truman's civil rights program is just as vicious as that imposed on us by the carpetbaggers."[14]

The civil rights issues endorsed by Truman in 1948 that stirred such controversy in the South were the elimination of the poll tax, desegregation in the ranks of the military and an anti-lynching law. Although widely editorialized about, the text of the Democratic civil rights plank of 1948 was printed in only two of the Mississippi daily newspapers. It read:

> The Democratic Party is responsible for the great civil rights gains made in recent years in eliminating unfair and illegal discrimination based on race, creed or color. The Democratic Party commits itself to continuing its efforts to eradicate all racial, religious and economic discrimination.
>
> Basic rights are (1) the right of full and equal political participation, (2) the right to equal opportunity employment, (3) the right of security of person, and (4) the right of equal treatment in the service and defense of our nation.[15]

One of the "basic rights" of the National Democratic Party platform, "the right of full and equal political participation," meant the right to vote. In Mississippi, the poll tax kept many people, particularly blacks, from voter registration. Instituted in 1890, the two-dollar poll tax had to be paid two years in advance and by the first of February on an election year. The tax was a severe hardship on the poor, which included most blacks and many whites in the state, and the number of registered voters dropped because of it.[16] Funds brought into Mississippi coffers by the poll tax were marked for education and roads, and the tax was defended on that basis. Six other states had poll taxes in 1948: Alabama, Arkansas, South Carolina, Tennessee, Texas, Virginia and New Hampshire.[17] Many of the editors of the Mississippi daily press viewed the poll tax as a necessary evil. Edgar Harris of the West Point *Times-Leader* wrote, "We need the revenue from Poll Tax."[18]

A congressional vote on an anti–poll tax law, urged by Republican sponsors,[19] was headed for a long Southern filibuster following the Democratic National Convention in late July 1948. Senator John Stennis (D-Miss.) took the floor at the onset and made front-page news back home,[20] declaring that the anti–poll tax law was a political act to gain votes.[21] One interesting headline in this regard came from the Meridian paper, where Skewes' style for unusual verbiage was evident, "Stennis Dixie Fight Head."[22] Although there was a great deal of support in the state for the poll tax and the filibuster against the anti–poll tax law, not everyone in Mississippi could see the use in such a protest. The *Hattiesburg American* voiced its disgust over what appeared a futile effort with the headline, "Anti-Poll Tax Debate Drones On in Capital's Cave of Winds,"[23] while the McComb *Enterprise-Journal* printed similar concerns raised by James Eastland, Mississippi's other U.S. senator.[24]

Harriett Gibbons at the *Laurel Leader-Call* was one of the few editors of the Mississippi daily press who advocated elimination of the tax. "We might as well abolish the poll tax as a matter of pride and prejudice," she wrote. In the same editorial, however, she continued to express doubt about legalized social changes forced on a community. "Better treatment, more rights, and more privileges for any or all of us, will not come by legal fiat but by us gradually growing into deserving these," she wrote.[25]

Truman and the bi-partisan anti-lynching campaign were another story. With origins in frontier America, lynching is vigilante justice that usually imposes a sentence of death without a legal trial. Before the Civil War, the majority of lynch victims in the South were white, but after the Civil War, emancipated blacks became the primary targets. Most whites in the South accepted lynching as a means to "keep blacks in their place," and most lynch mobs were never brought to justice. In Mississippi between 1882 and 1952, there were almost 600 reported lynchings, 40 of white people and 500 of black people. Nationally during that time period, there were nearly 5,000 reported lynchings, 1,200 of whites and nearly 4,000 of blacks.[26]

None of the Mississippi daily newspapers encouraged lynching in 1948, but when Truman's anti-lynching law was proposed, there were few voices raised in support. Gibbons in Laurel wrote, "Most Southerners don't approve of lynching anymore than Northerners do, and they don't resort to lynching with any great frequency."[27] A week later she was back. "The *Leader* is now and forever opposed to lynching," she wrote. "But the anti-lynch bill is aimed at the South and 'this is not fair.' "[28]

Editorial hostility toward the proposed anti-lynching and anti–poll tax laws was evident. Trimble in Natchez addressed the issues with his usual flare for esoteric logic. "Anti-lynch, anti–poll tax, and anti-segregation are all aimed at negro votes and the death of white supremacy," he wrote. "These measures do not better the condition of the negro. They place them in greater jeopardy for they will certainly inflame and alienate the very people who for decades have been the negroes' best friend."[29] Skewes in Meridian shared Trimble's views and railed against the anti-lynching and anti–poll tax laws in his editorial, "For Fight—We Must!"[30]

Truman was also working to eliminate segregation practices in the military, and General Omar Bradley, who disagreed with the concept, was saluted in July 1948 by the Mississippi daily press when Harris of West Point referred to him as "What a man!"[31] The Jackson *Clarion-Ledger* praised Bradley once,[32] and the *Natchez Democrat* used the issue of military desegregation to promote its racial views. "The latest executive orders of President Truman represent another foolhardy fling into the sordid world of racial equality that will bring nothing but chaos to the government and the armed forces," Trimble wrote. "By and large, the white race is the superior in educated mentality and in the civilized arts and trades, including the military. This does not mean that the other races may not someday rise to the level of the white."[33]

Harris of West Point seemed the most bent on convincing his readers that integration was wrong. Several times in July 1948 he voiced his position. In an editorial titled, "Says Segregation Law of God," Harris quoted J. Rice Williams of Houston, Mississippi, as saying, "The only way to improve the lot of the Negro is to imbue him with racial pride," after which Harris went on to remark, "Most thoughtful citizens will agree with Dr. Williams."[34] Harris often used biblical references as defense for his racial views. "Race segregation is older than civilization," he wrote. "It began with creation."[35] Later in the month, Harris reported, "According to a recent Gallup Poll, forty percent of Americans think races should be segregated on trains and buses. In the South, the vote was eighty percent for segregation."[36] No mention is made of who was polled in the sampling. Harris also wrote about a black man who claimed that he was against integration. "An intelligent Negro friend is very much concerned about President Truman's proposal to prohibit race segregation," Harris wrote. "The Negro wants his own schools, his own churches and the right to maintain his own social standards."[37]

Prior to the Democratic National Convention in 1948, anti-Truman sentiment was rampant in the editorial columns of the Mississippi daily press. Tom Shepherd of the *Greenwood Commonwealth* criticized Truman's choice of political allies when he warned the president, "Quit playing politics with the slum and alien elements of the country."[38] Harris of West Point found great pride in the South's efforts to replace Truman. "Dixie Democrats can claim the distinction of having started the Ditch Truman movement," he wrote, and in a statement that would lack prophetic accuracy he continued, "Party leaders realize that the nomination of Truman means certain defeat."[39]

THE "DRAFT IKE" MOVEMENT

This anti-Truman sentiment was a major factor in the 1948 "Draft Ike" movement. General Dwight D. Eisenhower, home from victory in World War II, became a name bantered about as the possible savior of the Democratic Party in 1948, even though he was not a declared Democrat and showed little interest in the nomination. Most of the Mississippi daily press jumped on the "Draft Eisenhower" bandwagon to varying degrees, either with reportorial coverage or with editorials. Any supporters of Eisenhower for president with name recognition who defended the idea made the news. "Arkansas Governor Ben Laney Says Ike Can Unite All," the Clarksdale paper headlined,[40] and "Georgia Adopts 'Draft General Eisenhower' for President,"[41] the Corinth paper reported. Popular Mississippi Senator John Stennis stumped for the general during a stop in Vicksburg, where Eisenhower had spoken in 1947. "One Year After He Spoke at Vicksburg, He Is Endorsed There for President by Stennis," the Greenville paper headlined.[42] "Stennis Hopes Ike Will Accept" was the word in the Greenwood *Morning Star*.[43] "Stennis Booms Eisenhower Presidential Candidacy at Dixie Festival Address,"[44] and "Stennis Backs Gen. Eisenhower,"[45] were the accounts from Vicksburg.

Not all Mississippi Democrats were quite so sure. T.M. Hederman, Jr., editor of the Jackson *Clarion-Ledger* wondered why public sentiment held that Eisenhower would support Southern tradition. "We don't know where this information was gotten," he wrote.[46] Mississippi Governor Fielding Wright also expressed doubts based on Eisenhower's unknown civil rights stance.[47] The *Greenwood Commonwealth* published Wright's concerns. "Gov. Fielding Wright made no comment last night after General Dwight Eisenhower announced his refusal to run for high political office," the paper reported. "He said, 'I never recognized this Eisenhower thing. I never knew how he stood on states' rights.' "[48] The Associated Press reported similar reactions over the wire: "Some of Eisenhower's support in the South appears to be entirely conditional. It depends largely upon the general's yet unexpressed views on such matters as civil and states' rights."[49] Harris in West Point was the only Mississippi editor who did not question Eisenhower's commitment to the traditional Southern way of life. "Ike wants segregation,"[50] he opined confidently, although he never mentioned where he gained his insight.

The Draft Ike movement was fodder for the Mississippi editorial columns, and opinions varied, although the general notion was that anybody who could beat Truman should be considered. "Could he beat Dewey? We believe he could, hands down," Carter of Greenville wrote. "There's nothing to lose by shouting for Ike."[51] Trimble of Natchez saw Eisenhower as the Democrats' "only hope to retain the presidency."[52]

Eisenhower refused to run as a Democrat for president in 1948. Birney Imes, Jr., editor of the Columbus *Commercial Dispatch*, mourned Eisenhower's decision. "There is little doubt that if he could have been convinced to run, the cause of the Southern Democrat would have had a strong shot in the arm," Imes wrote.[53]

DIXIECRAT PROTEST AT THE DEMOCRATIC NATIONAL CONVENTION

The 1948 Democratic National Convention, the thirtieth in American history, opened its doors on Monday, 12 July, in Philadelphia. The Laurel *Leader-Call* published what would seem to be a reasonable plank for any candidate for the White House, but it was unacceptable to the states' rights proponents in 1948, who found their demands for state autonomy rejected. "President Truman has asked for civil rights measures that give minorities the right to live, develop, and vote equally with all citizens and share the rights that are guaranteed by our constitution," the AP reported.[54] Objection to Truman's platform was headline news in the Mississippi daily press during the four days of convention coverage,[55] and the editors were quick to respond to what they saw as disrespect for the Southern way of life. C.B. McAbee of the Corinth *Daily Corinthian* wrote, "The party leaders are trying to make Mississippi the whipping boy of present day politics,"[56] and Shepherd in Greenwood observed, "The racial problem in the South is showing betterment through state enforcement and improved attitudes, all without duress from Washington."[57] In Greenville, Carter thought the concepts of civil rights had merit but that the timing was not right. "Maybe that is the basis for the argument we ought to use, you can't rush democracy," Carter wrote. "The Southerner's affection for the Negro is a solid foundation for a deep understanding. But the change can't come overnight. It must come slowly if there is to be real progress instead of demanded change. Tragedy comes from rapid change not wanted and not understood."[58]

In the first two weeks of July 1948, the topic of a States' Rights Party was news in most Mississippi daily newspapers, although the probable walkout from the national convention by the Mississippi delegates was mentioned in just a few prior to its occurrence. On the first day of July, the findings of an International News Service survey were published that indicated that the Southern Democrats would not leave the convention,[59] but ten days later the headline "Dixie Set to Walk, South Will Fight from Birmingham,"[60] contradicted the earlier announcement. The Greenville *Delta Democrat-Times* predicted the Dixiecrat protest with its headline, "All State Delegates Pledged to Walk Out if States' Rights Issue Is Flouted at Convention, Wright Says on Eve of Trip,"[61] while the Gulfport *Daily Herald* announced rejection of the party by another state's delegates in the banner, "Virginia Democrats Told Not to Bolt by Party Chairman."[62] In the editorial pages, references were fewer. Emmerich in McComb, who was an at-large delegate to the convention, was the only editor who opted to discuss the issue in depth prior to the meeting, and his statement was to criticize a Mississippi legislator who did not support the protest. "Congressman Will Whittington is quoted as saying that he will not walk out of the Democratic convention," Emmerich wrote. "We have a great deal of respect and admiration for Congressman Whittington, but he must not take the position that he is bigger than his own state Democratic party."[63] McLean in Tupelo also foresaw the impending walk but laid no individual blame.[64]

One Mississippi delegate, Charles Hamilton of Aberdeen, had the political audacity to question the loyalty of the state's delegation to the national party and raised the issue to the entire national convention. A front-page story in the Columbus paper, just a few miles from Hamilton's hometown, reported: "Charles Hamilton of Aberdeen, Mississippi, said the states' righters should be unseated unless they agree to the national plank. Hamilton wants to be seated. He declined to make public the names of the delegates who agree with his stance saying it would cost them or their relatives their state jobs."[65] Hamilton became an object of scorn in several Mississippi daily newspapers. "Friend Charlie Hamilton is out of order again," wrote Imes in Columbus. "He tried to discredit the Mississippi Delegation to the Democratic convention. Just what his motive was is not known, but this is a colossal blunder for Charles who has been beaten in more political races than any man in north Mississippi."[66] In Laurel, Gibbons was less kind. "Hamilton is a preacher without a church, a politician without an office, a Mississippian who is a relative newcomer to us who knows little about our customs and doings," she wrote.[67] The Jackson *Clarion-Ledger* ran a photo of Hamilton on the front page with a staff-written story by managing editor Purser Hewitt, who reported, "Mississippi's delegation to the Democratic convention was seated tonight over the protests of a negro lawyer from Missouri, a white preacher from Aberdeen, Mississippi, and a shouting minority at the national convention."[68]

Truman's nomination, combined with the Democratic platform on civil rights, was the last straw for many of the editors, regardless that Truman brought Kentucky Senator Alben Barkley on board as vice president. Initially, Barkley was praised as a "Best-Loved Senator,"[69] and his hour-long speech at the onset of the convention had been applauded as "comprehensive, detailed, eloquent,"[70] but by accepting the Democratic nomination to run with Truman, he became a "traitor" and "a bootlicker."[71]

Besides chagrin with Barkley, many of the Mississippi daily editors were completely disillusioned with the Democratic Party. In Columbus, Imes penned bitterly that the Democratic plank had become a "socialist platform which was foist upon the convention."[72] Shepherd in Greenwood unleashed his segregationist frustration: "For many years we have witnessed the infiltration of aliens, scum, slum renegades and 'South baiters,' into Democrat ranks simply because they could vote for the party in power."[73] In Grenada, Frank Jones, Sr., shared Shepherd's anger. "Truman was nominated by combined minorities, each of which has engaged itself in efforts to destroy the representative form of government during their stranglehold under New Deal days," he wrote.[74] Sullens in Jackson agreed but was willing to get personal and specific. "For two years, Walter White of the NAACP and his co-workers, in behalf of social and political equality for the negro, have been playing President Truman and his followers for a bunch of suckers," he wrote.[75] Across town, the Jackson *Clarion-Ledger* preached gloom and doom. "Anger and resentment smolder in the hearts and minds of a legion of Southern Democrats, sorrow and regret dwell there, too," Hederman wrote. "The Democratic Party, controlled and stampeded by extreme 'liberal' and 'New Deal' elements, prostituted by big city bosses willing to bid anything for votes in pivotal states, has formally and officially repudiated the fundamental principles which commanded Southern loyalty, including defense of constitutional states' rights."[76]

THE DIXIECRATS WALK

The Mississippi delegation was finally seated at the convention, but the next day they walked out in disgust, taking Emmerich of McComb with them. A front-page editorial by Emmerich explained his views of why the Dixiecrats walked:

> The Mississippi delegates to the Democratic convention walked out because they could not maintain their self respect and stay in the convention. (1) The Mississippi Democratic leaders recognized that the convention was determined to nominate Harry Truman and they knew that Harry Truman could not win; (2) The Southern Democrats recognize that they have been kicked around, abused, ignored at times and generally treated with a lack of dignity and consideration at the hands of a party that owes its very existence to the "Solid South"; (3) Many minority groups have taken over control of the Democratic Party. The Negroes of the East have far more influence in the Democratic Party than do all the white people in the South. Naturally, the Southerners are determined that this situation shall be corrected; (4) The fundamental principles upon which the Democratic Party was founded have been excluded from the 1948 platform. Instead, the Party is using every device to appeal to Northern Negroes and city bosses; (5) The basic freedoms of our people depend upon the preservation of states' rights and protection from a centralization of government in Washington. Therefore, the South feels it is fighting a possible dictatorship when it fights those who would deprive our citizens of these principles.[77]

The Dixiecrat walkout from the 1948 Democratic National Convention included all twenty-two Mississippi delegates and thirteen from Alabama, not quite the numbers or the support from the other Southern states that the Dixiecrats were anticipating. The incident was front-page news in every Mississippi daily newspaper, although the headlines varied: "Mississippi, Alabama Stalk Out of Convention in Defiance,"[78] "Dixie Democrats Take Walk at Philadelphia,"[79] "Truman Is Nominated, Mississippi Takes Walk."[80] Purser Hewitt was sent to cover the convention for the Jackson *Clarion-Ledger*. "Mississippi made history in Democratic annals tonight when the state delegation walked out of the national convention," he wrote. "But the Mississippians were deserted when the testing time came by all but Alabama, and some members of even that state's delegation refused to walk. Thus collapsed the States' Rights campaign in the national convention."[81] Trimble in Natchez concurred with Hewitt's complaints but voiced his respect for the protest. "We must have great pride in the staged walkout," he wrote. "If the states' rights movement becomes the salvation of the nation, history will record that Mississippi led the way."[82] Editor L.P. Cashman in Vicksburg considered the walkout an understandable conclusion to the convention, since the Southern Democrats had been renounced and thus humiliated. "The Philadelphia convention was emphatic in its denunciation of the Southern viewpoint on states' rights, civil rights and incidentally, what might be termed 'Southerners' rights,' " he wrote.[83] Editor G.P. Money in Gulfport reminded his readers, "History seems to be flashing back eighty years to another bitter party split over the race issue."[84] At that time, President Abraham Lincoln was installed in the White House.

The only daily press in Mississippi that conducted a local survey to find whether there was grassroots support for the Dixiecrat walkout was the *Meridian Star*. The paper found nearly total support among the people polled,[85] and, although not stated, those surveyed were probably white. Bursting with states' rights enthusiasm, Emmerich of McComb voiced the same support. "This movement has the concern of the grass roots," he wrote. "The people are behind it in dead earnest and that is why it is destined to succeed."[86] Who the grassroots people were specifically or how he knew of this support, Emmerich never said.

THE DIXIECRAT CONVENTION IN ALABAMA

The Mississippi delegates who walked out of the Democratic National Convention in 1948 were headed for Birmingham, Alabama, where the national States' Rights Democrats convention was scheduled to take place during the weekend of 17 July to nominate a presidential ticket. Emmerich of McComb, who attended the convention, proclaimed in a front-page headline, "It's On to B'ham! Mississippi and Alabama Take a Walk as Truman is Nominated, Harsh Civil Rights Anti-South Program Is Adopted."[87] Along with nearly 8,000 States' Rights Democrats, Mississippians John Stennis and James Eastland were the only U.S. senators to attend the Dixiecrat convention.[88]

On 18 July, after two days of states' rights rhetoric and Confederate flag-waving, South Carolina Governor J. Strom Thurmond and Mississippi Governor Fielding Wright made headline news in the Mississippi daily press by emerging as the presidential and vice presidential nominees, respectively, of the States' Rights Party.[89] The platform of the States' Rights Party was simply: "We oppose all efforts to invade or destroy individual rights. We stand for segregation of the races and the racial integrity of each race, the constitutional right to choose one's associates, to accept private employment without government interference. We oppose and condemn a civil rights program calling for the elimination of segregation."[90]

THE MISSISSIPPI DAILY PRESS RESPONDS

During and after the Dixiecrat convention in Birmingham, most editors of the Mississippi daily press supported the party and the Southern protest, though several thought Mississippi Democrats had rushed into abandoning their national party. Prior to the 1948 convention, Carter in Greenville wrote, "Disintegration of the Democratic Party is unhealthy,"[91] while Gibbons in Laurel admonished, "If we start a new party, a small one comprising a handful of states in this immediate section, we will lose patronage and prestige."[92]

The day following the first meeting of the Dixiecrats in Birmingham, Imes in Columbus wrote, "Now is a good time for Southerners to show the northern political dictators that they will not be pushed around."[93] The next day, Imes declared, "The South's fight against the Democratic civil rights platform is beginning to take shape."[94] Emmerich of McComb truly believed the States' Rights Party would be successful, or perhaps he was trying to convince himself and his readers, when he sub-headed his front-page column, "Chance of Growing to Major Political Party Seen for Dixie Group."[95] Harris in West Point agreed with Emmerich: "We're pretty certain the Dixie Democrat ticket will get more electoral votes than the ticket nominated in Philadelphia."[96] Trimble in Natchez encouraged his readers to get involved with the States' Rights Party.[97] James Alsop of the Greenwood *Morning Star* viewed the States' Righters through Jeffersonian ideals. "The fight is against the centralized control of someone all powerful in Washington," he wrote.[98]

Most editors of the Mississippi daily press during the Dixiecrat revolt agreed with Andrews Harmon at the *Hattiesburg American*. "Throughout the black period of Reconstruction, our Southern fathers did not lose hope, but worked quietly to establish what we now know as our Southern Way of Life," he wrote. "We are now called upon to exhibit courage and a similar determination to work quietly for re-establishment of our right to control our own affairs of government."[99] Trimble at the *Natchez Democrat* expressed great pride in the Dixiecrat walkout and Southern patriotism. He viewed the states' rights movement of 1948 as reminiscent of earlier times. "There is no other course open to the states' rights adherents than to hold their own convention, nominate their own candidates and draw the battle lines for the first time since the Civil War," Trimble wrote.[100] At the Greenwood *Morning Star*, Alsop supported the states' rights campaign and voiced concern about Truman's civil rights plank. "The Democrats, if elected, will certainly put white folks in the same class as Negroes," he wrote.[101]

Across town at the *Greenwood Commonwealth*, Shepherd kept the Dixiecrats in the news. He saw the creation of the States' Rights Party as imperative. "Here in the deep South we usually vote the Democratic ticket for reasons that are generally understood," he wrote. "This year, however, when the leading Democratic candidate has declared himself against the principles and traditions that are vital to the South, an independent candidate may be nominated."[102] At the Corinth *Daily Corinthian*, McAbee was a staunch supporter of states' rights and viewed the Democratic Party's civil rights platform as "laws that would subject its people to scorn and ridicule."[103] When the Mississippi Democrats walked out of the Democratic convention, he believed they had no choice and that revenge would be theirs. "Those who manipulated the rape of the South at Philadelphia," McAbee warned, "will live to rue the day."[104] At the Columbus *Commercial Dispatch*, Imes, who attended the Dixiecrat convention in Birmingham, published front-page "Convention Notes" from Jimmy Arrington, the editor of the weekly Collins (Mississippi) *News-Commercial*. "We met the enemy last night but we still ain't his," Arrington reported. "We are Alabama bound today on the Southern railroad."[105]

Jones, the prohibitionist editor of the Grenada *Sentinel-Star*, saw the "demon alcohol" as the only reason for there not being a mass exodus from the national convention in support of the Dixiecrat protest. "Many other Southern delegations will follow when they get down to sober thinking," he wrote, and with an afterthought he penned, "Or just plainly speaking, sober."[106] At the conclusion of the convention, a bitter and frustrated Jones wrote, "The National Democratic Party platform now, and Communism, are surely one and the same thing."[107] In Corinth, McAbee saw the development of the states' rights movement as a show of Southern force in his editorial, "South's Leadership Expands."[108] In Natchez, Trimble saw no other recourse. "Perhaps we shall not see victory in our own time," he wrote, "but neither did the Founding Fathers live to witness the crystallization of their dreams into a vigorous, free nation that was at one time the beacon light of the world."[109]

Gibbons of Laurel looked at things a bit more allegorically. "The Democratic party today is like Humpty Dumpty," she wrote. "Nobody can put the pieces back together again. Not right now."[110] Harris in West Point agreed and harked back to the Civil War. "The split in the Democratic Party over states' rights issues is admittedly the most serious since 1860," he wrote. "The states should be asked to do nothing the individual can do for himself."[111]

On the Mississippi Gulf Coast, Gulfport *Daily Herald* editor Money offered readers the following opinion, which would have raised the ire of a more traditional readership than that of the Coast. "We believe the South is not solid on the subject of civil rights but is solid on states' rights," he wrote.

Cashman at the *Vicksburg Evening Post* and the *Vicksburg Herald* seemed uncertain regarding his position on the formation of the Mississippi States' Rights Party. Only once did he mention the issue in a *Vicksburg Evening Post* editorial.[112] In the *Vicksburg Herald* he kept the same noncommittal tone. "It will be interesting to see what happens,"[113] Cashman wrote, but he never mentioned the States' Rights Party by name.

Joseph F. Ellis, Jr., at the *Clarksdale Press Register*, had nothing to say in his editorial column regarding the Mississippi States' Rights Party or the

Dixiecrat walkout of the Democratic National Convention. Ellis instead printed several guest editorials, all of which supported the Dixiecrat position, including one from the Tunica *Times-Democrat* that protested, "The Democrats can't kick the South around."[114]

Gibbons was one of the few editors of the Mississippi daily press who questioned the actions of the protesters. "We don't believe Mississippi gained anything in particular by walking out," she wrote in the *Laurel Leader-Call*.[115] Carter at the Greenville *Delta Democrat-Times* agreed and argued for Southerners to remain within the Democratic Party. He voiced his fear that the states' rights issue was being handled in such a way as to "give misunderstanding outsiders the impression that we are truly guilty of mass bigotry."[116] At the *Tupelo Journal*, McLean concurred with Gibbons and Carter in questioning the Southern rejection of the national Democratic Party platform. McLean tried to encourage his readers to look at the larger picture. "The key to justice, tolerance and brotherhood lies in the improvement of the people of America," he wrote, "not in some complicated political formula."[117] McLean also asked his readers to seriously ponder the consequences of the states' rights that many of them were so eager to acquire. "We may be thrown so completely on our own, that we discover how disagreeable are the state responsibilities which inevitably go with states' rights," he wrote.[118] McLean was no social reformer bent on altering the traditional Southern way of life, however. He was a Southern Democrat who disagreed with the path being taken by the Democrats in 1948, a political party that he viewed as having become "little more than an assembly of minorities."[119]

Harris at the West Point *Daily Times-Leader* editorialized about the situation more than any other Mississippi editor. In his front-page "March of Events" column, Harris allied himself with the Dixiecrats as anti-Truman and for states' rights. He was the only editor of the Mississippi daily press who was optimistic about a States' Rights victory in the national election. "We're pretty certain the Dixie Democrat ticket will get more electoral votes than the ticket nominated in Philadelphia," he wrote.[120]

The chance for a national victory by the States' Rights Party was seen as a pipe dream by several editors of the Mississippi daily press. Cashman in Vicksburg, refusing to voice his total support or optimism for the States' Righters, observed, "While the possibilities for victory by Southerners are remote, their party creation appeared to be the only avenue left."[121] Sullens in Jackson recognized the futility of the States' Rights ticket but remained a staunch supporter of their ideals. "Southern Democrats, of course, realize their cause is hopeless, they know the Thurman-Wright ticket named at Birmingham cannot possibly win in November," he wrote. "But they have written a new chapter in the political history of the United States. They have put the nation on notice that we cannot be intimidated."[122] Sullens was an angry man in 1948. "We will not surrender our most sacred constitutional rights in order to placate a vicious minority that seeks to rupture present racial relations and establish social equity," he wrote. "If damn fool Democrats in other sections want to eat, drink and sleep with negroes that is their business. We can only deplore their degeneracy and declare we will have none of it."[123]

McLean in Tupelo, although a states' rights advocate and traditional conservative Southerner, did not foresee a future for the States' Rights Party in the country and failed to see the practicality in placing Thurmond and Wright on a ticket. In "Only Kidding Themselves and the Public," he wrote, "There is little likelihood that they will capture the presidency in the near future or that they will bring fame and glory for themselves."[124] A letter from three students at Mississippi College in Clinton was published in the Jackson *Clarion-Ledger* regarding similar concerns about the Dixiecrat ticket. One of the students, Jesse Howell, Jr., who now resides in Jackson and taught in the Jackson public schools from 1949 to 1970, said following the appearance of their letter in the Jackson *Clarion-Ledger* that the president of Mississippi College received several telephone calls threatening loss of alumni revenue.[125] "We believe states' rights should be tempered with more tolerance and reasonableness," the students wrote. "We are Southern college students and live in the South; proud to be called Southerners, but still prouder to be called Americans. Look around you, weigh the facts, and see for yourselves that there isn't much hope or place to go in the Dixiecrat program."[126]

Another letter castigating the concept of a renegade Democratic Party appeared in the *Meridian Star*. "We had just as well get ready to carry out the Supreme Court's mandates," the unsigned letter read. "All this talk about going over to the Republicans, or going over to a third party, is just d—— fool poppycock!"[127]

The last time in July 1948 that Carter in Greenville mentioned the States' Rights Party in an editorial was soon after Gerald K. Smith, director of the Oklahoma-based conservative Christian National Crusade, offered his assistance in working toward a Dixiecrat victory at the polls. Smith, who was quoted in the Mississippi daily press as saying, "We believe the negro and the Jew are exerting too much control in American politics,"[128] was not the type of person whom Carter or many of the other editors of the Mississippi daily press wanted associated with the States' Rights Party. In referencing his editorial "No Thanks, Mr. Smith," Carter wrote, "The good, legal basis upon which the states' rights issue is founded needs no aid from rabble rousers."[129] Gibbons in Laurel also praised the States' Rights rejection of Smith in an editorial: "More trouble can be stirred up in the South with a lot of rabble-rousing, race-baiting talk than we can live down in the next 50 years."[130] Skewes in Meridian, one of the most avowed traditional segregationists among the Mississippi daily editors, took the same stand, but with the perspective of calling into question Smith's manhood. "We don't need Gerald Smith," Skewes wrote. "Dixie Democrats want only He-Americans."[131]

Carter, Gibbons and Skewes were joined in their pronouncements against Smith by news articles in McComb, "Dixiecrats Spurn Offer from Smith"[132]; in Meridian, "Thurmond Blasts Smith Support"[133]; and in Tupelo, "Gerald Smith's Help Rejected by Dixiecrats."[134] An AP story in Columbus, "Thurmond Spurns Rabble-Rousers," reported that Thurmond had rejected Smith's support, saying the States' Rights Party "is not based on racial prejudice or hatred."[135]

The query raised here would seem to be why these editors would renounce Smith. Did they not see themselves as racists, with their condescending attitudes toward blacks? The difference may have been the level of anger. Most Southerners held no general anger toward blacks, so when someone like Smith came along with his attitude of "we'll make sure they know their place right quick," many white Southerners were repulsed. They preferred the "Happy Negro" theme in Mississippi. Emmerich in McComb reflected toward the end of the month about race relations in Mississippi and the impact on the States' Rights campaign. "The thing that hurts most in the states' rights fight is that the colored people of the South are badly confused," he wrote. "The difference between the North and the South insofar as race relations are concerned is the white people and the colored of the South feel kindly toward one another, in the North the race hatred is akin to viciousness."[136] Emmerich returned to finish his thoughts the next day. "There are millions of good Negroes in the South and it is to be regretted that Northern demagogues are seeking to hurt their cause by trying to win the approval of some Negro voters," he wrote. "There is no infringement on any race, white or colored, when its leaders insist upon maintaining race integrity through living with its own."[137]

Truman's chance at a second term in the White House was slim to nil, according to several editors of the Mississippi daily press. Harris of West Point wrote, "If Chairman Howard McGrath of the Democratic National Committee really believes Truman can be re-elected in November, then he ranks as one of the world's greatest optimists."[138] Sullens of Jackson reported, "Sen. Eastland may be right that the Truman/Barkley ticket will not carry a single state."[139] Gibbons in Laurel, who had not supported the concept of a new political party, agreed with Sullens and displayed his lack of prophetic accuracy. "The Dixiecrats in Birmingham on Saturday made it perfectly sure that Truman would not be elected," she wrote. "We doubt they will be successful, though we are sure the Democrats will lose the election."[140]

SUMMARY OF DIXIECRAT COVERAGE

The major issue of concern raised by editors of the Mississippi daily press during the 1948 Democratic presidential campaign was the Democratic civil rights platform and its commitment to the equal treatment of all Americans, regardless of race. The Mississippi Democrat delegation did not endorse that platform, and neither did the majority of the Democratic editors of the Mississippi daily press. Based on their editorials during July 1948, the idea of the social equality of blacks was a concept unacceptable at the time.

The propensity toward reporting civil rights issues in Mississippi daily newspapers during the 1948 Dixiecrat walkout ranged from daily news coverage of the Democratic campaign with only one editorial, in the *Hattiesburg American*, to almost daily editorials and daily news coverage in the West Point *Times-Leader*. Without a doubt, the presidential election of 1948 was a top story in the Mississippi daily press during July 1948. Most of the nineteen Mississippi daily newspapers covered the events of the Democratic national campaign daily on their front pages in July 1948, and they averaged an editorial every three days.

News articles in several of the Mississippi daily newspapers were quite different from the editorials, in that some were nothing more than fund-raising efforts and free political advertisements for the Dixiecrat cause.[141] This may have been the manner in which the editors justified their obvious political bias—by parading the States' Rights Democratic bid for power as legitimate news, rather than as editorial opinion and personal patronage.

Contrary to what media critics have noted about the promotion of violent suppression of civil rights activity in a small sampling of Southern newspapers,[142] the Mississippi daily press in 1948 did not advocate violence during the Dixiecrat protest that year. Not once was this found in any of the nineteen newspapers. However, the Mississippi daily press, as an aggregate, rejected the civil rights platform of the Democrats during the 1948 presidential campaign, and the usual rationalization was the states' rights argument, a convenient and tolerated camouflage for rejection of equal rights for all people.

In their news coverage of the civil rights issues pertaining to the 1948 Dixiecrat protest, the two most widely circulated Mississippi daily newspapers, the Jackson *Clarion-Ledger* and the Jackson *Daily News*, were representative, for the most part, of the Mississippi daily press. All the newspapers subscribed to at least one of the three major wire services available at the time, AP, UP or INS, and they ran the copy relatively unrevised, except for the sometimes lowercased word "negro."[143] The headlines of these wire service articles, although widely varied, did not misrepresent the stories. Because the Jackson *Clarion-Ledger* and the Jackson *Daily News* were able to send correspondents to cover the 1948 Democratic National Convention, news articles from their reporters were often more one-sided in favor of the Dixiecrats than wire service stories printed by the other newspapers.[144]

Likewise, editorial opinion in the other seventeen daily newspapers regarding the 1948 Dixiecrat protest was not drastically different from that in the Jackson *Clarion-Ledger* and the Jackson *Daily News*. The *Clarion-Ledger*, however, was alone in expressing doubt about the proposed presidential candidacy of General Dwight Eisenhower, a hesitancy based on lack of knowledge of Eisenhower's civil rights stance.

The Mississippi daily press personalized and localized the civil rights struggle during the Dixiecrat walkout in 1948, although there was little local activity reported pertaining to the protest. The general editorial concept in support of the states' rights movement and in opposition to the civil rights movement of Truman was an "us against them" theme. This notion created a connection to, and protest of, the national Democratic campaign, and thus the objection was localized, even if only on the philosophical level. Following the Democratic convention, local support groups for the States' Rights Party received news coverage.[145]

The events covered by the Mississippi daily press regarding the Dixiecrat walkout from the 1948 Democratic National Convention chronicle a turning point in Mississippi, Southern and national history. But that November, when cheesecake photos and Red Scare stories were headline news, other political events occurred that would also change the face of America forever. A U.S. Senate seat from Texas was won by a young schoolteacher named Lyndon Baines Johnson, who, as a future president, would sign into law the Civil Rights Acts of 1964 and 1968. Other incoming freshman senators included Hubert Humphrey, a social reformer known as "the crusading former mayor of Minneapolis," and Paul Douglas, "the liberal intellectual from Chicago,"[146] both dedicated and influential civil rights activists.

In November 1948, Harry Truman was re-elected, although with less than fifty percent of the popular vote. Only four Southern states—Mississippi, Louisiana, Alabama and South Carolina—were solid behind the States' Rights Party that November. The South would never be the same. And the Dixiecrats would never walk again.

NOTES

1. Neil R. McMillen, *Dark Journey: Black Mississippians in the Age of Jim Crow* (Urbana: University of Illinois Press, 1990), 303.
2. Ibid.

3. John Dittmer, *Local People: The Struggle for Civil Rights in Mississippi* (Urbana: University of Illinois Press, 1994), 18.

4. James Loewen and Charles Sallis, eds., *Mississippi: Conflict and Change* (New York: Pantheon Books, 1974), 245.

5. Neil R. McMillen, *The Citizens' Council: Organized Resistance to the Second Reconstruction 1954–1964* (Urbana: University of Illinois Press, 1971), 189.

6. James Marlow, "Democrats Dreary Outlook," Columbus *Commercial Dispatch*, 12 July 1948, 6.

7. Hodding Carter, Jr., "Democrats Will Put on Show," Greenville *Delta Democrat-Times*, 8 July 1948, 4.

8. J.O. Emmerich, "Highlights in the Headlines," McComb *Enterprise-Journal*, 1 July 1948, 1.

9. James H. Skewes, "Whistling in the Wind," *Meridian Star*, 1 July 1948, 1.

10. Fred Sullens, "Harry Truman, Renegade," Jackson *Daily News*, 28 July 1948, 4.

11. Frank Jones, Sr., "Briefed by Editor," Grenada *Sentinel-Star*, 6 July 1948, 1.

12. Ibid., 20 July, 1948, 1.

13. Elliott Trimble, "Southern Disservice," *Natchez Democrat*, 17 July 1948, 4.

14. L.O. Cosby, Sr., "Truman Ruined Nation's Economy," Jackson *Daily News*, 20 July 1948, 4.

15. "Text of Civil Rights Plank," Grenada *Sentinel-Star*, 15 July 1948, 1; Greenwood *Morning Star*, 16 July 1948, 4.

16. Loewen and Sallis, *Mississippi*, 185.

17. James Marlow, "Poll Tax Battle: What's It About?" Columbus *Commercial Dispatch*, 29 July 1948, 8.

18. Edgar Harris, "March of Events," West Point *Times-Leader*, 30 July 1948, 1.

19. "Push Anti-Poll Tax, GOPs Will Make Every Effort to Pass Measure, Southern Democrats Have Promised Long Filibuster," AP, Gulfport *Daily Herald*, 28 July 1948, 1; "Republicans Vote to Push Anti-Poll Tax Bill," AP, Columbus *Commercial Dispatch*, 28 July 1948, 1.

20. "Sen. Stennis Begins Dixie Filibuster, Anti-Poll Tax Bill Sparks Debate in Congress, Twenty [Other Dixiecrats] to Aid Stennis," AP, Greenville *Delta Democrat-Times*, 29 July 1948, 1; "Anti-Poll Tax Bill Their Target," AP, *Hattiesburg American*, 30 July 1948, 1; "Stennis Challenges Congress to Enact Anti-Poll Tax Bill, Senator First to Take Floor in Filibuster," AP, Corinth *Daily Corinthian*, 29 July 1948, 1; "Southern Democrats Ready to Fight Anti-Poll Tax Legislation," UPI, Greenwood *Morning Star*, 28 July 1948, 1; "Senator Prepares for Filibuster," AP, *Meridian Star*, 31 July 1948, 1.

21. "Stennis Flays Motive of Anti-Poll Tax," AP, *Meridian Star*, 30 July 1948, 1.

22. "Stennis Dixie Fight Head," *Meridian Star*, 28 July 1948, 1.

23. "Anti-Poll Tax Debate Drones On in Capital's Cave of Winds," AP, *Hattiesburg American*, 30 July 1948, 1.

24. "Eastland Makes Flat Prediction That Anti-Poll Tax and Anti-Lynch Bills Will Pass," McComb *Enterprise-Journal*, 27 July 1948, 1.

25. Harriet Gibbons, *Laurel Leader-Call*, 27 July 1948, 4.
26. Dittmer, *Local People*, 13; Loewen and Sallis, *Mississippi*, 178–179.
27. Harriet Gibbons, *Laurel Leader-Call*, 20 July 1948, 4.
28. Ibid., 27 July 1948, 4.
29. Elliott Trimble, "Mississippi Leads Nation," *Natchez Democrat*, 16 July 1948, 10.
30. James H. Skewes, "For Fight—We Must!" *Meridian Star*, 30 July, 1948, 4.
31. Edgar Harris, "March of Events," West Point *Times-Leader*, 28 July 1948, 1.
32. T.M. Hederman, Jr., "Army's Chief of Staff Defends Military Segregation," Jackson *Clarion-Ledger*, 30 July 1948, 6.
33. Elliott Trimble, "Off the Deep End," *Natchez Democrat*, 28 July, 1948, 8.
34. Edgar Harris, "Says Segregation Law of God," West Point *Times-Leader*, 13 July 1948, 4.
35. Edgar Harris, "March of Events," West Point *Times-Leader*, 19 July 1948, 1.
36. Ibid., 27 July 1948, 1.
37. Ibid., 10 July 1948, 1.
38. Tom Shepherd, "Democrats Not Whipped," *Greenwood Commonwealth*, 2 July 1948, 4.
39. Edgar Harris, "March of Events," West Point *Times-Leader*, 6 July 1948, 1.
40. "Laney Says Ike Can Unite All," AP, *Clarksdale Press Register*, 5 July 1948, 1.
41. "Georgia Adopts 'Draft Eisenhower' for President," AP, Corinth *Daily Corinthian*, 2 July 1948, 1; "Georgians Back Ike," AP, West Point *Times-Leader*, 2 July 1948, 1.
42. "One Year After He Spoke at Vicksburg," AP, Greenville *Delta Democrat-Times*, 5 July 1948, 2.
43. "Stennis Hopes Ike Will Accept," UPI, Greenwood *Morning Star*, 6 July 1948, 1.
44. "Stennis Booms Eisenhower," *Vicksburg Herald*, 6 July 1948, 1.
45. "Stennis Backs Gen. Eisenhower," *Vicksburg Evening Post*, 5 July 1948, 1.
46. T.M. Hederman, Jr., "General Eisenhower Presented as a States' Rights Man," Jackson *Clarion-Ledger*, 4 July 1948, 4.
47. "Truman Pleased as Ike Says No," AP, *Greenwood Commonwealth*, 6 July 1948, 1; James Ewing, "Wright Continues Skeptical of 'Draft Ike' Boom," Jackson *Daily News*, 6 July 1948, 1; "Views Ike Boom with Skepticism," INS, *Meridian Star*, 3 July 1948, 1.
48. "Truman Pleased as Ike Says No," 1.
49. "Dixie Awaits Ike's Yes or No Reaction," AP, Jackson *Clarion-Ledger*, 6 July 1948, 1.
50. Edgar Harris, "March of Events," West Point *Times-Leader*, 31 July 1948, 1.
51. Hodding Carter, Jr., "Maybe He's Available," Greenville *Delta Democrat-Times*, 4 July 1948, 4.

52. Elliott Trimble, "Eisenhower," *Natchez Democrat*, 7 July 1948, 8.

53. Birney Imes, Jr., Columbus *Commercial Dispatch*, 12 July 1948, 6.

54. "Platform Fight Looming," AP, *Laurel Leader-Call*, 12 July 1948, 1.

55. "Southerners Balk at Civil Rights Plank," AP, *Clarksdale Press Register*, 13 July 1948, 1; "Convention Split over Civil Rights Issue," AP, Columbus *Commercial Appeal*, 14 July 1948, 1; "Democrats Go to Philadelphia with Bad Case of Split Personality," AP, Greenville *Delta Democrat-Times*, 12 July 1948, 2; "Civil Rights Issue May Divide Party," AP, *Greenwood Commonwealth*, 12 July 1948, 1; "Civil Rights Issue May Divide Party," AP, *Greenwood Commonwealth*, 12 July 1948, 1; "Democratic Party Splits Wide Open," UPI, Greenwood *Morning Star*, 13 July 1948, 1; "Argue over Civil Rights," AP, Gulfport *Daily Herald*, 14 July 1948, 1; "Party Suffers from Split Personality," AP, *Hattiesburg American*, 12 July 1948, 1; "Issue on Civil Rights Toughest Facing Convention," AP, Jackson *Daily News*, 10 July 1948, 1; "Platform for Democrats Causes Break," AP, *Laurel Leader-Call*, 12 July 1948, 1; "Truman's Civil Rights Program Endorsed, Democratic Convention Deals Double Blow to South by Rejecting States' Rights Plank," AP, *Natchez Democrat*, 15 July 1948, 1; "Democratic Civil Rights Plank Watered Down, Little Support for States' Rights," UPI, Tupelo *Daily Journal*, 14 July 1948, 1; "Civil Rights Fight Flares into Open," AP, *Vicksburg Herald*, 10 July 1948, 1; "Southerners Rise to Cause as Platform Fight Shapes Up," AP, West Point *Times-Leader*, 10 July 1948, 1.

56. C.B. McAbee, "Southerners Kindle Democratic Fire," Corinth *Daily Corinthian*, 14 July 1948, 4.

57. Tom Shepherd, "Much Ado about Nothing," *Greenwood Commonwealth*, 22 July 1948, 4.

58. Hodding Carter, Jr., "Don't Rush Us," Greenville *Delta Democrat-Times*, 15 July 1948, 4.

59. "Will Dixie Bolt? Press Survey Indicates No," INS, Jackson *Clarion-Ledger*, 1 July 1948, 1.

60. "Dixie Set to Walk," Jackson *Clarion-Ledger*, 11 July 1948, 1.

61. "All State Delegates Pledged to Walk," AP, Greenville *Delta Democrat-Times*, 8 July 1948, 1.

62. "Virginia Democrats Told Not to Bolt," AP, Gulfport *Daily Herald*, 2 July 1948, 1.

63. J.O. Emmerich, "Highlights in the Headlines," McComb *Enterprise-Journal*, 8 July 1948, 1.

64. George McLean, "Dixie Congressmen May Duck Convention," Tupelo *Daily Journal*, 9 July 1948, 4.

65. "Move to Upset Mississippi Made," AP, Columbus *Commercial Dispatch*, 13 July 1948, 1.

66. Birney Imes, Jr., "Convention Notes," Columbus *Commercial Dispatch*, 16 July 1948, 6.

67. Harriet Gibbons, *Laurel Leader-Call*, 14 July 1948, 4.

68. Purser Hewitt, "Convention Report," Jackson *Clarion-Ledger*, 14 July 1948, 1.

69. Drew Pearson, "Barkley Best-Loved Senator," Tupelo *Daily Journal*, 20 July 1948, 6.

70. G.P. Money, "The Barkley Keynote Speech," Gulfport *Daily Herald*, 14 July 1948, 1.

71. Birney Imes, Jr., "The Philadelphia Glory," Columbus *Commercial Dispatch*, 15 July 1948, 8.

72. Ibid.

73. Tom Shepherd, "South without a Party," *Greenwood Commonwealth*, 16 July 1948, 4.

74. Frank Jones, Sr., "Briefed by Editor," Grenada *Sentinel-Star*, 16 July 1948, 1.

75. Fred Sullens, "Negroes in the Saddle," Jackson *Daily News*, 16 July 1948, 4.

76. T.M. Hederman, Jr., "A Hurt and Angered South Is Pondering These Questions," Jackson *Clarion-Ledger*, 16 July 1948, 6.

77. J.O. Emmerich, "We Will Win the Party," McComb *Enterprise-Journal*, 15 July 1948, 1.

78. "Mississippi, Alabama Stalk Out," AP, Columbus *Commercial Dispatch*, 15 July 1948, 1.

79. "Dixie Democrats Take Walk," AP, Corinth *Daily Corinthian*, 15 July 1948, 1.

80. "Truman Is Nominated," INS, Jackson *Clarion-Ledger*, 15 July 1948, 1.

81. Purser Hewitt, "Mississippi Makes History," Jackson *Clarion-Ledger*, 15 July 1948, 1.

82. Elliott Trimble, "Mississippi Leads Nation," *Natchez Democrat*, 16 July 1948, 10.

83. L.P. Cashman, Sr., "The Fourth Party," *Vicksburg Evening Post*, 20 July 1948, 4.

84. AP, Gulfport *Daily Herald*, 15 July 1948, 1.

85. "Most Meridianites for Delegate Walk," *Meridian Star*, 15 July 1948, 1.

86. J.O. Emmerich, "Highlights in the Headlines," McComb *Enterprise-Journal*, 21 July 1948, 1.

87. Howard Suttle, "It's on to B'ham!" McComb *Enterprise-Journal*, 15 July 1948, 1.

88. "Mississippi Briefs," UPI, Greenwood *Morning Star*, 22 July 1948, 1.

89. "Carry States' Rights Banner," AP, *Clarksdale Press Register*, 19 July 1948, 1; "Southerners Give Ovation to Thurmond–Wright Ticket," AP, Columbus *Commercial Dispatch*, 18 July 1948, 1; "Dixie Democrats Select Thurmond and Wright to Head Rights' Ticket," AP, Corinth *Daily Corinthian*, 18 July 1948, 1; "Thurmond, Wright Lead South, Dixiecrats Campaign in Fourteen States," AP, Greenville *Delta Democrat-Times*, 18 July 1948, 1; "Carry States' Rights Banner," AP, *Greenwood Commonwealth*, 19 July 1948, 1; "Thurmond, Wright Accept Dixiecrat Nomination," AP, Greenwood *Morning Star*, 18 July 1948, 1; "Our Leaders," Gulfport *Daily Herald*, 19 July 1948, 1; "Gov. Wright, Dixie Rebel Leader," AP, *Hattiesburg American*, 17 July 1948, 1; "Thurmond, Wright Hoist Dixie Banner," Jackson *Clarion-Ledger*, 18 July 1948, 1; "Thurmond, Wright Accept Dixiecrat Draft, Party Leaders Named in Riotous Session," UPI, Jackson *Daily News*, 18 July 1948, 1; "Nominees of Dixie, Thurmond and Wright," AP, *Laurel Leader-Call*, 19 July 1948, 1; "Southern Nominees for Highest Offices Get Together for Strategy Meeting," McComb *Enterprise-Journal*, 15 July 1948, 1; "Dixiecrats Name Thur-

mond and Wright," *Meridian Star*, 18 July 1948, 1; "Thurmond and Wright States' Rights Candidates," *Natchez Democrat*, 18 July 1948, 1; "Dixiecrats to Invade Home States of Truman and Barkley, Will Run Rebel Ticket in Both South and North," UPI, Tupelo *Daily Journal*, 17 July 1948, 1; "Revolting Southern Democrats," AP, *Vicksburg Herald*, 17 July 1948, 1; "Dixie Revolt Is Last Hope," AP, West Point *Times-Leader*, 20 July 1948, 1.

90. "Dixie Democrats Select Thurmond and Wright to Head Rights' Ticket," AP, Corinth *Daily Corinthian*, 18 July 1948, 1; "Southerners Map Truman Challenge," *Hattiesburg American*, 17 July 1948, 1.

91. Hodding Carter, Jr., "Looking at the South," Greenville *Delta Democrat-Times*, 11 July 1948, 4.

92. Harriet Gibbons, "Nothing More," *Laurel Leader-Call*, 12 July 1948, 4.

93. Birney Imes, Jr., "A Good Chance," Columbus *Commercial Appeal*, 18 July 1948, 6.

94. Birney Imes, Jr., "The Birmingham Meeting," Columbus *Commercial Dispatch*, 19 July 1948, 2.

95. J.O. Emmerich, "Highlights in the Headlines," McComb *Enterprise-Journal*, 16 July 1948, 1.

96. Edgar Harris, "March of Events," West Point *Times-Leader*, 19 July 1948, 1.

97. Elliott Trimble, "Get behind It," *Natchez Democrat*, 20 July 1948, 2.

98. James Alsop, "The Fight Outlined," Greenwood *Morning Star*, 27 July 1948, 4.

99. Andrews Harmon, "Grave Days Ahead," *Hattiesburg American*, 27 July 1948, 2.

100. Elliott Trimble, "No Other Course," *Natchez Democrat*, 11 July 1948, 6.

101. James Alsop, Greenwood *Morning Star*, 13 July 1948, 4.

102. Tom Shepherd, "The Silent Majority," *Greenwood Commonwealth*, 6 July 1948, 4.

103. C.B. McAbee, "Southerner Rekindles Democratic Fire," Corinth *Daily Corinthian*, 14 July 1948, 4.

104. C.B. McAbee, "South Gets Read Out of Party," Corinth *Daily Corinthian*, 15 July 1948, 4.

105. Jimmy Arrington, "Convention Notes," Columbus *Commercial Dispatch*, 15 July 1948, 1.

106. Frank Jones, Sr., "Briefed by Editor," Grenada *Sentinel-Star*, 15 July 1948, 1.

107. Ibid., 19 July 1948, 1.

108. C.B. McAbee, "South's Leadership Expands," Corinth *Daily Corinthian*, 4 July 1948, 4.

109. Elliott Trimble, "No Other Course," *Natchez Democrat*, 11 July 1948, 6.

110. Harriet Gibbons, *Laurel Leader-Call*, 10 July 1948, 2.

111. Edgar Harris, "March of Events," West Point *Times-Leader*, 8 July 1948, 1.

112. L.P. Cashman, Sr., "The Fourth Party," *Vicksburg Evening Post*, 20 July 1948, 4.

113. L.P. Cashman, Sr., "It Will Be Interesting to See What Happens," *Vicksburg Herald*, 9 July 1948, 4.

114. *Clarksdale Press Register*, 30 July 1948, 4.

115. Harriet Gibbons, "It's Over," *Laurel Leader-Call*, 15 July 1948, 4.

116. Hodding Carter, Jr., "No Thanks, Mr. Smith," Greenville *Delta Democrat-Times*, 21 July 1948, 4.

117. George McLean, "The Biggest Flaws Are in Human Nature," Tupelo *Daily Journal*, 10 July 1948, 6.

118. George McLean, "How Lonesome It's Getting Down Here," Tupelo *Daily Journal*, 24 July 1948, 4.

119. George McLean, "A Chance to Make History in Losing," Tupelo *Daily Journal*, 14 July 1948, 4.

120. Edgar Harris, "March of Events," West Point *Times-Leader*, 19 July 1948, 1.

121. L.P. Cashman, Sr., "The Fourth Party," *Vicksburg Evening Post*, 20 July 1948, 4.

122. Fred Sullens, "Southern Democracy," Jackson *Daily News*, 19 July 1948, 4.

123. Ibid.

124. George McLean, "Only Kidding Themselves and Public," Tupelo *Daily Journal*, 21 July 1948, 4.

125. Jesse Howell, Jr., unpublished telephone interview by Susan Weill, 1 July 1997.

126. Joe Steinwinder, Dalton McCullar, and Jesse Howell, Jr., letter to editor, "College Students Entering Dissent," Jackson *Clarion-Ledger*, 27 July 1948, 4.

127. Unsigned letter to the editor, *Meridian Star*, 22 July 1948, 4.

128. "Gerald K. Smith for Southerners," AP, *Greenwood Commonwealth*, 19 July 1948, 1.

129. Hodding Carter, Jr., "No Thanks, Mr. Smith," 4.

130. Harriet Gibbons, *Laurel Leader-Call*, 20 July 1948, 4.

131. James H. Skewes, "We Choose Our Own," *Meridian Star*, 21 July 1948, 4.

132. "Dixiecrats Spurn Offer from Smith," McComb *Enterprise-Journal*, 20 July 1948, 1.

133. "Thurmond Blasts Smith Support," *Meridian Star*, 19 July 1948, 1.

134. "Gerald Smith's Help Rejected by Dixiecrats," Tupelo *Daily Journal*, 20 July 1948, 1.

135. "Thurmond Spurns Rabble Rousers," AP, Columbus *Commercial Dispatch*, 20 July 1948, 1.

136. J.O. Emmerich, "Highlights in the Headlines," McComb *Enterprise-Journal*, 28 July 1948, 1.

137. Ibid., 29 July 1948, 1.

138. Edgar Harris, "March of Events," West Point *Times-Leader*, 9 July 1948, 1.

139. Fred Sullens, "Lowdown on Higher Ups," Jackson *Daily News*, 21 July 1948, 1.

140. Harriet Gibbons, "What They Did," *Laurel Leader-Call*, 19 July 1948, 4.

141. "States' Righters Need Funds, Call for Contributions," Columbus *Commercial Dispatch*, 23 July 1948, 1; "States' Righters Ask Contributions," *Greenwood Commonwealth*, 22 July 1948, 1.

142. "Dilemma in Dixie," *Time*, 20 February 1956, 76; "Dixie Flamethrowers," *Time*, 4 March 1966, 64; "Moderation in Dixie," *Time*, 19 March 1965, 71; Edwin W. Williams, "Dimout in Jackson," *Columbia Journalism Review* 9 (Summer 1970): 56.

143. "President's Machinery Being Oiled," AP, *Clarksdale Press Register*, 8 July 1948, 1; "Gerald K. Smith for Southerners," AP, *Greenwood Commonwealth*, 19 July 1948, 1; "Grant Bus Permit to Jackson Negro," AP, Gulfport *Daily Herald*, 9 July 1948, 1; "Highlights in the Headlines," McComb *Enterprise-Journal*, 28 July 1948, 1.

144. Purser Hewitt, "Dixiecrat Caucus," Jackson *Clarion-Ledger*, 12 July 1948, 1; Purser Hewitt, "The Rev. Charles Hamilton," Jackson *Clarion-Ledger*, 14 July 1948, 1; Purser Hewitt, "Dixiecrat Choice Bolsters Strength for Showdown," Jackson *Clarion-Ledger*, 14 July 1948, 1; Purser Hewitt, "Wright Delegation Gets Okay after Brisk Floor Fight," Jackson *Clarion-Ledger*, 14 July 1948, 1; Jack Hancock, "States' Righters Seek Solid Citizen of South for Presidency," Jackson *Daily News*, 11 July 1948, 1; Jack Hancock, "Mississippi Delegates Walk Out Wednesday, They're 'Bama Bound," Jackson *Daily News*, 13 July 1948, 1.

145. "Locals Attend Dixiecrat Meeting on Saturday," Corinth *Daily Corinthian*, 20 July 1948, 6; "Most Meridianites for Walk," *Meridian Star*, 15 July 1948, 1.

146. Doris Kearns Goodwin, *Lyndon Johnson and the American Dream* (New York: St. Martin's Press, 1976), 101–102.

Chapter 3

1954: *Brown v. Board of Education* and the Mississippi Daily Press

When the U.S. Supreme Court declared segregated public schools illegal with its 1954 *Brown v. Board of Education* decision, the mandate was considered "a sort of second emancipation proclamation."[1] An end to public school segregation had become a goal of the National Association for the Advancement of Colored People because in seventeen Southern states black and white students attended segregated schools that were definitely "separate," but certainly not "equal."[2] In 1950, black students constituted nearly sixty percent of the public school pupils in Mississippi, but they received less than thirty percent of public school funds.[3] Salaries for black teachers in Mississippi averaged $1,000 annually, compared to nearly $2,000 annually for white teachers.[4] Knowledge is power, and according to Mississippi historian Neil McMillen, "Throughout the Jim Crow era, the single greatest impediment to better Afro-American schools was white fear of the revolutionary and economic implications of educating a subservient workforce."[5]

Historically, black public schools in Mississippi were severely underfunded. In the early 1900s, black children accounted for more than fifty percent of Mississippi's public school students but received less than twenty percent of the state's public school allocations. By the time of the *Brown v. Board of Education* decision in 1954, the same proportion of black students were receiving about a quarter of the state's educational funding. "In the field of public education, the doctrine of separate but equal has no place," the *Brown v. Board of Education* decision stated. "Separate education facilities are inherently unequal."[6]

Many Southern blacks feared reprisal from the white community because of the mandate. H.H. Humes, a black minister, expressed his concerns to

Mississippi Governor Hugh White and a group gathered to discuss White's plan for voluntary segregation to counter *Brown*. "You should not be mad at us," Humes said. "Those were nine *white* men who rendered the decision. Not one colored man had anything to do with it." The real trouble, according to Humes, was that black schools in the state were in such dilapidated condition that students "study the earth through the floor and the stars through the roof."[7]

EDITORIAL RESPONSE TO *BROWN*

Wire service stories announced the decision as front-page news in all twenty Mississippi daily newspapers,[8] but the editors responded to *Brown v. Board of Education* with less than half the editorial opinion with which they had addressed the Dixiecrat protest of 1948. Perhaps the rationale was that words seemed futile against a Supreme Court decision, whereas a political ideology can sometimes be modified through verbal debate. Or possibly, the lack of more editorial opinion regarding *Brown* was that the editors knew the "separate but equal" decree of *Plessy v. Ferguson* had not been enforced for fifty years, and they, like Fred Sullens at the Jackson *Daily News*,[9] assumed that *Brown* would not be enforced, either. To these editors, *Brown v. Board of Education* may have appeared as simply another token attempt at change that would bear no consequences.

The percentage of blacks in the communities served by the Mississippi daily press, which ranged from fourteen to seventy percent, seemed to have no impact on editorial opinion regarding civil rights in 1954. In Clarksdale, for instance, where the Coahoma County black population was one of the highest in the state at seventy percent,[10] editor Joseph Ellis, Jr., followed his pattern from 1948 by publishing the opinions of guest editors and columnists rather than writing his own editorials. The day after the *Brown v. Board of Education* decision, the *Clarksdale Press Register* published a syndicated column by James Marlow denouncing the Court order as a violation of both the Fourteenth Amendment and *Plessy v. Ferguson.*[11] In Corinth, on the other hand, where Alcorn County's black population was the smallest represented in this study at fourteen percent,[12] Jack Waldon, the newly appointed editor of the Corinth *Daily Corinthian*, also utilized Marlow to address the issue on the opinion page.[13]

On the Mississippi River in Greenville, where the Washington County population was nearly seventy percent black,[14] editor Hodding Carter, Jr., was alone among the Mississippi daily press editors in advocating the desegregation of the state's school system on the college level.[15] Carter displayed a global consciousness unusual for the times and urged his readers to consider the positive aspects of the Supreme Court's decision. "Let's keep our shirts on," he wrote. "Whatever the South thinks of it, there is no doubt that it will raise America's prestige in the world, and especially in the world of brown and yellow and black people. And to us in the South, it gives a challenge to replace trickery and subterfuge in our educational structure with an honest realization that every American child has the right to an equal education."[16]

Two days later, Carter was back, praising his community in the editorial, "Delta Shows Good Sense." He applauded his readers for their "calm compliance coupled with determination to work things out."[17] In late August, as the public schools were enrolling students, the Greenville *Delta Democrat-Times* published Carter's front-page editorial, "What Next for Our Schools?" clearly stating his views on the desegregation of schools below the college level. "It would be tragic if in the deep South any widespread or concentrated effort is made this fall or in the immediate future to enroll Negro children in hitherto all-white schools," he wrote. "This is not said as a threat or warning, but as a basic fact. A majority of Southerners are not ready for the reality of integration."[18]

In neighboring Greenwood, where the Leflore County population in 1954 was also nearly seventy percent black,[19] Virgil Adams of the Greenwood *Morning Star* disagreed with Carter's tolerant view of *Brown v. Board of Education*. Adams viewed the decision as "inevitable," but he also considered the consequences of the decision detrimental to both blacks and whites. In his editorial "A Real Test for the South," published the day after the decision, Adams pleaded for calm on all fronts until a "solution" could be found. "Unless advocates of segregation in the South come up with some new angle to the laws regarding segregation, it is only a matter of months, or perhaps a year, until enforcement of the new ruling will be put into effect," he wrote. "We fully expect there will be a greater intermarriage of the races and some other evil effects which are not good for either race." Adams then called on "cool leadership" from the "levelheaded thinking leaders of both races."[20]

The next day, Adams complained that the high court had overstepped its intended purpose of interpreting laws and had cast itself, instead, as a maker of laws with *Brown v. Board of Education*.[21] Within the week, Adams published a guest editorial from Austin Walden, a black writer in Atlanta who did not endorse desegregation. "Negro Attorney Says Those Favoring Integration Are Emotionally Unstable," headlined Walden's argument.[22]

In August, as school was about to begin, Adams continued his role as a peacekeeper and optimist. In "Greenwood People Worried about School Problem," he wrote, "Our advice is to look to the future with confidence that these problems can and will be worked out fairly and satisfactorily for both races."[23] Later in the month, he tried to explain his support of segregation. "The South's stand on separate schools stems from the long experience which Southerners have in race relations," he wrote. "It is not prejudice, but a measure which has proven itself best for both races."[24]

Across town, Tom Shepherd of the *Greenwood Commonwealth* published an editorial every three days during the Dixiecrat protest. He had only one observation to offer pertaining to *Brown v. Board of Education*, and that was on the last day of May. "Abolition of segregation required by the recent Supreme Court decision would not of itself remove the deficiencies in our schools," he wrote. "It would simply mean, under present conditions, that some negro children would go to better schools and some white children would go to worse."[25]

In Columbus, where half the Lowndes County population was black,[26] Birney Imes, Jr., discussed the Dixiecrat walkout in 1948 every other day in the *Commercial Dispatch*. In May 1954, he mentioned *Brown v. Board of Education* only twice in his editorial column. The first time was the day after the 17 May decision, when he observed without explanation on the front page, "I think the Supreme Court decision was born a hundred years too soon."[27] The headline to the AP story announcing the decision in the Columbus *Commercial Dispatch* included an alternative to *Brown*: "Abolish Public School System Declares Sillers."[28] Walter Sillers was the speaker of the Mississippi House of Representatives in 1954. He proposed closing down the state's public school system rather than desegregating.

In Grenada, where the Grenada County population was fifty percent black,[29] editor M.M. Grimes of the *Sentinel-Star* made no editorial comment in May 1954 regarding *Brown v. Board of Education*. Six years earlier, during the Dixiecrat protest, then editor Frank Jones, Sr., had published an editorial at least twice a week pertaining to the Dixiecrat controversy. Despite publishing no opinions regarding the decision, Grimes did cover *Brown* in front-page news articles from UP and AP wire services throughout the month in which he localized headlines to make his point.[30]

On the Mississippi Gulf Coast, where the population was about twenty percent black in 1954,[31] E.P. Wilkes of the Gulfport *Daily Herald* offered a single editorial opinion in May 1954 following *Brown vs. Board of Education*. "In spite of the historic background embodied in the word, segregation, we feel the Negro and the white desire to go right ahead in shaping the schools of the South into the best in the United States for each race to use as its own," he wrote.[32]

In Forrest County, where the population was thirty percent black in 1954,[33] the *Hattiesburg American* published only two opinions from editor Andrews Harmon in May 1954 pertaining to the Supreme Court decision. Harmon had not been prolific during the Dixiecrat movement of 1948, with only one editorial concerning that issue. Four days after news of *Brown v. Board of Education* hit the press, however, Harmon attempted to convince his readers that it was in the best interests of everyone, black and white, to keep the schools segregated. "The truth is that ninety-eight percent of the Negroes in the South do not want to attend schools with white people," he wrote. "One of the South's great crises can be lessened if the honest, faithful Negroes resist efforts by outside agitators."[34]

Harmon made no reference to where he acquired his information about what blacks "want," but his pronouncement that most desired segregated schools was certainly contrary to what the NAACP reported.[35] In August that summer, prior to schools opening for the 1954–1955 school year, Harmon was back to encourage his readers to act on their beliefs. "If all the people of Mississippi want to retain racial segregation in the public schools they can do it simply by standing together," he wrote. "No power on earth can compel more than a million people to do something that is against the law of God and nature."[36]

In Hinds County, where the state capital is located and where the population was forty percent black in 1954,[37] the Jackson *Clarion-Ledger* averaged an opinion pertaining to *Brown v. Board of Education* every three days, primarily in letters to the editor. The number of opinion columns in the Jackson *Clarion-Ledger* was similar to that during the Dixiecrat protest, but in 1948 there were several more staff-written editorials than in 1954 and not quite as many letters to the editor. The Jackson *Clarion-Ledger* was never hesitant to proclaim its convictions and did so on the day after *Brown v. Board of Education*, with "Segregation Crisis Faces Us," in which the Supreme Court was harshly criticized. "Stunning as the decision is, it creates no immediate crisis," Hederman wrote. "May 17, 1954, may be recorded by future historians as a black day of tragedy for the South, and for both races, but we can conduct ourselves in such a fashion as to cause historians to record that we faced that tragedy and crisis with wisdom, courage, faith and determination such as our fathers would have applauded."[38]

During the rest of the month, the only staff-written opinion pertaining to the decision came from Charles M. Hills in his "Affairs of State" column. Hills was prophetic beyond his racially motivated imagination when he suggested an alternative for Mississippi children in order avoid desegregation in Mississippi's public schools. "If integration becomes a painful fact one of these days and we of the white race just can't take it, why not look into television education?" he wrote. "Children could get their education right in their own homes, and certainly there is no law yet that could force us to invite negro children into our living rooms."[39]

Letters to the editor of the Jackson *Clarion-Ledger* displayed personal angst concerning *Brown* in 1954. Grover Hewell of Canton wrote in anger and dismay, "The Supreme Court, in its deadly coil, is about to strike down our sacred traditions."[40] Blanche Gregory of Pickens agreed. "Under heaven let there be no brother and sister incestation between races," she wrote. "Sociology informs us that the white blood of the South, including that in the black belt, has a higher percentage of racial purity than that of any other section of the country."[41]

Jack Garellick of Vicksburg wrote one of the few published letters of support for the elimination of segregation. "We are all God's children and he ignores the distinctions made by men," he wrote. "Segregation was man-made. For the answer to whether or not segregation is right or wrong, look not to the lawmakers or politicians, look to God."[42] Garellick was supported by L.G. Patterson of Jackson. "There are those of us who believe that the Negro will act and behave like a human being only when he is educated and treated like one," he wrote. " 'Jim Crow' laws are not in harmony with the love for one another taught in the Bible."[43]

Edwin White, a member of the Mississippi House of Representatives from Holmes County, also used the Bible to make his point, but it was completely opposite from the one made by Garellick and Patterson. "The question might be asked, if the white man is a true friend to the colored man, then why is he not willing to abide by the Supreme Court Decision?" he wrote. "The answer is plain and simple. There is only one thing in the whole situation which the white man asks for and that is the privilege of his children, and his children's children, continuing to be white people. It's God's law."[44]

Evelyn Riley, a black woman from Itta Bena, wrote to express her support of segregation based on white attitudes. "We are proud of our race and do not want to go to school with your children if you do not want us there," she wrote. "Frankly, I feel the same about the whites as they feel about me."[45]

A letter from "Concerned Taxpayers" responded to Riley the next day. "Why doesn't the Negro do for himself?" the letter said. "No, we the white people have helped, pampered, and cared for this race for so long they have become like a youngster who has been given too much. The time comes when you can't satisfy his wants. Let the Negro build his own schools with his own taxes, let the white man build his with his."[46]

Across town, the Jackson *Daily News* made news itself in August 1954 after being purchased by the rival Hedermans of the Jackson *Clarion-Ledger*.[47] Fred Sullens, who continued as editor after the Hederman acquisition, voiced his interpretation of *Brown v. Board of Education* in May as the final insult from a Supreme Court that was, in his mind, determined to destroy the Southern way of life regardless of the confusion and carnage that it left behind. Eight front-page stories, mostly staff-written, reported Sullens' own prejudice in the guise of news with headlines such as "South Will Not Obey Political Court"[48] and "[Mississippi Lieutenant Governor Carroll] Gartin Says Negroes Want Separate Schools."[49] In his front-page editorial, "Low Down on Higher Ups," Sullens vented his wrath. The decision was "the worst thing that has happened to the South since carpetbaggers and scalawags took charge," he wrote. "It means racial strife of the bitterest sort. Mississippi will never consent to placing white and Negro children in the same public schools." Sullens thought that he could speak for all people in Mississippi. "The white people and the thinking Negro people did not want that to happen. Both look on the decision as a calamity," he wrote. "White and Negro children in the same schools will lead to miscegenation. Miscegenation leads to mixed marriages and mixed marriages lead to mongrelization of the human race."[50]

The next day, Sullens continued his outraged uproar. He, like Harmon in Hattiesburg, had suddenly become an insider on what blacks wanted for themselves and their children. "An overwhelming majority of the Negro parents in Mississippi do not want their children to attend white schools," he wrote. "They prefer to have their children taught by teachers of their own race. They are not seeking any form of social equality."[51]

Throughout May 1954, Sullens continued to blast the Supreme Court and to declare that *Brown* would be ignored in Mississippi. In his editorial "We Are Not Acquiescent," he wrote, "There may be many doubts as to what other states intend to do, but the people of Mississippi have always had the intelligence and courage sufficient to manage their own destiny."[52] Sullens' "Low Down on Higher Ups" column offered encouragement to those who agreed with him, and perhaps those who did not, with one-line sentences such as "Rebel!"[53] Sullens believed that blacks were mentally inferior to whites.[54] He also believed that Mississippi would not abide by *Brown*. "The white people of the South will evade the Supreme Court decision," he wrote.[55] Sullens praised "thinking" blacks who supported segregation. "The great masses of the Negroes in Mississippi, numbering less than one million, are happy and contented in their schools, churches and social activities," he wrote. "Thoughtful, hardworking peace-loving Negroes prefer their own schools, churches and places of entertainment. Why not let them have what they want?" He spoke for blacks but never said where he received his information. "Public sentiment among Negroes is against the abolition of segregation," he wrote. "Public sentiment is the law, regardless of what may be written in statute books."[56]

Later in the summer, as the beginning of the 1954–1955 school year approached, Sullens was back with his virulent pen. "No matter how the Supreme Court may phrase its final decree, that decree will not be obeyed by the people of Mississippi," he wrote. "Public sentiment is still the law and our minds are still governed by common sense."[57]

Letters to the editor of the Jackson *Daily News* in May and August 1954 were of an intriguing and varied assortment pertaining to *Brown*. Interestingly, Sullens responded to his own threatening approach to the NAACP with an appeal to letter writers not to use the same tactics. In late May, Sullens had published a front-page warning to the organization, suggesting to NAACP officials, "Trouble is never hard to find."[58] A few weeks later, Sullens admonished letter writers to calm their own rhetoric. "No matter whether written by white persons or Negro, the *Daily News* will not print communications on the subject of segregation that contain violent, abusive or intemperate language," he wrote. "It must be dealt with in a cool, calm, common sense manner. Please do not send us communications written in the heat of passion."[59]

The Jackson *Daily News* published many letters, most in support of segregation. Black writers who supported segregation found ready access to the pages of the Jackson *Daily News*. One front-page missive, "Negro Teacher Asks Dual School System Remain as Best Policy for the South," was written by C.W. Falconer of Shubuta, Mississippi. "I truthfully believe my race should not advocate mixing of schools at this time because it would have a tendency to bring disunity between the races, a thing which the Communist Party desires," Falconer wrote. "We must not cut our own throats on this issue."[60] Another black Mississippian, Viola Prine, wrote to complain. "We know that they [white people] have taught their children that they are superior to Negroes," she wrote. "Why put our black children through this?"[61] Professor E.T. Hawkins, principal of the "colored" Hawkins High School in Forest, Mississippi, for twenty years, was hailed as a "Respected Negro Educator" for "warning" his black students, "Don't allow yourselves to be misled by wild rumors, know the source of your information."[62]

In Laurel, where the Jones County population was about thirty percent black,[63] Harriet Gibbons had only one editorial in May 1954 concerning *Brown v. Board of Education*, quite different from Sullens. She remained the only woman editor of a Mississippi daily newspaper during this time period and was remarkably quiet considering how often she had addressed the Dixiecrat protest in 1948. In May 1954, the *Laurel Leader-Call* published her single editorial. "We are glad to see that Mississippi's public officials have spoken with restraint and discretion, because nothing is gained by politicians taking this subject as an opportunity for inflaming passion and arousing prejudice," she wrote. "That Mississippi is in for a period of most difficult and trying times is conceded by us all. Such an era must be met with an even temper, with self-control, with a determination to work out what faces us in the spirit of Americanism and true Christianity."[64]

In McComb, where the Pike County population was forty percent black,[65] J.O. "Oliver" Emmerich continued his defense of the traditional South and called for his community to remain calm in the face of *Brown*. In the McComb *Enterprise-Journal*, Emmerich's editorials voiced support for a Mississippi law to more equitably fund the black schools, legislation rushed into passage to counteract *Brown*. "The Negro leadership that is opposed to the separate but equal plans is doing its people a vast disservice," he wrote. "It would be a serious mistake to plunge our two races together in our schools at this hour."[66] Emmerich thought the black children would "suffer the most" from desegregation. "Time is essential to apply any reform," he wrote. "There is need of many adjustments and the outlawing of segregation would bring disastrous conditions."[67]

Emmerich failed to elaborate on the "disastrous conditions" that desegregation of the public schools would cause to the students of Mississippi or how the black students "would suffer the most." The next day, he announced in his front-page editorial column, "Highlights in the Headlines," "Neither race wants an integrated school system in Mississippi"[68] but failed to attribute the information. Although Emmerich supported the concept of "separate but equal," he knew that the disparity in funding between the black and white schools in Mississippi was wrong. "The rule of discrimination must be abolished, this we have held for many years," he wrote. "No constitutional ruling is required to make this duty obvious. But we believe that both of the races in the McComb area prefer to have colored children in colored schools and white children in white schools."[69] Later in the month, Emmerich published his "5-Part Plan to Help Maintain Segregated Schools in Mississippi," which was reprinted in the Jackson *Clarion-Ledger*.[70] Emmerich's plan stated:

(1) Cultivate the spirit that can develop common consent for approval of the equal-but-separate schools in Mississippi; (2) Remember that a Supreme Court decision is a cold but dynamic force that cannot be set aside short of war unless conflicting views are solved through common consent; (3) Provide the spirit by which Negroes will vote as citizens, not as a Negro bloc. If Negroes vote as a racial bloc, we will inevitably surrender our state into the hands of demagogues; (4) Recognize that the preliminary discussions proposed to find a solution of our problem can, if mishandled, be the means of destroying the will for "common consent"; (5) Remember, too, that Mississippi's own leaders are competing with an out-of-state, out-of-South leadership that is seeking to direct our Negro people into a channel contrary to the will of the majority of the white people of Mississippi, and that if that radical leadership succeeds, we fail. We must not contribute to the success of this hostile influence by failing to recognize the forceful events confronting us at the moment.[71]

In August 1954, in what seemed a desperate last effort to maintain segregation, Emmerich again proposed "equalizing" the black and white schools in Mississippi. Once that was done, he reasoned, the Supreme Court would relax the demands of *Brown*. "The unprecedented decision of the United States Supreme Court, which ignored the Constitutional police powers of the state, has created a school dilemma in Mississippi and the South," he wrote. "Mississippi should seek immediately (1) to equalize our school facilities and (2) to delay the enforcement of segregation rules long enough to permit the new equalized school facilities to function."[72]

In searching for rationalization of his traditional Southern views, Emmerich, like most other editors of the Mississippi daily press, sought credible black allies. He found one in Davis Lee, the black publisher of the *Newark* (New Jersey) *Telegraph*, whose editorial on *Brown* was published on the front page of the McComb paper. "Southern Negroes may lose a lot more than they gain," Lee wrote. "Integration in the North and East is not a howling success. This movement to integrate the schools of the South is loaded with more racial dynamite than appears on the surface and the Negro will be the one who is blown away."[73]

In Meridian, where James H. Skewes continued as editor, Lauderdale County was almost forty percent black in 1954.[74] Skewes' staunch Southern conservatism was played out in his editorial pages, although he penned only two opinions regarding *Brown v. Board of Education* compared to nine for the Dixiecrat protest. Two days after the 1954 decision, the *Meridian Star* published Skewes' opinion on the matter. "We violently disagree with Supreme Court school segregation politics," he wrote. "Neither average Southern white, or Southern black, approves. However, law is whatever the Supreme Court says law is. We sing 'Star Spangled Banner' ahead of 'Dixie' however, we shall by any and all means or expedience preserve our Mid-South heritage."[75]

Toward the end of the month, after a ten-day silence on the decision, Skewes was back, with his peculiar, fragmented editorial style. "Mid-South ponders look-see in regards segregation ruling," he wrote. "We hear very few violent outbursts of word or threat. However, most Southerners accept high court ruling with good grace based on threefold Supreme Court provisions. First: justices decree school segregation is unconstitutional. Second: court offers time aplenty wherein to work out the situation. Third: invites Dixie suggest ways and means to do the job. We propose fairness to both races."[76]

In Adams County, where the population was nearly fifty percent black in 1954, the two Natchez daily newspapers displayed divergent editorial approaches to *Brown v. Board of Education*. The *Natchez Democrat* published one of the few editorials supporting the Supreme Court's decision. In "Still Much Uncertain on Segregation," Trimble, or an unnamed editorial writer, stepped beyond the usual traditional Southern views of the paper.

> A very great many people have been convinced for generations that segregation was inherently wrong, law or no law, and a violation of national morals. But they haven't known what to do about it until now. Certainly there can be pride that the Supreme Court has finally faced up to what has obviously been the law all the time. Administered with goodwill, it may prove an important step in clearing up the whole matter of segregation. Children growing up together can hardly maintain the deep suspicions which have so complicated this problem.[77]

Two days later, however, a different voice emerged. In "The Supreme Court's Decision on Segregation," it seemed as if someone else had taken the editorial reins of the newspaper. "It is our considered opinion that we shall live to regret this Supreme Court decision," the editorial stated. "Not necessarily because formal segregation has been abolished, but because the court reasoned and acted capriciously without due regard to its position in the division of power among the three branches of government and because of the non-judicial considerations which guided it."[78]

In the weeks just before school started in August, Trimble continued with this line of editorial thought. "There is no basic conflict between whites and negroes on this issue of segregation," he wrote. "The only conflict is that which has been engendered by ratical [sic] minority elements seeking to impose their will upon the majority."[79]

Why the tone changed so drastically in the editorials in the *Natchez Democrat* may never be known, because Trimble died in 1997, shortly before being contacted for an interview.[80] Perhaps advertisers pressured the newspaper or threats of bodily harm were made, or community outrage was overwhelming. Whatever the reason, the editorial pen was definitely refocused. Despite what appeared to be, initially, a sympathetic editorial slant toward *Brown*, the *Natchez Democrat* published other material to the contrary. Conservative columnist Thurman Sensing wrote that the decision was "the worse thing for Negroes," and "Segregation is simply recognition of the fact that there are certain natural laws that have resulted in different races, and the practice of segregation is based on that fact."[81] A few days later, Trimble continued his diatribe against government interference in the Southern way of life. "When the power of the government is used, or sought to be used, for the purpose of changing human nature, customs and mores," he wrote. "it has lost its American characteristics."[82] His concerns seemed to focus primarily on the states' rights issue more than on the race issue.

Across town at the *Natchez Times*, founded in 1949, a full-page "News of Negro Activities" appeared regularly, and the mood was initially supportive of *Brown*, as had been the case earlier at the *Natchez Democrat*. Herman Moore, editor of the *Natchez Times*, was silent in May regarding the decision. He did, however, publish in the *Natchez Times* a letter to the editor of the *Christian Science Monitor*, an unsigned missive that supported *Brown*. The letter also cautioned that black children should not be made to suffer simply to boost the egos of black leaders. "I do not believe it just or right to pour millions of ignorant Negro children into our white schools in order that a handful of upperclass Negroes may be freed from a sense of inferiority," the letter said. "We say, however, that the Supreme Court decision was fundamentally right."[83]

Later in August 1954, the Mississippi Supreme Court upheld the decision of a lower court's finding the *Natchez Times* guilty of libel and awarded Mary Dunigan, a white woman, $5,000 for having been referred to erroneously in the paper as a "Negro."[84] The case was the first of its kind in the state. The *Natchez Times* was soon defunct.

In Tupelo, where the Lee County population was nearly thirty percent black in 1954,[85] editor George McLean of the Tupelo *Daily Journal* continued to be a voice of reason as well as of conservatism. He had an immediate response to *Brown*. "The South will no doubt respond with a gradual reaction to the Supreme Court ruling rather than changing its school system overnight," he wrote. "This is not a time for high emotion or thoughtless action. It is above all a time for sanity and for Christianity."[86]

McLean was the only editor of the Mississippi daily press in 1954 who raised the issue of non-compliance to *Brown* in terms of loss of federal funding for Mississippi's public schools in an editorial,[87] although the issue was reported in news stories in several of the other state dailies.[88] Similar to the other editors of the Mississippi daily press in 1954, however, McLean was eager to publish support for his stance on segregation by anyone from the black community. Like Emmerich in McComb, McLean published the letter from Lee, the black publisher of the *Newark* (New Jersey) *Telegraph*, in which Lee warned that integration could prove harmful to black business.[89] Unlike Emmerich, however, McLean published Lee's letter on page eleven, rather than page one.

In Vicksburg, where the Warren County population was fifty percent black in 1954,[90] The *Vicksburg Evening Post* retained its calm approach to crisis and continued to voice its support of traditional Southern segregation as it had during the Dixiecrat protest of 1948. In "Word of Caution," editor L.P. Cashman, Sr., advised readers to follow his plan. "We will deliberately take some time to study the decision and to fully comprehend its effects," he wrote. "Until that has been done, we will voice no opinion on the matter, and we urge our readers to follow the same course."[91] A few days later, Cashman responded again to *Brown*, and this time, his views on segregation were clear. "Basically, we disagree with the decision," he wrote. "We do not believe either colored or white Mississippians will ever be happy under a system of non-segregation. By their very natures, the races are apart."[92]

At the *Vicksburg Herald*, which Cashman also owned and edited, less opinion in the editorial columns pertaining to *Brown* was published than had been written regarding the Dixiecrats. No editorial by Cashman addressed *Brown* in May 1954.

In West Point, where the Clay County population was nearly sixty percent black in 1954,[93] W.H. Harris had taken the editorial helm of the *Times-Leader* and continued the rabid, anti-integration conservatism that the newspaper supported during the 1948 Dixiecrat protest against civil rights. The day after *Brown v. Board of Education* was announced, he published his first editorial on the matter. "None of us think for one minute that we are about to throw white schools open to Negro children now," he wrote. "Your writer firmly believes that he will some day see non-segregated schools in the South. But first, we must pass through a lengthy period of equalized school facilities which will lift the Negro onto a higher level—mentally, socially and morally."[94] Harris, along with Sullens of the Jackson *Daily News*, was vehement in his denunciation of *Brown*. He was also certain that school desegregation would never be enforced in Mississippi. "We know for certain that Negro children are not going to be admitted to our white schools for a long, long time," he wrote.[95]

MISSISSIPPI LEADERSHIP RESPONDS TO *BROWN*

How Mississippi's elected officials reacted to *Brown v. Board of Education* was a topic of major news interest for the state's daily press in May 1954. Mississippi Governor Hugh White was reportedly "disappointed"[96] and "sad"[97] about the decision, and he told the media that he preferred to study the case before making a statement.[98] The next day, however, White had apparently had time to "study the case," and he doubted that the schools in Mississippi would be affected by Brown "for fifty years,"[99] just as *Plessy v. Ferguson* had not been enforced for a half century after it was declared law by the U.S. Supreme Court. White also believed that there were myriad legal maneuvers with which the state could avoid the desegregation of its public schools.[100]

Other Mississippi elected officials were not so reserved. U.S. Senator James Eastland told the wire services, "The South will not abide by, nor obey, this legislative decision by a political court."[101] He also stated confidently that the high court had little actual power. "A court decree is worthless unless it is supported by public opinion," he said.[102] U.S. Senator John Stennis agreed but offered a different criticism. "The justices abandoned their role as judges of the law and organized themselves into a group of social engineers," he said.[103] Later in the summer, Eastland, who served in the U.S. Senate from 1939 to 1972, proposed an amendment to the U.S. Constitution that would give each state "exclusive jurisdiction" over the regulation of "health, morals, education, marriage and good order."[104] Stennis chose a different approach, telling the wire services, "I feel that most of our colored people would appreciate a plan which would result in harmony between the two races."[105]

U.S. Representative John Bell Williams, a future governor of Mississippi (1968–1972),[106] said, "The ruling will lead the Southern Negro to go it alone and probably will mean the end of public school systems in several states." U.S. Representative William Colmer responded, "It is unfortunate that the harmonious relations and the splendid progress being made in racial relations in the South now are threatened by this precipitous action."[107]

Mississippi Lieutenant Governor Carroll Gartin referred to *Brown* as "a grave blow to our Southern way of life," and Walter Sillers, the Speaker of the Mississippi House of Representatives, reported that Mississippi would certainly "abolish public schools to maintain segregation."[108] Paul B. Johnson, Jr., a future governor of Mississippi (1964–1968), was not subtle. "The white people in Mississippi are not in any mood to accept Negroes in our schools," he said. "I, for one, will fight against that to my dying day. The whites of this state want no colored in-laws."[109] Former Mississippi Governor Fielding Wright, the failed vice presidential candidate of the States' Rights Party in 1948, came forward with a plan to use police force to maintain segregation in the public schools, and he was soon followed in this concept by Governor White.[110] Gartin agreed. "If Mississippi Negroes listen to troublemakers, we will use our police power to maintain segregation and the colored race will suffer a great and tragic loss," Gartin said. "If they cooperate, they will get good schools."[111] Segregation "is our last, most important, states' right," Gartin said in a front-page story in the Jackson *Daily News*. "We must use police force to maintain segregation."[112]

A letter to the editor of the Jackson *Daily News* from Mary Taylor of Jackson, however, strongly disagreed. "Such remarks as Fielding Wright and Governor White make about using police force are absolutely ridiculous and only stir up hard feelings and antagonism between the races," she wrote. "I hate to think of the contempt the rest of the nation must have for the South if they have read the front pages of the Mississippi newspapers."[113]

Mississippi Attorney General J.P. Coleman, who later served as governor of the state (1956–1960),[114] agreed with Taylor regarding White's suggestion to use police powers to maintain segregation in the public schools. "Segregation can be maintained without it," Coleman told the wire services.[115] Coleman knew the legal realities of using state police power to avoid a national mandate. At the Neshoba County Fair that summer he told a crowd, "State police power is subject to the 14th amendment and every commissioned officer could be enjoined by injunction and rendered useless."[116]

The opinions of other Southern leaders were front-page news in the Mississippi daily press following *Brown*. Governor Herman Talmadge of Georgia told the wire services, "We must insure the continued and permanent segregation of the races"; Governor James Byrnes of South Carolina said, "South Carolina will refuse to go along with a decision to end segregation"; Governor Allan Shivers of Texas said the decision would "take years to comply to"; and Governor Lawrence Weathersby of Kentucky said his state "will try to adjust its public education system to comply."[117]

"DAMN FOOL REMARKS"

Most editors of the Mississippi daily press had nothing to say in response to elected officials, other than giving their wire service stories front-page placement. But Carter in Greenville could not resist the opportunity to take a crack at the group against whom he often had complaints. "Every responsible individual with whom we have talked about the matter is using his good sense and refuses to be stampeded into making damn fool remarks," he wrote. "This isn't so of our politicians and state observers."[118] Carter also criticized the governor of a neighboring state for the same infraction. "We rather doubt that Georgia is going to furnish much leadership of an intelligent nature after noting the utterances of Governor Herman Talmadge," he wrote.[119]

McLean in Tupelo went even further. Though he did not support the desegregation of the state's school system, McLean disapproved of politicians using the issue for personal gain. "Southern politicians are occupied full time nowadays denouncing the Supreme Court," he wrote. "But when the novelty has worn off this sport, they will seek something more spectacular to keep their names before the public as guardians of Dixie education."[120]

"SEPARATE BUT EQUAL" PROPOSED AND DEBATED

A few days after the *Brown* decision was announced, Mississippi Governor White attempted to convince black leaders that the state's schools for blacks would be upgraded, or "equalized."[121] White informed black Mississippians that it would be in their "best interest" to support "voluntary" segregation.[122] This notion, although widely played in the Mississippi daily press, did not receive much support from leaders of the Mississippi or national NAACP,[123] whose ideas and meeting places were suddenly front-page news. Walter White, national president of the NAACP, offered a statement to the press that most Mississippians were not ready to admit in 1954. "The South is more ready for the change from segregation to integration than the professional politicians believe it to be," he said.[124] Mississippi NAACP leader E.J. Stringer of Columbus had other concerns to air. "There is no hate in this, no animosity," he told the AP and UP. "We feel we are entitled to it and we intend going about getting it the American way."[125]

Two black educators endorsed White's plan for "equalized schools" and "voluntary segregation." One was a former president of the Mississippi Negro Teacher's Association, J.D. Boyd. "New buildings for our schools would solve ninety percent of our problems," he said in a story that received wide coverage in the Mississippi daily press.[126] Percy Greene, editor of the weekly black Jackson *Advocate*, also supported the "separate but equal" concept. If the schools "equalized," Greene said, "[t]here is not going to be a mad rush of Negro parents to send their children to so-called white schools just to have their children going to school with white folks."[127]

Carter in Greenville found Governor White completely out of touch with the black community to even suggest "voluntary" segregation. "Governor Hugh White said he was stunned the other day when he learned that the state's Negroes did not in fact plan to go along with his plan for 'voluntary segregation' in the public schools," Carter wrote. "Granting the news was unpleasant at best, for the governor to be 'stunned' indicates that he hasn't had his ear to the ground."[128]

Imes in Columbus agreed with Carter's disdain for White, but for different reasons. "To date, state leadership's handling of the segregation issue presents a dismal picture," Imes wrote. "The governor's effort to 'please everyone' with a 'calm' approach to the problem has flopped dismally. He got a flat turndown from a group of negroes in his proposal to preserve segregation in schools on a voluntary basis."[129]

Within a week of the *Brown* decision, Governor White began committee appointments for a newly created twenty-five-member Mississippi Legal Education Advisory Committee (LEAC) to investigate ways to maintain segregation in the state's public schools, an action widely reported in the Mississippi daily press.[130] LEAC appointee Thomas Tubb of West Point said, "Gradual integration of the races would ultimately lead to the destruction of the white race."[131] Not all members of the LEAC shared Tubb's view, however, and the committee was described as "wildly split on school issues."[132]

ABOLISHMENT OF PUBLIC SCHOOLS CONSIDERED

One consideration before the LEAC was a recommendation to abolish the public school system and organize a private system supported by tax dollars through amendment to the state constitution. After much debate at a statewide convention in August, the idea was unanimously accepted by 800 white superintendents of Mississippi schools as a "last resort" to maintain segregation.[133] This was an amendment worth considering, according to several editors of the Mississippi daily press, and a notion akin to total insanity, according to several others. Waldon at the Corinth *Daily Corinthian* was particularly vehement in his denouncement of the idea and wrote three editorials in protest. "The proposal to wipe out a hundred years of educational progress in this state would set us back to pioneer days if we allowed it," he wrote. "We do not believe that the proposal to abolish public education is a good, well thought-out answer to the problem of segregation in the schools. It is obviously a move of desperation. We don't think the legislators would vote something so harmful to their constituents."[134]

A week later Waldon was back to warn his readers that they should seriously question the proposed "last resort" solution to end the public schools being considered by state leaders. "The people should not be hoodwinked by this 'last resort' promise," he wrote. "Like suicide, abolishing the state's public schools is the easy way out."[135] Waldon also praised state Representative Dexter Lee of Alcorn County, where the Corinth *Daily Corinthian* was published, for his opposition to the abolition of schools, even though Lee believed that all segregation should be maintained.[136] Exactly how Lee intended to maintain public schools in a segregated manner following *Brown* was never explained.

Carter in Greenville agreed with Waldon that segregation should somehow be maintained but that the public school system should not be abolished. "The fact that none of the other Southern states is now considering abolition of the public schools would certainly indicate to us that the system isn't calculated to be the best one," he wrote.[137] Emmerich in McComb, who had drafted his own plan for maintaining segregated schools, also thought abolition of the public schools was preposterous. "All this talk about private schools with private funds in Mississippi is sheer nonsense," he wrote.[138] Emmerich addressed the issue in a front-page editorial. "Already it has been made public in political circles in Mississippi that the purpose of attempting to abolish the public schools is to circumvent the recent decision of the United States Supreme Court," he wrote. "This preannounced purpose admits subterfuge. Thus already the teeth have been removed from this plan."[139]

Moore at the *Natchez Times* agreed and was willing to consider other avenues to maintain segregation. "Possible, more desirable, methods of opposing the integration order are through application of state police powers, through school districting policies and by giving school boards the authority to assign pupils to their respective schools," he wrote. "A move at this time to prepare for wrecking the public school system seems ill-advised."[140]

McLean at the Tupelo *Daily Journal* supported Waldon, Carter, Emmerich and Moore in denouncing the abolition of the public school system. McLean's line of thought, however, was that some black leaders supported the idea. "We must not be stampeded into abolishing our public schools by the pressure of a few colored leaders when for more than eighty years we have resisted all such pressure from white politicians," he wrote.[141] State Senator George Owens, who represented Tupelo at the time, was concerned that if the public schools were closed, the poor white students would not be able to attend private schools.[142] No concern of this type was voiced for the black students.

In support of the abolition of the state's public school system to maintain racial segregation were Hills of the Jackson *Clarion-Ledger* and Harris of the West Point *Times-Leader*. "That the people of Mississippi are prepared to go to any end to keep the Negro out of white schools is evidenced from the rounds of applause that every speaker who touches on the subject receives," Hills wrote.[143] It is interesting to note that Hills referred to the "people of Mississippi" and "the Negro" as two divergent groups.

Harris at the West Point *Times-Leader* responded with his usual white supremacist views. "Most of us would quickly and willingly approve the abolition of our public schools before we would permit our children to become involved in any bloody integration system," he wrote.[144]

As the Mississippi school year began in late August 1954, none of the Mississippi public schools had begun to desegregate as ordered by *Brown v. Board of Education*. Nor was the Mississippi public school system abolished or a private school plan amended to the state constitution. Also at the end of the summer, Governor White began a campaign in the Mississippi Legislature to pass a bill "forbidding anyone from stirring up race trouble by filing lawsuits against schools, except for relatives of children in that school."[145]

Schools in four states affected by *Brown* did abide by the mandate in 1954: Arkansas, West Virginia, Missouri, and Maryland, as did schools in the District of Columbia.[146] In Fayetteville, Arkansas, School Superintendent Wayne White said that the desegregation of the Fayetteville school district "will affect about nine Negro students and save the district five thousand dollars a year in federal funds."[147] A decade later, as the schools in Mississippi grudgingly began to comply with *Brown*, federal funds were the primary motivation.

SUMMARY OF COVERAGE OF *BROWN V. BOARD OF EDUCATION*

The major issues of concern raised by editors of the Mississippi daily press following *Brown v. Board of Education* were (1) that black and white children should not be schooled in the same facilities as this could lead to integrated socializing, which would be unacceptable by traditional Southern standards, (2) that black and white children should not be schooled together because black children would not be able to compete academically with the white children, and (3) that the public schools in the state should not be abolished to prevent this. According to their editorials during May and August 1954, the notion that blacks and whites should be educated together based on the equality of the two races was a concept that remained unacceptable.

The propensity toward reporting civil rights issues in Mississippi daily newspapers following *Brown v. Board of Education* in 1954 ranged from daily news coverage with only one editorial, such as in the *Greenwood Commonwealth*, the Gulfport *Daily Herald*, the *Hattiesburg American*, the *Laurel Leader-Call*, and the *Vicksburg Herald*, to an editorial every three days and daily news coverage in the Jackson *Clarion-Ledger* and the Jackson *Daily News*. Most of the twenty Mississippi daily newspapers published only two or three editorials in May and August 1954 pertaining to *Brown v. Board of Education*, but the issue was unquestionably a top story on the front pages of the Mississippi daily press during those two months.

Contrary to what media critics have noted about the promotion of violent suppression of civil rights activity in a small sampling of Southern newspapers,[148] the Mississippi daily press in 1954 did not advocate violence following *Brown v. Board of Education.* Not once was this found in any of the twenty newspapers. However, the Mississippi daily press, as an aggregate, did reject the *Brown* mandate, and the usual rationalization was the preservation of the traditional Southern way of life.

In their news coverage of the civil rights issues pertaining to *Brown v. Board of Education,* the two most widely circulated Mississippi daily newspapers, the Jackson *Clarion-Ledger* and the Jackson *Daily News,* were not representative of the Mississippi daily press as they had been during the 1948 Dixiecrat protest. Although all the daily newspapers subscribed to at least one of the three major wire services available at the time, AP, UP or INS, and they ran the copy relatively unrevised, staff-written stories by the Jackson *Clarion-Ledger* and the Jackson *Daily News* were much more virulent, for the most part, than those of the other newspapers. The editorials of Sullens at the Jackson *Daily News* and Hills at the Jackson *Clarion-Ledger* certainly earned their reputation for propagating racial polarization and intensifying the opposition of Mississippi whites to desegregation.[149] But except for Harris of the West Point *Times-Leader* and Skewes at the *Meridian Star,* this blatant racism was not generally true of the editorials written by the other editors of the Mississippi daily press in 1954.

The Mississippi daily press personalized and localized the civil rights struggle following *Brown v. Board of Education* in 1954, although there was little local activity reported in response to the mandate during the months of this study. The editorial consensus in opposition to *Brown* was the "us against them" theme proposed during the 1948 Dixiecrat protest. This notion reaffirmed a commitment to the preservation of the traditional South and a local version of the states' rights controversy of 1948—the right of each community, or rather the local whites in power, to manage their educational institutions without outside interference.

NOTES

1. "South Faces Enormous Problems in Ending Segregation," AP, *Laurel Leader-Call,* 21 May 1954, 12.
2. James Loewen and Charles Sallis, eds., *Mississippi: Conflict and Change* (New York: Pantheon Books, 1974), 247; Neil R. McMillen, *Dark Journey: Black Mississippians in the Age of Jim Crow* (Urbana: University of Illinois Press, 1990), 73.
3. McMillen, *Dark Journey,* 73.
4. Loewen and Sallis, *Mississippi,* 247.
5. McMillen, *Dark Journey,* 90.
6. "Court Strikes Down School Segregation," AP, Gulfport *Daily Herald,* 17 May 1954, 1.

7. Loewen and Sallis, *Mississippi*, 252.

8. "By Unanimous Vote, High Court Rules Out School Segregation," AP, *Vicksburg Herald*, 18 May 1954, 1; "Court Ends Segregation," AP, *Meridian Star*, 17 May 1954, 1; "Court Overrules Color Bar," AP, West Point *Times Leader*, 17 May 1954, 1; "Court Strikes Down School Segregation," AP, Gulfport *Daily Herald*, 17 May 1954, 1; "High Court Strikes Down School Segregation," AP, *Clarksdale Press Register*, 18 May 1954, 1; "Mississippi Will Adopt Cautious, Slow Approach to School Segregation Ruling," UP, Greenwood *Morning Star*, 18 May 1954, 1; "Nation's Highest Court Rules Segregation Unconstitutional," UP, Tupelo *Daily Journal*, 18 May 1954, 1; "Order End of Segregation," AP, Columbus *Commercial Dispatch*, 17 May 1954, 1; "Public School Segregation Declared Unconstitutional," UP, Grenada *Sentinel-Star*, 17 May 1954, 1; "Public School Segregation Ruled Out Unanimously by Supreme Court," AP, *Natchez Democrat*, 17 May 1954, 1; "Racial Segregation in Schools Ruled Against by Supreme Court," AP, McComb *Enterprise-Journal*, 17 May 1954, 1; "School Segregation Is Held Illegal," UP, Greenville *Delta Democrat-Times*, 17 May 1954, 1; "School Segregation Upset," AP, *Vicksburg Evening Post*, 17 May 1954, 1; "Segregation Action May Be Delayed for Years," *Natchez Times*, 17 May 1954, 1; "Segregation Ended by Highest Court," AP, *Laurel Leader-Call*, 17 May 1954, 1; "Segregated Schools Outlawed," AP, *Hattiesburg American*, 17 May 1954, 1; "State Seeks Answer to Adverse Ruling on School Segregation," AP, Jackson *Clarion-Ledger*, 18 May 1954, 1; "Supreme Court Says Segregation Must End," Corinth *Daily Corinthian*, 17 May 1954, 1; "U.S. Supreme Court Bans Segregation in Schools," AP, *Greenwood Commonwealth*, 17 May 1954, 1; "Will Not Obey Supreme Court," AP, Jackson *Daily News*, 17 May 1954, 1.

9. Fred Sullens, "Mississippi Will Not Be Bound by Ruling of United States Supreme Court on Segregation before Lawsuits in Each District," Jackson *Daily News*, 24 May 1954, 5.

10. Ibid.

11. James Marlow, "Negroes Will Try to End Segregation," *Clarksdale Press Register*, 19 May 1954, 4.

12. Mississippi Power and Light Company Economic Research Department, *Mississippi Statistical Summary of Population, 1800–1980* (Jackson: Mississippi Power and Light Company, 1983).

13. James Marlow, "Negroes Will Try to End Segregation," Corinth *Daily Corinthian*, 18 May 1954, 4.

14. Mississippi Power and Light Company Economic Research Department, *Mississippi Statistical Summary of Population, 1800–1980*.

15. Hodding Carter, Jr., "The Moment of Decision Is Here," Greenville *Delta Democrat-Times*, 12 September 1962, 4; see also Harry D. Marsh, "Hodding Carter's Newspaper on School Desegregation, 1954–1955," *Journalism Monographs* 92 (May 1985).

16. Hodding Carter, Jr., "The Court's Decision," Greenville *Delta Democrat-Times*, 18 May 1954, 4.

17. Hodding Carter, Jr., "Delta Shows Good Sense," Greenville *Delta Democrat-Times*, 20 May 1954, 3.

18. Hodding Carter, Jr., "What Next for Our Schools?" Greenville *Delta Democrat-Times*, 22 August 1954, 1.

19. Mississippi Power and Light Company Economic Research Department, *Mississippi Statistical Summary of Population, 1800–1980.*

20. Virgil Adams, "A Real Test for the South," Greenwood *Morning Star*, 18 May 1954, 6.

21. Virgil Adams, "Supreme Court Exceeding Its Intended Role," Greenwood *Morning Star*, 19 May 1954, 4.

22. Virgil Adams, "Negro Says Those Favoring Integration Are Emotionally Unstable," Greenwood *Morning Star*, 22 May 1954, 4.

23. Virgil Adams, "Greenwood People Worried about School Problem," Greenwood *Morning Star*, 1 August 1954, 4.

24. Virgil Adams, "The Real Story of How Southerners Treat the Negroes," Greenwood *Morning Star*, 24 August 1954, 4.

25. Virgil Adams, "Schools in the South," *Greenwood Commonwealth*, 31 May 1954, 4.

26. Mississippi Power and Light Company Economic Research Department, *Mississippi Statistical Summary of Population, 1800–1980.*

27. Birney Imes, Jr., "Supreme Court Decision," Columbus *Commercial Dispatch*, 18 May 1954, 1.

28. "Abolish Public School System," AP, Columbus *Commercial Dispatch*, 17 May 1954, 1.

29. Mississippi Power and Light Company Economic Research Department, *Mississippi Statistical Summary of Population, 1800–1980.*

30. "Public School Segregation Declared Unconstitutional, South Ponders Racial Problem Now in View," UP, Grenada *Sentinel-Star*, 17 May 1954, 1; "Dixie Readies Fight to Preserve Separate Schools Despite Ruling," AP, Grenada *Sentinel-Star*, 17 May 1954, 1; "Slow, Cautious Moves Planned by Mississippi," AP, Grenada *Sentinel-Star*, 17 May 1954, 1.

31. Mississippi Power and Light Company Economic Research Department, *Mississippi Statistical Summary of Population, 1800–1980.*

32. E.P. Wilkes, "Working Together," Gulfport *Daily Herald*, 20 May 1954, 4.

33. Mississippi Power and Light Company Economic Research Department, *Mississippi Statistical Summary of Population, 1800–1980.*

34. Andrews Harmon, "Example," *Hattiesburg American*, 21 May 1954, 2.

35. "Jobs, Housing Are Next, Says NAACP," AP, Greenville *Delta Democrat-Times*, 18 May 1954, 1; "NAACP Council Speaks in Jackson, Residential Segregation Blasted," *Clarksdale Press Register*, 7 May 1954, 1; "State NAACP Wants Action," AP, Corinth *Daily Corinthian*, 31 May 1954, 1; "State Negroes to Start Drive on Segregation," AP, Grenada *Sentinel-Star*, 31 May 1954, 1; "Will Petition School Boards to End Segregation," AP, Gulfport *Daily Herald*, 24 May 1954, 1.

36. Andrews Harmon, "Strength of People," *Hattiesburg American*, 2 August 1954, 2.

37. Mississippi Power and Light Company Economic Research Department, *Mississippi Statistical Summary of Population, 1800–1980.*

38. T.M. Hederman, Jr., "Segregation Crisis Faces Us," Jackson *Clarion-Ledger*, 18 May 1954, 6.

39. Charles Hills, "Affairs of State," Jackson *Clarion-Ledger*, 25 May 1954, 2.

40. Grover Hewell, letter to the editor, Jackson *Clarion-Ledger*, 19 May 1954, 12.

41. Blanche Gregory, letter to editor, Jackson *Clarion-Ledger*, 28 May 1954, 8.

42. Jack Garellick, letter to editor, Jackson *Clarion-Ledger*, 22 May 1954, 6.

43. L.G. Patterson, letter to editor, Jackson *Clarion-Ledger*, 10 August 1954, 8.

44. Edwin White, letter to editor, Jackson *Clarion-Ledger*, 12 August 1954, 14.

45. Evelyn Riley, letter to editor, Jackson *Clarion-Ledger*, 5 August 1954, 12.

46. Concerned Taxpayers, letter to editor, Jackson *Clarion-Ledger*, 9 August 1954, 6.

47. "*Clarion-Ledger* Buys *Daily News*," AP, *Hattiesburg American*, 9 August 1954, 1; "*Clarion-Ledger* Buys Control of Jackson *Daily News*," AP, *Vicksburg Herald*, 8 August 1954, 1; "Jackson Daily News Sold to Hedermans," Columbus *Commercial Dispatch*, 8 August 1954, 1; "Newspaper Suit Settled," Jackson *Daily News*, 8 August, 1954, 1.

48. "South Will Not Obey Political Court," AP, Jackson *Daily News*, 17 May 1954, 1.

49. "Gartin Says Negroes Want Separate Schools," Jackson *Daily News*, 17 May 1954, 1.

50. Fred Sullens, "Bloodstains on the White Marble Steps," Jackson *Daily News*, 18 May 1954, 1.

51. Fred Sullens, "The Segregation Decision," Jackson *Daily News*, 19 May 1954, 8.

52. Fred Sullens, "We Are Not Acquiescent," Jackson *Daily News*, 23 May 1954, 10.

53. Fred Sullens, "Low Down on Higher Ups," Jackson *Daily News*, 21 May 1954, 1.

54. Ibid., 5 August 1954, 1.

55. Ibid., 4 August 1954, 1.

56. Fred Sullens, "It's Time for Thinking," Jackson *Daily News*, 1 August 1954, 8.

57. Fred Sullens, "Yes, We Are Defiant," Jackson *Daily News*, 8 August 1954, 8.

58. Fred Sullens, "Low Down on Higher Ups," Jackson *Daily News*, 25 May 1954, 1.

59. Fred Sullens, "No Heat, If You Please," Jackson *Daily News*, 9 August 1954, 4.

60. C.W. Falconer, "Negro Teacher Asks Dual School System Remain as Best Policy for South," Jackson *Daily News*, 2 August 1954, 1.

61. Viola Prine, letter to editor, Jackson *Daily News*, 19 August 1954, 2.

62. E.T. Hawkins, letter to editor, Jackson *Clarion-Ledger*, 21 May 1954, 3.

63. Mississippi Power and Light Company Economic Research Department, *Mississippi Statistical Summary of Population, 1800–1980.*

64. Harriet Gibbons, "Take It Easy," *Laurel Leader-Call*, 18 May 1954, 4.

65. Mississippi Power and Light Company Economic Research Department, *Mississippi Statistical Summary of Population, 1800–1980.*

66. J.O. Emmerich, "A Time to Be Cool, Calm and Dispassionate," McComb *Enterprise-Journal*, 17 May 1954, 2.

67. Ibid.

68. J.O. Emmerich, "Highlights in the Headlines," McComb *Enterprise-Journal*, 18 May 1954, 1.

69. Ibid., 19 May 1954, 1.

70. J.O. Emmerich, "Editor Suggests Ways to Maintain Segregation," Jackson *Clarion-Ledger*, 4 August 1954, 4.

71. J.O. Emmerich, "A 5-Part Plan to Help Maintain Non-Segregated Schools in Mississippi," McComb *Enterprise-Journal*, 4 May 1954, 2.

72. J.O. Emmerich, "A Suggestion to Solve School Dilemma," McComb *Enterprise-Journal*, 2 August 1954, 1.

73. Davis Lee, *Newark* (New Jersey) *Telegraph*, quoted in the McComb *Enterprise-Journal*, 9 August 1954, 1.

74. Mississippi Power and Light Company Economic Research Department, *Mississippi Statistical Summary of Population, 1800–1980.*

75. James H. Skewes, "Find Way or Make It," *Meridian Star*, 19 May 1954, 6.

76. James H. Skewes, "The Will and the Way," *Meridian Star*, 29 May 1954, 4.

77. Elliott Trimble, "Still Much Uncertain on Segregation," *Natchez Democrat*, 17 May 1954, 4.

78. Elliott Trimble, "The Supreme Court's Decision on Segregation," *Natchez Democrat*, 19 May 1954, 4.

79. Elliott Trimble, "We Should Be Unified on This Important Issue," *Natchez Democrat*, 15 August 1954, 4.

80. Mrs. Elliott Trimble, unpublished telephone interview by Susan Weill, 7 September 1997.

81. Thurman Sensing, "What Does Segregation Really Mean?" *Natchez Democrat*, 23 May 1954, 5.

82. Elliott Trimble, "Alternative to Slow Progress Is Going Backward," *Natchez Democrat*, 26 May 1954, 6.

83. Letter to the editor, *Christian Science Monitor*, in the *Natchez Times*, 23 August 1954, 4.

84. "Mississippi Supreme Court Declares Erroneous Designation of Race Libelous," AP, *Clarksdale Press Register*, 24 May 1954, 1; "Mississippi Supreme Court Holds to Write of White Person as Negro Libelous," *Vicksburg Herald*, 25 May 1954, 1; "Supreme Court Rules That to Write of White Person as Negro Is Libelous," AP, *Natchez Democrat*, 25 May 1954, 1; "Uphold Damages in Erroneous Race Designation," AP, Gulfport *Daily Herald*, 24 May 1954, 1.

85. Mississippi Power and Light Company Economic Research Department, *Mississippi Statistical Summary of Population, 1800–1980.*

86. George McLean, "South Thinking Can Find South's Solution," Tupelo *Daily Journal*, 18 May 1954, 11.

87. George McLean, "Federal Funds for Schools," Tupelo *Daily Journal*, 18 August 1954, 4.

88. "Believe Ruling May Speed U.S. School Aid Funds," AP, Gulfport *Daily Herald*, 28 May 1954, 1; "Congressional Battle over School Aid Money," AP,

Natchez Democrat, 11 August 1954, 4; "Dixie Democrats Seek Federal School Aid," AP, West Point *Times-Leader*, 28 May 1954, 1; "Federal Aid: Defiant Dixie Schools Wouldn't Get Any," AP, *Hattiesburg American*, 21 May 1954, 15; "Tippah Legislator Says Private School Plan Dangerous," AP, Jackson *Daily News*, 22 August 1954, 1.

89. Davis Lee, "Negro Editor Asks His Race to Think Twice," from the *Newark* (New Jersey) *Telegraph*, in the Tupelo *Daily Journal*, 16 August 1954, 11.

90. Mississippi Power and Light Company Economic Research Department, *Mississippi Statistical Summary of Population, 1800–1980.*

91. L.P. Cashman, Sr., "Word of Caution," *Vicksburg Evening Post*, 17 May 1954, 4.

92. L.P. Cashman, Sr., "The Supreme Court Decision," *Vicksburg Evening Post*, 21 May 1954, 4.

93. Mississippi Power and Light Company Economic Research Department, *Mississippi Statistical Summary of Population, 1800–1980.*

94. W.H. Harris, "The Supreme Court Ruling," West Point *Times-Leader*, 18 May 1954, 4.

95. W.H. Harris, "We Know for Certain," West Point *Times-Leader*, 18 May 1954, 4.

96. "White Delays Statement, Says Court Ruling Is Disappointing," AP, *Clarksdale Press Register*, 17 May 1954, 1; "Gov. White Urges Go Slow Attitude, Disappointed over High Court Ban on Segregation," AP, *Vicksburg Herald*, 18 May 1954, 1; "Gov. White Is Disappointed but Defers Statement," AP, *Vicksburg Evening Post*, 17 May 1954, 1.

97. "Decision Saddens Gov. White," AP, *Hattiesburg American*, 17 May 1954, 1; "White Saddened by News," AP, Jackson *Daily News*, 17 May 1954, 1.

98. "No Comment Until I Get the Facts, Says Miss. Gov. White," AP, Greenville *Delta Democrat-Times*, 17 May 1954, 1; "White Silent," AP, *Meridian Star*, 17 May 1954, 1; "How Governors Reacted to School Ruling," AP, *Natchez Democrat*, 17 May 1954, 1; "White Refuses Rash Statement about Ruling," UP, Tupelo *Daily Journal*, 18 May 1954, 1.

99. "Mississippi Will Adopt Cautious, Slow Approach to School Segregation Ruling, Gov. White Sees Continuation of Present Program for Fifty Years," UP, Greenwood *Morning Star*, 18 May 1954, 1; "Slow, Cautious Moves Planned by Mississippi," AP, Grenada *Sentinel-Star*, 18 May 1954, 1.

100. "Endless Variety of Ways to Maintain Segregation in Schools of Mississippi," AP, Gulfport *Daily Herald*, 18 May 1954, 1; "Gov. White Acts to Avert Segregation Ban, Racial Ruling Poses Vast Social, Economic Problems for South," AP, *Hattiesburg American*, 18 May 1954, 1.

101. "Congressmen from Mississippi Blast Decision," AP, *Vicksburg Evening Post*, 18 May 1954, 1; "Congressmen, Senators View Opinions," AP, *Clarksdale Press Register*, 18 May 1954, 1; "Decision Bitterly Assailed by Southern Solons," AP, Grenada *Sentinel-Star*, 18 May 1954, 1; "Dixie Congressmen React to Decision," AP, *Natchez Democrat*, 18 May 1954, 1; "Dixie Congressmen React Sharply to Segregation Edict," AP, *Vicksburg Herald*, 18 May 1954, 1; "Dixie Democrats View Ruling with Alarm," AP, Corinth *Daily Corinthian*, 18 May 1954, 1; "Eastland Declares South Will Not Obey," AP, Jackson *Daily News*, 17 May 1954, 1; "Eastland: Won't Abide by Ruling," AP, Greenville *Delta Democrat-Times*, 18 May

1954, 1; "Many Southern Congressmen Assail Segregation Decision," AP, *Natchez Times*, 18 May 1954, 1; "Mississippi Congressmen View Ruling with Alarm," AP, West Point *Times-Leader*, 18 May 1954, 1; "State Leaders Declare Segregation Will Stay," Columbus *Commercial Dispatch*, 18 May 1954, 1; "State's Congressional Delegation Views with Alarm Segregation Act," AP, *Laurel Leader-Call*, 18 May 1954, 1; "State's Congressmen View With Alarm Anti-Segregation Ruling," AP, *Meridian Star*, 18 May 1954, 1; "U.S. Supreme Court Decision Draws Bitter Attacks from Southern Congressmen," AP, Tupelo *Daily Journal*, 18 May 1954, 1; "White Leaders See Enforcement Delay," AP, *Natchez Democrat*, 17 May 1954, 1.

102. "Segregation Order Useless, Eastland Tells U.S. Senate," AP, Columbus *Commercial Dispatch*, 28 May 1954, 1.

103. "Congressmen from Mississippi Blast Decision," AP, *Vicksburg Evening Post*, 18 May 1954, 1; "Congressmen, Senators View Opinions," AP, *Clarksdale Press Register*, 18 May 1954, 1; "Decision Bitterly Assailed by Southern Solons," AP, Grenada *Sentinel-Star*, 18 May 1954, 1; "Dixie Congressmen React to Decision," AP, *Natchez Democrat*, 18 May 1954, 1; "Dixie Congressmen React Sharply to Segregation Edict," AP, *Vicksburg Herald*, 18 May 1954, 1; "Dixie Democrats View Ruling with Alarm," AP, Corinth *Daily Corinthian*, 18 May 1954, 1; "Eastland Declares South Will Not Obey," AP, Jackson *Daily News*, 17 May 1954, 1; "Eastland: Won't Abide by Ruling," AP, Greenville *Delta Democrat-Times*, 18 May 1954, 1; "Many Southern Congressmen Assail Segregation Decision," AP, *Natchez Times*, 18 May 1954, 1; "Mississippi Congressmen View Ruling with Alarm," AP, West Point *Times-Leader*, 18 May 1954, 1; "State Leaders Declare Segregation Will Stay," Columbus *Commercial Dispatch*, 18 May 1954, 1; "State's Congressional Delegation Views with Alarm Segregation Act," AP, *Laurel Leader-Call*, 18 May 1954, 1; "State's Congressmen View with Alarm Anti-Segregation Ruling," AP, *Meridian Star*, 18 May 1954, 1; "U.S. Supreme Court Decision Draws Bitter Attacks from Southern Congressmen," AP, Tupelo *Daily Journal*, 18 May 1954, 1; "White Leaders See Enforcement Delay," AP, *Natchez Democrat*, 17 May 1954, 1.

104. "Eastland Hits Supreme Court for Disregard of Public Duty, Wants Constitution Amended to Preserve Segregation in the South," UP, Greenwood *Morning Star*, 28 May 1954, 1; "Eastland Proposes Amendment to Permit Segregation Choice," AP, Jackson *Clarion-Ledger*, 25 May 1954, 1; "Eastland Tries to Keep Segregation and States' Rights," AP, Columbus *Commercial Dispatch*, 25 May 1954, 1; "Sen. Eastland's School Proposal Lauded," Jackson *Clarion-Ledger*, 6 August 1954, 1; Untitled editorial, Jackson *Clarion-Ledger*, 30 May 1954, 12.

105. "Milder Attitude Taken by Stennis, Says Colored Folks Will Suffer Unless Separate School Continue," AP, Columbus *Commercial Dispatch*, 28 May 1954, 1.

106. Loewen and Sallis, *Mississippi*, 351.

107. "Congressmen from Mississippi Blast Decision," AP, *Vicksburg Evening Post*, 18 May 1954, 1; "Congressmen, Senators View Opinions," AP, *Clarksdale Press Register*, 18 May 1954, 1; "Decision Bitterly Assailed by Southern Solons," AP, Grenada *Sentinel-Star*, 18 May 1954, 1; "Dixie Congressmen React to Decision," AP, *Natchez Democrat*, 18 May 1954, 1; "Dixie Congressmen React Sharply to Segregation Edict," AP, *Vicksburg Herald*, 18 May 1954, 1; "Dixie Democrats

View Ruling with Alarm," AP, Corinth *Daily Corinthian*, 18 May 1954, 1; "Eastland Declares South Will Not Obey," AP, Jackson *Daily News*, 17 May 1954, 1; "Eastland: Won't Abide by Ruling," AP, Greenville *Delta Democrat-Times*, 18 May 1954, 1; "Many Southern Congressmen Assail Segregation Decision," AP, *Natchez Times*, 18 May 1954, 1; "Mississippi Congressmen View Ruling with Alarm," AP, West Point *Times-Leader*, 18 May 1954, 1; "State Leaders Declare Segregation Will Stay," Columbus *Commercial Dispatch*, 18 May 1954, 1; "State's Congressional Delegation Views with Alarm Segregation Act," AP, *Laurel Leader-Call*, 18 May 1954, 1; "State's Congressmen View with Alarm Anti-Segregation Ruling," AP, *Meridian Star*, 18 May 1954, 1; "U.S. Supreme Court Decision Draws Bitter Attacks from Southern Congressmen," AP, Tupelo *Daily Journal*, 18 May 1954, 1; "White Leaders See Enforcement Delay," AP, *Natchez Democrat*, 17 May 1954, 1.

108. "Erase Public Education Says Sillers," AP, West Point *Times-Leader*, 17 May 1954, 1; "Only Thing to Do, Sillers Believes, Is Private Schools," Jackson *Daily News*, 17 May 1954, 1; "Quick Action Promised," AP, *Clarksdale Press Register*, 18 May 1954, 1; "Sillers Advocates Immediate End of Public Education," AP, *Natchez Democrat*, 17 May 1954, 1.

109. "Paul Johnson Firm in Segregation Stand," Jackson *Clarion-Ledger*, 12 August 1954, 1.

110. "Fielding Wright Expresses His Opinion on the Subject of Enforcing Segregation," Jackson *Daily News*, 2 August 1954, 1; "Fielding Wright Would Use Police to Keep Segregation,," AP, *Laurel Leader-Call*, 2 August 1954, 1; "Former Gov. Wright Backs Up Segregation, Urges Police Power," AP, Jackson *Clarion-Ledger*, 2 August, 1954, 1; "Former Gov. Wright Backs Up Segregation, Urges Police Power to Separate Schools," Jackson *Clarion-Ledger*, 2 August 1954, 1; "Gov. White Says State Police Will Be Used to Ban Negroes from White Schools," AP, *Vicksburg Herald*, 3 August 1954, 1; "Police Powers of State Suggested in School Issue," AP, Grenada *Sentinel-Star*, 2 August 195, 1; "Urge State to Use Police Powers to Prevent Any Mixing of Races," AP, *Greenwood Commonwealth*, 1 August 1954, 1; "Urges Police Power to Block Segregation," AP, *Meridian Star*, 2 August 1954, 1; "White Follows Wright, Police Power," AP, McComb *Enterprise-Journal*, 3 August 1954, 1; "Use of Police Powers Urged in Segregation," AP, Greenville *Delta Democrat-Times*, 2 August 1954, 1; "White Urged to Use Police Powers to Preserve Segregation in Schools," AP, Tupelo *Daily Journal*, 2 August 1954, 1; "Wright Would Use Police Power to Stop Integration," AP, Corinth *Daily Corinthian*, 3 August 1954, 1; "Wright Urges Use of Police Powers to Maintain Dual Schools," AP, Hattiesburg *American*, 2 August 1954, 1; "Wright Supports Move to Use Police Power in Segregation," AP, West Point *Times-Leader*, 2 August 1954, 1.

111. "Gartin Urges Police Power in School Issue," AP, *Vicksburg Evening Post*, 7 August 1954, 1.

112. "Fielding Wright Is Right," Jackson *Daily News*, 3 August, 1954, 1.

113. Mary Taylor, letter to editor, Jackson *Clarion-Ledger*, 13 August 1954, 10.

114. Loewen and Sallis, *Mississippi*, 351.

115. "Coleman Opposes Police Powers," AP, Columbus *Commercial-Dispatch*, 11 August 1954, 1; "Coleman: Police Powers Alone Won't Keep Segregation," UP, Greenville *Delta Democrat-Times*, 11 August 1954, 1; "Police Cannot Assure Sep-

arate Schools," Grenada *Sentinel-Star*, 11 August 1954, 1; "Police Power No Solution," AP, Tupelo *Daily Journal*, 11 August 1954, 1.

116. "Coleman Warns against Use of Police Power," AP, *Vicksburg Evening Post*, 11 August 1954, 1.

117. "Future of State's Schools Pondered after Court Decision, States Take Wait and See Attitude," AP, *Clarksdale Press Register*, 18 May 1954, 1; "Hasty Action Not Needed, Gov. Kennon, Louisiana," AP, *Vicksburg Evening Post*, 18 May 1954, 1; "How Governors Reacted to School Ruling," AP, *Natchez Democrat*, 17 May 1954, 1; "Momentous Edict Confronts South," AP, Jackson *Daily News*, 18 May 1954, 1; "Most of the South Plans to Proceed Carefully against School Edict," AP, McComb *Enterprise-Journal*, 18 May 1954, 1; "Southern Chiefs Seek Ways to Maintain Dual System," AP, Columbus *Commercial Dispatch*, 18 May 1954, 1.

118. Hodding Carter, Jr., "Delta Shows Good Sense," Greenville *Delta Democrat-Times*, 20 May 1954, 3.

119. Hodding Carter, Jr., "Not the Best Company," Greenville *Delta Democrat-Times*, 24 May 1954, 4.

120. George McLean, "He Guessed Too Wrong to Follow Again," Tupelo *Daily Journal*, 20 May 1954, 11.

121. "Equalization Talks Begin in Jackson," AP, *Clarksdale Press Register*, 18 May 1954, 1; "School Plan Explained by Educators," AP, *Vicksburg Herald*, 19 May 1954, 1; "School Leaders Talk Cost of School Program," AP, *Natchez Democrat*, 19 May 1954, 1; "School Superintendents Study Equalization in Face of Ruling," AP, West Point *Times-Leader*, 18 May 1954, 1.

122. "Negroes Refuse Consent Plan," Columbus *Commercial Dispatch*, 3 August 1954, 1.

123. "NAACP Leaders Will Petition Public Schools," UP, Tupelo *Daily Journal*, 24 May 1954, 1; "NAACP Reveal Intent to Fight All the Way on School Decision," AP, West Point *Times-Leader*, 31 May 1954, 1; "NAACP to Ask Court to Hasten Erasure of Color Bar in Schools," AP, West Point *Times-Leader*, 24 May 1954, 1; "NAACP to Seek Enforcement of Ruling in State" AP, Gulfport *Daily Herald*, 31 May 1954, 1; "NAACP to Seek Immediate End of Segregated Schools," UP, Greenville *Delta-Democrat Times*, 24 May 1954, 1; "Quick End to Segregation Is NAACP's Aim," AP, Jackson *Clarion-Ledger*, 24 May 1954, 1; "State NAACP Demands Total Desegregation," AP, *Hattiesburg American*, 29 May 1954, 1; "State NAACP Pledges Unsegregated Schools," UP, Greenville *Delta Democrat-Times*, 31 May 1954, 1; "State NAACP Wants Action," AP, Corinth *Daily Corinthian*, 30 May 1954, 1; "State Negroes to Start Drive on Segregation," AP, Grenada *Sentinel-Star*, 31 May 1954, 1; "Supreme Court Decision Hailed by NAACP," AP, *Vicksburg Herald*, 18 May 1954, 1.

124. "NAACP to Ask Quick Segregation," AP, *Clarksdale Press Register*, 24 May 1954, 1.

125. "Mississippi NAACP to Meet Sunday in Jackson," AP, *Clarksdale Press Register*, 27 May 1954, 1; "Negro Leaders Announce Goal on Segregation," AP, *Vicksburg Evening Post*, 29 August 1954, 1; "Negroes Ready to Act in Mississippi Courts," UP, Tupelo *Daily Journal*, 31 May 1954, 1; "State Negro Leaders Meet Here Sunday," Jackson *Clarion-Ledger*, 30 May 1954, 1; "State Negro Meet Called," AP, West Point *Times-Leader*, 26 May 1954, 1; "Total Abolition of Racial

Segregation to Be Goal of NAACP Here," AP, Jackson *Daily News*, 29 May 1954, 1.

126. "Adequate Schools to Solve Problem," AP, *Greenwood Commonwealth*, 12 August 1954, 1; "Call for Patience," AP, *Hattiesburg American*, 12 August 1954, 1; "Negro Education Leader Calls for Patience on Issue," Jackson *Daily News*, 12 August 1954, 1; "Negro Educator Urges New Buildings as Solution," AP, West Point *Times-Leader*, 12 August 1954, 1; "Negro Leader Asks Patience in School Issue," AP, Gulfport *Daily Herald*, 12 August 1954, 1; "Private School Plan Explained to Educators," AP, *Clarksdale Press Register*, 12 August 1954, 1; "State's Patience Is Needed over School Problem," AP, *Laurel Leader-Call*, 12 August 1954, 1.

127. "Percy Greene Outspoken Supporter of Segregation," Jackson *Daily News*, 27 May 1954, 1; "White to Confer with Negro Leaders," AP, Columbus *Commercial Dispatch*, 25 May 1997, 1.

128. Hodding Carter, Jr., "The White Proposal," Greenville *Delta Democrat-Times*, 2 August 1954, 2.

129. Birney Imes, Jr., "Dismal Picture," Columbus *Commercial Dispatch*, 3 August 1954, 6.

130. "Advisory Group Will Get Action Soon on Ways to Dodge Decision on Segregation," AP, *Laurel Leader-Call*, 18 May 1954, 1; "Eight Men Appointed to Legal Education Advisory Committee," AP, *Natchez Democrat*, 19 May 1954, 1; "Gov. White Will Select Committee for School Study," *Vicksburg Evening Post*, 18 May 1954, 1; "Governor Moves to Set Up Committee to Find Ways of Retaining Segregation," AP, West Point *Times-Leader*, 18 May 1954, 1; "Governor Names Laymen Members to Advisory Group," Jackson *Daily News*, 18 May 1954, 1; "Group Plans to Keep Segregation," AP, *Greenwood Commonwealth*, 19 May 1954, 1; "Group to Dodge Court Decision Will Roll Soon," Gulfport *Daily Herald*, 18 May 1954, 1; "Legal Parley to Meet June 2," *Meridian Star*, 20 May 1954, 1; "Pro-Segregation Leaders Plan Quick Action, Southern Chiefs Seek Ways to Maintain Dual System," AP, Columbus *Commercial Dispatch*, 18 May 1954, 1; "Quick Action Promised, Find Ways to Dodge the U.S. Supreme Court Decision Outlawing Segregation in Public Schools," AP, *Clarksdale Press Register*, 18 May 1954, 1; "South Segregationists to Fight to Bitter End against Court's Decision, See No Enforcement Soon in Most States," AP, Greenville *Delta Democrat-Times*, 18 May 1954, 1; "Special State Group to Sidetrack Segregation Ban," *Vicksburg Herald*, 20 May 1954, 3; "State Board to Find Ways to Dodge Court's Anti-Segregation Decision Appointed by White," AP, McComb *Enterprise-Journal*, 19 May 1954, 1; "State Leaders Plan First Conference," AP, Columbus *Commercial Dispatch*, 20 May 1954, 1; "White Appoints Advisory Board in Evasion of Segregation Ruling," UP, Greenwood *Morning Star*, 19 May 1954, 1; "White Appoints School Advisors," Jackson *Clarion-Ledger*, 19 May 1954, 1.

131. "Segregation Most Vital Issue," AP, Columbus *Commercial Dispatch*, 5 August 1954, 1.

132. "Slow Action Seen on Segregation Ban as State Legal Advisory Committeemen Wildly Split on School Issues," AP, Greenville *Delta Democrat-Times*, 23 May 1954, 1.

133. "800 School Leaders Almost Unanimous for Abolishing Public Schools as Last Resort," UP, Greenwood *Morning Star*, 13 August 1954, 1; "800 White

School Leaders Vote for End of Public Schools Bill," UP, Greenville *Delta Democrat-Times*, 12 August 1954, 1; "Leaders Okay Abolishing Schools," *Meridian Star*, 12 August 1954, 1; "School Groups Pledge to Support Bid for Erasing Public Education System," West Point *Times-Leader*, 12 August 1954, 1; "School Leaders Reverse Position on Public Schools After Building Plan Assured," Jackson *Daily News*, 15 August 1954, 1; "School Teachers, Officials Give Approval of Proposed Amendment," AP, *Natchez Democrat*, 13 August 1954, 1; "School Teachers Pledge Support of Amendment," Corinth *Daily Corinthian*, 13 August 1954, 1; "Segregation Proposal Endorsed by Leaders," UP, Grenada *Sentinel-Star*, 13 August 1954, 1; "State Teachers Pledge Support of School Plan," AP, Gulfport *Daily Herald*, 13 August 1954, 1; "Teachers Approve School Amendment," AP, *Hattiesburg American*, 13 August 1954, 1.

134. Jack Waldon, "Danger Is Seen," Corinth *Daily Corinthian*, 9 August 1954, 4.

135. Jack Waldon, "Don't Be Fooled," Corinth *Daily Corinthian*, 13 August 1954, 4.

136. Jack Waldon, "Kudos Offered," Corinth *Daily Corinthian*, 18 August 1954, 4.

137. Hodding Carter, Jr., "The White Proposal," Greenville *Delta Democrat-Times*, 2 August 1954, 2.

138. J.O. Emmerich, "A 5-Part Plan to Help Maintain Segregated Schools in Mississippi," McComb *Enterprise-Journal*, 24 May 1954, 2; J.O. Emmerich, "A Suggestion to Solve School Dilemma," McComb *Enterprise-Journal*, 2 August 1954, 1.

139. J.O. Emmerich, "Why Our Public Schools Should Not Be Abolished," McComb *Enterprise-Journal*, 10 August 1954, 1.

140. Herman Moore, "Practical, Not Hasty, Planning Needed," *Natchez Times*, 19 August 1954, 4.

141. George McLean, "Why Give Negroes a Death Grip on Schools?" Tupelo *Daily Journal*, 2 August 1954, 11.

142. "Dangerous, Says Sen. Owens of School Plan," Tupelo *Daily Journal*, 28 August 1954, 1.

143. Charles Hills, "Affairs of State," Jackson *Clarion-Ledger*, 15 August 1954, 9.

144. W.H. Harris, "Cart before Horse," West Point *Times-Leader*, 16 August 1954, 4.

145. "Gov. White Plans Law to Prevent Race Trouble," AP, *Vicksburg Herald*, 27 August 1954, 1; "White Proposes Segregation Barrier," AP, *Hattiesburg American*, 27 August 1954, 1; "White Reveals Another Plank in Program to Maintain Segregation," AP, Corinth *Daily Corinthian*, 27 August 1954, 1; "White Reveals Plank in Segregation Program," AP, *Laurel Leader-Call*, 27 August 1954, 1.

146. "Arkansas School Will Integrate White, Colored," AP, Gulfport *Daily Herald*, 22 May 1954, 1; "Five Border States Open Unsegregated Schools Soon," UP, *Meridian Star*, 29 August 1954, 1; "Historic Steps End Segregation in Five State's Schools This Fall," UP, Greenville *Delta Democrat-Times*, 29 August 1954, 1; "Schools in Five States to Mix Races, Mississippi Will Remain Segregated," UP, Grenada *Sentinel-Star*, 31 August 1954, 1.

147. "Arkansas White Schools to Admit Negroes, First Break in Southern Front," AP, *Hattiesburg American*, 22 May 1954, 1.

148. "Dilemma in Dixie," *Time*, 20 February 1956, 76; "Dixie Flamethrowers," *Time*, 4 March 1966, 64; "Moderation in Dixie," *Time*, 19 March 1965, 71; Edwin W. Williams, "Dimout in Jackson," *Columbia Journalism Review* 9 (Summer 1970): 56.

149. "Belting One Down for the Road," *Nation*, 6 October 1962, 190; Charles Butts, "Mississippi: The Vacuum and the System," in *Black, White and Gray: 21 Points of View on the Race Question*, ed. Bradford Daniel (New York: Sheed and Ward, 1964), 104; "Dilemma in Dixie," 76; "Dixie Flamethrowers," 64; "Moderation in Dixie"; Ted Poston, "The American Negro and Newspaper Myths," in *Race and the News Media*, ed. Paul Fisher and Ralph Lowenstein (New York: Praeger, 1967), 63; Pat Watters and Reese Cleghorn, *Climbing Jacob's Ladder: The Arrival of Negroes in Southern Politics* (New York: Harcourt, Brace and World, 1967), 73; Simeon Booker, *Black Man's America* (Englewood Cliffs, N.J.: Prentice-Hall, 1964), 15; Roger M. Williams, "Newspapers in the South," *Columbia Journalism Review* 6 (Summer 1967): 27; James Boylan, "Birmingham Newspapers in Crisis," *Columbia Journalism Review* 2 (Summer 1963): 30.

Chapter 4

1962: The Desegregation of Ole Miss and the Mississippi Daily Press

Almost a century before the University of Mississippi, known as Ole Miss, was forced by federal decree to enroll a black student in 1962, Chancellor John Waddel said in 1870, "Should the University be required to receive and admit applicants of the Negro race to University classes, the members of the present faculty would instantly tender their resignations."[1]

A hundred years later, as the first black student was preparing to move into a dormitory at Ole Miss under the protection of federal troops and U.S. marshals,[2] Chancellor John Williams voiced a distinctly different concern from that of Waddel. Williams urged Ole Miss students to be peaceful and reasonable and "to go about their business as normal."[3]

The U.S. Supreme Court ruled in early September 1962 that James Howard Meredith should be admitted to Ole Miss, and the controversial matter was front-page news in every Mississippi daily newspaper.[4] "Supreme Court Justice Hugo L. Black today set aside an order blocking admission of James H. Meredith, 29, a Negro seeking to enter the University of Mississippi at Oxford next month," the UPI reported. "The 5th Circuit Court ordered Meredith admitted to the university on the grounds that he had been kept out for reasons of race only. Meredith has been trying for fourteen months to get into the all-white university."[5]

Meredith was born in Attala County, Mississippi, in 1933, the seventh of thirteen children born to Cap and Roxie Meredith. He graduated from high school in St. Petersburg, Florida, and served in the U.S. Air Force from 1951 to 1960. He was enrolled at the historically black Jackson State College in Mississippi's capital city when he applied for admission to Ole Miss in 1961.[6]

GOVERNOR ROSS BARNETT RESISTS THE COURT

The day after Justice Black's decision to admit Meredith to Ole Miss, Mississippi Governor Ross Barnett was in the news proclaiming that Meredith would never be admitted and that the state would close the university system before it would allow desegregation of the campuses.[7] Student leaders at Ole Miss did not agree with Barnett, which was widely reported in the Mississippi daily press.[8]

Barnett addressed the Meredith decision on statewide television and radio the evening of 13 September. An announcement of the planned speech was published in most of the Mississippi daily newspapers,[9] but not the Greenville *Delta Democrat-Times*, where Hodding Carter, Jr., and his son, Hodding Carter III, had a particular disdain for Barnett.[10]

On 14 September, excerpts from Barnett's speech, a defiant stance against the desegregation of Ole Miss, was front-page news in the Mississippi daily press. He was praised by Jackson *Clarion-Ledger* staff writers. Tom Etheridge labeled Barnett "courageous."[11] Gene Wirth, who died of a heart attack six days later,[12] referred to Barnett as "fearless."[13]

Barnett blamed "professional agitators, an unfriendly liberal press and other troublemakers" for the desegregation order. With a staggering lack of foresight he pledged, "No schools in Mississippi will be integrated while I am your governor."[14]

Two chaotic weeks later, Meredith attended his first class at Ole Miss.

BARNETT PROPOSES INTERPOSITION: "BAYING AT THE MOON"

Barnett was born in 1899, the son of a Confederate soldier, and he told state officials they should go to jail rather than obey federal desegregation orders. "We will not drink from the cup of genocide," he was quoted by the UPI. "There is no page in history where the Caucasian race has survived social integration."[15]

The primary means by which Barnett proposed to defy the federal court order was "interposition," a theoretical concept whereby a state "places, or interposes, its sovereignty between the court's ruling and the state, thereby bringing on a contest to be settled by constitutional amendment."[16] Interposition was not a legal protest by Barnett but rather "an illegal defiance of a constitutional order."[17] The last time in the nation that interposition was attempted on a regional scale—and it failed—was during the Civil War.[18] Prior to that time, South Carolina had declared interposition, and the Mississippi Legislature in 1832 rejected that state's action as "a heresy, fatal to the existence of the Union, contrary to the letter and spirit of the Constitution."[19] Consequently, Barnett's enthusiasm for interposition in 1962 was headline news in the Mississippi daily press,[20] despite the fact that the procedure had been tried unsuccessfully in Alabama following *Brown v. Board of Education* to maintain segregation in that state's public schools.[21]

When Barnett declared his determination to "interpose" himself between Meredith and Ole Miss, Alabama Governor James Folsom described the futility of the measure. "It's like a dog baying at the moon and claiming it got it treed," he said.[22]

CROSS BURNED, EFFIGY HANGED AT OLE MISS

The day after Barnett's televised speech of defiance, the Mississippi daily press reported that an effigy of Meredith was hanged on a flagpole at Ole Miss.[23] Earlier, a cross was burned near the campus apartments where Meredith was to be housed if accepted into the school.[24] A front-page photo of the burning cross in the Jackson *Daily News* was captioned, "Greeting for Negro."[25]

The cross-burning at Ole Miss was contrived and blown out of proportion, according to Russell Barrett, a political science professor at Ole Miss when the incident occurred. Barrett recollected that a crowd was not at the scene or dispersed by campus police as reported the next day in the media. "The cross-burning was staged to produce a newspaper story so written to inflame feelings at the University and throughout the state," he wrote.[26]

INJUNCTION AND LEGISLATION AGAINST MEREDITH

A week after Justice Black issued his order, nearly fifty parents of Ole Miss students filed a lawsuit seeking an injunction from a state court to keep Meredith out of the university. Chancery Judge L.B. Porter of Newton ruled in their favor, a decision widely reported in the Mississippi daily press.[27] Porter's authority, of course, was soon overshadowed by the Fifth Circuit Court of Appeals in New Orleans.

Another attempt to keep Meredith from enrolling at Ole Miss involved publicizing a voter registration fraud case against him.[28] The Mississippi Legislature quickly passed a bill forbidding a person with a criminal record from gaining admittance to a state university, and an attempt to use this bill to keep Meredith out of Ole Miss was made.[29] The ploy, however, was defused by the Fifth Circuit Court of Appeals in New Orleans.[30]

REACTION BY MISSISSIPPI OFFICIALS

During this time, Barnett had the fairly solid support of Mississippi's elected officials,[31] including U.S. Senators John Stennis and James Eastland.[32] On 19 September, the Mississippi House of Representatives voted 130–2 in support of Barnett, with only Joe Wroten of Greenville and Karl

Weisburg of Pascagoula in opposition.[33] The next day, when a vote was taken in the House on whether to arrest Meredith in order to prevent him from enrolling at Ole Miss, the vote was 122–1, with only Weisburg in opposition.[34]

State Representative Frank Smith, however, was an outspoken opponent of Barnett and accused the governor of "leading the state down a blind alley."[35] A popular representative from the Delta for a decade, Smith was voted out of office in November 1962, "for being a friend of President John F. Kennedy, allegedly favoring integration, supporting liberal trade programs with foreign nations and 'opposing the Mississippi way of life.' "[36] In a front-page article in the Jackson *Clarion-Ledger* headlined, "All but Smith Support Ross," the congressman was reported to be one of the few white Mississippians to publicly criticize the governor for his stance on Ole Miss. "Whether we like it or not, the question of state versus Federal law was settled a hundred years ago," Smith said.[37]

QUANDARY OF STATE COLLEGE BOARD

Caught in the cross fire of the Meredith case was the twelve-member state college board, all traditional Southerners but men who took their positions seriously as guardians of the state's institutions of higher learning. Barnett was demanding that they refuse Meredith entry to Ole Miss or resign from the board. He was also suggesting that the state's university system be closed down to avoid desegregation, an idea with which the college board was not ready to comply.[38] Board member Thomas Tubb supported Barnett in his desire to maintain a segregated school system, but he questioned whether closing the schools to defy a court order was legal.[39] Because the board refused to comply with Barnett's immediate demands, they were under a great deal of pressure, as reported in the Tupelo newspaper under the headline, "College Board Showdown on Meredith Is Due Today, Group's Failure to Back Ross Stirs Anger."[40]

Members of the college board also faced jail terms if they failed to comply with the federal court order to enroll Meredith, a possibility widely covered in the Mississippi daily press.[41] Interestingly, Vernon Holmes, vice president of the board, came bravely forward. "Yes, I will go to jail," Holmes said. "But it will be to keep Ole Miss open."[42]

On 20 September, Barnett received a handwritten death threat by mail from Vicksburg that said, "You won't live three weeks."[43] That same day, the college board and several Ole Miss officials were summoned to the Federal District Court in Meridian on contempt charges for allowing Barnett to act as the registrar and deny entrance to Meredith.[44] Barnett had appointed himself into that capacity over the protestations of several board members who disapproved the tactic.[45] The governor was not party to the charges.

On 22 September 1962, the centennial anniversary of the Emancipation Proclamation,[46] Ole Miss administrators were freed from responsibility by the district court,[47] and the college board was held solely accountable. An eight-judge panel of the Fifth Circuit Court of Appeals heard the case in New Orleans, where an agreement was reached with the board that Meredith be allowed to register for admission to Ole Miss by 25 September 1962.[48] The board was told by the panel that if they all resigned in protest, the court would appoint a new board. Barnett would not be allowed to do the appointing.[49]

OLE MISS ACCREDITATION AT STAKE; BARNETT FINED FOR CONTEMPT

In the midst of the chaos that week, the loss of the university's accreditation for failure to comply with the federal court order to enroll Meredith became an issue with the Southern Association of Colleges.[50] This dilemma, in conjunction with Barnett's threat to close the state's universities, created a major controversy among Ole Miss students, faculty and alumni, most of whom wanted to keep Ole Miss open, segregated or not.[51] Also that week, Barnett was charged with contempt by the Fifth Circuit Court of Appeals in New Orleans and fined $10,000 a day, beginning 2 October, until he "ceased resistance of court orders, maintained law and order at Ole Miss, and let Meredith enter."[52]

MEREDITH GOES TO OLE MISS

On 19 September, Ed Noel, a staff writer for the Jackson *Clarion-Ledger*, was in Oxford to cover Meredith's attempt to register. "Meredith didn't show up on Wednesday," he wrote. "We waited on him, me and the faculty, seventy Highway Patrolmen, fifty sheriffs and all of Mississippi."[53]

The next day, Meredith tried to enter the Ole Miss campus accompanied by U.S. marshals and jeering students. He was turned away quietly by Barnett. "An attempt by deputy U.S. marshals to usher the Air Force veteran into the school through throngs of booing students was stymied personally Thursday by Gov. Barnett, who has sworn to go to jail rather than allow integration," the UPI reported. "There were no signs of trouble and the students seemed more curious than angry."[54]

William Miles, a staff reporter for the Tupelo *Daily Journal*, was at Ole Miss that day. "In general, the crowd was orderly," Miles wrote. "There were about a thousand students and a hundred media."[55] Bill Simpson of the Corinth *Daily Corinthian*, was also there. "Gov. Barnett was clearly the most popular man on campus yesterday as he appointed himself registrar and personally refused negro James H. Meredith's application to enroll at the University," Simpson wrote. "There were cries from the crowd of 'Go home, nigger.' "[56] The incident was front-page news in some, but not all, Mississippi daily newspapers.[57]

During the last week in September 1962, Meredith was officially registered in Jackson as a student at Ole Miss, and he tried twice more, unsuccessfully, to gain entrance to the campus at Oxford. He was portrayed in the Mississippi daily press during this time as a calm, somewhat naive individual who considered himself safe from harm. "I don't think I'll need any federal marshals," Meredith said, and he spoke understandingly of Barnett. "He's doing what he feels is his duty."[58]

Meredith did, however, need protection. Barnett was at Ole Miss to turn him away the first two times that month, but Lieutenant Governor Paul Johnson, Jr., backed by hundreds of Mississippi Highway Patrol officers and county sheriffs, stood in the doorway during Meredith's third attempt. The wire services reported the incident as the state's third "deliberate defiance" of the federal government. "The confrontation started calmly but ended in a tense, almost eerily quiet, pushing and shoving contest," AP and UPI reported. "Few students were there. Johnson said, 'I refuse to allow you to enter because of imminent breach of peace.' "[59]

The next day, U.S. marshals, sent by President John Kennedy and his brother, U.S. Attorney General Robert Kennedy, began arriving on campus to aid Meredith. The buildup of federal troops at the school was widely covered by the Mississippi daily press in wire service copy that described Chief U.S. Marshal James McShane as he "tried to push his way through Mississippi Highway Patrol officers and could not."[60] Barnett complained to the media about federal interference and issued his only accurate prediction during the entire conflict, "A gun battle could erupt."[61]

THE RIOT

On 30 September, Barnett agreed to have Meredith escorted onto campus and secured in his dormitory room. The prospect of a $10,000-a-day fine was probably quite daunting to Barnett. By early that evening, a crowd was milling near the Lyceum building on campus, where several hundred U.S. marshals and several thousand federalized Mississippi National Guardsmen were positioned. As a showdown became imminent, into the fray came General Edwin A. Walker, a Texan and former major general in the U.S. Army who referred to the U.S. Supreme Court as "the anti-Christ." He arrived in Jackson in late September, eager to do battle rather than allow the desegregation of Ole Miss. Walker, who had been in charge of federal troops in Little Rock following *Brown v. Board of Education* in 1954, was vehemently opposed to federal interference in what he considered states' rights.[62]

As dusk settled over the campus, a riot broke out that lasted for eight hours into the night. Most of the rioters were not students, but had come to heed the call of Walker, who was "ushered out of Courthouse Square at bayonet point" during the melee.[63] Many people were injured, and two were killed, Roy Gunter, a Mississippian in his twenties, and Paul Guihard, a photographer for a French news agency, who was shot in the back.[64]

The morning after the riot, the Ole Miss campus was littered with burned-out automobiles, tear gas canisters and broken glass. Martial law was declared, and seventy-five arrests were made, including some members of the American Nazi Party from Georgia.[65]

Sidna Bower, editor of the Ole Miss student newspaper, the *Mississippian*, said the riot "brought shame and dishonor" to the school.[66]

The next day, the state flag was flown at half-staff over the capital in Jackson.[67] Whether the flag was lowered to honor the two men who were killed or to mourn the loss of segregation at the university was not officially designated.

Meredith remained at Ole Miss and attended classes.[68] He was guarded constantly by federal marshals or bodyguards[69] and graduated in August 1963.[70]

THE EDITORS RESPOND

Editorials pertaining to the court-ordered desegregation of Ole Miss began to roll off the presses at most Mississippi daily newspapers soon after Justice Black's decision in mid-September. Unlike the *Brown v. Board of Education* decision in 1954, the desegregation of Ole Miss was immediate. Only three of the nineteen daily newspapers published no opinion pertaining to the Meredith decision in September 1962, the Grenada *Sentinel-Star*, the Gulfport *Daily Herald* and the *Natchez Democrat*. All three newspapers did, however, cover the Meredith case extensively with wire service stories.

In Columbus, Birney Imes, Jr., continued as editor of the *Commercial Dispatch*. The possible desegregation of Ole Miss inspired his editorial pen much more often than had *Brown v. Board of Education* in 1954. "Our freedom is in great danger," he wrote in a front-page editorial. "The threat is more imminent now than at any other point in our history. A federal government, growing ever more powerful, is slowly smothering the life from individual freedoms. Will we measure up in the hour of the state's great crisis?"[71] Another front-page editorial by Imes, "Gutless Mississippians?" directed his anger toward the state's college board. Imes thought the board should defy the court order, even if it meant going to jail. "We sincerely hope every single one will stand firm," he wrote.[72] Imes encouraged his readers to support Barnett. "We think the governor is eminently correct," he wrote. "We hope our readers will agree and give Governor Barnett complete support."[73] Later in the month, Imes expressed his appreciation for those who supported the Columbus *Commercial Dispatch* in its most recent endorsement of states' rights, this time in opposing the forced desegregation of the state's universities.[74]

In agreement with Imes was J.O. "Oliver" Emmerich, who remained as editor of the McComb *Enterprise-Journal*. Barnett found all the support he needed in Pike County. When the governor announced that he would speak to the state on television to address the Ole Miss "crisis," Emmerich offered him front-page coverage. "The people of Mississippi stand behind their officials in this crisis," he wrote.[75] The next day, in his front-page editorial column, "Highlights in the Headlines," Emmerich praised Barnett's speech as "unflinchingly courageous" and expressed veneration for the governor. "In his determined will to stand up for what he believes to be right, we as Mississippians must admire him," he wrote.[76]

Emmerich voiced his concern about closing the state's universities, however.[77] He did not want to see this happen. "What good would it accomplish?" he asked his readers. "Would it keep Mississippi's schools all white this year and the next year and for the decade and the decades to come?"[78] Toward the end of the month, Emmerich began to question whether Barnett was able to keep his promise of barring the doors of the state's white universities to blacks. "Will Governor Barnett be successful?" he asked. "Will he be the first governor to brush aside a Supreme Court decision?"[79] At the same time, Emmerich remained convinced that Barnett was the most popular man in Mississippi, at least among the white population.[80]

At the *Meridian Star*, James B. Skewes had replaced his father as editor and publisher when James H. Skewes died in 1958.[81] The younger Skewes was a shy, introverted man with a speech impediment who left the business of the paper to others. "His peers in newsrooms around the state are often puzzled by his behavior," historian Robert Hooker wrote. "Even a former managing editor under him calls him 'a genius with no common sense.' "[82]

During the early 1960s, the younger Skewes was a member of the Citizens' Council, a group founded in Mississippi in 1953 to maintain segregation. The Citizens' Council was supported by most Mississippi legislators and the Hederman family, who controlled the Jackson *Clarion-Ledger* and the Jackson *Daily News*.[83] Wide coverage by the state's daily newspapers provided credibility and free advertising to the Citizens' Council, a group that greatly influenced Mississippi government until the end of Ross Barnett's gubernatorial tenure in 1964.[84]

Skewes believed that if Ole Miss was to be forcibly desegregated, then federal troops should be responsible for the job. "The order to integrate the school came from the federal government and therefore doing the 'dirty work' of carrying it out is not the responsibility of the state of Mississippi," Skewes wrote. "Neither Mississippi law enforcement nor Mississippi National Guardsmen should be asked to escort Meredith at any time. The health and lives of our own people should not be endangered because of the whims of federal officials seeking to gain political advantage."[85] Skewes believed that the attempt to desegregate Ole Miss was a blatant and insidious effort by the U.S. Supreme Court to destroy traditional Mississippi society. "They are attempting to pollute the very blood in our veins, to destroy one of the things that we hold most sacred, our racial integrity," he wrote.[86]

Skewes agreed with Barnett that state officials should work to resist all efforts to enroll Meredith, even if it meant going to jail. He also concurred with Barnett that if state officials were not willing to face jail, they should resign. "We agree with the governor one hundred percent for racial integrity," he wrote.[87]

In his final editorial column for the month, Skewes told his readers that if Ole Miss was forced to desegregate, then socialism had taken over as the country's political ideology. "If the government uses force to bring about the integration of Mississippi, we will know that there is no longer a democratic government but a government which is determined to remove the cherished freedoms we have known and substitute in their place a socialist state where the individual loses his identity and perhaps his soul," he wrote.[88]

In Greenwood, Thatcher Walt was the newly appointed editor at the *Greenwood Commonwealth*. The first news story concerning the mandated desegregation of Ole Miss in the *Greenwood Commonwealth* in September 1962 was an AP story about J.W. Jones, a black Mississippi educator who made a name for himself in the Mississippi daily press following *Brown v. Board of Education* by supporting segregated schools.[89] In a front-page story in the *Greenwood Commonwealth*, "Negro Editor Says Mixing Ole Miss Won't Help Us," Jones, then editor of the semi-monthly black *Community Citizen*, said, "James Meredith is not a Patrick Henry, but a pied piper."[90]

At the *Greenwood Commonwealth*, Walt offered no editorial guidance regarding Meredith until the middle of the month, when his first comment was to praise Barnett, referring to him as "a knight on a white charger."[91] Walt also suggested that a statue be built to honor the governor. "Governor Barnett's shrine in American history is already sculpted," he wrote. "His unflinching stand on principle will be studied by school boys as long as there is a free United States."[92] President Kennedy, on the other hand, was only seeking to gain black votes with his support of the Meredith decision, according to Walt.[93]

In his only front-page opinion pertaining to the Meredith decision in September, Walt placed a heavy burden on Barnett, calling on him to force the nation's hand. "Make them use troops, Governor," he wrote. "Make them reveal the lengths to which a government will go to suppress its own people to perpetuate itself in power. Unless you do, nothing you have told the people up to now will make sense."[94] Although Walt appeared willing to go to any lengths to maintain a segregated system in Mississippi, he drew the line at closing down the state's universities.[95]

At the *Hattiesburg American*, Leonard Lowrey had become editor, and his advice on the opinion page was to pray as Ole Miss prepared for desegregation. "The state of Mississippi today began what is pretty certain to be the most eventful and crucial week in history," he wrote. "We urge a calm attitude on the part of the public, allowing our elected and appointed officials and law enforcement officers to handle whatever situations occur. We can support them with prayers for divine guidance in their decisions and for acceptable solutions to our problems."[96] Lowrey agreed with Walt that President Kennedy supported civil rights issues primarily because the number of registered black voters was growing in the country. Syndicated columnist David Lawrence found a willing publisher in Hattiesburg for his column, "JFK Pushes Some Civil Rights for Votes."[97]

Keeping the state's universities open, however, was Lowrey's primary concern, and, despite his Southern conservatism, he asked his readers in a front-page editorial to settle down and take the long view. "Along with most other Mississippians, we are anxious to see segregation maintained in the schools of our state from the University of Mississippi, on down, if it's at all possible," he wrote. "Grave concern has been expressed by some that the university will be closed or that it will lose its accreditation as a result of the Meredith matter. No matter what else, Ole Miss, and all of our other state institutions of higher learning, should be kept open and in good standing."[98]

In the state's capital, front-page editorials in the Jackson *Clarion-Ledger* were common during the Ole Miss crisis. T.M. Hederman, Jr., remained as editor, and readers were urged to back Barnett. State officials were directed to stand by the governor or resign. Schools are state business, not federal, Hederman exhorted. "By authority of the federal constitution this is true, regardless of misinterpretations of the constitution in recent years," he wrote. "As the governor said, it is apparent this state is the keystone in this battle for states' rights. We must neither falter nor fall in this supreme test."[99]

In a plea to the state college board to deny access to Meredith despite the federal court order, another front-page headline in the Jackson *Clarion-Ledger* proclaimed, "United We Stand."[100] Charles M. Hills, the fire-breathing conservative who was with the *Clarion-Ledger* in 1954, continued his "Affairs of State" column. A few days after the Meredith decision, he wrote, "The yankee philosophy that the government can do no wrong isn't taking here."[101] Most editorial comment pertaining to the Meredith case in the *Clarion-Ledger*, however, was addressed in Tom Etheridge's "Mississippi Notebook." Etheridge was anti-Kennedy, both John and his brother, Robert.[102] He was also a staunch states' rights supporter.

"At stake is more than a single Negro at Ole Miss," Etheridge wrote. "The main issue is states' rights."[103]

Across town at the Jackson *Daily News*, editor James "Jimmy" Ward had replaced Fred Sullens, who died in 1957 after being at the helm of the newspaper for fifty years. Ward maintained Sullens' propensity for conservative Southern opinion but was not nearly as prolific. He commented the day after the court order to admit Meredith in his front-page "Crossroads" column, "Meredith is a Negro with a nervous stomach."[104] A few days later, Ward praised Barnett and his defiant stand as "courageous"[105] and announced, "We Support Governor Barnett."[106] The Jackson *Daily News* continued to denounce violence as it had in 1954. In his editorial, "Let the Crackpots Scream," Ward wrote, "Any act of violence will only serve the agitators."[107] Ward recommended, "Determination, calmness and courage will mean victory"[108] and suggested that Mississippi's opposition to desegregation was because in regions of the nation that were integrated there was more crime. "We think the price of appeasement is too high," Ward wrote.[109] In another front-page "Crossroads," Ward angrily suggested that the name "Ole Miss" be changed to "the United States Academy for Negroes."[110]

Another newly appointed editor of the Mississippi daily press was at work in Jones County at the *Laurel Leader-Call*, which was sold in 1959 to Thomson Newspapers.[111] J.W. "Jay" West replaced Harriet Gibbons at the paper and persisted with Gibbons' vague distrust of politicians. West wrote only three editorials in September 1962 pertaining to the Meredith case. In his first, a week after Black issued his decree to force Meredith's admission to Ole Miss, West pointed a critical finger at the governor in "Barnett's Action Goads State's Sad Situation." He questioned Barnett's attempt at interposition. "Barnett is a lawyer by profession," he wrote. "He knew, or should have known, that the theory of interposition has been rejected by the courts since 1792." West also questioned Barnett's demand to the college board that they support him or resign. "According to Barnett, the members of the state college board either go to jail for contempt of a federal court order, or get off the board," he wrote. "Really, what skin is it off his neck if somebody else goes to jail? Whatever the ultimate outcome of the issue, it is believed Barnett would have served the course of Mississippi education better if he had left the matter with those entrusted with it."[112]

In the last days of September 1962, as the admission of Meredith to Ole Miss appeared imminent, and the threat of bloodshed was in the air, West published an editorial, "Violence Is No Answer," from the Memphis *Commercial Appeal*. "Mississippi's governor has been independent and forthright in a regrettable situation," the writer observed. "But is it worth it if it puts a headstone over you?"[113]

In 1962, one of the most traditional and angry Southerners among the editors of the Mississippi daily press was W.H. Harris, who continued as editor and publisher of the West Point *Times-Leader*. He was also the publisher of the *Starkville Daily News*, which he founded in 1960, ten miles south of West Point in Starkville. Sherrill Nash was the editor of the *Starkville Daily News*, but Harris' conservative editorials were published in both newspapers, usually in the West Point *Times-Leader* a day before appearing in the *Starkville Daily News*. Two days after the Meredith decision was announced, Harris expressed his support of Barnett and was confident that if Meredith was allowed to enter Ole Miss, he would soon be gone because of his inability to meet the academic standards.[114]

Harris voiced his support of Barnett,[115] believed in the feasibility of interposition, and questioned the Southern patriotism of those who did not. "We respect any man's right to his own opinion, but we wonder what those who would obey Black's directive would have done in the early days of the Civil War," he wrote. "No, we're certainly not suggesting that Mississippi should start cessation action. That shouldn't be necessary. But we are saying that the basic matter of principle, regarding the fundamental rights of the separate and sovereign states, is just as real today as it was a hundred years ago."[116]

Harris often published his "Pencil Shavings" column in the Starkville paper, as well as the West Point *Times-Leader*. Harris loathed President Kennedy with a passion, and he took advantage of the Kennedy support of the Meredith decision to express his disdain. "While we're convinced that the Kennedy brothers would like to see a Negro in every Southern school, we're also convinced that they don't want violence connected with it," he wrote. "The Democratic Party knows it can't depend on bloody voters. It's time for calm thinking."[117] Toward the end of the month, as federal marshals assembled at the university in anticipation of Meredith's arrival on campus, Harris continued his diatribe against the Kennedys, chiding them for their concern about Mississippi's Highway Patrol, or "peace officers," who were gathering at the campus. "The peace officers assembled en masse on the Ole Miss campus Thursday carried no guns, only wooden night sticks and tear gas bombs," he wrote. "Do we need Little Bobby to bring armed marshals against Mississippi's unarmed peace officers? Governor Barnett has JFK on the spot. For political reasons he can't invade the South with troops."[118]

In late September, when it appeared that Barnett might be jailed for defiance of the court order to enroll Meredith and that Lieutenant Governor Paul B. Johnson, Jr., might have to fill the gubernatorial shoes, Harris commented in "Take Note, Paul," that the job would be no easy task. "You could become governor before this day, or this week, is over," he wrote. "Mississippi will expect, and demand, the same bravery and determination displayed by Ross Barnett."[119]

When Meredith's arrival at the Ole Miss campus as an officially admitted student occurred on 30 September, Harris took a final jab at the president. "There's a silver lining in every cloud," he wrote. "John F. Kennedy is about to cut the throat of his personal political future."[120]

In Tupelo, Harry Rutherford had replaced George McLean as editor at the *Daily Journal*, although McLean remained with the paper as publisher. Rutherford offered only two editorials concerning the Meredith decision in September, and the first was to criticize the notion of closing the state's universities rather than desegregating them. In 1954, the Tupelo *Daily Journal* had proffered the same advice when then Mississippi Governor Hugh White suggested abolishing the state's public school system rather than abide by *Brown v. Board of Education.* "Surely, the Board of Trustees, regardless of pressure from the governor, will, at the last minute, stand up for the reasonable expectation of every young Mississippian to get an education," Rutherford wrote. "Surely, they will not throw five thousand students out into the streets with small chance of entering college elsewhere."[121]

Toward the end of the month, Rutherford advised his readers to accept the inevitable. "The young people of our state are being made pawns in the battle as thoughtless opposing forces rush toward the point of no return," he wrote. "Nothing except disaster can now be achieved by pushing the issue past the explosion point." Rutherford also appealed to common sense. "Governor Barnett is a good lawyer," he wrote. "He knows that no person, agency or state has ever been able to defy the authority of the government of the United States."[122]

The next day, as if to reassure his readers that acceptance of a desegregated university system was the right thing to do because of its inevitability, Rutherford borrowed a quote from W.J. Cash, author of *The Mind of the South* (1941). In an editorial he titled, "For the South, the Future Has Arrived," Rutherford published Cash's words, "In the coming days, the South is likely to have to prove its capacity for adjustment far beyond what has been true in the past."[123]

West to the Mississippi River in the Delta at the *Clarksdale Press Register*, Joseph Ellis, Jr., remained at the helm. He had few opinions to offer his readers regarding the Ole Miss crisis. In September 1962, he made mention of the Meredith case just once, and that was toward the end of the month as Meredith's enrollment was assured. "As in a Greek tragedy, we know that a major disaster is impending, and like the murmuring extras on the stage, helpless to avert it," Ellis wrote. "The doomed heroes in this case are several, the republican concept of a Federal government of limited powers, the rights of the people of several states to control and regulate, rightly or wrongly, wisely or unwisely, their own affairs, and most important, the status of a great university."[124] Ellis blamed many parties for the situation, including "a pushing, militant minority determined to obtain their 'rights' even if in the process they destroy the governmental concepts which must ultimately ensure all rights" and "a somewhat confused state administration, trying to protect a great and sound principle, without quite knowing how to do it."[125]

Less than a week later, the day after the riot at Ole Miss left two dead and many injured, Ellis was back with "Appeal to Reason." He was critical of the defiance shown by the state and had harsh words for Barnett:

> The emotional forces of violence, defiance and mass hysteria which have been unleashed in Mississippi by the obstinate stupidity of politically-motivated national and state leadership on opposing sides of the controversy will be difficult, if not impossible, to check and control. We must start looking for new leadership, on the national and state level. Both have failed this nation and state to a miserable, shameful degree. A "banzai" charge against an impregnable position is not an act of courage, it is an act of suicide and insanity.[126]

Ellis advised the students at Ole Miss to return to their classes and get on with their academic goals.

Northeast toward the Tennessee and Alabama border, the Corinth *Daily Corinthian* was edited by Bill Simpson, who went to Ole Miss to gather eyewitness reports. His front-page "Talk of Town" editorials portrayed an Old South view congruent with that of the previous editors at the *Daily Corinthian.* Beginning the third week of September 1962, Simpson kept the Meredith case in the opinion columns. His first mention was a racially condescending story from Ole Miss told by an unnamed reporter: "A fine old negro gentlemen employed as a janitor at the university was asked how he felt about Meredith by a reporter from the North. The reporter was surprised by the answer. 'That nigger is just stirring up misery for us poor colored folks.' "[127]

The next day, Simpson reported that untruths were being spread by the media regarding an incident at Ole Miss. Simpson said that he was on the campus, standing near Meredith, when news reports said a rock or brick was thrown. Simpson said he never saw anything to match that description. "The malicious lies about what went on at Ole Miss yesterday are already being spread by newspapers and radio and TV networks hostile toward Mississippi segregation laws," he wrote.[128]

Simpson joined Nash of the *Starkville Daily News* and Harris in Westpoint in denouncing the Kennedy administration following the Meredith decision. Toward the end of the month, he conceded, "The federal government with Robert Kennedy and the NAACP at the forefront is almost certain to win the war by enrolling negro James Meredith at Ole Miss." He also urged that the university not be closed to avoid desegregation because "our students would be forced to seek their educations in other states, probably with negroes."[129]

Simpson degraded blacks in general and the NAACP in particular whenever he found a chance, such as the janitor story, which was one of the only instances that the word "nigger" was found in the Mississippi daily press between 1948 and 1968 in the issues examined for this book. Toward the end of September 1962, when he was complaining about the plea the NAACP was making for civil rights, Simpson wrote, "The NAACP is demanding that the first astronaut on the moon be a negro on de moon by June."[130]

At the *Vicksburg Evening Post*, Louis P. Cashman, Jr., had replaced his father as editor. The day after the Meredith decision, Cashman directed his angst toward the U.S. Supreme Court, just as his father had directed anger toward the Court following *Brown v. Board of Education* in 1954. "It is utterly amazing that reference to color could bring such prompt and wonderful service from our federal courts," he wrote. "There is no doubt that the appeal of 'discrimination' on racial lines, whether founded on fact or not, will get the best de-luxe service from our government, our Justice Department and most of our federal judiciary, and it is now standard procedure to inject the racial issue into every case."[131]

As his father had done before him, Cashman advanced the states' rights argument in attacking the Meredith decision. He praised Barnett's televised address. "This was no political tirade, no inflammatory appeal to passion," he wrote. "The Meredith decision is a much deeper issue than integration. We must lead the fight."[132] Two days later, Cashman returned with more concern about the states' rights issue. "Political expediency in the field of so-called civil rights has long ago overthrown any devotion to principle, in the relentless drive to consolidate the power which now rests in Washington," he wrote.[133]

Interestingly, even though the paper expressed support for Barnett and his attempt to keep Meredith from being admitted to Ole Miss, a column by syndicated columnist James Marlow was published in the *Vicksburg Evening Post* that referred to the governor as "just a Johnny-come-lately for states' righters."[134]

On the Mississippi River in the Delta, the often controversial Hodding Carter, Jr., known for his commitment to equal justice for all people regardless of race, had handed over the helm of the Greenville *Delta Democrat-Times* to his son. Hodding Carter III, who went on to his own distinguished career as a journalist, followed in his father's philosophical footsteps. "I returned to Greenville in 1959, and started writing editorials immediately," he said. "Dad was out of the country on a fellowship in South Africa during the Ross Barnett election, so I had one hell of a great time."[135] Carter III, along with Ira Harkey of the Pascagoula *Chronicle*, was one of only two editors of the Mississippi daily press who openly endorsed allowing blacks to attend Mississippi's traditionally white institutions of higher learning. "Before the 1954 Supreme Court desegregation decree, we said that qualified Negro students should be admitted to our institutions of higher learning," Carter III wrote. "In the name of common sense, if nothing else, Mississippi should abandon massive resistance, for events have demonstrated time and time again since 1954 that it is an impossible policy to maintain."[136]

Five days later, Carter III was back. He aired his view that even though most white Mississippians voiced support for Barnett, none truly believed that he would be successful in keeping Meredith from enrolling at Ole Miss. He also raised the specter of sedition. "Few people really believe the federal government can be successfully defied," he wrote. "We even doubt that the Mississippi legislature, which yesterday voted with scarcely a dissenting voice to endorse Governor Barnett's position on interposition, is so blinded by political necessity as to be able to ignore the record which stands plainly in view. It will also take us to the edge of treason."[137]

As the controversy landed in the laps of the state college board, Carter III expressed his disgust of "Barnett's dramatic but essentially meaningless rejection" of Meredith's attempts to register at Ole Miss.[138] As troops gathered at Ole Miss in preparation for Meredith's enrollment on 1 October, Carter III warned his readers that Barnett was a leader who deserved no respect. "In the western hemisphere today there are two men whose actions and attitudes are an unending source of embarrassment to the United States," he wrote. "One is Fidel Castro. The other is Ross Barnett."[139] On the last day of the month, Carter implored his readers to publicly voice their concerns if they disagreed with the governor's handling of the Ole Miss situation. In "Silence Must Be Broken," he wrote, "People should speak out who don't support Barnett."[140]

Carter had an ally on the Mississippi Gulf Coast, where Ira Harkey had been at the editorial helm of the Pascagoula *Chronicle* since June 1949 and remained until he sold the paper in July 1963, "after white intimidation and violence were directed toward him."[141] The Pascagoula *Chronicle* did not become a daily newspaper until after *Brown v. Board of Education.*

In 1963, Harkey was awarded a Pulitzer Prize for his "hard-hitting" editorials prior to, and following, the Ole Miss riot on 30 September 1962.[142] He was no traditional Southern journalist, and his early years at the New Orleans *Times Picayune* greatly impressed him with the ways that he would never edit his own newspaper. Harkey did not endorse the white supremacist view, and he remembered with disdain a practice during the early 1950s at the New Orleans *Times Picayune* that dictated no black person was to appear, not even as a blurred face in a crowd, on the pages of the newspaper. "Photos of street scenes were scrupulously scanned by picture editors and every perceivably black face was either incised by scissors or erased by air brush," he wrote.[143]

Harkey went to Mississippi in 1948 and purchased the Pascagoula *Chronicle*, which he published twice weekly for many years. A few days prior to Justice Black's handing down his judgment in the Meredith case, Harkey published an editorial from the *Christian Science Monitor* titled, "Racial Evolution and Pure Humbug," which denounced a book that stated, "The Negro race is 200,000 years behind that of the white."[144] Harkey was no racist. He believed in the equality of all people, and he believed *Of Race and Reason*, by Carlton Putnam, was a fabrication with destructive intent.[145]

In response to Barnett's televised speech regarding how he would not "back down" from blocking Meredith's admission to Ole Miss, Harkey appealed to his readers. "Mississippians are mature enough to recognize the inevitable, to accept it and adapt to it with good enough grace. The political faction that rules them, however, is not," he wrote. "It is not the Kennedy administration that is making demands upon Mississippi. It is the United States of America, it is democracy itself, it is the whole of humanity. These surely will not back down, either."[146]

A week after Justice Black instructed the state college board to enroll Meredith at Ole Miss, Harkey published his second and final editorial for the month leading up to the 30 September arrival of Meredith as a student on the Ole Miss campus. In "Confusing Times, Dangerous Times," he chided Barnett for declaring that he would keep the doors of Ole Miss closed to black students:

> A pall of contradiction covers our state as if every one of us had schizophrenia.
>
> The newspapers and politicians who hailed Governor Barnett's address call upon us citizens not to resort to violence. Do they really mean it? is the question, for some papers and people who have long been advocates of a "fight to the finish," and now they must just see what it is they have raised up. How can we defy the law "to the finish" without resorting to violence?
>
> Then there is the call upon the United States of America not to send marshals into our state to enforce the law. How can we make such a demand without appearing devoid of all sense? Does the burglar announce to the police that he will not observe the anti-burgling statutes because they violate his way of life and then expect the police to issue him an exemption?
>
> Governor Barnett knows full well how laws are enforced when the lawless are defiant. He himself has sent troops into counties to search out a bottle of whiskey here, to shatter a crap table there. Federal marshals enforce the law except in rebellions which are tended to by troops. How do we think the United States will enforce the law now? By sending in the Peace Corps? Postmen? Soil conservationists? When orders are ignored, force is applied. Governor Barnett knows that.
>
> In a madhouse's din, Mississippi waits.
>
> God help Mississippi.[147]

Following his coverage of the desegregation of Ole Miss, Harkey was boycotted by his advertisers. His newspaper carriers were threatened by thugs. His business became, according to him, "a disaster."[148] Harkey sold the Pascagoula *Chronicle* in 1963, moved out of the state, and wrote a book about his experiences as a Mississippi newspaperman, *The Smell of Burning Crosses* (1967).

SUMMARY OF COVERAGE OF THE DESEGREGATION OF OLE MISS

As evidenced by the majority of the editors of the Mississippi daily press, the major issues of concern raised following the legal decree to desegregate Ole Miss were the same as those following *Brown v. Board of Education* in 1954: (1) black and white students should not be schooled in the same facilities, as this could lead to integrated socializing, which would be unacceptable by traditional Southern standards, (2) black and white students should not be schooled together because the black students would not be able to compete academically with the white students and (3) the public schools in the state should not be abolished to prevent this. According to editorials during September 1962, the notion that blacks and whites should be educated together based on the equality of the two races was a concept that remained unacceptable. Interestingly, the editors of the Mississippi daily press had an ally in Percy Greene, the editor of the black Jackson *Advocate*, who repudiated Meredith's goal of attending Ole Miss. On 29 September, Greene wrote that separate but equal facilities "are a far better answer than racial tension, confusion and hatred engendered by integration attempts," and he suggested that repeal of the U.S. Supreme Court decision might be the answer.[149] The Jackson *Advocate* was not, according to Hooker, "representative of the new black awakening, nor were the other four black newspapers in the state."[150]

The propensity toward reporting civil rights issues in Mississippi daily newspapers in the weeks prior to the desegregation of Ole Miss ranged from daily news coverage with no editorials, such as in the Grenada *Sentinel-Star*, the Gulfport *Daily Herald*, and the *Natchez Democrat*, to an editorial every three days and daily news coverage in the Jackson *Clarion-Ledger* and the Jackson *Daily News*. Most of the nineteen Mississippi daily newspapers published between two and nine editorials in September 1962 concerning the desegregation of Ole Miss, but the issue was unquestionably a top news story on the front pages of the Mississippi daily press during the month.

Contrary to what media critics have noted about the promotion of violent suppression of civil rights activity in a small sampling of Southern newspapers,[151] the Mississippi daily press in 1962 did not advocate violence to prevent the desegregation of Ole Miss. Not once was this found in any of the nineteen newspapers. On the contrary, an appeal for non-violence was the norm. However, the Mississippi daily press, as an aggregate, did reject desegregation of the state's universities, and the usual rationalization was the preservation of the traditional Southern way of life and states' rights.

In their news coverage of the civil rights issues pertaining to the desegregation of Ole Miss, the two most widely circulated Mississippi daily newspapers, the Jackson *Clarion-Ledger* and the Jackson *Daily News*, were not representative of the Mississippi daily press as they had been during the 1948 Dixiecrat protest. Although all the state's daily newspapers subscribed to at least one of the two major wire services available at the time, AP or UPI, and published the copy relatively unrevised, staff-written stories by the Jackson *Clarion-Ledger* and the Jackson *Daily News* were much more virulent than those of the other newspapers. Also, the editorials of Hills at the Jackson *Clarion-Ledger* deserved a reputation for propagating racial polarization and intensifying the opposition of Mississippi whites to desegregation.[152] Except for Harris of the West Point *Times-Leader* and Skewes of the *Meridian Star*, this was not true for any of the other editors of the Mississippi daily press in 1962.

The Mississippi daily press personalized and localized the civil rights struggle pertaining to the desegregation of Ole Miss, although there was little local activity reported. The editorial consensus in opposition to the federally mandated desegregation of Ole Miss was the "us against them" theme proposed during the 1948 Dixiecrat protest and the 1954 *Brown v. Board of Education* decision, particularly after federal law enforcement officials were sent to the state. This "attack from the outside" reaffirmed a commitment to the preservation of the traditional South and a local version of the states' rights controversy of 1948 and 1954—the right of each state, or rather the white power structure, to manage its university system without outside interference.

NOTES

1. James Loewen and Charles Sallis, eds., *Mississippi: Conflict and Change* (New York: Pantheon Books, 1974), 7.

2. "4,000 Armed Troops Occupy Ole Miss Campus after Forced Registration of Negro Student," AP, *Vicksburg Evening Post*, 1 October 1962, 1; "At Least Two Dead in Ole Miss Riot," AP, *Laurel Leader-Call*, 1 October 1962, 1; "Bayonets Protect Men," AP, *Greenwood Commonwealth*, 1 October 1962, 1; "Blame Riot on Trigger Happy Marshals," AP, *Natchez Democrat*, 1 October 1962, 1; "Meredith Enrolled as Student at UM," *Hattiesburg American*, 1 October 1962, 1; "Meredith Enrolled, Riots Wreck Ole Miss Campus, Two Dead, 75 Hurt," UPI, West Point *Times-Leader*, 1 October 1962, 1; "Meredith Enrolls, Two Die, Riots Continuing," UPI, Pascagoula *Chronicle*, 2 October 1962, 1; "Mississippi Invaded, Says Gov. Barnett," UPI, Columbus *Commercial Dispatch*, 1 October 1962, 1; "Riot Aftermath Leaves Two Dead," AP, *Starkville Daily News*, 2 October 1962, 1; "Violence Surges in Oxford after Meredith Enrollment," AP, McComb *Enterprise-Journal*, 1 October 1962, 1.

3. "Chancellor Asks Calm at Ole Miss," UPI, West Point *Times-Leader*, 17 September 1962, 1; "Chancellor Calls for Reason," Greenville *Delta Democrat-Times*, 17 September 1962, 1; "Most Critical Time, Says Chancellor," UPI, Grenada *Sentinel-Star*, 16 September 1962, 1.

4. "Black Orders Ole Miss Mix," AP, *Laurel Leader-Call*, 10 September 1962, 1; "Black Orders UM to Admit Meredith, Ross Not Surprised," AP, Jackson *Daily News*, 10 September 1962, 1; "Black Rules Ole Miss Must Admit Meredith, Says Little Chance of Appeal," UPI, West Point *Times-Leader*, 10 September 1962, 1; "Black Rules on Meredith Case," AP, *Natchez Democrat*, 11 September 1962, 1; "Feds Force Meredith in Ole Miss, States' Rights Thrown Away," UPI, Grenada *Sentinel-Star*, 10 September 1962, 1; "Governor Vows Negro Won't Enter Ole Miss, Hugo Black Orders Meredith Admitted," UPI, Jackson *Clarion-Ledger*, 10 September 1962, 1; "Judge Tells Ole Miss to Register Meredith," AP, *Greenwood Commonwealth*, 10 September 1962, 1; "Justice Acts to Let Negro Enter Ole Miss," UPI, *Clarksdale Press Register*, 10 September 1962, 1; "Justice Black Clears Way for Integration at Ole Miss," UPI, *Meridian Star*, 1 September 1962, 1; "Justice Black Clears Way for Meredith at Ole Miss, Barnett Says He'll Be Barred," UPI, Tupelo *Daily Journal*, 11 September 1962, 1; "Meredith Gets Nod," UPI, Pascagoula *Chronicle*, 10 September 1962, 1; "Must Admit Meredith Black Tells Ole Miss, NAACP Hints MSU Next Target," AP, *Starkville Daily News*, 11 September 1962, 1; "Negro Plans to Enter Ole Miss Next Week, Upheld by High Court, Barnett Says He'll Be Stopped," UPI, Corinth *Daily Corinthian*, 11 September 1962, 1; "Ole Miss Ordered to Admit Negro This Fall, Black Rules in Favor of Meredith," AP, *Hattiesburg American*, 10 September 1962, 1; "Ole Miss Ordered to Enroll Meredith," AP, Gulfport *Daily Herald*, 10 September 1962, 1; "Ole Miss Ordered to Enroll Negro," UPI, Greenville *Delta Democrat-Times*, 10 September 1962, 1; "Ole Miss Ordered to Take Negro," AP, McComb *Enterprise-Journal*, 10 September 1962, 1; "Order Stopping Negro's Entrance Set Aside," AP, Columbus *Commercial Dispatch*, 10 September 1962, 1; "U.S. High Court Orders Ole Miss to Admit Negro," AP, *Vicksburg Evening Post*, 10 September 1962, 1.

5. "Black Rules Ole Miss Must Admit Meredith, Says Little Chance of Appeal," UPI, West Point *Times-Leader*, 10 September 1962, 1; "Feds Force Meredith in Ole Miss, States' Rights Thrown Away," UPI, Grenada *Sentinel-Star*, 10 September 1962, 1; "Governor Vows Negro Won't Enter Ole Miss, Hugo Black Orders Meredith Admitted," UPI, Jackson *Clarion-Ledger*, 10 September 1962, 1; "Justice Acts to Let Negro Enter Ole Miss," UPI, *Clarksdale Press Register*, 10 September 1962, 1; "Justice Black Clears Way for Integration at Ole Miss," UPI, *Meridian Star*, 1 September 1962, 1; "Justice Black Clears Way for Meredith at Ole Miss, Barnett Says He'll Be Barred," UPI, Tupelo *Daily Journal*, 11 September 1962, 1; "Meredith Gets Nod," UPI, Pascagoula *Chronicle*, 10 September 1962, 1; "Negro Plans to Enter Ole Miss Next Week, Upheld by High Court, Barnett Says He'll Be Stopped," UPI, Corinth *Daily Corinthian*, 11 September 1962, 1; "Ole Miss Ordered to Enroll Negro," UPI, Greenville *Delta Democrat-Times*, 10 September 1962, 1.

6. "The Meredith File," Jackson *Clarion-Ledger*, 20 September 1997, 13A.

7. "Barnett Holds Key to Negro's Entry," UP, Greenville *Delta Democrat-Times*, 12 September 1962, 1; "Battle against Integration Is Expected," UP, *Meridian Star*, 12 September 1962, 1; "Negro Making Plans to Enter Ole Miss, Governor

Vows to Stop Entry, State Law Gives Barnett Authority to Close State Schools," UPI, Columbus *Commercial Dispatch*, 11 September 1962, 1; "Negro Plans to Enter Ole Miss Next Week, Upheld by High Court, Barnett Says He'll Be Stopped," UPI, Corinth *Daily Corinthian*, 11 September 1962, 1.

8. "Barnett to Review Case of Meredith," AP, Gulfport *Daily Herald*, 12 September 1962, 1; "Barnett Vows to Bar Negro from Ole Miss, Plans to Defy High Court," AP, Clarksdale *Press Register*, 11 September 1962, 1; "Barnett Won't Tell Plans for Meredith," AP, *Hattiesburg American*, 12 September 1962, 1; "Governor, Officials Discuss Meredith Case, Report College Board Will Block Admission," AP, Jackson *Clarion-Ledger*, 12 September 1962, 1; "State Plans Legal Steps on Mix Order," AP, *Laurel Leader-Call*, 12 September 1962, 1; "State Prepares Meredith Blocks, 'Surprise' Legal Acts Expected," AP, McComb *Enterprise-Journal*, 12 September 1962, 1; "State to Fight Meredith Ruling, Legal Plans under Wraps," AP, *Starkville Daily News*, 12 September 1962, 1; "Surprise Legal Moves Set to Prevent Ole Miss Mixing," AP, *Vicksburg Evening Post*, 12 September 1962, 1; "Surprise Moves Seen in Meredith Case," AP, *Greenwood Commonwealth*, 12 September 1962, 1.

9. "Barnett May Reveal Strategy Via Radio, TV," Tupelo *Daily Journal*, 13 September 1962, 1; "Barnett on TV Tonight, Expected to Discuss Ole Miss," *Meridian Star*, 13 September 1962, 1; "Barnett to Address State over TV, Radio, 7:30 Tonight," Columbus *Commercial Dispatch*, 13 September 1962, 1; "Barnett to Speak to State Thursday on Meredith Case," Pascagoula *Chronicle*, 12 September 1962, 1; "Barnett Schedules Address to Public Thursday Night," Jackson *Clarion-Ledger*, 13 September 1962, 1; "Barnett Speaks Tonight," McComb *Enterprise-Journal*, 13 September 1962, 1; "Barnett to Deliver Statewide Message," Jackson *Daily News*, 12 September 1962, 1; "Barnett to Make Statewide Talk on Meredith Case," *Greenwood Commonwealth*, 13 September 1962, 1; "Barnett to Review Case of Meredith, Statewide Talk Slated on Thursday," AP, Gulfport *Daily Herald*, 12 September 1962, 1; "Governor May Reveal Meredith Plan Tonight, Scheduled Speech over Radio, TV," *Hattiesburg American*, 13 September 1962, 1; "Governor to Speak on Ole Miss Mixing," *Natchez Democrat*, 13 September 1962, 1; "Ole Miss Integration Attempt, Barnett to Discuss James Meredith on Statewide Radio, TV Tonight," Corinth *Daily Corinthian*, 13 September 1962, 1; "Mississippi Awaits Barnett's Message," Clarksdale *Press Register*, 13 September 1962, 1; "Ross Speaks on Radio, TV," *Laurel Leader-Call*, 12 September 1962, 1; "Ross Will Talk on TV," *Starkville Daily News*, 13 September 1962, 1.

10. Hodding Carter, Jr., "The Bitter Harvest Will Be Reaped," Greenville *Delta Democrat-Times*, 26 September 1962, 4.

11. Tom Etheridge, "Courageous Speech," Jackson *Clarion-Ledger*, 15 September 1962, 1.

12. "Heart Attack Fatal to City Editor Wirth," Jackson *Clarion-Ledger*, 21 September 1962, 1.

13. Gene Wirth, "Place Assured in History for Fearless Ross Barnett," Jackson *Clarion-Ledger*, 15 September 1962, 1.

14. "Text of Barnett Speech," Gulfport *Daily Herald*, 14 September 1962, 1; "Text of Gov. Barnett's Speech on Meredith Case," AP, *Hattiesburg American*, 14 September 1962, 1.

15. "Barnett in Open Defiance of Integration Order, I'll Go to Jail before Mix-

ing Schools," UP, Corinth *Daily Corinthian*, 14 September 1962, 1; "Barnett Leads Mississippi in Constitutional Fight, Schools Not to Be Mixed Is Pledged," UPI, West Point *Times-Leader*, 14 September 1962, 1; "Barnett Prefers Jail to Obeying U.S. Court Order, Directs Officials to Resist Desegregation," UPI, Greenville *Delta Democrat-Times*, 14 September 1962, 1; "Fight or Quit, Barnett Tells State Officials, Says Ole Miss Will Not Be Integrated," UP, *Meridian Star*, 14 September 1962, 1; "High Court Challenged by Barnett, Governor Defies Order to Enroll Negro at Ole Miss," UPI, Clarksdale *Press Register*, 14 September 1962, 1; "Ole Miss Will Not Mix, Says Barnett, Governor Calls for Resignation of Officials Unwilling to Fight," UPI, *Greenwood Commonwealth*, 14 September 1962, 1; "Ross Tells Officials to Defy Court Order," UPI, Columbus *Commercial Dispatch*, 14 September 1962, 1; "We Will Never Integrate, to Jail First—Barnett," UP, Pascagoula *Chronicle*, 14 September 1962, 1.

16. "Interposition Move Is Expected, Old Procedure to Be Revived," AP, *Clarksdale Press Register*, 13 September 1962, 1.

17. "Interposition Doctrine Mulled," AP, *Greenwood Commonwealth*, 13 September 1962, 1.

18. "Interposition to Keep Segregation Never Fully Tested," UPI, Pascagoula *Chronicle*, 13 September 1962, 1; "Interposition Untried since 19th Century," UPI, Tupelo *Daily Journal*, 14 September 1962, 1.

19. Arthur Schlesinger, *A Thousand Days: John F. Kennedy and the White House* (Greenwich, Conn.: Fawcett Publications, 1967), 860.

20. "Barnett Orders Interposition," *Natchez Democrat*, 14 September 1962, 1; "Doctrine May Be State's Best Weapon, Bobby Will Be Mad," UP, Grenada *Sentinel-Star*, 13 September 1962, 1; "Gov. Barnett Interposes Self, Feds," Jackson *Clarion-Ledger*, 14 September 1962, 1; "Gov. Barnett to Invoke Unconstitutional Order," UPI, Grenada *Sentinel-Star*, 14 September 1962, 1; "Interposition, Can It Prevent Integration? Mississippi Last Chance?" UPI, Corinth *Daily Corinthian*, 13 September 1962, 1; "Interposition Doctrine Last Tested by Civil War, State May Test Again," UP, Greenville *Delta Democrat-Times*, 13 September 1962, 1; "Interposition Is Being Discussed Again," UPI, West Point *Times-Leader*, 13 September 1962, 1; "Interposition Looms as Possible Meredith Roadblock," UPI, Tupelo *Daily Journal*, 14 September 1962, 1; "Interposition Move Is Expected, Old Procedure to Be Revived," AP, Clarksdale *Press Register*, 13 September 1962, 1; "Interposition to Keep Segregation Never Fully Tested," UPI, Pascagoula *Chronicle*, 13 September 1962, 1; "Mississippi Mix? Ross Says Never! Doctrine of Interposition Invoked," Jackson *Daily News*, 14 September 1962, 1; "Ole Miss Application," AP, Gulfport *Daily Herald*, 13 September 1962, 1; "Ross Issues Proclamation Based on Interposition," *Laurel Leader-Call*, 14 September 1962, 1.

21. "Interposition Move Is Expected, Old Procedure to Be Revived," AP, Clarksdale *Press Register*, 13 September 1962, 1.

22. Ibid.

23. "Effigy Is Burned at Ole Miss," *Starkville Daily News*, 15 September 1962, 1; "Hang Effigy of Meredith," Gulfport *Daily Herald*, 14 September 1962, 1; "Meredith Lynched in Effigy," AP, *Clarksdale Press Register*, 14 September 1962, 1; "Meredith Hanged in Effigy," *Greenwood Commonwealth*, 13 September 1962, 1; "Meredith Is Hung in Effigy at University of Mississippi," AP, *Hattiesburg Amer-*

ican, 14 September 1962, 1; "Negro Hung in Effigy," AP, McComb *Enterprise-Journal*, 14 September 1962, 1.

24. "Cross Burned at Ole Miss," UP, Greenville *Delta Democrat-Times*, 12 September 1962, 1; "Cross Burned at Ole Miss," UPI, West Point *Times-Leader*, 12 September 1962, 1; "Cross Burned on University Campus, Around 100 Gather to See Blaze," UPI, Columbus *Commercial Dispatch*, 12 October 1962, 1; "Fiery Cross Burned at Ole Miss," Jackson *Clarion-Ledger*, 13 September 1962, 1; "No Action by Governor, Cross Burned at University," UPI, Grenada *Sentinel-Star*, 12 September 1962, 1; "Ole Miss Cross Fired," UP, Pascagoula *Chronicle*, 12 September 1962, 1.

25. "Meredith Cross Blazes at Oxford," photograph, Jackson *Daily News*, 12 September 1962, 1.

26. Russell Barrett, *Integration at Ole Miss* (Chicago: Quadrangle Books, 1965), 92–93.

27. "Chancery Judge Issues Order Banning Meredith," *Meridian Star*, 19 September 1962, 1; "Injunction Granted to Block Meredith, Judge Acts on Request of Parents," Columbus *Commercial Dispatch*, 19 September 1962, 1; "Injunction Would Bar Meredith," *Hattiesburg American*, 19 September 1962, 1; "Issue New Injunction on Negro," *Natchez Democrat*, 19 September 1962, 1; "Judge Grants Injunction in Ole Miss Case," UP, Clarksdale *Press Register*, 19 September 1962, 1; "Judge Issues Injunction to Bar Meredith from Ole Miss," West Point *Times-Leader*, 19 September 1962, 1; "Judge Porter Restrains Meredith's Mix Attempt," *Laurel Leader-Call*, 19 September 1962, 1; "New Injunction Bars Meredith's Admission," McComb *Enterprise-Journal*, 19 September 1962, 1; W.C. Shoemaker, "State Judge Rules Meredith Out," Jackson *Daily News*, 19 September 1962, 1; "Showdown Looms on Ole Miss Mix, Injunction Okayed to Halt Action," AP, *Vicksburg Evening Post*, 19 September 1962, 1; "Sign Injunction to Bar Meredith Entry," Gulfport *Daily Herald*, 19 September 1962, 1; "State Judge Bucks U.S.," Greenville *Delta Democrat-Times*, 19 September 1962, 1; "State Judge Orders Ban," *Greenwood Commonwealth*, 19 September 1962, 1; "State Judge Tries to Bar Meredith from Ole Miss," Pascagoula *Chronicle*, 19 September 1962, 1; "To Prevent Meredith's Admission, Judge Issues Injunction," *Starkville Daily News*, 19 September 1962, 1.

28. "Justice of Peace Orders Arrest of Meredith," *Meridian Star*, 20 September 1962, 1; "Meredith Could Face Jail and $500 Fine," UP, Corinth *Daily Corinthian*, 20 September 1962, 1; "Meredith Sentenced to Jail Term," UPI, Columbus *Commercial Dispatch*, 20 September 1962, 1; "State Court Convicts Meredith in Abstentia," UPI, Grenada *Sentinel-Star*, 20 September 1962, 1; "State Goes All Out to Stop Enrollment," *Laurel Leader-Call*, 20 September 1962, 1.

29. "Legislature Sets Up Last Minute Roadblock," Tupelo *Daily Journal*, 20 September 1962, 1; "New Legal Roadblock," West Point *Times-Leader*, 20 September 1962, 1; "To Prevent Meredith's Admission, Legislature Passes Bill," *Starkville Daily News*, 20 September 1962, 1.

30. "Don't Arrest Meredith, Court Tells Mississippi," AP, *Greenwood Commonwealth*, 20 September 1962, 1; "JP Court Calls for Meredith Arrest," Gulfport *Daily Herald*, 20 September 1962, 1; "Judges Say State Can't Arrest Meredith," AP, *Hattiesburg American*, 20 September 1962, 1; "State Given Order, Don't Nab Meredith," Pascagoula *Chronicle*, 20 September 1962, 1; "Two Federal Judges

Order Ole Miss and State Leaders to Enroll Negro," AP, *Vicksburg Evening Post*, 20 September 1962, 1; "U.S. Court Order Would Halt Arrest of Meredith," McComb *Enterprise-Journal*, 20 September 1962, 1; "U.S. Seeks to Prohibit Arrest of Meredith," AP, Jackson *Daily News*, 20 September 1962, 1.

31. "Barnett Gets Solid Support in Challenge," AP, Clarksdale *Press Register*, 15 September 1962, 1; "Governor's Position Praised by Officials," AP, *Hattiesburg American*, 14 September 1962, 1; "Legislators Praise Ross' Stand," *Laurel Leader-Call*, 19 September 1962, 1; "Officials Back Stand of Barnett," McComb *Enterprise-Journal*, 14 September 1962, 1; William Peart, "Barnett Receives All-Out Support," Jackson *Daily News*, 14 September 1961, 1; "Political, State Leaders behind Barnett," UP, Columbus *Commercial Dispatch*, 16 September 1962, 1; "Reaction to Barnett Talk," Gulfport *Daily Herald*, 14 September 1962, 1; "Ross Backed by State Legislature," West Point *Times-Leader*, 18 September 1962, 1; "Solons Support Barnett," UP, Greenville *Delta Democrat-Times*, 18 September 1962, 1; "Solons Back Barnett on Stand against Ole Miss Integration," UPI, Tupelo *Daily Journal*, 19 September 1962, 1; "United Support Pledged," AP, *Vicksburg Evening Post*, 17 September 1962, 1.

32. "Senators Back Ross, Eastland, Stennis," Jackson *Clarion-Ledger*, 27 September 1962, 1; "Stennis Appeals to Federal Authorities to Keep Agitators Out," AP, *Hattiesburg American*, 17 September 1962, 1; "Stennis Asks U.S. to Bar Agitators," AP, *Greenwood Commonwealth*, 17 September 1962, 1; "Stennis Urges Curb of Outside Agitators," AP, Jackson *Clarion-Ledger*, 18 September 1962, 1; "Stennis Urges Outsiders Not to Interfere," AP, *Natchez Democrat*, 18 September 1962, 1; "Stennis Urges Outsiders to Stay Out," *Meridian Star*, 17 September 1962, 1.

33. Charles Hills, "J.P. Coleman Supports Barnett," Jackson *Clarion-Ledger*, 19 September 1962, 1.

34. Charles Hills, "State Lawmakers Move to Prevent Integration," Jackson *Clarion-Ledger*, 20 September 1962, 1; "Legislature Backs Ross' Opposition," AP, *Starkville Daily News*, 20 September 1962, 1.

35. "Smith Says Barnett Plan a Blind Alley," AP, *Greenwood Commonwealth*, 13 September 1962, 1.

36. Loewen and Sallis, *Mississippi*, 262.

37. "All but Smith Support Ross," AP, Jackson *Clarion-Ledger*, 15 September 1962, 1.

38. "Barnett, Board, Discuss Meredith Case Today," AP, *Hattiesburg American*, 17 September 1962, 1; "Barnett Prods Board to Reject Meredith," AP, Clarksdale *Press Register*, 17 September 1962, 1; "Barnett to Appear before State College Board Today," Columbus *Commercial Dispatch*, 17 September 1962, 1; "Barnett to Tell Strategy of College Board Action," AP, *Vicksburg Evening Post*, 17 September 962, 1; "Board, Governor, in Action on Meredith Case," AP, *Greenwood Commonwealth*, 20 September 1962, 1; "Board, Governor, to Scan Meredith Case," AP, Gulfport *Daily Herald*, 17 September 1962, 1. "College Board Hears Barnett's Views on Ole Miss, Tubb Says No Vote Yet," AP, Jackson *Clarion-Ledger*, 17 September 1962, 1; "College Board Split on Integration Order," UPI, Pascagoula *Chronicle*, 17 September 1962, 1; "Decision on Meredith Postponed by Trustee," *Starkville Daily News*, 16 September 1962, 1; "Gov. Barnett to Meet with State College Board," UPI, Corinth *Daily Corinthian*, 17 September 1962, 1; "No An-

nouncement from College Board," Jackson *Clarion-Ledger*, 15 September 1962, 1; "No Word from Board Meeting," UP, West Point *Times-Leader*, 17 September 1962, 1; "Ole Miss Regents Reportedly Balking over Barnett's Ultimatum," UPI, Greenville *Delta Democrat-Times*, 16 September 1962, 1; "Ross Barnett to Voice Appeal to State College Board Today," UP, *Meridian Star*, 17 September 1962, 1; "State College Board Ponders Meredith," Pascagoula *Chronicle*, 18 September 1962, 1; "School Board's Day of Decision Near," UPI, Grenada *Sentinel-Star*, 18 September 1962, 1; "Strategy Remains Secret," AP, *Vicksburg Evening Post*, 20 September 1962, 1.

39. "Tubb Doubts Right to Close Ole Miss," AP, *Meridian Star*, 17 September 1962, 1.

40. "College Board Showdown on Meredith," Tupelo *Daily Journal*, 17 September 1962, 1.

41. "Segregation Test Faces University," UPI, Clarksdale *Press Register*, 18 September 1962, 1; "Board to Jail, Not Barnett, Marshals Will Escort Negro," UP, Columbus *Commercial Dispatch*, 18 September 1962, 1.

42. "Board Member Says He'd Go to Jail to Keep Integrity," AP, Jackson *Daily News*, 18 September 1962, 1; "College Board Quiet on Plans," McComb *Enterprise-Journal*, 18 September 1962, 1.

43. "Barnett's Life Is Threatened," UPI, Corinth *Daily Corinthian*, 21 September 1962, 1; "Barnett Threatened in Letter," McComb *Enterprise-Journal*, 21 September 1962, 1; "Governor Is Guarded after Death Threat," Tupelo *Daily Journal*, 21 September 1962, 1; "Governor's Life Threatened in Letter," West Point *Times-Leader*, 21 September 1962, 1; "Governor's Life Threatened in Note," AP, *Hattiesburg American*, 21 September 1962, 1; Charles Hills, "Death! Gov. Barnett Threatened," Jackson *Clarion-Ledger*, 21 September 1962, 1.

44. "College Board Is Caught in Middle," AP, *Hattiesburg American*, 20 September 1962, 1; "College Board Caught in Middle of Fight to Bar Meredith," AP, Gulfport *Daily Herald*, 21 September 1962, 1; "Contempt Hearing Set for Ole Miss Officials," AP, *Natchez Democrat*, 23 September 1962, 1; "Court Moves against College Trustees," McComb *Enterprise-Journal*, 21 September 1962, 1; "Crucial Court Battle Looms for Ole Miss," UPI, Columbus Commercial Dispatch, 23 September 1962, 1; "Desegregation Case Shifts to New Site," AP, Clarksdale *Press Register*, 22 September 1962, 1; "IHL Faces Contempt," AP, *Greenwood Commonwealth*, 21 September 1962, 1; "Ole Miss Officials and College Board Cited, No Move Is Pointed at Governor," UP, West Point *Times-Leader*, 21 September 1962, 1; "Ole Miss Officials Face Contempt Citations," UPI, Corinth *Daily Corinthian*, 21 September 1962, 1; "State Officials Face U.S. Contempt Trials," AP, Pascagoula *Chronicle*, 21 September 1962, 1; "U.S. Cites 16 State Officials in Meredith, Ole Miss Squabble," UP, Greenville *Delta Democrat-Times*, 21 September 1962, 1; "Ole Miss Officials Face U.S. Action," UPI, *Meridian Star*, 21 September 1962, 1; W.C. Shoemaker, "Board Faces Contempt Charges," Jackson *Daily News*, 21 September 1962, 1.

45. "Ole Miss Board Faces U.S. Court, Tubb Says Vote Not Unanimous," *Laurel Leader-Call*, 21 September 1962, 1.

46. "Mark 100th Anniversary of Emancipation Proclamation," Gulfport *Daily Herald*, 22 September 1962, 12.

47. "Judge Mize Clears Ole Miss Officials, Board Due in Court," AP, Gulfport *Daily Herald*, 22 September 1962, 1.

48. "Appeals Court Orders Meredith Registered for Ole Miss Today," AP, Tupelo *Daily Journal*, 25 September 1962, 1; "Blanket Order Protects Meredith," UPI, Corinth *Daily Corinthian*, 25 September 1962, 1; "Board Agrees to Register Meredith Today at Jackson," *Starkville Daily News*, 25 September 1962, 1; "Board Did Its Best, Acted in Unity," UPI, Greenville *Delta Democrat-Times*, 25 September 1962, 1; "Board Orders Ole Miss to Admit James Meredith," AP, Gulfport *Daily Herald*, 25 September 1962, 1; "Board Requests Understanding," UPI, West Point *Times-Leader*, 25 September 1962, 1; "Board's Ouster Hinted," AP, *Vicksburg Evening Post*, 25 September 1962, 1; "College Board Bows to Court Pressure, Agrees to Register Negro Here Today," AP, Jackson *Clarion-Ledger*, 25 September 1962, 1; "Counter Moves Pit State vs. U.S., Board Bows to Decision," AP, *Laurel Leader-Call*, 25 September 1962, 1; "Court of Appeals Orders Mississippi Not to Interfere," UPI, Grenada Sentinel-Star, 25 September 1962, 1; "State College Board Orders Him Accepted," AP, *Hattiesburg American*, 25 September 1962, 1; "State Ordered to Take Meredith," UPI, Pascagoula *Chronicle*, 25 September 1962, 1; "University Board Backs Down," *Natchez Democrat*, 25 September 1962, 1.

49. "College Board Yields to Judge," AP, McComb *Enterprise-Journal*, 25 September 1962, 1.

50. "Accreditation Group Threatens State's Colleges," AP, *Vicksburg Evening Post*, 29 September 1962, 1; "Accreditation Hit for All Colleges," Jackson *Clarion-Ledger*, 29 September 1962, 1; "Accreditation in Danger," *Laurel Leader-Call*, 24 September 1962, 1; "Accreditation Loss Faces University," AP, *Greenwood Commonwealth*, 29 September 1962, 1; "Accreditation of University to Be Studied, Ole Miss Standing Could Be Lost," UPI, Clarksdale *Press Register*, 27 September 1962, 1; "All Mississippi State Colleges Risk Loss of Accreditation," UP, Tupelo *Daily Journal*, 29–30 September 1962, 1; "Former President of Board Fears Accreditation Loss," Jackson *Daily News*, 23 September 1962, 1; "Review Slated for Accreditation of University," UPI, Pascagoula *Chronicle*, 27 September 1962, 2; "Schools Face Loss of Accreditation," AP, *Hattiesburg American*, 29 September 1962, 1; "State Schools Rating Studied, Ole Miss May Lose Accreditation," Columbus *Commercial Dispatch*, 30 September 1962, 1.

51. "Alumni Urge Ole Miss to Stay Open," Grenada *Sentinel-Star*, 28 September 1962, 1; "County Alumni Group Says Ole Miss Must Be Kept Open," Greenville *Delta Democrat-Times*, 26 September 1962, 1; "Reaction Is Anger and Dismay," UPI, Pascagoula *Chronicle*, 26 September 1962, 1.

52. "$10,000 a Day Fine for Gov. Barnett Mentioned in Contempt," AP, *Natchez Democrat*, 29 September 1962, 1; "Court Holds in Contempt," UP, Tupelo *Daily Journal*, 29–30 September 1962, 1; "Court Ponders Case for Citing Johnson," UPI, Clarksdale *Press Register*, 29 September 1962, 1; "Court Prepares for Barnett's Arrest," AP, *Starkville Daily News*, 29 September 1962, 1; "Gov. Barnett Convicted in U.S. Court of Contempt," AP, Jackson *Clarion-Ledger*, 29 September 1962, 1; "Gov. Barnett, Johnson, Convicted of Contempt," Greenville *Delta Democrat-Times*, 30 September 1962, 1; "RFK Continues Troop Buildup for Possible Use at Ole Miss," AP, *Vicksburg Evening Post*, 29 September 1962, 1; "Ross Found Guilty, Faces Huge Fine," AP, *Laurel Leader-Call*, 29 September 1962, 1.

53. Ed Noel, "Beloved University in Hurricane's Eye," Jackson *Clarion-Ledger*, 20 September 1962, 1.

54. "Federal Government Acts in Desegregation Case, Contempt Citations Seen after Meredith Turned Away," UPI, *Clarksdale Press Register*, 21 September 1962, 1.

55. William Miles, "Barnett Bars Meredith from Ole Miss," Tupelo *Daily Journal*, 21 September 1962, 1.

56. Bill Simpson, "Students Back Barnett as Meredith Turned Down, Governor Cheered by Excited Crowd," Corinth *Daily Corinthian*, 21 September 1962, 1.

57. "Barnett Bars Meredith from Ole Miss, Takes Over for Officials at University," Tupelo *Daily Journal*, 21 September 1962, 1; "Barnett Tells Meredith 'No' at Ole Miss Campus, Admissions Denied at College," AP, *Starkville Daily News*, 21 September 1962, 1; "Feds Seek to Force Negro's Entrance," UPI, Columbus *Commercial Dispatch*, 21 September 1962, 1; "Governor Moves on Two Fronts at Ole Miss," UP, Grenada *Sentinel-Star*, 21 September 1962, 1; Ed Noel, "Barnett Rejects Meredith, Keeps His Word to State's Citizens," Jackson *Clarion-Ledger*, 21 September 1962, 1; "Refuses to Register Meredith, Gov. Barnett Defies Federal Edict," AP, *Natchez Democrat*, 21 September 1962, 1.

58. "Meredith Answers Questions Calmly," UPI, Grenada *Sentinel-Star*, 19 September 1962, 1; "Meredith Doesn't Believe Marshals Will Be Needed," UP, Columbus *Commercial Dispatch*, 19 September 1962, 1; "Meredith Doubts Need for Federal Marshal Escort," UPI, *Meridian Star*, 19 September 1962, 1; "Meredith Not Worried on Need for Protection," UPI, Pascagoula *Chronicle*, 19 September 1962, 1; "Meredith Remains Calm as Time to Move Nears," UPI, Clarksdale *Press Register*, 19 September 1962, 1; "My Goal Is to Study at the University of Mississippi," Clarksdale *Press Register*, 19 September 1962, 1; "Negro States That Guards Unnecessary," UPI, Corinth *Daily Corinthian*, 19 September 1962, 1; "Violence Ruled Out by Negro," UPI, Greenville *Delta Democrat-Times*, 19 September 1962, 1.

59. William Miles, "Barnett Is Late, Johnson Bars Meredith from Campus," Tupelo *Daily Journal*, 26 September 1962, 1; "Johnson Bars Meredith, Troops May Halt Gravest Crisis since Civil War," UPI, Pascagoula *Chronicle*, 26 September 1962, 1; "Johnson Blocks Negro from Ole Miss Campus, Third Try to Enroll Repulsed," UPI, Greenville *Delta Democrat-Times*, 26 September 1962, 1; Johnson, Highway Patrol Bar Negro," AP, *Vicksburg Evening Post*, 26 September 1962, 1; "Johnson, Patrolmen, Block Meredith's Third Attempt," *Starkville Daily News*, 26 September 1962, 1; "Lt. Gov. Acts for Barnett, Johnson Holds Meredith at University Gates," UPI, Clarksdale *Press Register*, 26 September 1962, 1; "Meredith Barred in Third Attempt," AP, Jackson *Clarion-Ledger*, 26 September 1962, 1; "Meredith Blocked by Paul Johnson," UPI, *Meridian Star*, 26 September 1962, 1; "Meredith Fails at Third Attempt," UPI, Grenada *Sentinel-Star*, 26 September 1962, 1; "Meredith Is Denied Entry to Campus, Johnson Bars Third Attempt," AP, *Laurel Leader-Call*, 26 September 1962, 1; "Meredith's Path Barred Third Time, Johnson, Patrolmen Halt Entry," AP, McComb *Enterprise-Journal*, 26 September 1962, 1; "Meredith Is Turned Down for Third Time," AP, Gulfport *Daily Herald*, 26 September 1962, 1; "Meredith Turned Down for Third Time! Paul Johnson Pinch Hits for Barnett at University," UPI, Corinth *Daily Corinthian*, 26 September 1962, 1; "Meredith Turned Away Third Time," *Natchez Democrat*, 26 September

1962, 1; "Negro's Entrance Blocked for Third Time," UPI, Columbus *Commercial Dispatch*, 26 September 1962, 1; "Negro Turned Back at UM Gates," *Hattiesburg American*, 26 September 1962, 1; "Patrolmen Block Negro, Scuffle with Marshals," AP, *Greenwood Commonwealth*, 26 September 1962, 1; W.C. Shoemaker, "Paul Johnson Stops Negro at Gateway to Ole Miss, Marshals Attempt to Elbow Way In," Jackson *Daily News*, 26 September 1962, 1.

60. "Army of Law Officers Awaits New Attempt by Meredith," *Hattiesburg American*, 26 September 1962, 1; "Barnett Rushes to Ole Miss, Lawmen Descend," UPI, Greenville *Delta Democrat-Times*, 26 September 1962, 1; "Federal Marshals Flock to Ole Miss," UPI, *Clarksdale Press Register*, 27 September 1962, 1; "Federal, State Forces Pour into Oxford," UP, Corinth *Daily Corinthian*, 27 September 1962, 1; "Officers Given Gas Masks, Helmets," UP, *Meridian Star*, 27 September 1962, 1; "Ross at Ole Miss Meeting with Officials, Campus Ringed with Officers," UPI, Columbus *Commercial Dispatch*, 27 September 1962, 1; "Sheriffs, Police, Gather at Ole Miss to Keep Meredith Out," Gulfport *Daily Herald*, 27 September 1962, 1; "Sheriffs, Police Up Campus Guard, Helmets and Masks Issued," AP, *Laurel Leader-Call*, 26 September 1962, 1; "State, Federal Officers Mass near Ole Miss for Showdown," AP, *Vicksburg Evening Post*, 26 September 1962, 1; "State's Lawmen, 500 Strong, Gather at Oxford," Jackson *Daily News*, 27 September 1962, 1, "State Officers Guard Campus," AP, McComb *Enterprise-Journal*, 27 September 1962, 1.

61. "Big Risk Seen at Ole Miss," UPI, Clarksdale *Press Register*, 27 September 1962, 1; "Fight Likely at Ole Miss," UPI, Corinth *Daily Corinthian*, 26 September 1962, 1; "Gun Battle Possible at Ole Miss," UPI, Greenville *Delta Democrat-Times*, 26 September 1962, 1.

62. "10,000 Men Pledged to Gen. Walker's Plea," UPI, *Meridian Star*, 28 September 1962, 1; "Bring Your Flags, Boys," UPI, West Point *Times-Leader*, 28 September 1962, 1; "General Walker Calls for Army of 10,000," UPI, Clarksdale *Press Register*, 28 September 1962, 1; "Massive Resistance Urged by Walker," AP, *Vicksburg Evening Post*, 27 September 1962, 1; "Time to Move, Says Walker," UPI, Grenada *Sentinel-Star*, 28 September 1962, 1; "Walker Arrives at State Capital to Offer Support," AP, Columbus *Commercial Dispatch*, 30 September 1962, 1; "Walker Calls for Assistance," AP, *Laurel Leader-Call*, 27 September 1962, 1.

63. "4,000 Armed Troops Occupy Ole Miss Campus after Forced Registration of Negro Student," AP, *Vicksburg Evening Post*, 1 October 1962, 1; "At Least Two Dead in Ole Miss Riots," *Laurel Leader-Call*, 1 October 1962, 1; "Bayonets Protect Men," AP, *Greenwood Commonwealth*, 1 October 1962, 1; "Blame Riot on Trigger Happy Marshals," *Natchez Democrat*, 1 October 1962, 1; "Federalized State Troops Break Up Oxford Rioters," *Hattiesburg American*, 1 October 1962, 1; "Meredith Now Attending Ole Miss Classes, Debris Cleared in Wake of Bloody Violence," UPI, Clarksdale *Press Register*, 1 October 1962, 1; "Meredith Enrolls, Riots Wreck Ole Miss Campus," UPI, West Point *Times-Leader*, 1 October 1962, 1; "Meredith Enrolls, Two Die," UP, Pascagoula *Chronicle*, 1 October 1962, 1; "Negro Enrolls at Ole Miss, Abernethy Says Federal Marshal Fired First Shots," UPI, Columbus *Commercial Dispatch*, 1 October 1962, 1; "Riot Aftermath Leaves Two Dead," *Starkville Daily News*, 2 October 1962, 1; "Violence Surges in Oxford after Meredith Enrollment," McComb *Enterprise-Journal*, 1 October 1962, 1.

64. "Meredith Now Attending Ole Miss Classes, Debris Cleared in Wake of Bloody Violence," *Clarksdale Press Register*, UPI, 1 October 1962, 1.

65. Ibid.

66. "Students Urged to Halt Rioting," UPI, *Clarksdale Press Register*, 1 October 1962, 1.

67. "Flag Flying over State Capital at Half Mast," UPI, *Clarksdale Press Register*, 1 October 1962, 1.

68. Robert Hooker, "Race and the News Media in Mississippi, 1962–1964" (Master's thesis, Vanderbilt University, 1971), 127–128; Earl Lively, Jr., *The Invasion of Mississippi* (Belmont, Mass.: American Opinion, 1963), introduction; Schlesinger, *A Thousand Days: John F. Kennedy in the White House*, 858–866.

69. Erle Johnston, *Mississippi's Defiant Years, 1953–1973: An Interpretive Documentary with Personal Experiences* (Forest, Miss.: Lake Harbor Publishers, 1990), 158.

70. "The Meredith File," Jackson *Clarion-Ledger*, 20 September 1997, 13A.

71. Birney Imes, Jr., "The Decisive Round?" Columbus *Commercial-Dispatch*, 14 September 1962, 1.

72. Birney Imes, Jr., "Gutless Mississippians?" Columbus *Commercial-Dispatch*, 14 September 1962, 1.

73. Birney Imes, Jr., "With the Governor," Columbus *Commercial-Dispatch*, 14 September 1962, 1.

74. Birney Imes, Jr., "Thanks," Columbus *Commercial-Dispatch*, 27 September 1962, 6.

75. J.O. Emmerich, "Governor Barnett Speaks Tonight," McComb *Enterprise-Journal*, 13 September 1962, 1.

76. J.O. Emmerich, "Highlights in the Headlines," McComb *Enterprise-Journal*, 14 September 1962, 1.

77. J.O. Emmerich, "Newspapers Fear Ole Miss Closing," McComb *Enterprise-Journal*, 24 September 1962, 4.

78. J.O. Emmerich, "Let's Not Sacrifice Ole Miss," McComb *Enterprise-Journal*, 25 September 1962, 4.

79. J.O. Emmerich, "Highlights in the Headlines," McComb *Enterprise-Journal*, 26 September 1962, 1.

80. Ibid., 28 September 1962, 1.

81. "The *Meridian Star*," in *Mississippi Press Association 125th Anniversary Report*, 58.

82. Hooker, "Race and the News Media in Mississippi," 40.

83. Ibid., 25.

84. Loewen and Sallis, *Mississippi*, 255.

85. James B. Skewes, "Federal Responsibility," *Meridian Star*, 13 September 1962, 4.

86. James B. Skewes, "Ross Barnett's Finest Hour," *Meridian Star*, 16 September 1962, 4.

87. James B. Skewes, "Risk Jail or Resign," *Meridian Star*, 18 September 1962, 4.

88. James B. Skewes, "For Freedom," *Meridian Star*, 30 September 1962, 4.

89. "J.W. Jones of Jeanse School, New Albany, Keep Segregated Schools," Jackson *Clarion-Ledger*, 25 August 1954, 8; "Negro Education Leader Urges Equal

Schools," Tupelo *Daily Journal*, 30 August 1954, 1; "Negro Leader Appeals to Race," *Greenwood Commonwealth*, 23 August 1954, 1; "Negro Supervisor Appeals to Teachers," Grenada *Sentinel-Star*, 27 August 1954, 1.

90. J.W. Jones, "Negro Says Mixing Ole Miss Won't Help Us," AP, *Greenwood Commonwealth*, 19 September 1962, 1.

91. Thatcher Walt, "The Times Have Made Him Great," *Greenwood Commonwealth*, 21 September 1962, 6.

92. Ibid.

93. Thatcher Walt, "A Look at JFK's Racial Thinking," *Greenwood Commonwealth*, 24 September 1962, 6.

94. Thatcher Walt, "One Mississippian's Thinking," *Greenwood Commonwealth*, 25 September 1962, 1.

95. Thatcher Walt, "Don't Close Ole Miss," *Greenwood Commonwealth*, 26 September 1962, 4.

96. Leonard Lowrey, "Crucial Week," *Hattiesburg American*, 17 September 1962, 8.

97. David Lawrence, "JFK Pushes Some Civil Rights for Votes," *Hattiesburg American*, 20 September 1962, 8.

98. Leonard Lowrey, "The Long View," *Hattiesburg American*, 27 September 1962, 1.

99. "Governor Barnett Interposes Self, Feds," Jackson *Clarion-Ledger*, 14 September 1962, 1.

100. "United We Stand," Jackson *Clarion-Ledger*, 17 September 1962, 1.

101. Charles Hills, "Affairs of State," Jackson *Clarion-Ledger*, 17 September 1962, 5.

102. Tom Etheridge, "Mississippi Notebook," Jackson *Clarion-Ledger*, 19 September 1962, 8.

103. Ibid., 28 September 1962, 6.

104. James "Jimmy" Ward, "Crossroads," Jackson *Daily News*, 11 September 1962, 1.

105. Ibid., 13 September 1962, 1.

106. James "Jimmy" Ward, "We Support Governor Barnett," Jackson *Daily News*, 14 September 1962, 6.

107. James "Jimmy" Ward, "Let the Crackpots Scream," Jackson *Daily News*, 15 September 1962, 6.

108. James "Jimmy" Ward, "Mississippi Stands Unified," Jackson *Daily News*, 19 September 1962, 10.

109. James "Jimmy" Ward, "Why Mississippians Unite," Jackson *Daily News*, 20 September 1962, 10.

110. James "Jimmy" Ward, "Crossroads," Jackson *Daily News*, 21 September 1962, 1.

111. "*Laurel Leader-Call* Focuses on Local," in *Mississippi Press Association 125th Anniversary Report*, 50.

112. Jay West, "Barnett's Action Goads State's Sad Situation," *Laurel Leader-Call*, 18 September 1962, 4.

113. "Violence Is No Answer," from the Memphis *Commercial Appeal*, in the *Laurel Leader-Call*, 29 September 1962, 4.

114. W.H. Harris, "Stand Firm," West Point *Times-Leader*, 11 September 1962, 4; W.H. Harris, "Stand Firm," *Starkville Daily News*, 12 September 1962, 4.

115. W.H. Harris, "History Is Being Made Now in Mississippi," West Point *Times-Leader*, 15 September 1962, 4; W.H. Harris, "History Is Being Made Now in Mississippi," *Starkville Daily News*, 15 September 1962, 4.

116. W.H. Harris, "Important Week," West Point *Times-Leader*, 19 September 1962, 4; W.H. Harris, "Important Week," *Starkville Daily News*, 19 September 1962, 4.

117. W.H. Harris, "Pencil Shavings," *Starkville Daily News*, 19 September 1962, 4.

118. Ibid., 29 September 1962, 1, 4.

119. W.H. Harris, "Take Note, Paul," West Point *Times-Leader*, 26 September 1962, 4; W.H. Harris, "Take Note, Paul," *Starkville Daily News*, 27 September 1962, 4.

120. W.H. Harris, "Cheer Up!" West Point *Times-Leader*, 28 September 1962, 4; W.H. Harris, "Cheer Up!" *Starkville Daily News*, 29 September 1962, 4.

121. Harry Rutherford, "No One Has Right to Destroy Our Colleges," Tupelo *Daily Journal*, 18 September 1962, 4.

122. Harry Rutherford, "Point Is Made, Now Let's Stop and Think," Tupelo *Daily Journal*, 27 September 1962, 4.

123. Harry Rutherford, "For the South, the Future Has Arrived," Tupelo *Daily Journal*, 28 September 1962, 4.

124. Joseph Ellis, Jr., "The Final Act," *Clarksdale Press Register*, 26 September 1962, 6.

125. Ibid.

126. Joseph Ellis, Jr., "Appeal to Reason," *Clarksdale Press Register*, 1 October 1962, 6.

127. Bill Simpson, "Talk of Town," Corinth *Daily Corinthian*, 20 September 1962, 1.

128. Ibid., 21 September 1962, 1.

129. Ibid., 24 September 1962, 1.

130. Ibid., 28 September 1962, 1.

131. L.P. Cashman, Jr., "Service De-Luxe," *Vicksburg Evening Post*, 11 September 1962, 4.

132. L.P. Cashman, Jr., "The Governor's Address," *Vicksburg Evening Post*, 14 September 1962, 4.

133. L.P. Cashman, Jr., "Expediency and Principle," *Vicksburg Evening Post*, 16 September 1962, 4.

134. James Marlow, "Barnett Is a Johnny-Come-Lately for States' Righters," *Vicksburg Evening Post*, 28 September 1962, 4.

135. Hodding Carter III, interview via e-mail with Susan Weill, 1999.

136. Hodding Carter III, "The Moment of Decision Is Here," Greenville *Delta Democrat-Times*, 12 September 1962, 4.

137. Hodding Carter III, "Mississippi Ignores History," Greenville *Delta Democrat-Times*, 17 September 1962, 4.

138. Hodding Carter III, "State Colleges Approach a Dead End," Greenville *Delta Democrat-Times*, 24 September 1962, 4.

139. Hodding Carter III, "The Bitter Harvest Will Be Reaped," Greenville *Delta Democrat-Times*, 26 September 1962, 4.

140. Hodding Carter III, "Silence Must Be Broken," Greenville *Delta Democrat-Times*, 30 September 1962, 4.

141. William Lance Conn, "Crisis in Black and White: The McComb *Enterprise-Journal*'s Coverage of Racial News, 1961–1964" (Master's thesis, University of Mississippi, 1991), 127–128.

142. Loewen and Sallis, *Mississippi*, 295.

143. Ira B. Harkey, *The Smell of Burning Crosses* (Jacksonville, Ill.: Harris-Wolfe and Co., 1967), 52.

144. "Racial Evolution and Pure Humbug," from the *Christian Science Monitor*, in the Pascagoula *Chronicle*, 10 September 1962, 4.

145. Johnston, *Mississippi's Defiant Years*, 401.

146. Ira Harkey, "Governor Reaches Point of No Return," Pascagoula *Chronicle*, 14 September 1962, 6.

147. Ira Harkey, "Confusing Times, Dangerous Times," Pascagoula *Chronicle*, 18 September 1962, 6.

148. Johnston, *Mississippi's Defiant Years*, 400–401.

149. Hooker, "Race and the News Media in Mississippi," 111.

150. Ibid., 22.

151. "Dilemma in Dixie," *Time*, 20 February 1956, 76; "Dixie Flamethrowers," *Time*, 4 March 1966, 64; "Moderation in Dixie," *Time*, 19 March 1965, 71; Edwin W. Williams, "Dimout in Jackson," *Columbia Journalism Review* 9 (Summer 1970): 56.

152. "Belting One Down for the Road," 190; Charles Butts, "Mississippi: The Vacuum and the System," in *Black, White and Gray: 21 Points of View on the Race Question*, ed. Bradford Daniel (New York: Sheed and Ward, 1964), 104; "Dilemma in Dixie," 76; "Dixie Flamethrowers," 64; "Moderation in Dixie"; Ted Poston, "The American Negro and Newspaper Myths," in *Race and the News Media*, ed. Paul Fisher and Ralph Lowenstein (New York: Praeger, 1967), 63; Pat Watters and Reese Cleghorn, *Climbing Jacob's Ladder: The Arrival of Negroes in Southern Politics* (New York: Harcourt, Brace and World, 1967), 73; Simeon Booker, *Black Man's America* (Englewood Cliffs, NJ: Prentice-Hall, 1964), 15; Roger Williams, "Newspapers in the South," *Columbia Journalism Review* 6 (Summer 1967): 27; James Boylan, "Birmingham Newspapers in Crisis," *Columbia Journalism Review* 2 (Summer 1963): 30.

Chapter 5

1964: Freedom Summer and the Mississippi Daily Press

In 1964, a decade after *Brown v. Board of Education* ordered desegregation in public schools, Mississippi's primary and secondary educational institutions remained segregated, as did most of the state's society. Movie theaters had balconies known as the "colored section." Waiting rooms in professional offices were segregated by race. The only contact that most white Mississippians had with black Mississippians was through the relationships of "colored maids," yardmen or field hands. As news of the Freedom Summer project reached the state, the people braced. From the governor's mansion, to the state legislature, to county sheriffs, to the editors of the Mississippi daily press, the civil rights activities of the federal government and the "invading agitators" consumed many waking moments. One major concern was that the national and world media were watching closely. Beatings, arrests, bombings and church burnings were suddenly being documented regularly by the Associated Press and United Press International, as well as television network news. As Mississippi's "closed society" was tested and challenged on a daily basis, the state's editors were called upon for explanation and analysis as never before.

THE CIVIL RIGHTS ACT OF 1964

In June 1964, as the Mississippi daily press was preparing to deal with the impending Freedom Summer project, the 1964 Civil Rights Act was about to be signed into law by President Lyndon Johnson. The most significant civil rights legislation since the post–Civil War period, the act was ratified primarily for three reasons. A change in the national attitude and awareness about civil rights had been initiated by more black activism. The assassination of President John Kennedy in November 1963, a known supporter of equal rights, gave activists a memorial cause, and Johnson, a conservative Texan who became president following the death of Kennedy, underwent a metamorphosis.[1] In his first State of the Union address, Johnson said, "Let this session of Congress be known as the session which did more for civil rights than the last hundred sessions combined."[2]

The Civil Rights Act of 1964 barred racial discrimination in restaurants, entertainment enterprises and all public accommodations with more than five rooms. It was intended to guarantee blacks and other minorities equal access to public facilities. One controversial aspect of the 1964 act was the section that reduced qualifications for voter eligibility, an issue about which Lyle Wilson of the AP wrote, "A sixth grade education is not good enough."[3] An editorial from the *Manchester* (New Hampshire) *Union Leader* criticized the reduced voter qualifications in a derogatory criticism of blacks and was reprinted in several of the Mississippi daily newspapers. "Mississippi's racial problem, we should try to realize, is unique," the editorial said. "Forty percent of its population is colored. Northerners cannot imagine, let alone understand, what this is like. Naturally, Mississippians resist radical change because it would throw the balance of political power into the hands of people who are by no stretch of the imagination capable of voting intelligently."[4]

A Southern filibuster of the act raged in Congress for nearly three months before its passage in July.[5] When Senator Robert Byrd (D-W.Va.) held the floor for fourteen hours to protest the act, his marathon talk was front-page news in several of the Mississippi daily newspapers.[6] Mississippi Senator John Stennis led the charge for his home state, and also received wide coverage in the Mississippi press.[7]

A "counter-filibuster" was initiated in early June by Senator Hubert Humphrey, the Democratic Whip from Minnesota, who successfully led congressional supporters to the signing of the bill on 2 July.[8] Gaining "cloture" of the Southern filibuster, however, so that Congress could vote on the act took nearly a month,[9] and from the cloture debate arose an unlikely Southern hero. A Republican senator from Arizona, Barry Goldwater, not only supported the filibuster but intended to vote against the act because of its effect on individual rights.[10] When the Senate filibuster ended, the seventy-four-day protest was praised by the Mississippi press for the verbosity of its attempt (over 8 million words)[11] and for the fact that it was the "longest debate in history."[12]

In mid-June, President Johnson declared his goal of a Fourth of July signing of the act, and the information was heralded across many front pages in the Mississippi daily press.[13] In late June and early July, it appeared evident that Johnson would meet his deadline.[14] The U.S. House of Representatives approved the bill by a vote of 289–126, and the U.S. Senate approved it by a vote of 73–27.[15] Sent to Johnson in the White House on

2 July, the Civil Rights Act of 1964 was signed in a dramatic, televised ceremony that night. As reported by the UPI and printed in several of the Mississippi daily newspapers, "The House finally passed and sent to the White House today far-reaching legislation born of race violence, bombings, vote curbs and continued resistance to school integration."[16]

Mississippi Governor Paul B. Johnson, Jr., labeled the act "unconstitutional,"[17] and advocated "noncompliance,"[18] a stance considered "dangerous" by the NAACP.[19] The Mississippi Legislature voted 113–0 to "to fight the rights bill" by budgeting half a million dollars to the Sovereignty Commission, a state agency created in 1956 to propagandize the segregationist position.[20] In neighboring Alabama, Governor George Wallace predicted that the act would be repealed "within two to four years."[21]

MISSISSIPPI EDITORS REACT TO THE CIVIL RIGHTS ACT OF 1964

Editorial reaction among the Mississippi daily press to the Civil Rights Act of 1964 varied. In Clarksdale, editor Joseph Ellis, Jr., of the *Clarksdale Press Register* addressed passage with the editorial, "Law but Not Fact." Ellis was outraged. "President Johnson's plea to every American to join in enforcing the so-called Civil Rights Bill to 'bring justice and hope to all people and bring peace to our land,' has not died out," he wrote. "Responsible voices are raised against it."[22] In Columbus, editor Birney Imes, Jr., of the *Commercial Dispatch* published an opinion column by Al Kuettner of the AP, who complained that of the nine blacks he interviewed, "only two had a 'more than general idea' about what the Act meant."[23] Another editorial in the Columbus *Commercial Dispatch*, reprinted from the *Dixie Lumberman*, complained that "the Kennedy idea of civil rights is to take them from the majority and give them to the minority."[24] In Corinth, editor Bill Simpson of the *Daily Corinthian* was angry. "There are very few, if any, who ever really believed the civil rights bill would not eventually pass," he wrote. "The shock will come later, and not for Southerners alone. The tears will roll, the fears will turn into nightmares when officials, federal, state and otherwise, begin actual enforcement of some of the provisions of this monstrosity." Simpson did not direct all his anger toward the federal government, however. "The South was not blameless with its bevy of segregation laws, many of which were uncalled for and only a method of insulting the already humble Negro," he wrote. "Now humility has been lost by all groups as legislation is adopted to war against legislation and tradition."[25]

A couple weeks later, on the eve of the signing of the act by President Johnson, Simpson addressed it again in his front-page "Talk of Town" column. "By tomorrow morning, Americans will have lost their right of jurisdiction over most private property with the exception of their homes, and possibly, that will be covered in a later bill," he wrote.[26]

In Greenville, editorial concern was how the act would be complied with, and reacted to. In "The Day of Cloture," Hodding Carter III wrote, "How the citizenry votes in its everyday observance of the law will be the crucial test, and there are strong indications that resistance to some of its features will not be confined to the South."[27] On the morning after the act was signed by Johnson, Carter asked his readers to comply peacefully until the issue had been examined in the courts. "Let us today resolve that the testing ground for the law shall be in the courts and not in the streets," he wrote. "Let us also resolve that as the law is applied, we demonstrate again that we are following the law, much as many may resent or dislike it."[28]

Carter was the only editor of the Mississippi daily press who made it a point to inform his readers that peaceful acquiescence to the new civil rights legislation was widespread. "What is extraordinary about the national and Southern reaction to the new civil rights law is not that there has been scattered violence, but that there has been such a high degree of compliance," he wrote. Carter was also the only editor of the Mississippi daily press in 1964 to encourage his readers to give the Civil Rights Act a chance. "What civil rights groups and whites alike need to do now is to give the bill a chance to work before running pell mell into the streets with angry accusations, ultimatums and impassioned speeches," he wrote,[29] cautioning those who felt compelled to resist the new law to voice their protest in a way that was "orderly and legal."[30]

In Hattiesburg, editor Leonard Lowrey of the *Hattiesburg American* was far less supportive and more prone to doomsaying. "We greatly fear that an era of federal control, strife and racial trouble such as this country has never seen before is ahead for the entire nation, and that it can be dated from June 10, 1964, when the cloture vote assured passage of this civil rights bill," he wrote.[31] Lowrey did, however, urge his readers to be patient with businesspeople who felt they had to comply. His editorial was reprinted in the *Laurel Leader-Call*. "Above all else, fair-minded Mississippians should guard against unfair treatment and criticism of their long-time neighbors and proven good citizens who recognize that they have no choice, at this time under the law, but to comply," he wrote.[32]

In Jackson at the *Clarion-Ledger*, editor T.M. Hederman, Jr., shared his disdain and criticism. The 1964 Civil Right Act, he said, "flouts the letter and spirit of the federal constitution"[33] and "kills more liberty than it gives."[34] The mind-set at the Jackson *Clarion-Ledger* was that "the civil rights bill would take away far more rights than it would protect."[35] Jackson *Clarion-Ledger* writer Tom Etheridge, in his traditional white Southern view, published what he said was an anonymous poem sent to his "Mississippi Notebook" column: "Lyndon gave the signal, Hubert rang the bell, Bobby shouted all aboard, and the country went to . . . pot."[36]

Across town at the Jackson *Daily News*, Etheridge had a supporter, at least on the issue of civil rights, with editor James "Jimmy" Ward, who warned that "liberals" would "rue the day" the Civil Rights Act became law.[37] Ward also described "the evil consequences of the fiendishly-concocted civil rights legislation" and detailed "the blackness of thorough and crushing domination."[38] In early June, the Jackson *Daily News* began propagating the notion that the civil rights movement was Communist-inspired and -supported,[39] an idea that was spread by many, including Representative James Utt of California, who received extensive coverage in the Mississippi daily press for his *Congressional Record* report.[40] Utt's description of the "sinister force at work in Mississippi"[41] was a front-page endorsement of their own convictions that many editors of the Mississippi press simply could not resist publishing.

In McComb, editor J.O. "Oliver" Emmerich at the *Enterprise-Journal* questioned the constitutionality of the Civil Rights Act.[42] The day after the act was signed, Emmerich offered his own explication, which was reprinted in the *Clarksdale Press Register*.[43] "Mississippi opposed the legislation, we still oppose the idea," he wrote. "Some phases of the law, we believe, will be held by the courts to be invalid. Other phases of it doubtlessly will be held to be Constitutional. In the interim, we must hope for the maximum in patience and common sense. A newspaper could say defiantly in protest of the law, 'Let us rise up in arms against it.' But this could not be said responsibly."[44]

In Meridian, editor James B. Skewes of the *Meridian Star* raved on with his conservative anti-integration outlook as the Civil Rights Act of 1964 became a looming reality. He referred to the act as "The most vicious congressional bill ever perpetrated on the American people"[45] and "another step in the direction toward a dictatorship in this country."[46] Skewes considered the Civil Rights Act of 1964 "another step toward ending freedom in the United States and toward a totalitarian state."[47] In "The Ultimate Result? It's Mongrelization," Skewes voiced a near paranoid fear of the new law. "Integration will eventually produce an attitude that is blind to race differences," he wrote. "It is for our children's sake that we must dedicate ourselves to the preservation of segregation now, segregation tomorrow, segregation forever."[48] Skewes was obviously distraught with the passage of the Civil Rights Act in 1964, as evidenced by his editorial, "God Help the USA."[49]

In Natchez, editor James Lambert of the *Natchez Democrat* addressed the Civil Rights Act of 1964 in an editorial, "Our New Slavery." Lambert described how the law would control businesses, which was "un-American" to him.[50] Lambert thought the Civil Rights Act was "obnoxious,"[51] and primarily a means "to punish the South."[52] He wanted blacks to know that the Civil Rights Act would not guarantee them jobs. "What Negroes need is more racial pride, pride in their racial characteristics, in their native talents, in their capacity to achieve if they will only apply themselves," he wrote.[53]

On the Gulf Coast, W. David Brown had taken the helm as editor of the Pascagoula *Chronicle*, and he was as staunchly conservative as former editor Ira Harkey had been liberal on the race issue. Brown agreed with Lambert that the "so-called Civil Rights Bill" was "aimed at the South"[54] and termed it a "monstrosity."[55] Brown believed that the U.S. Senate "yielded in shameful fashion to the rankest sort of coercion, blackmail and intimidation"[56] in passing the bill and that to sign it on 4 July was a "desecration" of that national holiday.[57] He thought the act was "full of evil" and that it would usher in "a second reconstruction."[58] In terms of whether his readers should comply with the act or not, Brown advised them to "let reason guide" and to "weigh the consequences" of their actions.[59] West of Pascagoula in Gulfport, editor E.P. Wilkes of the *Daily Herald* never addressed the Civil Rights Act of 1964 during Freedom Summer from an editorial perspective.

North in Starkville, editor Sherrill Nash of the *Starkville Daily News* referred to "a war" between Washington and the South.[60] "Sure, we can see some reasoning behind the claims of an individual who says he should be permitted to enter a business establishment which is operated as a public facility," he wrote. "Not that we can understand how or why any person would want to enter any business establishment where he knows he would not be welcomed." Harris raised an interesting question when he asked his readers, "Clients can be turned down, why can't customers?"[61]

At the West Point *Times-Leader*, editor W.H. Harris harked back to the Civil War. "This whole mess of racial trouble and 'civil rights' has evolved into a war between Washington and the South," he wrote. "How long will it take for the South to be forgiven?"[62] Harris considered the act "unworkable, unenforceable and, by the majority, unwanted."[63]

Northward in Tupelo, editor Harry Rutherford at the *Daily Journal* never directly addressed the Civil Rights Act of 1964 in an editorial during Freedom Summer. At the *Vicksburg Evening Post*, on the other hand, editor Louis P. Cashman, Jr., referred to the "civil wrongs bill."[64] Cashman advised his readers to comply with the law until it was tested in the courts, but "it seems unconstitutional."[65]

PRESIDENT LYNDON JOHNSON AND THE MISSISSIPPI DAILY PRESS

The Civil Rights Act of 1964 was criticized almost as much as President Lyndon Johnson (1963–1969) by the Mississippi daily press. A Southerner by birth, Johnson was rapidly losing favor among the Mississippi editors for his outward support of civil rights for all Americans. When the states' rights issue was raised in protest of the Civil Rights Act of 1964, Johnson said, "The concept of the fifty states being fifty 'countries' is as out-of-date as dinosaurs."[66] When Johnson announced that he would no longer accept speaking engagements at events with segregated audiences, the Jackson *Clarion-Ledger* and *Natchez Democrat* accused the president of "pouring salt into the South's wounds"[67] and being a "real double talker."[68] The Pascagoula *Chronicle* accused the president of a "leftish collaboration" with the Supreme Court[69] and said the civil rights workers in Mississippi during Freedom Summer were his "emissaries."[70] The *Starkville Daily News* encouraged Johnson to draft Robert Kennedy as a running mate for the 1968 presidential election. "We would like to see it," Harris wrote. "It would be like throwing an anchor at a drowning man."[71] In an AP story, Johnson was referred to as "a counterfeit Confederate" by former Mississippi Governor Ross Barnett.[72] Syndicated columnist Tom Anderson reported that Johnson, as a U.S. senator from Texas, had established "a socialist voting record" and that "only ten percent of the time he voted for safeguarding the God-given rights of the individual."[73]

When Johnson announced that U.S. postal workers would no longer be allowed to attend segregated meetings during work hours, he once again became the object of scorn for several of the Mississippi daily editors and a multitude of readers. The Jackson *Daily News* accused him of "extremism,"[74] while a reader sarcastically inquired whether a postal employee could still attend his segregated church.[75]

CIVIL RIGHTS COMPLIANCE AND THE MISSISSIPPI DAILY PRESS

In late June, just prior to the signing of the Civil Rights Act of 1964, NAACP leader Roy Wilkins announced at the national NAACP convention that the group wanted to "make the white folks mad, but not too mad"[76] by testing compliance to the act as soon as it was passed. Within a day of the signing of the Act, the NAACP was planning a tour of the South.[77] A group of black leaders arrived in Mississippi during the Fourth of July week, and several clashes between them and locals, including one in Laurel involving fifty whites and thirty blacks, were reported in the daily press.[78] In Clarksdale, a group of blacks were turned away from the local Holiday Inn.[79] In Meridian, the touring NAACP leaders were given rooms at the Holiday Inn without incident.[80] The same day, the nation's nearly 500 Holiday Inns were instructed by management to comply with the new law.[81]

The NAACP's determination to force compliance to the law was front-page news in the Mississippi daily press,[82] as were the NAACP description of the state as "Hell" and the suggestion to President Johnson that "the federal government should take over the government of Mississippi and withdraw federal funds."[83] Mississippi Governor Johnson said he thought that the group was "adding fuel to the fire" by being in the state and refused to meet with them.[84] Conservative syndicated columnist Jack Lotto referred to the NAACP as "Commies."[85]

In response to the NAACP recommendation that the federal government take over the government of Mississippi, Brown at the Pascagoula *Chronicle* thought a better idea "would be for Mississippi to take over the federal government."[86] The Jackson *Clarion-Ledger* reprinted an editorial from the *Ft. Worth* (Texas) *Telegram* that declared that the NAACP's suggestion was "not the answer."[87]

In Clarksdale, Ellis at the *Clarksdale Press Register* voiced his outrage over an incident at a local hotel where an attempt "to integrate" was "staged" for the news media:

> Mississippi and its citizens are being treated with utmost and unjustified contempt by national political leaders, by national television and news media, by sarcastic, martini-sipping pseudo-intellectuals of every breed, whose opinions do not matter a tinker's dam [*sic*] except that they are somehow accepted as the new gospel by those of influence whose past testaments have destroyed nearly every worthwhile attribute and heritage in American political, social and economic life. The ultimate indignity is typified by yesterday's charade at a Clarksdale motel, when an unknown, unnamed, undereducated lout from Columbia Broadcasting System literally stage-directed an absurd little demonstration drama for the benefit of his previously placed television cameras.

Ellis referred to "Negro puppets" and "a sanctimonious sermon on these 'horrid Mississippians' by Walter Cronkite."[88]

An individual protest in Georgia against the mandates of the Civil Rights Act made Lester Maddox, an Atlanta restaurant owner, a household name and hero to some who agreed that the law eliminated the rights of some to give to others. Maddox had no intention of serving black customers alongside his white customers at his Pickrick Cafe and vowed to go to jail before he would do so. He garnered a moment of fame for "strapping on a six shooter" and disbursing ax handles at his restaurant with which he and other white patrons drove away potential black customers. Maddox's case, which he took to the U.S. Supreme Court and lost, was covered extensively in the Mississippi daily press.[89] True to his word, Maddox closed the Pickrick rather than serve black customers alongside white,[90] and in an interesting twist, he told the U.S. Supreme Court, "You just put forty black people out of work."[91]

Three Mississippi restaurants in the state's capital, Primos, H.L. Green and Woolworth's, were in court almost immediately following passage of the act, sued by blacks who had been denied service.[92] Many other restaurants in Mississippi decided to avoid compliance and thus keep blacks away, by redefining themselves as "private" clubs.[93]

Another commercial protest that received wide coverage in the Mississippi daily press was the closure of the Robert E. Lee Hotel in Jackson, a move praised by the state legislature.[94] Rather than opening its doors to black customers, as mandated by the new law, the establishment closed down.[95] A few days later, however, the Robert E. Lee was back in the news when it reopened to offer free accommodations to Mississippi legislators, all of whom were white, staying in the capital during legislative sessions.[96] Interestingly, not long after re-opening, the hotel was the target of an undercover raid for illegal liquor sales.[97] Three other commercial lodging facilities in Jackson, the King Edward, the Sun-N-Sand and the Heidelberg, began immediate compliance with the act and received substantial daily press coverage through AP and UPI reports.[98] The Mississippi Innkeepers Association instructed individual members to comply or not to comply with the Civil Rights Act of 1964 as they believed appropriate, while the organization publicly questioned whether the accommodations clause was constitutional.[99]

Jackson Mayor Allen Thompson created a controversy by advocating compliance with the act, although he described it as "repugnant."[100] Senator Stennis, who had filibustered against passage of the act, also recommended acquiescence, "until the bill was tested in the courts."[101] The Jackson Chamber of Commerce offered the same stance and was "condemned" by the state legislature.[102]

The only editor of the Mississippi daily press who openly supported Thompson, Stennis and the Jackson Chamber of Commerce, was Carter III at the Greenville *Delta Democrat-Times*. "Decent people in the state are tired of abdicating leadership to the demagogues and the haters," he wrote. "The shackles of fear which have for so long bound white as well as Negro can be removed once and for all if the good people will at last join those who have now taken the lead in the attempt."[103]

The statewide Citizens' Councils, on the other hand, urged total noncompliance.[104] The Mississippi Legislature agreed with the Citizens' Council and voted to advise their constituents to resist the mandates of the act, the Senate, 24–13, and the House, 69–3.[105]

MISSISSIPPI FREEDOM DEMOCRATS AND THE MISSISSIPPI DAILY PRESS

Several statewide political challenges were front-page news during early June prior to the arrival of the Freedom Summer project. Senator Stennis faced a re-election challenge by Victoria Jackson Gray, a black Hattiesburg resident. Representative Jamie Whitten was challenged by Fannie Lou Hamer, a black Delta farmworker. Representative William Colmer was challenged by a black Hattiesburg minister, John Cameron, and Representative John Bell Williams was challenged by a black man, J.M. Holston. In a state with half a million registered white voters and only 30,000 registered black voters, all four black office seekers were "soundly defeated."[106] "Victoria Gray, a Negro housewife, polled fewer than five thousand votes in her race against Stennis," the UPI reported. "Representative Jamie Whitten routed Mrs. Fannie Lou Hamer, a Negro housewife from Ruleville."[107] The 1964 Civil Rights Commission found that less than seven percent of the state's voting-age blacks were registered, as compared to seventy percent of the whites.[108]

Hamer, although defeated by Whitten, was instrumental during the summer of 1964 in organizing the Mississippi Freedom Democratic Party (MFDP), a group of black activists and a few whites who were protesting black exclusion from the Mississippi Democratic Party.[109] Praised and criticized for her "I'm sick and tired of being sick and tired" speech at the Democratic National Convention in August 1964, Hamer helped focus national attention on the plight of black Mississippians.[110] Her televised presentation and the demands of the MFDP at the national convention were widely covered in the Mississippi press.[111] Aaron Henry, a Clarksdale pharmacist and president of the Mississippi NAACP, also attended the Democratic convention. The *Starkville Daily News* referred to him as a "renegade Mississippi Negro who somehow picked up the title of 'Dr.' between his sundry store in Clarksdale and Atlantic City."[112]

News reports on the Freedom Democrats in the Mississippi daily press focused primarily on a state injunction that sought to keep the MFDP from the national convention and forbade them from using the name "Mississippi Democrat."[113] Mississippi Attorney General Joe Patterson denounced the MFDP as a Communist front.[114] Gary Holland, who replaced W. David Brown at the Pascagoula *Chronicle* in August 1964, referred to the Freedom Democrats as "the Negro brand of Democrats" and wrote, "It would be a sight to behold if the few sturdy Democratic champions left get a stomach full and threw them out."[115] The *Starkville Daily News* defined the Freedom Democrats as a group representing "primarily those who are not now qualified to vote."[116] The Jackson *Daily News* revealed its opinion of the Freedom Democrats with a front-page photograph and caption as the preliminaries to the national convention in Atlantic City were getting started. The photo showed several members of the group, both black and white, relaxing in a hotel lobby. Their clothes were disheveled, many of the men had long hair, and the caption read, "They Want to Represent Mississippi."[117] Emmerich at the McComb *Enterprise-Journal* labeled the group "political liberals,"[118] which was no compliment from his perspective.

The only editor of the Mississippi daily press who had an openly positive thought for the Mississippi Freedom Democrats was Hodding Carter, Jr., retired from the Greenville *Delta Democrat-Times*. "They are squatters," he was quoted in the Jackson *Daily News*. "But they have a moral right to be there."[119]

In the end, practically no one represented Mississippi at the 1964 Democratic National Convention. The Freedom Democrats' delegation, composed of sixty-four blacks and four whites, rejected a compromise from the Johnson administration that would have given them two seats "at large."[120] All but three of the sixty-six regular Mississippi Democrats, Doug Wynn of Greenville, Fred Burger of Natchez and Randy Holladay of Picayune,[121] went home after refusing to sign an oath pledging support to the national ticket.[122] The three delegates who stayed were both praised and condemned in the Mississippi daily press. Carter III in Greenville supported the three men. "The state owes a debt of gratitude to them," he wrote.[123]

In Natchez, Lambert thought the Mississippi delegates should leave the convention in protest,[124] and he harshly criticized the delegate from Natchez, who was one of the three who remained. "We express our deep regret," Lambert wrote, "that Fred Burger, local attorney and alternate to the convention, chose to stay."[125] Emmerich in McComb was the only editor to question why a loyalty oath was required of the delegates at the convention, perhaps because he had been a delegate himself in the past.[126] Rutherford in Tupelo thought it was "ridiculous" for the Freedom Democrats to be seated at the convention and he chided the regular Democrats for returning to the state in protest and "sulking at home."[127]

Upon their return, the Mississippi delegates expressed dismay at the civil rights stance of the national Democrats, and many agreed that the party "was dead" in Mississippi.[128] Skewes at the *Meridian Star* referred to the national Democrats as the "Socialist Integrationist Party."[129] Mississippi Supreme Court Justice Tom Brady, a traditional Southerner and a disgusted delegate, argued that the loyalty oath initiated at the convention was "discrimination"[130] and that the Democratic Party had become the "national Negro party."[131] Earlier in the summer, Brady recommended an economic boycott to protest the mandates of the Civil Rights Act.[132] He was also the author of "Black Monday," a speech transcribed and disbursed throughout the South by the Citizens' Council. "Black Monday" condemned *Brown v. Board of Education* in 1954 and advocated continued segregation.[133]

EDUCATION CONTROVERSIES DURING FREEDOM SUMMER

In the Mississippi education arena, there were several controversies during Freedom Summer. Local Citizens' Councils began to organize their own system of private schools.[134] "Racial integration lowers educational standards for blacks and whites," said William J. Simmons, director of the Mississippi Citizens' Council.[135]

Ole Miss was back in the news with desegregation issues. The second black student of record at the university, Cleve McDowell, was expelled in July for having a pistol with him on campus during a class. He was refused readmission by the courts.[136] A third black, Cleveland Donald, was attempting to enroll at Ole Miss as a pre-law student.[137] Donald, who was supported in his efforts by Ole Miss political science professor Russell Barrett,[138] was admitted to the university by the state college board during the summer session and began classes, "with scarcely a glance from hundreds of white students."[139] An interesting legal aspect of Donald's acceptance to Ole Miss is that he was barred, by court order, from taking part in civil rights activities on the campus.[140]

In a related Ole Miss story, history professor James Silver, author of *Mississippi, the Closed Society*, was given a year's leave of absence to teach at Notre Dame following the publication of his book.[141] One of Silver's observations in *Closed Society* that raised the ire of many Mississippians was his assertion that no people, white or black, were "free" in the state.[142] Silver expected to lose his faculty position because of the book.[143] The Jackson *Daily News* accused Silver of "slashing" the state,[144] but the McComb *Enterprise-Journal* disagreed. "This book had to be written," wrote Emmerich. "Sharp and Penetrating."[145]

The desegregation of the South's colleges was becoming a reality. Without incident in June 1964, Northeast Louisiana State University admitted its first black student of record.[146] "Integration on college campuses is on the increase this summer," the AP reported. "And all entered peacefully."[147]

In 1964, Mississippi was the only state that had not made "at least a token start toward integration" in elementary and high schools, according to the UPI.[148] The state legislature, although "sharply divided,"[149] was considering a bill that would allow state funding of private schools as federal enforcement of the 1954 *Brown v. Board of Education* decision began to impact the state after a decade of non-compliance. The primary conflict within the state legislature regarding the plan was whether church schools should be eligible for student aid because, by definition, the Black Muslims would then qualify for tuition assistance in their church schools.[150] The state of Virginia had just been overruled by a federal court in a similar attempt to fund private schools with state money, but this did not deter the Mississippi legislators who supported Mississippi's plan.[151] They set up a special committee, headed by Governor Johnson, to investigate the possibility of dodging public school integration by financial support to private schools.[152] Later in the summer, Johnson told a crowd gathered to hear him speak at the Neshoba County Fair: "Integration is like prohibition. If the people don't want it, a whole army can't enforce it."[153]

Johnson's action in respect to public education was in answer to the impending desegregation of three school systems in the state by court decree: Biloxi, Jackson and Leake County.[154] The three schools had collaborated with a federal judge to create a "grade a year" plan, protested by many blacks,[155] in which the schools would begin desegregation during the 1964–1965 school term.[156] In July, a judge ruled that an integration plan be drafted in Clarksdale.[157] In August, however, no black students attempted to enroll at the white school in Clarksdale, or whites at the black. One white student attempted to register at the black elementary school, but he had no birth certificate, so he was denied admission.[158]

The public school system in the state was not the target of a totally negative campaign in 1964. Mississippians for Public Education, a newly established organization of white parents, was bent on preserving the state's public education and opposed the state legislature's determination to fund private schools.[159] The private tuition plan was also opposed by the Mississippi League of Women Voters,[160] as well as many educators and church leaders.[161] Carter in Greenville was certain the private tuition plan being explored by the Mississippi Legislature was doomed to failure, as it had been in Virginia. He complained that the state's leaders would "pass some form of private school plan anyway, all the while solemnly and hypocritically assuring the people of Mississippi that it will work."[162] Carter was also concerned about the state funds squandered on the issue and the negative impact on public schools. "We may well waste a lot of money, weaken our education system and lose a vast number of teachers in the process," he wrote.[163] Carter knew that in order for the state to maintain the proposed private school system, taxes would have to be increased, and he mentioned this fact several times over the summer as a means to support his adamant stand against the plan.[164] "Ten years after the Supreme Court decision of 1954, we are being called upon to face this self-evident fact," he wrote. "Our energies should be spent in facing it with honor and reason, not with strategies forever doomed to failure."[165]

Emmerich in McComb shared Carter's concerns. Refusing to take a pro or con position, however, he raised the specter of legal obstructions to the private tuition plan.[166] In Hattiesburg, Lowrey called for the state to "take its time" on major school decisions,[167] and requested that when the schools began to desegregate in the fall, the news media should stay away instead of creating a "three ring circus."[168] At the Tupelo *Daily Journal*, Rutherford was another outspoken proponent of maintaining Mississippi's public school system[169] and warned his readers that the experience of states like Virginia should "be a guide to us."[170] Rutherford was concerned that if private schools were funded in Mississippi, then a proposed NAACP school would be legally eligible to receive funds, a concept he found to be an "unbelievable offense."[171] He also thought the idea of supporting Black Muslim schools, "whose central teaching is that one God, the black man, will destroy the Devil, the white man," was setting the stage for "hatred and black supremacy."[172]

In late August, when the Jackson first grades desegregated without incident, the Jackson *Daily News* declared that the peaceful mood should not be construed as indicative of support for integration. "The lack of incidents should be taken as a manifestation of good behavior rather than approval of forced desegregation," Hederman wrote. "Jackson falls unwillingly as a bastion of segregation."[173]

School desegregation in Mississippi remained a controversial issue during Freedom Summer, even among parochial schools. In August, Bishop R.O. Gerow instructed the six Catholic schools in Mississippi to begin desegregation.[174] Several refused, including those in McComb[175] and Hattiesburg.[176]

WHITE SUPREMACIST GROUPS AND FREEDOM SUMMER

Another issue affecting Mississippi in early June, as the Civil Rights Act of 1964 began to appear certain of passage, was a resurgence of the Ku Klux Klan (KKK). Several editors of the Mississippi daily press spoke out against the Klan,[177] and none supported the group in their newspapers. In Hattiesburg, Lowrey wrote, "The men leading the Klan revival in Mississippi may be well intentioned and may feel such action is necessary, but we believe that they and those who join them are making a mistake that can only be harmful to the state and add to the difficulties of those seeking to solve our racial problems."[178] A news article in the Gulfport *Daily Herald* offered the Klan a chance to explain its position, which was the belief that most white people resented the civil rights movement.[179]

Also during Freedom Summer, the newly formed Americans for the Preservation of the White Race was back in the news. Known as APWR, the group was founded in a service station garage in Natchez in 1963 by W. Arsene Dick, who said the organization was "non-political, non-profit, and by all means, non-violent."[180] Carter in Greenville disagreed, however, noting that a member of the APWR had threatened a Greenville *Delta Democrat-Times* reporter.[181]

FREEDOM SUMMER VOLUNTEERS ARRIVE IN MISSISSIPPI

Into this already swirling chaos of discontent and anger came hundreds of Freedom Summer volunteers from all over the country. They were not in Mississippi, they said, to test the Civil Rights Act.[182] Most of them were idealistic college students, committed to the concept of equality for all people. They trained for their summer work at the Western College for Women in Oxford, Ohio,[183] and their goal was to assist blacks in registering to vote and to help establish "Freedom Schools" where blacks of all ages could enhance their reading and writing skills.[184] At the Freedom Schools, instruction was offered in traditional academic subjects, discussions were held on how to understand the white power structure and politics, and black cultural awareness programs were designed and carried out.[185] During Freedom Summer, fifty Freedom Schools were established in Mississippi, and more than 2,000 black students attended, ranging in age from pre-school to the elderly.[186]

From the middle of June, when they began to arrive in Mississippi, until late August, when most of them went back to school, the "civil rights workers" were viewed with skepticism and loathing. They faced an uphill battle for acceptance among most black Mississippians and hostility and opposition from most white Mississippians. They were considered outside agitators, part of an unwanted "invasion" on the state. Robert Moses, director of the statewide Freedom Summer project, said the volunteers planned to "move cautiously in areas of racial tension,"[187] which included most of Mississippi in 1964. Although calculations vary regarding violence in Mississippi during the Freedom Summer campaign, there were at least three Freedom Summer volunteers killed, eighty beaten, thirty homes and thirty churches burned or bombed and over 1,000 arrests made.[188]

The civil rights workers in Mississippi during Freedom Summer were unusual in a number of ways. First of all, they were much younger than the sit-in participants and court combatants of the 1950s.[189] Historian C. Vann Woodward noted that the young demonstrators and civil rights workers in the 1960s were particularly significant. "More than a black revolt against white, it was a generational rebellion, an uprising of youth against the older generation, against the parental 'Uncle Toms' and their inhibitions," he wrote.[190]

The protesters of the 1960s also realized the importance of national organization and economic support. Primary among the collaborating Freedom Summer groups were the Congress of Racial Equality (CORE), the Southern Christian Leadership Conference (SCLC), and the Student Nonviolent Coordinating Committee (SNCC).[191] CORE was involved in nonviolent demonstrations prior to the 1960s, and members applied this experience in training the Freedom Summer volunteers.[192] Lowrey at the *Hattiesburg American* expressed his disdain for CORE by publishing a column by Fitz McCoy. "The cause of progress for all Americans needs no enemies as long as it has friends like CORE, a militant, extremist organization with wild, often stupid, escapades," McCoy wrote.[193] The SCLC was headed by Martin Luther King, Jr., who helped organize a successful Alabama bus boycott in Montgomery in 1955.[194] During Freedom Summer, King involved himself in the civil rights struggle in St. Augustine, Florida,[195] then toured Mississippi briefly to promote the Freedom Democrats,[196] encourage black Mississippians to register to vote,[197] deny the civil rights movement was a Communist conspiracy,[198] and criticize the Federal Bureau of Investigation (FBI) for not locating three missing civil rights workers.[199] King also made front-page news in August for asserting that race relations were just as bad in the North as they were in the South.[200] During his civil rights work in St. Augustine, several of the Mississippi daily newspapers suggested that their readers take a vacation to that city to counteract King's economic boycott. "His tactics are to create an atmosphere of lawlessness, unrest and confusion," Imes in Columbus wrote. "If you are planning a trip South and are opposed to the likes of Martin Luther King and his followers, visit St. Augustine. It will be a blow to the economic blackmail being exerted against it."[201] The *Natchez Democrat* agreed,[202] as did a letter writer to the *Greenwood Commonwealth*.[203] The *Meridian Star* referred to "the miserable 'non-violent' street rabble led by the unspeakable Martin Luther King and his ilk."[204] In the Jackson *Daily News*, King was referred to as "the Extremist Agitator Martin Luther King junior."[205] Rutherford at the Tupelo *Daily Journal* labeled King a "false leader."[206]

The Freedom Summer volunteers who came to Mississippi during Freedom Summer were under the direction of the Council of Federated Organizations (COFO), which was staffed primarily by SNCC and CORE members.[207] They were sponsored, in part, by the National Council of Churches (NCC), a respected organization in Mississippi that became a pariah to many during Freedom Summer, including Governor Johnson.[208] In early June, the NCC held a press conference at the Jackson airport to officially begin its civil rights program in Mississippi. "Actually, they didn't say a great deal," wrote Lowrey in the *Hattiesburg American*. "NCC's civil rights workers won't lead protests or demonstrations, but rather the student volunteers will, to quote an AP story, 'help Negroes and white persons make the necessary changes in a new pattern of race relations without violence.' "[209] The *Hattiesburg American* often criticized the NCC. "We heatedly disagree that churches should be political,"[210] and it suggested, "Churches should stay out of the segregation battle."[211] The Jackson *Clarion-Ledger* agreed. "Presently, their goal seems to be to get out of the pulpit and swarm into the streets."[212] The Pascagoula *Chronicle* said the NCC was aiding "insurrectionists."[213] Several churches in the state that donated funds regularly to the NCC asked the organization to reconsider its support of the Freedom Summer project because of the "social upheaval being caused."[214] Galloway United Methodist Church in Jackson withdrew nearly $7,000 in annual funding from the NCC to protest Freedom Summer involvement,[215] as did other churches in the state.[216] A group of Methodist ministers in Mississippi requested that their ministers refrain from demonstrating with the summer workers,[217] as did several other Jackson-area churches.[218] M.G. Lowman, a Methodist circuit rider, traveled around the state to "warn" local church people about the "Communist activities" of the summer workers.[219] A Presbyterian church in Jackson, on the other hand, refused to criticize the NCC for its role in the civil rights movement.[220]

Despite the hostile response to the inaugural group of Freedom Summer volunteers, several hundred more arrived in Mississippi soon after the first group.[221] Senator Stennis had proposed a "Freedom Rider" amendment to the Civil Rights Act of 1964 that would have forbidden civil rights workers from coming to the state because "only violence would follow."[222] The Senate rejected the amendment, but Stennis was endorsed in his efforts by several editors of the Mississippi daily press, including Thatcher Walt in Greenwood. "Stennis' failed amendment to the civil rights bill would have, if adopted, halted the invasion of race agitators and integration zealots whose purposes have been to stir up strife and disturbances," he wrote.[223] Nash in Starkville thought Stennis' proposal to impose a $5,000 fine and five-year prison sentence on people caught crossing state lines for civil rights work, while commendable, was "too late."[224] In support of Stennis, the Mississippi Legislature passed an "anti-picket" law, a piece of legislation upheld as constitutional by the U.S. Supreme Court.[225] The state legislature also created a legal barrier to the formation of Freedom Schools by requiring a license.[226]

Percy Greene, editor of the black Jackson *Advocate*, agreed with Stennis that the civil rights workers should stay away.[227] The Mississippi Municipal Association (MMA), a group of sixty Mississippi mayors, urged the civil rights workers to "register" with local authorities "for their own protection,"[228] a request ignored by most volunteers. The Mississippi Bar Association enforced its mandate that only out-of-state attorneys with an in-state attorney-sponsor could practice law in Mississippi. This was an effort to impede the Constitutional Defense Committee, attorneys who came to Mississippi to assist the volunteers.[229]

THE MURDERED TRIO

Although the civil rights workers were ridiculed and threatened by many Mississippians during Freedom Summer, the fate that befell volunteers Michael Schwerner from New York City; Andrew Goodman from Brooklyn, New York; and James Chaney from Meridian, Mississippi, troubled and saddened most editors of the Mississippi daily press.[230] The three young men vanished in late June after being jailed for investigating a church burning near Philadelphia in Neshoba County, about twenty miles northwest of Meridian.

Editorial opinion regarding their disappearance varied in the Mississippi daily press. The voice of the *Manchester* (New Hampshire) *Union Leader* was used to address the disappearance in several of the newspapers. "Certainly, the persons responsible for the disappearance of the three civil rights workers in Mississippi have done a despicable thing," the editorial stated. "But to condemn the entire state because of this incident about which no facts are known is simply not fair. Indeed, it is rather strange that the persons in charge of the civil rights operations in Mississippi have so easily escaped blame."[231]

Carter in Greenville had no blame to lay, only fear for the future. "If our prayers are not answered, if murder has been committed," he wrote, "then the rest of this summer could well be pure hell."[232] Carter implored anyone with information regarding the missing trio to "come forward,"[233] and the Greenville *Delta Democrat-Times* conducted a survey in Neshoba County a few days later and found that most people there thought the trio had staged the disappearance. "The general feeling among people in the search area is that they are not concerned about whether the men are ever found," Carter wrote. "A feeling of 'let it be a lesson' is evident among the people interviewed."[234]

In Pascagoula, Brown showed no sympathy. "Nothing has been said about how much wiser the missing young men would have been had they stayed home and minded their own business," he wrote.[235] The *Starkville Daily News* commented, "If the three men are alive, and we pray they are, they're safer in Mississippi than anywhere else on earth."[236]

The search for the missing trio lasted forty-four days and was widely covered in the Mississippi daily press. President Johnson ordered an extensive search by the Federal Bureau of Investigation.[237] FBI Director J. Edgar Hoover obliged by coming to Mississippi to open a Jackson office,[238] which was considered an "insult" by the Jackson *Clarion-Ledger*[239] and the Pascagoula *Chronicle*.[240] Hoover redeemed himself to some extent, however, by asserting that "lawlessness in the South is no worse than lawlessness in the North."[241]

Mississippi Governor Johnson said he was satisfied with the search effort,[242] although it soon began to appear "futile."[243] Fear was widespread that the three young men had met with "foul play."[244] SNCC Director James Foreman told the AP he thought the trio had been murdered.[245] Hoover agreed.[246] Within a few days of the trio's disappearance, President Johnson sent 200 marines to comb the area,[247] and before long, 400 sailors arrived to assist.[248] Governor Johnson, a former Marine, was not consulted by LBJ prior to the decision and was insulted by the troops being sent to the state after he proposed to let the state's National Guard handle the case.[249] Imes in Columbus thought it was "silly" to use the military in the search. "The use of troops gives the already overworked publicity machines more fodder," he wrote. "They are making capital of the missing trio, largely at the state's expense."[250] Simpson in Corinth agreed. "If they have met with foul play, it is certainly regrettable," he wrote. "But when talk of sending troops comes up there appears to be other parts of the country where they are needed more."[251] Simpson believed the dispatch of troops to Mississippi would induce violence, not appease it. "Their concern about the safety of these people could be alleviated by the simple act of discouraging them from coming to Mississippi," he wrote.[252] Lowrey in Hattiesburg considered the sending of federal troops to Mississippi a political move.[253] Nash in Starkville wondered, "Why don't federal troops get sent to New York when someone there disappears?"[254] Ward at the Jackson

Daily News agreed,[255] as did Simpson in Corinth. "There appear to be other parts of the country where troops are needed more," Simpson wrote.[256] Harris in West Point thought that sending the federal troops to Mississippi was related to hard feelings lingering from the Civil War. "There was more racial violence in New York City over the weekend than is experienced in Mississippi during an entire year," he wrote. "But no federal troops were sent to New York. Nor will there be. This whole mess of racial trouble and 'civil rights' has evolved into a war between Washington and the South."[257]

Comedian Dick Gregory, with assistance from *Playboy* publisher Hugh Hefner, offered a $25,000 reward for information leading to the location of the missing men,[258] and the FBI offered $30,000 more.[259] For a month, many were optimistic that the three men would be found alive.[260] A few scattered sightings of the trio were reported in the press. Corinth Police Chief Art Murphy said that he saw Schwerner in the Corinth bus station café and that "the man gave him dirty looks."[261] Goodman was reported to have been spotted in Baton Rouge, Louisiana.[262] The *Vicksburg Evening Post* wondered in print whether the trio was dead or had fled.[263] In early July, a grave was located in Neshoba County in which a horse's body was found.[264] The *Meridian Star* penned a joking reference to the incident with the headline, " 'Righterless' Horse Found in Grave."[265] A human body discovered in the Mississippi River in mid-July was initially thought to be one of the volunteers.[266]

Mississippi Senator Eastland labeled the disappearance a "hoax" initiated by "plotting Reds" involved with the civil rights movement.[267] The *Starkville Daily News* and the West Point *Times-Leader* hailed Eastland for "exposing a number of civil rights workers as Communists."[268] Robert Shelton, Jr., the grand wizard of the Ku Klux Klan, also considered the disappearance a hoax,[269] as did Mississippi Representative Arthur Winstead.[270]

After more than two months and $3 million spent on the search,[271] the decomposing bodies of Chaney, Schwerner and Goodman were finally found buried in the red clay of Neshoba County.[272] At that moment, their names were forever engraved in history as the only fatalities of record related to the civil rights activities of Freedom Summer. Reports were common that an unknown informer had tipped off officials. *Newsweek* found that many people in Neshoba County seemed more concerned with the identity of the informer than of the killers. "For some, the triple murder seemed less shocking than the thought that the FBI might have paid for the tip," *Newsweek* reported.[273]

The *Meridian Star* waited only a day after the bodies were discovered to criticize the "liberals" and "slander mongers" who, the newspaper said, would "outdo themselves to find words vicious enough to use in vilifying every man, woman and child in Mississippi en masse." The "truth," according to the newspaper, was that "the overwhelmingly vast majority of our people repudiated violence" and that "no matter who the murderers are, the 'civil rights' organizations share the blame, inasmuch as they care nothing for how much violence they provoke."[274]

In the state capital, the Jackson *Daily News* was silent regarding the deaths until the last day of the summer, when criticism of the state in the national media roused Ward's ire. "So far there is not a shred of evidence that a Mississippian laid a hand on either one of the three civil rights workers who went to Philadelphia to meddle in local affairs," Ward wrote. "But all over the nation, loud racial agitators, self-serving politicians, long-haired liberals, Communists, misguided preachers, the leftist news media and other assorted groups have joined in howls of ugly and unfounded criticism of our state and its people." Ward was convinced that "the integrationists, the vote hunting politicians, the Communists, and others are determined to punish Mississippi for its policies and way of life."[275]

The Mississippi daily press coverage of the murders was equally extensive to that of the search. Gregory claimed he had forwarded a letter to the FBI that led them to the site,[276] a pronouncement denied by the FBI.[277] The *Meridian Star* and the Jackson *Daily News* reacted as if offended by Gregory's avowed involvement and what they considered his false claims in a vain attempt to gain notoriety for himself. The Meridian headline, "Tip-off Claim by Negro Dick Gregory Branded 'Worthless,' "[278] and the Jackson *Daily News* headline, "Probers Discount Comedian's Tip,"[279] expressed pleasure in Gregory's denunciation by the FBI. Two days later, Ward at the Jackson *Daily News* wrote that Gregory "tried to cash in on the announcement" and that Gregory "slipped to last place down the ladder, or about as low as whale droppings in the Pacific."[280]

Controversy encompassed the official coroner's autopsy reports of the murders, which stated that all three men had been shot to death, not beaten or tortured.[281] When a second autopsy was conducted at the request of the murdered men's parents, a brutal beating of Chaney was found that had not been reported in the state autopsy account. Chaney's "jaw was shattered, his left shoulder and arm reduced to pulp, his right forearm was broken in several points, his skull bones were broken and pushed in toward his brain," the autopsy reported.[282]

Governor Johnson told the press that he "deplored" the murders and went on to defend Mississippi for having a low crime rate, which "proves the segregated way of life is the way of peace."[283] Carter in Greenville criticized Johnson's assertion that racial segregation was the reason that Mississippi remained such a peaceful place. "Bunk," Carter wrote. "If Johnson's remark was, in fact, accurate, the three civil rights workers' bodies would never have been found. In fact, the trio would never have come to Mississippi because there would have been no reason for a militant civil rights movement here."[284]

Carter wanted the killers found. In "Justice Must Prevail," he wrote, "Let's not let another murder go unpunished."[285] Cashman in Vicksburg concurred. "We must track down the murderers of these men and bring them to justice," he wrote.[286] Harris at the West Point *Times-Leader*, despite his usual harsh words for the civil rights movement, was in agreement. "Like millions of other Americans, we were hoping that the three civil rights workers missing for six weeks would turn up alive and that the whole affair was a hoax," he wrote. "We must find who murdered them and bring them to justice."[287] In Tupelo, Rutherford grieved for the murdered men and the reputation of the state. "The slaying is a crime, a tragedy, a black eye for all Mississippi," he wrote.[288]

COVERAGE OF FREEDOM SUMMER ACTIVITIES

Although the disappearance and murders of Chaney, Schwerner and Goodman were daily front-page news in most Mississippi daily newspapers, other aspects of Freedom Summer were of newsworthiness, both statewide and locally. The content of the editorials addressing the civil rights workers during Freedom Summer primarily questioned the motives of the volunteers, criticized the organizations that supported them, requested patience and advocated non-violence. An editorial reprinted from the New Orleans *Times-Picayune* referred to the COFO summer project as "another Mississippi tragedy,"[289] and the Dallas *Morning Star* designated it "an invasion."[290]

Readers of the *Clarksdale Press Register* were urged to practice tolerance and humor while the civil rights workers were in the state. A recommendation to "meet the summer project with dignity and patience"[291] was published on the front page. Ellis shared his belief that "[t]he movement has, to a considerable degree, fallen on its face before it got started."[292] Clarksdale was ready, Ellis said, for "the immature collegians and over-ripe missionaries," and he advised his readers to "leave the law to law enforcement officials."[293] In his first editorial concerning Freedom Summer, "With Dignity and Restraint," Ellis advised his readers about the arrival of the "pitiful platoons," his description of the civil rights workers. "Northern students, through lack of something better to do with their vacation, have volunteered to conduct 'Freedom Schools' in Mississippi communities, including Clarksdale," he wrote. "Their program, while stupid, is one of non-violent and essentially legal activities."[294] Two days later, an editorial in the Clarksdale newspaper warned that the "Mississippi Project" would be a "summer-long program of agitation" and that the community must not "play into the civil rights workers' hands" by jailing them.[295] Within a week, a photo of the Freedom House in a converted Clarksdale store was published on the front page,[296] and a staff-written interview with civil rights worker Lew Sitzer was published in a front-page article that offered an in-depth look at the objectives of the summer project.[297]

The *Clarksdale Press Register* was fairly comprehensive in its coverage of local incidents during Freedom Summer, particularly those reported to the police that resulted in an arrest. On 22 June, four volunteers were arrested on vagrancy charges while organizing voter registration in Clarksdale.[298] The incident was reported in the *Clarksdale Press Register* in a front-page story.[299] When a local black pastor involved with the civil rights workers was arrested for driving under the influence on 23 June,[300] the story was not picked up by the *Clarksdale Press Register* until later in the month, when the case went to court, and the man was defended by Northern lawyers.[301] The incident remained front-page news after the attorneys volunteering on the case were denied the right to practice law in the state.[302]

Clarksdale was a hotbed of activity during Freedom Summer. In early July, a volunteer was arrested for taking photos in a Clarksdale courtroom, where the chief of police sprayed deodorant on two girls.[303] An NAACP member was turned away from Jenkins' Barber Shop at gunpoint,[304] and Jack Pratt, an attorney from New York working with the National Council of Churches, was "removed" from the Hamburger Café.[305] That eatery was where three summer workers were arrested for trespassing and fined $100 each in July.[306] The Clarksdale Youth Action Movement, a splinter group of the NAACP, was denied entrance to a white church,[307] and when a Freedom Rally was held in early July, the front-page coverage placed quotation marks around "witnesses" and "testimony," as if to question their authenticity.[308] A visit to Clarksdale by Martin Luther King, Jr., in support of the Freedom Democratic Party, was front-page news.[309] King's denial of a Communist influence in the civil rights movement, however, was buried on page twelve.[310]

Several incidents were not reported by the *Clarksdale Press Register* that were recorded by the summer workers. In early July, the driver of a pickup truck with the license plate covered by a rag tried to run down a SNCC volunteer. A local businessman told a group of blacks going to the county courthouse to register to vote that they would be fired from their jobs if they did.[311] A station wagon played "chicken" with a car full of civil rights workers, and the sheriff confronted a white minister driving a car with black passengers, "Are you married to them niggers?" he asked. "You ain't no minister, you're a SOB trouble maker."[312] A black civil rights worker was chased from a white laundromat, taken to jail and beaten by the sheriff, who told him, "You're a nigger and you're going to stay a nigger."[313] The registrar in Clarksdale closed the courthouse for voter registration in July and justified the action by saying that court was in session, and there was no time to register voters.[314] In August, Franklin Delano Roosevelt III was arrested and fined for speeding while he was conducting research for an aid project for the summer workers, and physicians Richard Moore and Les Hoffman of the Medical Committee for Human Rights were arrested for loitering outside the Clarksdale Freedom House.[315] The *Clarksdale Press Register* also failed to publish a story about a brutality charge against the Clarksdale police chief reported by the AP.[316]

Conversely, several incidents not reported by the summer volunteers were reported by the *Clarksdale Press Register*. In early July, state president and local NAACP leader Aaron Henry and several other blacks were "turned back" as they attempted to register for a room at the Clarksdale Holiday Inn and as they ventured to sit in the "white section" at the local movie theater.[317] The failed attempts at desegregation were front-page news with the headline, "Integrationists Probe for Breakthrough Here, Efforts Prove Futile in Most Tries So Far," with a story that reported, "The integration picture during the last hours in Clarksdale includes a little bit of everything, from ballots and books to pool halls to padlocked doors."[318] An act of vandalism at the Clarksdale Freedom House, in which a window was smashed out and garbage spread around the yard, was termed a "prank."[319]

Incidents related to the summer project that occurred in other areas of the state were reported in the *Clarksdale Press Register*, particularly those in Greenwood[320] and McComb.[321] The primary reason for that coverage was most likely that the wire services were covering them and that the reports were easily accessible. In late August, a front-page story reported that the summer project would continue on a "limited scale," although most of the eighteen workers in Clarksdale were leaving. The story also reported that the local Freedom House would remain open, that more than 100 blacks had been registered to vote in the county due to the civil rights workers efforts, and that only a few "minor" traffic violations had been committed by the civil rights workers.[322] A UPI article, "Summer Project Called Eminently Successful," hailed the formation of the Freedom Schools around the state and the organization of the Mississippi Freedom Democratic Party.[323]

Eastward to Columbus, the *Commercial Dispatch* published only one opinion column regarding the summer workers prior to the middle of July, when the bodies of Chaney, Schwerner and Goodman were found. In "What about Reverse Riders?" Imes suggested that blacks unhappy with the Southern way of life should be given a free ticket to the North.[324] The timing of this editorial coincided with the day that seven civil rights workers were arrested in Columbus for distributing literature without a license and fined $400 each.[325] The incident was not reported in the Columbus *Commercial Dispatch*, nor were many other incidents involving summer workers in Columbus. In late June, six carloads of whites drove their vehicles onto the lawn of the Columbus Freedom House. Five of the cars fled before police arrived, and the two men in the sixth car were questioned and released.[326] In early July, a black man from Missouri was mistaken for a civil rights worker and beaten by whites, after which he was fined $75 for disturbing the peace.[327] In mid-August, summer project attorney Tom Connelly was arrested on charges of reckless driving after a local white, Travis Hamilton, slammed his truck into Connelly's car, smashing it and injuring a passenger, law student Richard Wheeler. Connelly was arrested and released on $100 bond.[328] The Columbus *Commercial Dispatch* turned a blind eye, except to UPI stories from other areas of the state.[329]

Only one violent incident related to Freedom Summer was reported in the Columbus *Commercial Dispatch*. In early June, a group of blacks claimed that they were beaten by local police. The story was headlined, "Negroes Claim Beat by Police, Commie Type Propaganda Found in Car Says Sheriff."[330]

North of Columbus, the Corinth *Daily Corinthian* never offered an opinion regarding the summer workers who arrived in the state, other than to reprint an Iowa editorial, also published in several other Mississippi daily newspapers, that suggested to the volunteers that they return to their respective homes and leave Mississippi to settle its own matters.[331] No COFO office was established in Corinth that summer, and the primary complaint of Simpson at the Corinth *Daily Corinthian* was the Civil Rights Act. Although reports of activity in McComb[332] and other UPI-covered sites were published,[333] Freedom Summer never arrived in Corinth, Mississippi.[334] Editorially, Simpson's only advice to his readers was to inform them that they "are under no legal obligation to answer questions from the FBI unless so ordered in court."[335]

Freedom Summer hit like a tidal wave in Greenwood, a small Delta town to which the national headquarters for SNCC was relocated for the duration of the summer project. Walt, who edited the *Greenwood Commonwealth* during the 1962 desegregation of Ole Miss, advised his readers to keep calm and let the appropriate law enforcement officials handle any situation concerning the civil rights workers. "The long heralded summer of racial agitation has begun in Mississippi," he wrote. "Faced with the indifference, and probably in some instances the hostility, of the people they have come to 'free,' much of their idealism is bound to wilt. The law must prevail."[336] A few weeks later, an editorial from the *Dallas Morning News* that referred to the summer project as "the unjustified, uncalled-for invasion" appeared in the *Greenwood Commonwealth* and several other Mississippi daily newspapers.[337] The Greenwood City Council issued a statement through the *Greenwood Commonwealth* that warned residents, "Keep children away from dangerous situations created by the Civil Rights Act."[338]

Like the other Mississippi daily newspapers, the *Greenwood Commonwealth* reported wire service stories about other areas of the state[339] much less often than it did local activity. The first mention of the local summer project in the *Greenwood Commonwealth* was a headline story from the wire services in mid-June, "SNCC Says Headquarters Coming Here."[340] No staff-written article ensued. The next mention of the project was a week later after fourteen people were arrested for picketing a local store,[341] and a week after that when several summer workers told the *Greenwood Commonwealth* that they were in town to register voters and open a community school, not to test the mandates of the Civil Rights Act.[342] Many incidents of harassment were reported by the summer workers to the local police that were not reported in the *Greenwood Commonwealth*. Freedom House residents received a late night telephone call that warned, "You better not go to sleep or you won't wake up." Bomb threats were made. Six students who picketed the Greenwood jail with signs that said "stop police brutality" were arrested. A local insurance agent punched a volunteer working with voter registration. A SNCC staff member was arrested on a public profanity charge after a police officer overheard him say, "We've got to get some damn organization in our office." A local black woman was hit in the chest by a white man while in the company of two volunteers.[343]

In mid-July, the Greenwood Citizens' Council was given front-page placement to urge the white community to resist compliance with the Civil Rights Act,[344] and the next day a rural black church near Greenwood was burned down.[345] The summer project's local Freedom Day was announced as front-page news,[346] and the next day at the event, 111 people, including thirty juveniles and a seventy-eight-year-old man in ill health,[347] were arrested for picketing. That same evening, local black activist Silas McGhee was forced by three white men into their truck and beaten with an iron pipe after he tried to desegregate the local movie theater. FBI agents took him to the hospital.[348] The 111 people held in jail on picket charges, whose names were published in the *Greenwood Commonwealth*, attempted to have their trials moved to federal courts, where they thought their chances of a fair trial were much greater than on the local level, a story reported by the wire services.[349] The federal judge, however, remanded their cases back to the Greenwood police court, where each arrested picket was fined $100 and given thirty days in jail.[350] Several of the summer project volunteers' parents raised money for their legal fees,[351] and attorneys with the National Lawyers Guild who arrived in Greenwood to assist in the legal defense of the activists were classified as Communists on the front page of the *Greenwood Commonwealth*.[352]

Three men were eventually arrested for the attack on McGhee at the movie theater, a story reported by the AP and UPI as the first arrests under the Civil Rights Act of 1964.[353] McGhee was continually harassed. Gunshots were fired at his home, he and his brother, Jake, were mobbed by about 200 whites, and in August he was shot in the face while sitting outside Lulu's Café. The next day, several hundred angry blacks gathered at SNCC headquarters in Greenwood to protest the shooting. Police in full riot garb blocked the streets until the crowd dispersed.[354] The incidents related to McGhee were never reported in the *Greenwood Commonwealth*. The only mention of his family was when his brother, Clarence Robinson, was arrested for disturbing the peace,[355] and when his mother was being sought for slapping a Greenwood police officer.[356]

Martin Luther King, Jr., came to Greenwood to encourage voter registration, and his speech was not reported in the *Greenwood Commonwealth*, although his arrival made front-page news in the form of an AP story.[357] During King's speech to 1,000 people,[358] the KKK had an airplane fly over and drop disparaging and threatening leaflets throughout the crowd and town. The *Greenwood Commonwealth* failed to cover the incident, which was reported in several other Mississippi daily newspapers.[359]

In early August, controversy arose when the United States purchased land in Greenwood from white supremacist Byron De La Beckwith to build a new post office. The NAACP protested the purchase, but the episode was not reported in the *Greenwood Commonwealth*.[360] In mid-August, Greenwood was mentioned in the state and national news when actors Harry Belafonte and Sidney Poitier arrived to donate $70,000 to the SNCC project. Nearly 500 people were present at the ceremony, which received coverage in several of the Mississippi daily newspapers.[361]

Also in mid-August, Mrs. Joe Dobbs, one of the white owners of the Happy Day Grocery Store in Greenwood, fired a shotgun into a crowd of seventy black pickets.[362] According to the *Greenwood Commonwealth* report, "A camera was shot out of the hands of a white man by Mrs. Dobbs."[363] The next day, when pickets again gathered outside the store, they chose the sidewalk across the street from the Happy Day,[364] perhaps because Dobbs proved so adept with her firearm.

Westward into the Mississippi Delta at the Greenville *Delta Democrat-Times*, Carter III, like his father before him, was never one to dodge an issue of social importance. He quickly addressed his community's outspoken fear of the summer project prior to the arrival of the civil rights workers. "For the most part, we have felt that such a feeling was premature," he wrote. "Insofar as the project is concerned, we have believed that they represented a threat only to those who believe the Negro should be forever deprived of his constitutional rights. We still believe this." Carter appealed to his readers' desire for law and order. "Evenhanded justice when the law is broken, coupled with scrupulous regard for the constitutional rights of assembly, protest and the attempt to vote, are the best prescription for action in every community," he wrote. "This is as much a moral as a legal obligation, imposed by our American heritage and our Christian precepts. To follow the other course, to engage in total repression, is to evoke everything that is so feared.[365]

Carter was determined to do what he could to keep violence from breaking out. "The summer of 1964 should not go down in history as a synonym for violent discord in Mississippi," he wrote. "The time for militant opposition to the laws of the land are gone."[366] Although he referred to the influx of civil rights workers by the term "invasion," common among the Mississippi daily press during Freedom Summer, Carter advised his readers to try "peaceful acceptance."[367] He also published the "Yankee, Go Home" editorial from the *Oelwein* (Iowa) *Daily Register*.[368]

The amount of activity, particularly violent activity, in Greenville during Freedom Summer was much less than that of neighboring Greenwood, whose crises were reported more often in the Greenville *Delta Democrat-Times*[369] than in the *Greenwood Commonwealth*. Incidents in other areas of the state were also reported in the Greenville *Delta Democrat-Times* as they came across the UPI wire.[370] More than any other Mississippi daily newspaper, the Greenville *Delta Democrat-Times* offered extensive local reportage of Freedom Summer. Political activities were covered, such as the Democratic precinct meetings, which COFO members attended without incident.[371] Voter registration drives were announced,[372] as were numbers of newly registered voters.[373] Early into the summer, however, Carter was angered by misleading and inconsistent information that he was receiving from COFO members. In an editorial, "Questions Summer Project," Carter advised the local summer volunteers to drop their "double talk" but did not give specific examples.[374] "COFO statements have been contradictory, not only from day to day, but hour to hour," he wrote. Again, no specifics were provided.[375]

When the summer project workers arrived in Greenville, readers were offered statements by them, by the local police and by the mayor. Several of the fifty civil rights workers in Greenville told *Delta Democrat-Times* reporter John Childs that they were going to "push Greenville to the limits."[376] That same day, the newspaper reported that Greenville police were "thoroughly prepared" for the arrival of COFO.[377] Greenville Mayor Pat Dunne was also given front-page placement to ask the city's residents to "obey the law."[378]

A week later, as passage of the 1964 Civil Rights Act appeared imminent, Dunne's message was reiterated as he called for "patience."[379] Soon after, a COFO spokesperson was quoted on the front page saying that the group had no intention of testing the Civil Rights Act, that they were in Greenville to register voters.[380] When a black man was served without incident at the local Downtowner Motor Inn following passage of the act, the story was front-page news,[381] as was the report of the first group of local blacks to register to vote after the act was signed.[382]

Coverage of Freedom Summer by the Greenville *Delta Democrat-Times* was objective and comprehensive. Historian Robert Hooker concluded that the fair treatment that the summer volunteers received in the Greenville *Delta Democrat-Times* was based on scarce civil rights activity in that town. "Greenville was largely bypassed by the movement in the first place, and second, there were no potentially image-damaging incidents there," Hooker wrote. "The *Delta Democrat-Times*, therefore was never faced with the inevitable temptation of playing down news that might embarrass the town or incite white citizens."[383] Hooker, who evaluated only August and September issues of the Greenville *Delta Democrat-Times* for his thesis, would have concluded differently had he examined the entire summer.

Greenville, while not the hotbed of violent activity evidenced in neighboring Greenwood, was a site of diverse civil rights activity during Freedom Summer. At a COFO meeting in late June with 150 people in attendance, the discussion focused on employment issues.[384] This was how the story was reported, rather than as the "gathering of irate Negroes" stories in the *Greenwood Commonwealth*. A New Jersey schoolteacher working with COFO in Greenville for the summer, Nancy Schieffelin, was interviewed. She told Childs that race problems in the South were more evident than race problems in the North.[385] On Freedom Day in Greenville, over 100 blacks tested for voter registration,[386] and two reports about the event were published in the *Delta Democrat-Times*. Both were front-page news. One story described the rally and mentioned that 100 new voter applications were made "with no incidents."[387] The other, headlined "Freedom Day Has Surprises for Delta Civil Rights Units," described the quiet of the day's activities: "There were no disruptions, and pickets at the courthouse were ignored."[388]

In July, Carter responded to a local mistrial in the case of a black man being tried for the rape of a white woman. The jury had consisted of twelve whites. "This mistrial was not the first instance in which a Negro in Mississippi has not been convicted when accused of raping a white woman," Carter wrote. "But it was one of the few when the conviction has not been as automatic as the charge. The hung jury was a healthy omen for color-blind justice in Mississippi. That five men had the integrity to stick to an undoubtedly unpopular position, at this time and place, renews our pride in our county and its citizens."[389]

In early August, the Greenville *Delta Democrat-Times* could have been accused of being carried away by its commitment to equal justice for all people. Three local white men and a local black handyman, Jim Amos, were involved in an altercation. Amos was stabbed. The *Delta Democrat-Times* headlined the incident, "Three Whites Knife Negro Handyman."[390] No "alleged" was indicated. An editorial referred to the three assailants as "despicable at best."[391] The attorney for the three men complained that they were tried in the local press before their case went to court, a complaint that was published in the *Delta Democrat-Times*.[392]

Carter often used his editorial pulpit to praise his community. He commended local black leadership for helping to keep the peace during Freedom Summer.[393] He applauded the Greenville chief of police for "professionalism at its best."[394] He praised the local municipal court judge for his fairness.[395] He cheered the white community for allowing the Greenville Public Library to open its doors to the town's black citizens. "It has been done locally with no fanfare and without violence," he wrote. "And no one has felt any great loss in the process."[396] Carter kept the civil rights issue localized. In response to the burnings of several black churches in the Delta, Carter lambasted his white readers. "We white Mississippians talk righteously about the failure of citizens of the big cities of the East to offer aid as women are assaulted in the streets, or as men are mugged in broad daylight," he wrote. "But what of the one million whites of our own state who will do nothing as native-born thugs carry out a reign of terror against black fellow Mississippians, with the house of God as their favorite target?"[397]

As involved with Freedom Summer as Carter was, the opposite would be said of Joseph Lee in Grenada, about seventy miles northeast of Greenville. Lee, who had been with the Grenada *Sentinel-Star* during the 1962 desegregation of Ole Miss, remained at the newspaper. He expressed no published opinion concerning the Meredith case in September 1962 and had nothing to say editorially regarding the civil rights workers during Freedom Summer. The only editorial relating to civil rights activities during the summer in the Grenada *Sentinel-Star* was the "Yankee, Go Home"[398] reprint published in several of the other Mississippi daily newspapers. There was also only one Grenada incident related to the COFO project reported by the summer volunteers. On the day Interstate 55 opened to connect Grenada to Memphis,[399] a SNCC staff member was arrested there for speeding.[400] Little coverage was given to Freedom Summer stories from around the state,[401] unlike in the other Mississippi daily newspapers. When a civil rights worker in Jackson reported to police that he had been beaten, the Grenada *Sentinel-Star* published the UPI story under the head, "Exaggerates Story."[402] Rather than reporting that the mayor of Greenville issued a statement asking all people to leave the law to law enforcement officials, the Grenada *Sentinel-Star* headlined the article, "Greenville Officials Warn Group,"[403] as if the directive was aimed at COFO.

On the Coast, the Gulfport *Daily Herald* expressed the editorial opinion that the "real purpose" of Freedom Summer was to obtain federal intervention in Mississippi.[404] A variety of civil rights activities took place in Gulfport during Freedom Summer, but very little of it was reported in the Gulfport *Daily Herald*. Incidents in other areas of the state covered by the wire services, however, were often published, although usually buried deep inside the newspaper.[405] On the Coast, where desegregation had been accepted in some ways for years, the integration of dining establishments was relatively well accepted. The local restaurant owners announced that there was no "set policy" in motion following the 1964 Civil Rights Act but that every eatery was on its own.[406] Within days of the passage of the act, headlines proclaimed, "Coastal Facilities Are Mixed, No Incidents."[407] Voting rights and other civil rights were another matter. The first mention of COFO activity in the Gulfport area was when the local sheriff told the community, through the newspaper, to let him and his officers handle any situation arising from the summer project.[408] When the Gulfport Freedom School opened with thirty summer workers as teachers, the AP story was reported on page three.[409] The next day, an AP story listed many sites of the state's Freedom Schools, including Gulfport.[410] When the KKK dropped thousands of anti–civil rights leaflets from an airplane over the Gulf Coast, the front-page story merely reiterated the sheriff's concern.[411] Civil rights workers stationed in nearby Biloxi were interviewed for a story about the summer project and were portrayed as arguing among themselves and accused of being "intentionally vague."[412] In nearby Moss Point, a young black woman was wounded when gunshots were fired into a COFO meeting. She was referred to as a "girl" in the Gulfport *Daily Herald* reports.[413] In mid-July, a local judge told the summer volunteers that they would be charged with contempt if they continued to take blacks to the courthouse to register to vote.[414] A grand jury probe was launched to investigate whether blacks in Gulfport were being denied access to voter registration.[415] The findings of that probe were challenged a few days later by the local NAACP when the grand jury concluded that there had never been a case where a qualified black was not allowed to register to vote.[416]

Many incidents reported by the civil rights workers were ignored by the Gulfport *Daily Herald*. In July, Gulfport police allegedly threatened to hurt the children of a woman who was housing civil rights workers, so the workers moved elsewhere. Two voter registration workers were threatened, and four volunteers were arrested for refusing to cross a street on police orders as they neared the courthouse.[417] In August, several incidents occurred involving the civil rights workers that were not reported in the Gulfport *Daily Herald*. A local black volunteer was forced into a car one night at gunpoint, blindfolded, and taken to a location in Biloxi, where he was questioned by five men who offered to pay him for information about COFO. Volunteer Steve Miller was badly beaten by a white man as he left the local library, and a taxi refused to take him to the hospital.[418] Another incident that occurred in late August and was not reported in the newspaper seemed to summarize the Gulfport *Daily Herald*'s attitude toward Freedom Summer. Four local black voter registration workers were denied a meal at Albright and Woods Drug Store. They were served water, however, and asked to leave. When Luther Adams asked if the store was segregated, the waitress said, "You were served water, weren't you?"[419]

North of Gulfport about sixty miles, the *Hattiesburg American* expressed concern about the "behavior" of the arriving summer volunteers. "We hope the NCC had someone on hand who advised the young people of morality for morality's sake, not for the sake of the project," Lowrey wrote.[420] The newspaper endorsed the concept that the summer workers would have been much more useful working toward racial harmony in the North.[421] A letter from a group of Princeton University students reprinted in the *Hattiesburg American* condemned the summer workers in the state and concluded, "We wish to affirm our belief in the right of Mississippi to handle their own domestic affairs."[422] A letter from a black man in Jackson advising the summer workers to return home was also reprinted in the *Hattiesburg American*.[423]

As was the case with many other Mississippi daily newspapers, the *Hattiesburg American* published wire stories regularly regarding civil rights activities in other parts of the state.[424] The newspaper failed to report comprehensively about local events but did cover a few. Two cars owned by civil rights workers were shot full of holes in late June while they were parked outside the Hattiesburg Freedom House.[425] Then, until nearly two weeks later, when three volunteers were beaten with an iron pipe, and the story was picked up by the wire services, no other incidents were reported by the *Hattiesburg American*. According to the volunteers' records, however, many occurred. Hate literature was distributed in Hattiesburg that warned, "Beware good Negro citizens, when we come to get the agitators, stay away." The public school superintendent threatened to fire all janitors who were considering participation in local civil rights activity. Hattiesburg police stopped a black girl and five black boys who were walking home, cursed at them, threatened to arrest them, and slapped one of the boys. The wife of the owner of a local drive-in pulled a pistol on about twenty black youngsters who asked to be served, after which they were arrested, put in a drunk tank and "roughed up."[426]

The *Hattiesburg American* was one of the few Mississippi daily newspapers that offered the civil rights workers a chance to tell their side of Freedom Summer. In early July, Terri Shaw wrote that the main purpose of the summer project was to register voters. Shaw, who was the director of communications for COFO in Hattiesburg, said there were fifty volunteers in the Hattiesburg area and that nearly 600 blacks, ages eight to eighty-two, had enrolled in the local Freedom School.[427]

The wire services covered a mid-July incident in Hattiesburg in which three volunteers, including a rabbi from Ohio and two local teenagers, were attacked by two men with iron pipes as they walked in an uninhabited area. The assailants fled after attacking three of the men,[428] and the rabbi was hospitalized.[429] Kilmer Keys of Collins eventually turned himself in as the assailant, was tried and convicted and fined $500.[430] The rabbi, who left the state after being released from the hospital, told the media that Jews in Mississippi should "stand up for decency and freedom with all risks involved or leave the state."[431] Between the days in July when the attack occurred and when the arrest was made, Hattiesburg Mayor Claude Pittman released a statement to the press urging the people of Hattiesburg to refrain from violence.[432] A similar statement was published by Hattiesburg

Police Chief Hugh Herring.[433] Ten days later, a statement by the local Citizens' Council was published that urged resistance to the 1964 Civil Rights Act.[434]

Two other reports related to local civil rights activity were covered in the *Hattiesburg American.* One was the defeat by a group of local blacks in a picket lawsuit, a story reported by the wire services.[435] The second was the closure of the Hattiesburg Public Library twice after blacks attempted to use the facility and were arrested for vagrancy.[436] There were, however, many other incidents that could have been covered by staff writers at the *Hattiesburg American.* A white volunteer was beaten as he left a downtown bank with two other Freedom School teachers. The home of two local Freedom Democrats was bombed with a Molotov cocktail. Dorthea Jackson, a local black, was arrested when she would not give her seat on a bus to a white woman. Freedom School teacher Sandra Adickes was arrested for taking black students to the public library, and four voter registration workers were arrested for vagrancy.[437] The *Hattiesburg American* had many opportunities for news stories that it failed to cover during Freedom Summer.

The situation was similar in the state's capital, where the Jackson *Clarion-Ledger* referred to the COFO project as a "summer lark for youth"[438] and reprinted a *Nashville Banner* editorial that advised the summer workers to return from whence they came: "Students, Go Home!"[439] The Jackson *Clarion-Ledger* argued that the North needed the summer volunteers to solve their racial woes, but the South did not.[440] The newspaper reprinted the letter from Princeton University students who thought that the volunteers should have stayed home and worked toward racial peace in their own neighborhoods.[441] A favorite approach to civil rights issues by staff writer Charles M. Hills in his "Affairs of State" column was "too much emphasis on rights, and not enough emphasis on responsibility."[442]

The COFO workers in Jackson reported numerous violent incidents against themselves to the Jackson police, but few were covered in the Jackson *Clarion-Ledger*. In August, when blacks reported that KKK crosses were burned at several locations in Jackson, City Commissioner Tom Marshal told the press that the crosses were burned by the blacks to "agitate trouble."[443] Other incidents reported by the summer volunteers but never covered by the Jackson *Clarion-Ledger* included shots fired at the home of Robert L.T. Smith, a Jackson activist; a CORE field secretary taken to the Hinds County Jail and beaten; McCraven-Hill Missionary Baptist Church damaged by fire; a black woman attacked by an elderly white man at the Greyhound Bus Station Coffee Shop, after which she was charged with disturbing the peace; a black volunteer beaten with billy clubs by two whites at a major downtown intersection; a local volunteer denied service at a small café and then chased by a man in a pickup truck who fired two shots at him; two volunteers, one black and one white, chased by a man with pistol as they canvassed for voter registration; and a white volunteer beaten with a baseball bat at the Jackson COFO office.[444]

Unlike most other Mississippi daily newspapers, the Jackson *Clarion-Ledger* reported few civil rights activities from around the state, other than the disappearance and murder of Chaney, Schwerner and Goodman. Other stories were usually buried, rarely front-page news unless included in the condensed "On the Racial Front" column.[445] One of the few front-page articles concerning the summer project was written by staff reporter William Chaze, who visited the Hattiesburg COFO office. He claimed he was referred to as "just another yellow journalist," and his article was headlined, "Odor of Sweat, Dirt, Fill Hattiesburg COFO Office."[446] Chaze, who wrote several stories about Freedom Summer activities, reported that civil rights workers in Marshall County threatened blacks to coerce them into registering to vote and told them that their "welfare checks would be cut if they didn't." No COFO response to the allegations was included in the story.[447]

The Jackson *Clarion-Ledger* did publish, at least on a sporadic basis, letters to the editor that opposed the newspaper's stance. When several civil rights workers presented a talk to a sociology class at Ole Miss, two outraged readers responded to the newspaper's slanted coverage, which was headlined, "Ole Miss Students Get Lots of Civil Rights Propaganda."[448] Fred Taylor of Canton wrote, "May I congratulate you for, with unfailing accuracy, doing the wrong thing every single time?"[449] Kate Wilkinson of Jackson wrote, "May I demur to some of the hostile misrepresentations reported by your paper concerning guest visits by COFO workers to this university?"[450] A letter from D. Stephen Holbrook, a summer COFO volunteer from Utah, was also published. "Having been working on voter registration in the Mississippi Summer Project, I must say that it is an honor to have your opposition because your rhetoric is so childish and primitive in its provincial supposed self-interest," he wrote. "Before coming to Mississippi, I had thought the suggestion to send troops might be a little strong. I now wonder if it would be enough to ensure equal protection under the law."[451]

Toward the end of the summer, an editorial defense was made for the traditional Southern way of life, and racial troubles were blamed on the black population. "We have racial problems wherever we have concentrations of Negro populations," Hederman wrote.[452] Racial tolerance was blamed for the downfall of the nation in another reprinted editorial. "If prejudice means adhering to one's ideals and inherent beliefs, then we could use more prejudice in our nation. Tolerance is destroying our civilization," a reprinted editorial from Rayville, Louisiana, stated.[453] A front-page story, "Mississippi Project to Conclude August 24, Workers to Abandon State," incorporated derogatory comments gathered from officials in various towns and cities to downplay COFO's efforts.[454]

When the Jackson public schools were forced to desegregate the first grades in August, there was no opinion rendered by the Jackson *Clarion-Ledger*. When Jackson Mayor Thompson released a statement that "promised law and order" during the coming desegregation of the schools, the story was published on page three.[455] A week later, Thompson was quoted on page twelve as urging "peaceful desegregation of the schools or the federal government will come down here and run the schools just the way they want."[456] In late August, forty black first-graders enrolled in hitherto white public schools in the state's capital. The "calm" event was front-page news.[457]

Across town at the Jackson *Daily News*, the same negative attitude toward civil rights and the summer workers prevailed. Their arrival was heralded in a front-page story, "First Rider Wave Due This Weekend,[458] while another described the "shakes" that the "agitators" were having as Freedom Summer began.[459] The summer volunteers were referred to as "race mixing invaders"[460] and "racial zealots."[461] In July, during a protest in Jackson, civil rights workers who participated were described as "unkempt agitators" in Ward's front-page "Crossroads" column. "It was a nauseating scene," he wrote.[462] Ward used "Crossroads" all summer to degrade the volunteers with poems and puns and was particularly determined to discredit the "liberal" media. CBS was renamed the "Colored Broadcast System," ABC was the "African Broadcast Corporation," and NBC was the "Negro Broadcast Corporation."[463]

The COFO project was portrayed as an "agitation," rather than a civil rights project. Headlines read, "NCC Unveils Summer Agitation Plans"[464] and "CORE Regards Civil Rights Passage as New Signal for Agitation."[465] Like most other Mississippi daily newspapers, the Jackson *Daily News* covered activities around the state reported by the wire services more so than local civil rights activities. Similar to the Jackson *Clarion-Ledger*, most stories pertaining to Freedom Summer, other than the disappearance and deaths of Chaney, Schwerner and Goodman, were buried inside the newspaper rather than given front-page prominence.[466] Though many stories about bombings of churches and homes implicated or involved with the civil rights movement were published in the Jackson *Daily News*, an August editorial suggested that "bombings aren't news when the bombing sites are integrated love pads."[467] Any chance to discredit the civil rights workers by alleging a connection to the Communist Party was printed.[468]

When the desegregation of the Jackson public schools was mandated for the 1964–1965 school year by court decree, the front-page headline in the Jackson *Daily News* blared, "Mixing Ordered in Schools Here."[469] In late August, a Jackson *Daily News* editorial commended citizens for their "praiseworthy restraint" during the school registration but emphasized that it was "a manifestation of good behavior" rather than approval of forced desegregation. "As the event comes to pass, this city becomes a little bit pregnant with integration but the condition came about not voluntarily, but with Federalized rape," Ward wrote. "We view the succeeding years with gross pessimism as the problem of public schools becomes more one of maintaining order rather than schoolroom instruction. Such has been the experience of others in this ignoble experiment called race-mixing."[470]

In Laurel, Jay West at the *Laurel Leader-Call* began the summer by denying rumors that he was a Communist or had bombed his own newspaper a week earlier.[471] West's first and only editorial reference to the civil rights workers was in late June, when he advised President Johnson to "halt" the Freedom Summer project. "The general climate is not conducive to calm, reasoned thinking at a time when it is most needed," he wrote.[472] In late July, a news article reported that black voter registration had slowed in the Laurel area and that in order to vote in the November presidential election, an applicant had to have registered to vote two weeks earlier.[473]

Unlike the Jackson daily newspapers, the *Laurel Leader-Call* made an attempt to cover local civil rights activity and published wire service reports of incidents from around the state.[474] In the third week of June, when COFO workers began arriving in Laurel, a front-page headline advised readers, "Poise and Forbearance Urged for Local People," and the ensuing article reported that the Laurel Chamber of Commerce was requesting that people remain "calm and cool."[475] In early July, according to Doug McAdam's report from the summer workers, "the Laurel police were barely able to prevent a race riot" after two blacks attempted to desegregate the Laurel Burger Chef.[476] The incident, although covered in the *Laurel Leader-Call*, was referred to in the newspaper as "a slight altercation."[477] The AP account concurred with McAdam and described violent activity in which "fifty whites and thirty blacks clashed."[478] Following the incident, Laurel Mayor A.S. Scott met with local blacks in a closed session that the *Laurel Leader-Call* was excluded from covering.[479] A few days later, the *Laurel Leader-Call* reported on the "tests" in Laurel restaurants by the touring NAACP members. "Some local restaurants agree to deny service to Negroes, but not all," West wrote. "S.H. Kress, Holiday Inn and Woolworth served blacks with no trouble, and said it was acceptable if the Negroes request peaceable service."[480] Also in early July, Laurel was in UPI news when the Laurel Police Department added four blacks to the force.[481] The *Laurel Leader-Call* announced the decision in several supportive front-page articles.[482] The same day, the newspaper reported in a page-two article that the town had "returned to normal" since the NAACP tour departed.[483] One ongoing local story during Freedom Summer followed by the *Laurel Leader-Call* involved a civil rights worker from Iowa who was charged with vagrancy and tried as the first civil rights worker to face charges in Jones County. The woman's trial took only twenty minutes, and she was given a ten-day suspended sentence.[484] Two weeks later, she unsuccessfully appealed the decision.[485] In August, when three local blacks were beaten with baseball bats as they attempted to eat at S.H. Kress' lunch counter,[486] the incident was front-page news.[487] The next day, when a white volunteer was beaten unconscious at a Laurel gas station, that incident was also reported in a front-page story.[488] Toward the end of the summer, when COFO was evicted from its Laurel Freedom School location for "unsanitary conditions in a wooden, shotgun building," the story and an accompanying photo of the building confirmed the report.[489] The *Laurel Leader-Call*, while offering sparse editorial guidance to its readers, reported the events that occurred locally during Freedom Summer.

At the McComb *Enterprise-Journal*, Emmerich was an outspoken opponent of the 1964 Civil Rights Act and justified his stance with the notion that blacks and whites were inherently different. In an editorial in early July, "This Could Be a Case of Reality, Not Prejudice," he wrote, "Different races have different traits."[490] Emmerich's initial response to the impending summer project was to warn readers not to believe unsubstantiated rumors[491] and to maintain calm.[492] A republished editorial from the Perkinston Junior College *Bulldog Barks* in southern Mississippi advocated "reason."[493] In early July, Emmerich's front-page editorial column, "Highlights in the Headlines," reported that summer workers were in the area only to help register voters and that all residents should remain "peaceful."[494] In his editorials, derogatory statements directed toward the civil rights workers were never heard during Freedom Summer. The antagonistic opinions of others were, however, such as McComb Mayor Gordon Burt[495] and Governor Johnson,[496] and a statement by former Mississippi Governor Ross Barnett was headlined, "Ross Suggests Righters Bathe."[497] An editorial from the *Lowell* (Massachusetts) *Liberator* implied that the summer volunteers were the unsuspecting victims of "hard-boiled left wingers and Communists, part of an over-all scheme to destroy the United States by way of racial revolution."[498]

McComb, like Greenwood, was torn by racial trouble all summer, beginning in the spring and extending into the fall. Many acts of violent intimidation toward progressive blacks and whites were also recorded.[499] The first reported incident of racial violence during Freedom Summer in McComb happened in early June, when three Northern white men were "ambushed" in the county and beaten. The story was covered by the wire services, and the McComb *Enterprise-Journal* printed the AP version rather than a staff-written report.[500] A week later, when a local black mechanic was beaten with a leather strap by four white men who also questioned him about the NAACP, staff writer Charles Dunagin reported the story.[501] A few days later, Dunagin covered the first three in a series of bombings that occurred at the homes of McComb blacks, including the president of the local NAACP. The story was front-page news and offered photographs of the crime scenes.[502] The day after the bombings, a black police officer, Verhill Felder, was hired by the McComb Police Department "to work in Negro areas."[503] Within a month, Felder had been shot at, and missed, by an unknown assailant.[504] An article by Dunagin reported the continuing investigation of the three bomb attacks.[505] Within a few days of the McComb *Enterprise-Journal*'s coverage, a note in a bottle was thrown at Dunagin's house. The missive, signed "KKK" and printed in full on the front page of the newspaper, warned the reporter to keep his coverage of "anti-civil rights action off the front page."[506] Though denounced in the news article, Emmerich never mentioned the incident in his editorials.[507]

The McComb *Enterprise-Journal* was the voice of a community that wanted to maintain peace. A few days after passage of the Civil Rights Act, the local members of the Mississippi Restaurant Association released a statement announcing that they wanted to "get along with the public." No mention was made of whether this would entail compliance or defiance of the Civil Rights Act.[508] Mayor Burt declared his desire for a peaceful summer of "law and order,"[509] and the local Lion's Club offered its support.[510] The local Jaycees and the Rotary Club also "pledged law and order."[511]

In early July, COFO announced that no civil rights workers would be sent to the southwestern area of the state near McComb because of a history of "terror and vigilantism." The AP story was headline news in the McComb *Enterprise-Journal*.[512] Despite the COFO announcement, seven volunteers came to McComb in early July, and their arrival was reported in another front-page article.[513] The summer home of the group was bombed two days later. Only minor injuries were reported.[514]

The McComb *Enterprise-Journal* covered local stories related to Freedom Summer from staff reports and printed wire service stories regarding related activities around the state.[515] The reports of local COFO activity by staff writer Charles Gordon usually contained references to the summer volunteers' racially and sexually mixed living arrangements. In a mid-August story about an unsuccessful search by McComb police for illegal liquor in two COFO houses, Gordon wrote that a "large number of white man and Negro men were asleep in the house," including a white man and a black man who were sleeping together.[516] These "mixed quarters" greatly disturbed many white citizens and disgusted Mayor Burt, who was also the head of the local Citizens' Council.[517] "Niggers and whites, girls and boys together, unmarried and unchaperoned," Burt said later. "That's the one thing that set this town off."[518]

In mid-July, a civil rights worker was struck on the head by a white man when they both stopped their cars at a street light.[519] A few days earlier, a black church in the county, Mt. Zion Hill Baptist Church, was bombed and burned to the ground. The pastor had allowed COFO to use his other church building in McComb.[520] As the violent events began to occur more regularly, there was a possibility that the town would be placed under martial law. The front-page announcement of the action, which never materialized, reported that "the last time troops were sent to McComb was in 1911 during a union strike on the railroad."[521] Two days later, Mt. Vernon Missionary Baptist, a black church founded in the 1880s and not affiliated with the civil rights movement, was burned to the ground.[522] Emmerich's only editorial in relation to the church burnings was to reprint a column from the *Baptist Record*, "Church Burnings No Solution."[523] He made no mention of the KKK crosses burned during the summer,[524] although he reprinted an editorial from neighboring editor Paul Pittman of the *Tylertown Times*, who called the actions "cowardly attempts to intimidate good citizens."[525]

A report by Gordon in August dealt with a heavily publicized, but sparsely attended, voter registration drive in Magnolia, a small town about ten miles south of McComb. The event drew many journalists but only six potential black voters, and, according to Gordon's report, both groups were primarily concerned with "trying to keep from burning up under the merciless, absolutely equalized Mississippi sun." Gordon quoted Pike County Sheriff R.R. Warren's "kindly, deadly serious" warning that qualified blacks would get a "proper chance" to register but that there could be "no Nigerian tribal dancing."[526]

In late July, Albert "Red" Heffner, Jr., an insurance salesman in McComb and friend of Emmerich, invited two civil rights workers to his house. After the visit was reported to local police, harassment and threats began. Heffner released a statement that was published on the front page of the McComb *Enterprise-Journal* in which he explained that the meeting was an informational gathering, not "entertainment."[527] Within a month, the Heffners and their two teenage daughters, Jan, who was the reigning Miss Mississippi, and Carla, who wrote a teen column for the McComb *Enterprise-Journal,*[528] decided to leave town for good. They said that following the COFO visit to their home, their telephone was tapped, their dog was poisoned, and Heffner was evicted from his rented office space.[529] Emmerich never spoke out in the family's defense in his editorials during Freedom Summer and later said, "Red and Malva were better off without publicity at the time."[530]

Several incidents were recorded by the summer volunteers in McComb that were not reported by the McComb *Enterprise-Journal*. The owner of a local black club near the Freedom School was arrested and beaten by a police officer who told him, "Now that you have white people in here you're getting uppity." Two black boys got harassing phone calls from white girls, and then the boys were arrested and sent to jail. The house of the parents of a local black volunteer was burned. Three black voter registrants were told that they would be arrested if they didn't leave the county courthouse, and local voter registration workers were arrested for loitering.[531]

In late August, a COFO volunteer confessed to spreading a bomb rumor.[532] That single incident altered future reports of bombings in the newspaper. By the end of August, the McComb *Enterprise-Journal* was putting the words "bombed" and "bombing" in quotation marks nearly every time they were used in a story. The articles in the McComb *Enterprise-Journal* were almost exclusively drawn from interviews with law enforcement officials, never COFO staffers. Gordon later explained, "I trusted them [the COFO volunteers] as far as I trusted APWR, about as far as you could throw a bull."[533]

Emmerich may have offered editorial leadership to his readers in the fall of 1964 as the racial violence in McComb intensified,[534] but the McComb *Enterprise-Journal* provided little guidance to its readers in the heat of the summer. Although news coverage at the newspaper reported local and statewide events, the McComb *Enterprise-Journal* did not play a strong leadership role in the community during Freedom Summer.

At the *Meridian Star*, Skewes continued his Southern segregationist traditionalism,[535] referring to the Civil Rights Act as "another step toward ending freedom."[536] He called on his readers to maintain "law and order" during the coming COFO project[537] and published the "Yankee, Go Home!" editorial from the *Oelwein* (Iowa) *Register*.[538] He referred to the civil rights movement as "the so-called Negro revolution."[539] Other than that, the summer workers were ignored in the editorial columns of the *Meridian Star* until the bodies of Chaney, Schwerner and Goodman were discovered in August. *Meridian Star* executive editor Jerry Kerns observed later: "We killed off CORE purposively. There would be an attempted sit-in or something and those folks would be hauled off to the police station immediately. We didn't give it any publicity and if you don't get publicity for something like that, you cannot get far."[540]

Meridian, where the local Citizens' Council called for non-compliance to the Civil Rights Act until it was tested in court,[541] was the home of James Chaney, one of the three civil rights workers who disappeared in Philadelphia on 22 June. The story was one of the few covered by the *Meridian Star* concerning Freedom Summer, and the initial article after the three vanished was a UPI report headlined, "Clueless Trail Is Left by Interracial Trio."[542] A staff-written report focused on the fact that the disappearance was probably a publicity hoax,[543] and a UPI story raising the same suspicions followed.[544] Philadelphia, where the three disappeared, is about twenty miles northwest of Meridian. The communities are closely tied, and the *Meridian Star* offered daily coverage of the search for almost two weeks after the men disappeared. Staff writers covered the case with the articles "Neshoba Citizens Dislike Invasion of Newsmen"[545] and "Still No Trace of Missing Men, It's Possible They Left State."[546] The readers of the *Meridian Star* were continuously led to believe either that the disappearance was a publicity hoax or that the three men had fled in fear.

Three front-page stories addressed the finding of the bodies of Chaney, Schwerner and Goodman.[547] When Chaney was buried in Meridian three days later, the 700 people who attended his funeral and memorial made front-page news.[548] Editorially, Skewes placed the blame for the murders of the three men on the civil rights movement in general and on the workers themselves.[549]

Throughout Freedom Summer, incidents regarding civil rights activities in other areas of the state reported by the wire services were published in the *Meridian Star*.[550] More often than not, these stories had a derogatory, "you had it coming" headline, with the summer volunteers being described as "invaders," "mixers," and "righters," as if they deserved the problems and violence that often befell them. Many incidents were reported by the summer volunteers that were not reported in the *Meridian Star*. The Mount Moriah Baptist Church, a black church in a white neighborhood, was burned to the ground. A white volunteer was arrested and asked if he knew what race he was, and a city bus driver refused to let a passenger board who was wearing a CORE button.[551]

Skewes offered no editorial leadership to his readers during Freedom Summer, other than to congratulate and encourage those who opposed the Civil Rights Act. Although coverage at the newspaper reported local and statewide events, the *Meridian Star* did not play a strong role in the community during Freedom Summer, except to chide the summer project and volunteers. Toward the end of the summer, as three school systems in the state were forced to desegregate, Skewes described the "horrors of school integration" to his readers. "It is our sacred obligation to keep up the fight for our precious Southern way of life," he wrote. "We must never rest until this foul pollution of integration is forever banished from our soil."[552]

At the *Natchez Democrat*, the only mention of the summer workers in an editorial column was in early June, when readers were advised to "completely ignore them."[553] Lambert also warned, "Law and order are absolutely essential."[554] As Freedom Summer volunteers arrived in the state, Lambert declared that Mississippi had the best race relations in the country and that "thinking, responsible Negro citizens know this."[555] When the Mississippi Economic Council met in Natchez in June and called for residents of the state to "meet the summer project with dignity and patience," the event was covered by the *Clarksdale Press Register*,[556] but not by the *Natchez Democrat* or any of the other daily newspapers in the state.

Natchez was the birthplace of the Americans for the Preservation of the White Race. Meetings of the APWR were front-page news at the *Natchez Democrat*, including the election of officers at a gathering of 200 members.[557] In late June, the APWR accused the FBI of "smearing" the state because of the disappearance of Chaney, Schwerner and Goodman. The allegation, reported by the AP, was headline news in the *Natchez Democrat*.[558]

Wire service reports of civil rights activities from around the state were published, though infrequently, in the *Natchez Democrat.*[559] When Lambert directed his readers to "ignore" the volunteers, he took his own advice to heart. The *Natchez Democrat* reported when volunteers arrived in Meridian, on the other side of the state, but not when they arrived in Natchez.[560] The announcement in early July by SNCC director Bob Moses that workers would not be sent to southwestern Mississippi because it was "too dangerous" was one of the few times that the summer project was mentioned with a local perspective in the *Natchez Democrat.*[561]

Several incidents reported by the summer volunteers in Natchez were not reported by the *Natchez Democrat.* Within an hour after three SNCC workers arrived in Natchez to organize an office on 12 July, one was arrested for failure to halt at a stop sign. The COFO group in Natchez was under continual police surveillance, and a local black man was taken into police custody for walking with two SNCC staffers. A passing car fired shots at black businessman Archie Curtis' Funeral Home, and Curtis was later beaten. A tavern next door to the COFO office, owned by a white man and a black woman who lived together, was bombed, and the owner of a house rented by SNCC workers told the volunteers that he did not want them as boarders for fear of having his house blown up.[562]

When two black churches were burned down in the Natchez area in mid-July, Bethel Methodist and Jerusalem Baptist, the front-page report in the *Natchez Democrat* offered little information.[563] The next day, however, a fund-raising campaign by local white residents was being touted by the newspaper in order to replace the destroyed buildings,[564] and, according to the headlines, there was "Much Interest in Rebuilding."[565] The effort became the newspaper's own, with regular reminders and reports.[566] Less than two weeks into the drive, when the building fund reached more than $2,000, the *Natchez Democrat* applauded the generosity of the community,[567] as it did when the fund swelled to $4,000.[568] The Natchez City Bank was smothered with praise for donating $1,000.[569]

In mid-August, as the summer project was winding down, the KKK asked to use Liberty Park in Natchez for a rally. They were denied access based on a city law that no political rallies could be held in that park.[570] Just two weeks later, a front-page article reported that a crowd of 2,000 people gathered at Liberty Park to hear a speech by KKK grand wizard Robert Shelton, Jr. The crowd burned a cross, and Shelton gave, according to the report, a "very sane and sensible talk," including a reminder of the importance of maintaining segregation to "avoid the mongrelization of the race."[571] No mention was made of how the KKK obtained use of the park.

Lambert offered scarce editorial leadership to his readers during Freedom Summer, other than to suggest non-compliance with the newly enacted Civil Rights Act and ostracism of the civil rights workers in the area. News coverage at the *Natchez Democrat*, both local and statewide, failed to offer comprehensive information to the community.

At the Pascagoula *Chronicle*, W. David Brown replaced the open-minded Ira Harkey in 1963, and Gary Holland replaced Brown in August 1964, when Brown left for a position at the *Louisville* (Kentucky) *Times.*[572] Brown and Holland were no Harkey. A firm critic of the 1964 Civil Rights Act, Brown's idea regarding the summer civil rights workers was that they should have stayed at home and "minded their own business"[573] and that the entire project seemed "confused."[574] The Pascagoula *Chronicle* also reprinted the Jackson *Advocate* letter from Joseph Albright, a black man who advised the civil rights workers, or "saviors," to "go home."[575]

Civil rights activities from around the state reported by the wire services were published, though somewhat infrequently, in the Pascagoula *Chronicle.*[576] The COFO office closest to Pascagoula was about five miles north in Moss Point, but activity there was covered extensively by the Pascagoula *Chronicle*. The day when they arrived in Moss Point, two COFO workers were taken into "protective custody" by the Moss Point police, an incident covered as a front-page story in the Pascagoula *Chronicle.*[577] Two days later, Jackson County Sheriff Cecil Byrd and three of his eleven black deputies were featured in a photograph on the front page of the newspaper asking residents to "abide by the law." In the article, Byrd described the local COFO workers. "They are a shady bunch, usually poorly dressed and many appear emotionally unstable," the sheriff said. "We talked to one who did not believe in God and would not fight for his country."[578]

In early July, a black man, Jesse Gillespie, was in Moss Point distributing anti-COFO literature, "Views of Southern Negro Told."[579] The next day, Gillespie helped organize an anti-COFO group in Moss Point and again received front-page coverage.[580] In mid-July, Circuit Judge Darwin Maples announced his terms of compliance with the 1964 Civil Rights Act. He told the Pascagoula *Chronicle* that he would recommend that the mandates of the new law be followed, but only after "the Justice Department would condemn the activities of admitted Communists in Mississippi."[581] Exactly who these known "Reds" were or how the Justice Department was supposed to "stop" them, Maples did not say. The next day, the judge ordered a COFO volunteer with voter registration material to stay out of the county courthouse. No connection between the volunteer and the Communist Party was indicated in the news report.[582]

Most arrests of the summer volunteers were for petty offenses, real or fabricated, and many were reported by the Pascagoula *Chronicle*, particularly if the stories came from the wire services. There were often fines for illegal parking and vagrancy violations.[583] In early August, sixty local blacks and two white COFO volunteers were arrested in Pascagoula at a voter rally and charged with breach of peace.[584] At a trial the next day, charges were altered to "threatening breach of peace," a newly designated offense.[585] Several incidents were reported by the summer volunteers that were not reported in the Pascagoula *Chronicle*. The Knights of Pythias Hall in Moss Point, used for voter rallies, was firebombed. Moss Point police pressured black café owners not to serve civil rights workers; two Moss Point black men and one black woman were fired from their jobs for attending voter rallies, and a volunteer who left the project because of arrests and harassment returned from New York with $2,000 to assist COFO.[586]

As Freedom Summer came to an end, a UPI story reported that more than a half million blacks had been added to the voter registration rolls in the South in just a few months.[587] In response, newly appointed Pascagoula *Chronicle* editor Holland urged his white readers to register to vote and to remember to vote in every local, statewide and national election.[588] Brown and Holland offered little editorial leadership to their readers during Freedom Summer, other than to suggest non-compliance with the newly enacted Civil Rights Act and condemnation of the civil rights workers in the area. News coverage at the Pascagoula *Chronicle*, both local and statewide, failed to offer comprehensive information to its readers.

At the *Starkville Daily News*, the front-page "Pencil Shavings" column, written by publisher Harris, referred to the summer workers as "beatniks and nutniks,"[589] and "misguided young people."[590] When actor Harry Belafonte donated $70,000 to the COFO office in Greenwood, Harris wrote, "Hurrah, now these unkempt beatniks can buy their own soap." He went on to comment, "Cash, not conviction, is what brings the COFO workers into the state."[591] Syndicated columnist Paul Harvey warned that the summer workers would only cause trouble for black citizens,[592] while an unsigned editorial, possibly written by Nash, stressed, "We do not condone violence."[593] The ultraconservative Harris told his readers that, politically, "[a]s far as we're concerned, you can't get too far right,"[594] and he informed them that they were not legally bound to talk with FBI agents who were in town "digging through local records."[595] The Leflore County Bar Association supported Harris with a published response: "A citizen is under no legal obligation at any time to answer any questions asked by any investigator about anything except at a court hearing or at a court-connected proceeding."[596]

There was no COFO office in Starkville during Freedom Summer, and the only police activity directed toward any civil rights workers was when the Starkville police chief followed two volunteers from nearby Aberdeen and gave an "anti-agitator" speech to the local blacks talking with them.[597] Sheriff Bill Harpole released a statement to the *Starkville Daily News* in June regarding the "readiness" of county law enforcement to deal with any trouble stirred up by COFO,[598] but his office was never called upon. Harpole later told the local Chamber of Commerce that "civil rights work is Communist inspired."[599] Except for extensive coverage of the disappearance and murders of Chaney, Goodman and Schwerner, only a few wire reports regarding Freedom Summer activity from around the state were published in the *Starkville Daily News.*[600] Other than to editorially condemn the civil rights movement on all levels, the newspaper was silent.

In Tupelo, there was no COFO office during Freedom Summer, and the *Daily Journal* made no mention of the summer project in the editorials until the end of July, when readers were reminded that the civil rights workers would be leaving the state soon and urged to "show a little more patience."[601] The local district attorney, Jack Doty of Lee County, told the Tupelo Civitan Club in late June that any acts of violence toward the civil rights workers would only "play into the hands" of the civil rights "invaders."[602] In August, Rutherford expressed his support for "qualified" blacks being allowed to vote. He then told his black readers that a COFO campaign was not a substitute for a formal education and encouraged them to attend school.[603] He complained that more damage was done during Freedom Summer by COFO than good was gained[604] and told his community they should have pride in their state.[605] The only recorded incident related to civil rights in Tupelo during Freedom Summer was when the local voter registration office was the site of an arson attempt in late August.[606] Besides coverage of the disappearance and murders of Schwerner, Goodman and Chaney, the Tupelo *Daily Journal* also offered its readers extensive statewide reports from the wire services.[607]

On the Mississippi River, the *Vicksburg Evening Post* accused the civil rights workers of "turning their backs on responsibility" by causing racial agitation.[608] Cashman urged his community to leave law enforcement in the hands of law enforcement officials during Freedom Summer.[609] Except for coverage of the disappearance and murders of Chaney, Schwerner and Goodman, wire service reports of civil rights activities around the state were rarely published in the *Vicksburg Evening Post.*[610] As if to downplay the arrival of the COFO workers in late June, headline news in Vicksburg was, "Fighting Flares in Borneo."[611] The only local activity reported by the *Vicksburg Evening Post* was when eight blacks were served, without incident, at the local Woolworth's lunch counter.[612]

The big news in Vicksburg during the summer, according to the *Vicksburg Evening Post*, was the Miss Mississippi pageant, which was held there in late July. The even bigger news was that the newly elected Miss Mississippi was a hometown girl, Judy Simono.[613] When Martin Luther King, Jr., went to Mississippi in July for a four-day tour, his arrival in the state was reported by the *Vicksburg Evening Post,*[614] and his departure was reported,[615] but no coverage was offered of his stay or speech in Vicksburg.

Despite the lack of coverage of local civil rights activity by the *Vicksburg Evening Post*, many incidents were recorded by the summer volunteers. Several whites in a car chased and shot at a black motorcycle rider. A black woman was threatened for registering to vote. Several white boys threw a rock through the window of a car picking up a black child for Freedom

School. A homemade bomb was thrown through the window of a black café. A black milkman's assistant lost his job because he attended classes at the Freedom School, and a bottle was thrown through the window of a barbershop owned by a Freedom Democrat.[616] Basically, the *Vicksburg Evening Post* failed to offer its readers an overview of the local news regarding Freedom Summer civil rights activities.

In West Point at the *Times-Leader*, staunch conservative Harris was elected vice president of the Mississippi Press Association in 1964.[617] As Freedom Summer began, Harris warned his readers that the civil rights workers wanted to instigate violence and that the community should not respond. "You may be certain that all of these outsiders are coming into Mississippi with the hope that violence will erupt," he wrote. "We must not let this happen."[618] Mississippi Congressman Tom Abernethy of West Point concurred with Harris. "Their concealed aim is to beget strife and bloodshed, to provoke the federal government into some sort of occupancy by United States marshals or troops," he said.[619] Harris had no respect for the organizers of the summer project. He referred to the NAACP and COFO as "Communist-inspired groups,"[620] and he recommended to his white readers that they "stick together."[621] Despite his blatant Southern traditionalism, Harris did not advocate violence to maintain the social system in Mississippi. "This newspaper does not condone violence," he wrote.[622] Senator Stennis was also quoted in the West Point *Times-Leader* appealing for non-violence.[623] There were no COFO office in West Point during Freedom Summer and no reported incidents involving civil rights workers there.[624] Except for coverage of the disappearance and murders of Chaney, Schwerner and Goodman, wire service reports of activities in other areas of the state were rarely reported in the West Point *Times-Leader*. The words "civil rights" were always placed in quotation marks.[625]

SUMMARY OF COVERAGE

In the opening days of Freedom Summer, most Mississippi daily newspapers cost a nickel a copy, and several complex social issues already faced the state. Passage of the 1964 Civil Rights Act was imminent, the Equal Pay for Women Act of 1963 took effect,[626] and the Mississippi Legislature was about to end half a century of liquor prohibition in the state. Increased federal involvement with the war in Vietnam was beginning to cause concern for many Mississippians with sons and brothers of draft age, but not to any great extent until the end of Freedom Summer and the Gulf of Tonkin incident. According to historian Daniel Hallin, "Aside from a fleeting awareness of the Buddhist crisis of 1963, Vietnam probably entered the consciousness of most Americans for the first time in August 1964."[627]

As evidenced by the majority of the editors of the Mississippi daily press, the issues of concern addressed during Freedom Summer were the same as those addressed following the federal order to desegregate Ole Miss in 1962 and to desegregate the public schools following *Brown v. Board of Education* in 1954 and the Dixiecrat walkout of the Democratic National Convention in 1948: (1) black and white Mississippians were not ready for the reality of a desegregated society, and (2) national civil rights laws that supplanted states' and individual rights were probably unconstitutional. According to Mississippi daily press editorials during Freedom Summer, the notion that blacks and whites should dine at the same lunch counters or be educated and socialize together based on the equality of the races was a concept that remained inconceivable to most.

The propensity toward reporting civil rights issues in Mississippi daily newspapers during Freedom Summer ranged from daily news coverage with two or more stories, which was the norm, to virtual silence. The majority of the news stories reported about Freedom Summer activities and printed in the Mississippi daily press came from the wire services, AP and UPI. Most of the nineteen Mississippi daily newspapers published editorials at least once a week during Freedom Summer concerning some aspect of the civil rights movement, but the issue was unquestionably a top news story on the front pages of the Mississippi daily press during the summer.

Contrary to what media critics have noted about the promotion of violent suppression of civil rights activity in a small sampling of Southern newspapers,[628] the Mississippi daily press did not advocate violence to prevent civil rights activity during Freedom Summer. Not once was this found in any of the nineteen newspapers. However, the Mississippi daily press, as an aggregate, did reject the concept of desegregation of the state's society, and the usual rationalization was the preservation of the traditional Southern way of life.

In their news coverage of the civil rights issues during Freedom Summer, the two most widely circulated Mississippi daily newspapers, the Jackson *Clarion-Ledger* and the Jackson *Daily News*, were somewhat more representative of the Mississippi daily press than they had been during the desegregation of Ole Miss in 1962 or the *Brown v. Board of Education* decision in 1954. The staff-written stories in the Jackson *Clarion-Ledger* and the Jackson *Daily News* were much more virulent, however, than staff-written stories in the other newspapers, and the editorials of Ward at the Jackson *Daily News* and Hills at the Jackson *Clarion-Ledger* certainly deserved a reputation for propagating racial polarization, intensifying the opposition of Mississippi whites to racial integration, and condescension toward blacks.[629] Except for Harris at the West Point *Times-Leader*, Skewes at the *Meridian Star*, Brown at the Pascagoula *Chronicle* and Lambert at the *Natchez Democrat*, however, this was not true of the other editors of the Mississippi daily press during Freedom Summer. While not advocating support for the Civil Rights Act of 1964 or offering their encouragement to the efforts of the COFO volunteers in the state, most editors of the Mississippi daily press were not venomous in their approach to the civil rights workers or Freedom Summer.

The Mississippi daily press attempted, for the most part, to localize the civil rights struggles during Freedom Summer by reporting local activity, although the editors often focused on racial strife "all over the nation,"[630] including Chicago,[631] New York City,[632] Harlem,[633] Brooklyn,[634] Dallas,[635] Rochester,[636] St. Augustine,[637] Massachusetts[638] and New Jersey.[639] In St. Augustine, particularly, the wire services covered, and the Mississippi daily press published, story after story pertaining to racial strife. One interesting report in mid-July pertained to the son of a black activist in St. Augustine who disappeared after entering a white restaurant in that Florida city. Word was spread by the news media through the young man's father, "If he doesn't turn up by dark, there better not be a white face on the streets of St. Augustine tomorrow." The teenager was back home, unharmed, before sunset.[640]

Editorial consensus pertaining to Freedom Summer was the "us against them" theme proposed during the 1948 Dixiecrat protest, the 1954 *Brown v. Board of Education* decision, and the desegregation of Ole Miss in 1962. This "invasion" by outsiders reaffirmed a commitment to the preservation of the traditional South and a local version of the states' rights controversy of 1948 and 1954—the right of each state, or rather the white power structure, to manage their lives without interference.

Carter in Greenville was the only editor of the Mississippi daily press to encourage his readers to give the Civil Rights Act and its mandates a chance. "What civil rights groups and whites alike need to do now is to give the bill a chance to work before running pell mell into the streets with angry accusations, ultimatums and impassioned speeches," he wrote.[641]

The COFO project may not have accomplished as much as they had planned in Mississippi during Freedom Summer, but half a million Southern blacks were registered to vote in 1964, bringing the total to almost 2 million in eleven states.[642] Also in 1964, the American military, including the National Guard, was instructed to remove "racial designations" from documents, except casualty reports.[643]

Racial issues continued to raise controversy in the state during Freedom Summer, more so than ever before as equal rights for blacks became a looming reality. According to a Harris Poll following the presidential election that year, in which Johnson was re-elected, "Mississippi voters are dominated by the race question to the exclusion of almost any other political consideration."[644]

NOTES

1. Bernard Schwartz, ed., *Statutory History of the United States: Civil Rights Part I* (New York: McGraw-Hill, 1970), 1018.

2. Ibid.

3. "Sending Illiterates to Vote Is Poor Way to Grant 'Rights,' " AP, Jackson *Daily News*, 19 June 1964, 2B.

4. "Attack on Mississippi," from the *Manchester* (New Hampshire) *Union Leader*, in the *Clarksdale Press Register*, 18 July 1964, 4; "Attack on Mississippi," from the *Manchester* (N.H.) *Union Leader*, in the Columbus *Commercial Dispatch*, 23 July 1964, 3; "Attack on Mississippi," from the *Manchester* (N.H.) *Union Leader*, in the *Greenwood Commonwealth*, 14 July 1964, 4; "Attack on Mississippi," from the *Manchester* (N.H.) *Union Leader* in the *Starkville Daily News*, 22 July 1964, 2; "Attack on Mississippi," from the *Manchester* (N.H.) *Union Leader*, in the West Point *Times-Leader*, 21 July 1964, 4.

5. "Civil Rights Vote in July Forecast," *Clarksdale Press Register*, UPI, 1 June 1964, 1; "More Delaying Tactics Due over Rights Bill," AP, Jackson *Clarion-Ledger*, 21 June 1964, 1; "Rights Measure May Be Stalled by Southerners," UPI, Pascagoula *Chronicle*, 16 June 1964, 2; "Senate Postpones Filibuster Halt Try," AP, *Natchez Democrat*, 7 June 1964, 1; "Southerners Dash Cold Water on Civil Rights Bill," UPI, Columbus *Commercial Dispatch*, 16 June 1964, 1; "Southerners Delay Civil Rights Measure," AP, *Greenwood Commonwealth*, 16 June 1964, 1; "Southern Protests Delay Rights Bill," AP, *Hattiesburg American*, 22 June 1964, 1; "To Bitter End, Southern Senators Still Fight Civil Rights Bill," UPI, Grenada *Sentinel-Star*, 11 June 1964, 1; "Weary Dixie Forces Still Holding Out," UPI, Greenville *Delta Democrat-Times*, 11 June 1964, 1.

6. "West Virginian Holds Floor Fourteen Hours and Thirteen Minutes," UPI, *Clarksdale Press Register*, 10 June 1964, 1.

7. "Last Rights Will Go Under with the Civil Rights Bill," AP, *Natchez Democrat*, 7 June 1964, 1; "Says Civil Rights Bill Would Destroy Many Government Programs," AP, *Natchez Democrat*, 11 June 1964, 1; "Stennis Captains Team of Southern Opposition to Civil Rights," UPI, Greenville *Delta Democrat-Times*, 7 June 1964, 1; "Stennis Raps FEPC Section of Civil Rights Bill," UPI, Corinth *Daily Corinthian*, 19 June 1964, 1.

8. "Civil Rights Backers Try to Tire Southerners," UPI, West Point *Times-Leader*, 17 June 1964, 1; "Civil Rights Advocates Gag Foes," UPI, *Clarksdale Press Register*, 4 June 1964, 10; "Cloture Imposed by Four Votes," UPI, *Starkville Daily News*, 11 June 1964, 1; "Cloture Vote Seen on Tuesday," AP, McComb *Enterprise-Journal*, 5 June 1964, 1; "Dixie Move Blocked, Civil Rights Supporters Start Counter Filibuster," UPI, *Clarksdale Press Register*, UPI, 3 June 1964, 1; "Gag Petitions Filed, Civil Rights Issue Closer to Voting," AP, *Meridian Star*, 8 June 1964, 1; "Gag Vote on Civil Rights Set Today," UPI, *Starkville Daily News*, 10 June 1964, 1;"Gag Rule Voted, Clears Way to Okay Civil Rights Bill," UPI, Pascagoula *Chronicle*, 10 June 1964, 1; "Move Aimed at Shutting Off Civil Rights Debate," AP, *Natchez Democrat*, 9 June 1964, 1; "National Senate Postpones Civil Rights Bill Showdown," AP, Jackson *Clarion-Ledger*, 7 June 1964, 1; "Petition for Cloture Is Due Today," UPI, Tupelo *Daily Journal*, 6–7 June 1964, 1; "Petition to Vote on Cloture," AP, Gulfport *Daily Herald*, 8 June 1964, 1; "Senate Chokes Dixie Talkathon," UPI, Corinth *Daily Corinthian*, 10 June 1964, 1; "Senate Majority Continues Plowing Under Dixie Moves," UPI, *Meridian Star*, 14 June 1964, 1; "Senate Optimistic on Civil Rights Passage," AP, *Laurel Leader-Call*, 5 June 1964, 1; "Senate Slaps Gag on South, 71–29," UPI, Jackson *Daily News*, 10 June

1964, 1; "Senate Squelches Civil Rights Bill Filibuster," AP, *Greenwood Commonwealth*, 10 June 1964, 1; "Senate Votes to Halt Filibuster," AP, *Hattiesburg American*, 10 June 1964, 1; "Southerner Admits Gag May Stick," UPI, West Point *Times-Leader*, 2 June 1964, 1.

9. "Big Filibuster Broken," AP, Jackson *Clarion-Ledger*, 11 June 1964, 1; "Civil Rights Cloture Showdown on Wednesday," UPI, Grenada *Sentinel-Star*, 9 June 1964, 1; "Civil Rights Leaders Deny Cloture Plan Hurt," AP, *Laurel Leader-Call*, 4 June 1964, 1; "Cloture Is Passed," AP, *Meridian Star*, 10 June 1964, 1; "Cloture Showdown on Civil Rights Bill May Come in Senate Today," AP, *Natchez Democrat*, 10 June 1964, 1; "Cloture Move Gets Sufficient Backing," AP, Jackson *Daily News*, 5 June 1964, 1; "Cloture Vote Is Coming Tuesday," AP, *Greenwood Commonwealth*, 5 June 1964, 1; "Cloture Vote Postponed 24 Hours," UPI, *Clarksdale Press Register*, 6 June 1964, 1; "Cloture Vote on Civil Rights Bill," AP, Gulfport *Daily Herald*, 11 June 1964, 1; "End of Filibuster May Speed Up Other Bills," AP, McComb *Enterprise-Journal*, 11 June 1964, 8; "Filibuster Seems Doomed, Cloture Gains Support," UPI, *Clarksdale Press Register*, 2 June 1964, 1; "Senate Approves Cloture, 71–29," UPI, Grenada *Sentinel-Star*, 10 June 1964, 1; "Senate Approves Filibuster Gag," UPI, West Point *Times-Leader*, 10 June 1964, 1; "Senate Chokes Off Debate on Civil Rights Bill," AP, *Laurel Leader-Call*, 10 June 1964, 1; "Senate Closes Door against Filibuster," AP, McComb *Enterprise-Journal*, 10 June 1964, 1; "Senate Invokes Cloture on Civil Rights," AP, *Natchez Democrat*, 11 June 1964, 1; "Senators Vote Cloture on Rights Bill," UPI, Greenville *Delta Democrat-Times*, 10 June 1964, 1; "Six Republicans, 23 Democrats, Vote Vainly on Debate Curb," UPI, *Clarksdale Press Register*, 10 June 1964, 1.

10. "Barry to Nix Civil Rights Bill," AP, Gulfport *Daily Herald*, 19 June 1964, 1; "Barry's No Seen on Civil Rights," AP, Jackson *Daily News*, 18 June 1964, 1; "Goldwater Defends Civil Rights Vote," UPI, Grenada *Sentinel-Star*, 29 June 1964, 1; "Goldwater Explains Opposition to Civil Rights Bill," UPI, Corinth *Daily Corinthian*, 19 June 1964, 1; "Goldwater Plans to Vote Nay on Civil Rights Measure," AP, *Starkville Daily News*, 19 June 1964, 1; "Goldwater to Vote against Civil Rights Bill," UPI, *Tupelo Daily Journal*, 19 June 1964, 1; "Goldwater Will Vote against Civil Rights Bill," AP, *Natchez Democrat*, 19 June 1964, 1; "Goldwater Votes against Gag, Also May Vote against Bill," UPI, *Clarksdale Press Register*, 10 June 1964, 1; "Goldy's Friends to Urge Vote Yes on Civil Rights Bill," AP, *Laurel Leader-Call*, 17 June 1964, 1; "Thrusts Civil Rights Issue into Race," UPI, *Clarksdale Press Register*, 19 June 1964, 1.

11. "8,675,945 Words Spoken on Bill," UPI, *Clarksdale Press Register*, 10 June 1964, 1; "Senate Shuts Off Debate on Civil Rights Measure," UPI, Columbus *Commercial Dispatch*, 10 June 1964, 1.

12. "Civil Rights Bill Passes after Longest Debate in History," AP, *Natchez Democrat*, 20 June 1964, 1.

13. "Dixie Concedes Early Passage of Rights Bill," UPI, Greenville *Delta Democrat-Times*, 14 June 1964, 1; "Fast House OK Forecast for Civil Rights," AP, Jackson *Daily News*, 14 June 1964, 1; "Final Approval of Rights Bill Seen," UPI, Corinth *Daily Corinthian*, 25 June 1964, 1; "Final Debate on Civil Rights Bill," UPI, Corinth *Daily Corinthian*, 15 June 1964, 1; "House Gets Senate Civil Rights Bill," AP, McComb *Enterprise-Journal*, 22 June 1964, 1; "LBJ Predicts Passage of Civil Rights Legislature," AP, *Natchez Democrat*, 7 June 1964, 1; "Leaders

Jam Civil Rights Down Dixie," UPI, *Starkville Daily News*, 18 June 1964, 1; "May Make Bill Law by July 4," UPI, *Clarksdale Press Register*, 20 June 1964, 1; "Passage of Civil Rights Bill Near," AP, Gulfport *Daily Herald*, 18 June 1964, 1; "Rights Bill Hits Blocks," AP, *Laurel Leader-Call*, 23 June 1964, 2; "Rights Bill Endangers Liberty, Freedom, Says Dixie Leaders," AP, *Vicksburg Evening Post*, 20 June 1964, 1; "Rights Bill Passage Is Seen Tonight or Friday," AP, McComb *Enterprise-Journal*, 18 June 1964, 1; "Senate Approves Civil Rights Bill, Expect Final Okay," UPI, Pascagoula *Chronicle*, 18 June 1964, 1; "Senate Charges Full Steam Ahead to Pass Rights Bill," UPI, Columbus *Commercial Dispatch*, 11 June 1964, 1; "Says Rights Vote May Be Wednesday," UPI, Corinth *Daily Corinthian*, 12 June 1964, 1; "Senate Nears Civil Rights Bill Vote," AP, *Greenwood Commonwealth*, 18 June 1964, 1; "Senate Okay of Civil Rights Bill Expected Late Today or Friday, Southern Fight Ends in Failure," UPI, *Meridian Star*, 18 June 1964, 1; "Senate Prepares for Vote on Civil Rights Bill, AP, *Hattiesburg American*, 18 June 1964, 1; "Southern Senators Lose Fight, Civil Rights Bill Passage Due by Morning," AP, *Laurel Leader-Call*, 19 June 1964, 1; "Strong Arm Rights Bill Heads for Vote," UPI, Columbus *Commercial Dispatch*, 19 June 1964, 1; "Try Passage of Rights Bill by July 4," UPI, *Clarksdale Press Register*, 13 June 1964, 1.

14. "Civil Rights Bill Vote Scheduled Today," UPI, Grenada *Sentinel-Star*, 19 June 1964, 1; "Civil Rights Bill on Verge of Passing," UPI, Greenville *Delta Democrat-Times*, 19 June 1964, 1; "Civil Rights Bill Passed in Senate," AP, Gulfport *Daily Herald*, 20 June 1964, 1; "Civil Rights Debate Nearing Conclusion," AP, Jackson *Clarion-Ledger*, 19 June 1964, 1; "House Is Ready to Act on Civil Rights Bill," UPI, *Clarksdale Press Register*, 1 July 1964, 1; "Passage of Civil Rights Bill Expected by Nightfall," AP, *Hattiesburg American*, 19 June 1964, 1; "Time Running Out in Rights Struggle," UPI, Greenville *Delta Democrat-Times*, 18 June 1964, 1; "Senate Nears Civil Rights Bill Vote," AP, *Greenwood Commonwealth*, 18 June 1964, 1.

15. "Civil Rights Bill Passes Senate after Long Fight, 73 to 27," AP, *Starkville Daily News*, 20 June 1964, 1; "Civil Rights Measure Passes Senate, 73 to 27," AP, Jackson *Clarion-Ledger*, 20 June 1964, 1; "Democratic Roll Call Ends Civil Rights Vote, 73 to 27," UPI, Greenville *Delta Democrat-Times*, 21 June 1964, 1; "Senate Approves Civil Rights Bill, 73–27," UPI, Tupelo *Daily Journal*, 20–21 June 1964, 1; "Senate Approves 'Rights' Bill 73 to 27," AP, *Meridian Star*, 20 June 1964, 1; "Senate's Okay Puts Civil Rights Bill in House," UPI, Pascagoula *Chronicle*, 21 June 1964, 1.

16. "Civil Rights Bill by Congress, Needs Johnson's OK," *Laurel Leader-Call*, 2 July 1964, 1; "Civil Rights Bill Due to Become Law Today," AP, McComb *Enterprise-Journal*, 2 July 1964, 1; "Civil Rights Bill Goes to LBJ for Signature," AP, *Hattiesburg American*, 2 July 1964, 1; "Civil Rights Bill Clears Congress," AP, Jackson *Daily News*, 2 July 1964, 1; "Civil Rights Bill Is Passed, Sent to President," UPI, West Point *Times-Leader*, 2 July 1964, 1; "Civil Rights Bill Ready for LBJ Inking," UPI, Columbus *Commercial Dispatch*, 2 July 1964, 1; "Harsh Civil Rights Bill Clears Final Real Barrier," AP, *Natchez Democrat*, 1 July 1964, 1; "House Clears Measure, President Expected to Sign Bill Tonight," UPI, *Clarksdale Press Register*, 2 July 1964, 1; "House Ready to Put Okay on Rights Bill," UPI, Corinth *Daily Corinthian*, 2 July 1964, 1; "Johnson to Sign Civil Rights Bill Tonight," UPI, Pascagoula *Chronicle*, 2 July 1964, 1; "LBJ Plans to Sign Civil Rights Bill on TV

Tonight," UPI, Grenada *Sentinel-Star*, 2 July 1964, 1; "LBJ Rights Okay Predicted Today," AP, *Vicksburg Evening Post*, 2 July 1964, "LBJ to Sign Rights Bill Before 4th," AP, *Hattiesburg American*, 1 July 1964, 1; "Rights Bill Waiting Final OK," UPI, *Meridian Star*, 2 July 1964, 1; "Rights Bill Becomes Law Tonight," UPI, Greenville *Delta Democrat-Times*, 2 July 1964, 1; "Rights Bill Close to Climax," AP, McComb *Enterprise-Journal*, 1 July 1964, 1; "Signing of Civil Rights Bill Now Seen," AP, Jackson *Daily News*, 1 July 1964, 1.

17. "Civil Rights Bill Passes as Southern Leaders Stand Pat," AP, *Natchez Democrat*, 3 July 1964, 1; "Civil Rights Measure Becomes Law," AP, *Starkville Daily News*, 3 July 1964, 1; "Govs. Wallace and Johnson Rap Passage of 'Unconstitutional' Civil Rights Bill," UPI, Corinth *Daily Corinthian*, 3 July 1964, 1; "Johnson Signs Civil Rights Bill in Historic Ceremony," AP, Jackson *Clarion-Ledger*, 3 July 1964, 1; "LBJ Signs Civil Rights Bill," UPI, Grenada *Sentinel-Star*, 3 July 1964, 1; "Let Courts Rule on Civil Rights, Says Paul," AP, *Greenwood Commonwealth*, 3 July 1964, 1; "President Signs Bill, Urges Compliance by All," UPI, Tupelo *Daily Journal*, 3 July 1964, 1; "President Urges Justice for All in Signing Civil Rights Bill," AP, *Vicksburg Evening Post*, 3 July 1964, 1; "Two Johnsons, Two Different Views on Civil Rights," UPI, Grenada *Sentinel-Star*, 3 July 1964, 1; "Wallace Won't Obey New Law," AP, *Laurel Leader-Call*, 4 July 1964, 1.

18. "Don't Comply Is Advice of Gov. Johnson," AP, Jackson *Daily News*, 3 July 1964, 1; "Don't Comply Until Law Is Tested, PBJ Advises," AP, McComb *Enterprise-Journal*, 3 July 1964, 1; "Gov. Advises Citizens Not to Comply with Law Until Tested," AP, *Hattiesburg American*, 3 July 1964, 1; "Gov. Johnson Pledges New Civil Rights Law to Be Challenged," AP, Jackson *Clarion-Ledger*, 5 July 1964, 1; "Gov. Johnson Pledges New Civil Rights Law to Be Challenged," AP, Jackson *Daily News*, 5 July 1964, 1; "Governor Deplores Civil Rights Timing," AP, *Starkville Daily News*, 3 July 1964, 1; "Governor Says Strife to Come from Civil Rights Law," UPI, Pascagoula *Chronicle*, 3 July 1964, 1; "Governor Sees Chaos in Civil Rights Bill," UPI, Tupelo *Daily Journal*, 3 July 1964, 1; "House Backs Paul on Noncompliance Stand," AP, *Starkville Daily News*, 9 July 1964, 1; "Paul Predicts Real Trouble under Civil Rights Bill," AP, *Natchez Democrat*, 3 July 1964, 1; "PBJ Expects 'Civil Strife and Disorder,' " UPI, West Point *Times-Leader*, 3 July 1964, 1; "PBJ Tells State Not to Comply, Advises Wait for Court Test," AP, *Laurel Leader-Call*, 3 July 1964, 1; "Should Refuse, Pending Tests, PBJ Says," UPI, *Meridian Star*, 3 July 1964, 1; "State Businessmen 'On Their Own' in Dealing with Civil Rights Act," Jackson *Daily News*, 3 July 1964, 1.

19. "NAACP Says Paul's Stand Is Dangerous," UPI, Corinth *Daily Corinthian*, 10 July 1964, 1.

20. "Future of Sovereignty Commission Uncertain," UPI, Pascagoula *Chronicle*, 23 August 1964, 2; "Sovereignty Commission Gets Five New Members," UPI, Jackson *Clarion-Ledger*, 23 August 1964, 13; "State to Put $200,000 in Fight on Rights Bill," AP, McComb *Enterprise-Journal*, 3 June 1964, 1.

21. "Eventual Repeal Seen by Wallace," AP, *Vicksburg Evening Post*, 20 June 1964, 1; "Gov. Wallace Predicts People to Vote Repeal If Civil Rights Bill Is Enacted," AP, *Laurel Leader-Call*, 9 June 1964, 1; "Wallace Says Civil Rights Bill, If Enacted, Will Be Repealed," AP, Jackson *Daily News*, 9 June 1964, 5; "Wallace Says Nation Should Resist Civil Rights Bill," AP, McComb *Enterprise-Journal*, 9 June 1964, 8; "Wallace Sees Civil Rights Bill Repeal," UPI, *Greenwood Common-*

wealth, 9 June 1964, 1; "Wallace Sees Civil Rights Bill Repeal," UPI, Pascagoula *Chronicle*, 12 June 1964, 1.

22. Joseph Ellis, Jr., "Law but Not Fact," *Clarksdale Press Register*, 7 July 1964, 4.

23. "Few Negroes Understand Details of Rights Bill," AP, Columbus *Commercial Dispatch*, 11 June 1964, 4.

24. "The Idea Is . . . ," from *Dixie Lumberman* (a Jackson, Mississippi, publication), in the Columbus *Commercial Dispatch*, 9 July 1964, 6.

25. Bill Simpson, "Rights Handwriting Was on Wall," Corinth *Daily Corinthian*, 19 June 1964, 3.

26. Bill Simpson, "Talk of Town," Corinth *Daily Corinthian*, 1 July 1964, 1.

27. Hodding Carter III, "The Day of Cloture," Greenville *Delta Democrat-Times*, 10 June 1964, 3.

28. Hodding Carter III, "The Civil Rights Bill Becomes Law," Greenville *Delta Democrat-Times*, 4 July 1964, 4.

29. Hodding Carter III, "Time to Wait," Greenville *Delta Democrat-Times*, 19 July 1964, 4.

30. Hodding Carter III, "Senator Ellender's Wise Advise," Greenville *Delta Democrat-Times*, 9 July 1964, 4.

31. Leonard Lowrey, "National Tragedy," *Hattiesburg American*, 11 June 1964, 10.

32. Leonard Lowrey, "The Civil Rights Law," from the *Hattiesburg American*, in the *Laurel Leader-Call*, 20 July 1964, 4; Leonard Lowrey, "The Law," *Hattiesburg American*, 6 July 1964, 14.

33. T.M. Hederman, Jr., "Civil Rights Measures Flout Letter and Spirit of Federal Constitution," Jackson *Clarion-Ledger*, 10 June 1964, 10.

34. "West Agrees Civil Rights Bill Kills More Liberty Than It Gives," Jackson *Clarion-Ledger*, 16 July 1964, 10.

35. "Freedom under the Constitution Includes the Right to Be Left Alone," Jackson *Clarion-Ledger*, 16 June 1964, 16.

36. Tom Etheridge, "Mississippi Notebook," Jackson *Clarion-Ledger*, 15 June 1964, 1.

37. James "Jimmy" Ward, "Liberals Will Rue Day They Pass Civil Rights Bill," Jackson *Daily News*, 11 June 1964, 12.

38. James "Jimmy" Ward, "The Bleak Road Ahead," Jackson *Daily News*, 25 June 1964, 12.

39. James "Jimmy" Ward, "Communists and Race Issue," Jackson *Daily News*, 2 June 1964, 6.

40. "California Congressman Says Communists in Summer Project," AP, *Greenwood Commonwealth*, 29 July 1964, 1; "California Lawmaker Hits State Civil Rights Group," UPI, Jackson *Clarion-Ledger*, 29 July 1964, 1; "California Solon Says Civil Rights Workers Aiding Commies," UPI, Jackson *Daily News*, 29 July 1964, 1; "California Solon Sees Conspiracy," UPI, Pascagoula *Chronicle*, 29 July 1964, 1; "Civil Rights Drive Is Branded Communist Conspiracy," AP, *Meridian Star*, 29 July 1964, 1; "Claims State Invaders Do Work for Communists," Gulfport *Daily Herald*, 29 July 1964, 1; "Mississippi Invasion Commie Conspiracy, Lawmaker Claims," UPI, Corinth *Daily Corinthian*, 29 July 1964, 7; "Mississippi Invasion Is Red Conspiracy," UPI, Grenada *Sentinel-Star*, 30 July 1964, 1; "Reds

Infiltrate Ranks of Civil Rights Workers in Mississippi," UPI, *Natchez Democrat*, 11 July 1964, 1; "Representative Utt Renders Public Service by Exposing Red Front Influence," Jackson *Clarion-Ledger*, 6 August 1964, 10; "Righters Invaded by Reds," AP, *Vicksburg Evening Post*, 29 July 1964, 1; "Solon Says Mississippi Invasion Engineered by Commie Conspiracy," UPI, Tupelo *Daily Journal*, 29 July 1964, 14.

41. "Sinister Force at Work in Mississippi," AP, *Natchez Democrat*, 29 July 1964, 1.

42. J.O. Emmerich, "Positions Reversed in a Heated Contest," McComb *Enterprise-Journal*, 14 July 1964, 2.

43. J.O. Emmerich, "Agonizing Decision," from the McComb *Enterprise-Journal*, in the *Clarksdale Press Register*, 9 July 1964, 4.

44. J.O. Emmerich, "Analyzing Agonizing Civil Rights Program," McComb *Enterprise-Journal*, 6 July 1964, 1.

45. James B. Skewes, "Long, Bitter Battle," *Meridian Star*, 14 June 1964, 4.

46. James B. Skewes, "Gap Is Widening," *Meridian Star*, 5 July 1964, 4.

47. James B. Skewes, "A Body Blow," *Meridian Star*, 12 June 1964, 4.

48. James B. Skewes, "The Ultimate Result? It's Mongrelization," *Meridian Star*, 20 June 1964, 4.

49. James B. Skewes, "God Help the USA," *Meridian Star*, 12 July 1964, 4.

50. James Lambert, "Our New Slavery," *Natchez Democrat*, 16 June 1964, 4.

51. James Lambert, "Civil Rights Bill," *Natchez Democrat*, 23 June 1964, 4.

52. James Lambert, "People Are Ahead," *Natchez Democrat*, 17 June 1964, 4.

53. James Lambert, "Attainment by Merit," *Natchez Democrat*, 9 June 1964, 4.

54. W. David Brown, "Historic Hypocrisy," Pascagoula *Chronicle*, 15 June 1964, 4.

55. W. David Brown, "It Should Be Remembered," Pascagoula *Chronicle*, 9 June 1964, 4.

56. W. David Brown, "How Cloture Came," Pascagoula *Chronicle*, 16 June 1964, 1.

57. W. David Brown, "Desecration of the Fourth," Pascagoula *Chronicle*, 24 June 1964, 4.

58. W. David Brown, "A Second Reconstruction," Pascagoula *Chronicle*, 6 July 1964, 4.

59. W. David Brown, "Let Reason Guide," Pascagoula *Chronicle*, 10 July 1964, 4.

60. W.H. Harris, "Pencil Shavings," *Starkville Daily News*, 3 June 1964, 4.

61. Ibid., 8 July 1964, 4.

62. W.H. Harris, "Pencil Shavings," West Point *Times-Leader*, 2 June 1964, 1.

63. Ibid., 3 July 1964, 1.

64. L.P. Cashman, Jr., "Civil Wrongs Bill Irks," *Vicksburg Evening Post*, 5 July 1964, 5.

65. L.P. Cashman, Jr., "The Real American Approach," *Vicksburg Evening Post*, 12 July 1964, 12.

66. "LBJ Scoffs at Rights of States," AP, Gulfport *Daily Herald*, 19 June 1964, 1.

67. "LBJ Administration Pours Salt into Wounds Inflicted on South," Jackson *Clarion-Ledger*, 5 August 1964, 8; "Salt into Wounds," *Natchez Democrat*, 11 August 1964, 4; "Segregated Meetings Declared Off Limits," UPI, Jackson *Daily News*, 15 July 1964, 4.

68. James Lambert, "LBJ Real Double Talker," *Natchez Democrat*, 27 July 1964, 4.

69. W. David Brown, "Leftist Collaboration," Pascagoula *Chronicle*, 26 June 1964, 4.

70. W. David Brown, "Should Stay Home," Pascagoula *Chronicle*, 9 July 1964, 4.

71. W.H. Harris, "Pencil Shavings," *Starkville Daily News*, 1 August 1964, 4.

72. "Hang Together or Separately, Ross Barnett," AP, *Meridian Star*, 5 July 1964, 1.

73. Tom Anderson, "Senator Lyndon Had Socialist Voting Record," West Point *Times-Leader*, 12 June 1964, 4.

74. James "Jimmy" Ward, "Speaking of Extremism," Jackson *Daily News*, 4 August 1964, 4.

75. Nelson Cauthen, letter to editor, Jackson *Daily News*, 4 August 1964, 11.

76. "Make White Folks Mad, But Not Too Mad," UPI, Columbus *Commercial Dispatch*, 30 June 1964, 4; "Make White Folks Mad Is Integrationist Tactic," Corinth *Daily Corinthian*, 30 June 1964, 4; "Wilkins Admits NAACP Aim Is to Make White Folks Mad," UPI, West Point *Times-Leader* 30 June 1964, 3.

77. "Attempt to Test Vote Law," AP, Gulfport *Daily Herald*, 3 July 1964, 1; "Battles Cross South as Bill Passes," UPI, Columbus *Commercial Dispatch*, 6 July 1964, 1; "Both Sides Prepare to Test Rights Bill, LBJ Signs Measure," UPI, Columbus *Commercial Dispatch*, 3 July 1964, 1; "Civil Rights Measure Being Put to Test across Nation," AP, *Hattiesburg American*, 3 July 1964, 1; "Civil Rights Tests Loom, Negroes Say," UPI, *Clarksdale Press Register*, 3 July 1964, 1; "Early Testing of Civil Rights Law Begins," UPI, Pascagoula *Chronicle*, 3 July 1964, 1; "Further Integration Tests Due in State," AP, Jackson *Daily News*, 6 July 1964, 1; "Little Time Is Wasted in Testing New Civil Rights Bill," UPI, West Point *Times-Leader*, 3 July 1964, 1; "NAACP Announces Statewide Testing of New Civil Rights Bill," UPI, Tupelo *Daily Journal*, 6 July 1964, 1; "Negro Leaders Vow Quick Civil Rights Law Tests," UPI, Tupelo *Daily Journal*, 20–21 June 1964, 1; "Negroes Begin Test of Civil Rights Bill," UPI, Greenville *Delta Democrat-Times*, 3 July 1964, 1; "Negroes Seek Mix Speed-Up," UPI, Columbus *Commercial Dispatch*, 16 July 1964, 1; "Ready to Test Rights Bill," AP, Gulfport *Daily Herald*, 3 July 1964, 1; "Rights Law Test Awaited," AP, *Vicksburg Evening Post*, 3 July 1964, 1; "Testing of 'Rights' Law Continues across Dixie," UPI, Jackson *Clarion-Ledger*, 7 July 1964, 1.

78. "Civil Rights Group Touring Mississippi," UPI, *Clarksdale Press Register*, 6 July 1964, 1; "Civil Rights Leaders Continue Mississippi Tour," UPI, Greenville *Delta Democrat-Times*, 7 July 1964, 1; "Civil Rights Leaders Continue Tour of Mississippi," UPI, Pascagoula *Chronicle*, 7 July 1964, 3; "Civil Rights Testers Fan into Mississippi," AP, *Greenwood Commonwealth*, 6 July 1964, 1; "Laurel Has Race Flurry," AP, Jackson *Clarion-Ledger*, 5 July 1964, 1; "Laurel Has Race Flurry," AP, Jackson *Daily News*, 5 July 1964, 1; "Mix Group Continues State Tour," UPI, West Point *Times-Herald*, 8 July 1964, 1; "Mix Invasion Entering

State," AP, *Laurel Leader-Call*, 6 July 1964, 1; "NAACP Leaders Inspecting Cities during Tour," AP, *Meridian Star*, 6 July 1964, 1; "NAACP Sends Inspection Team to Mississippi," AP, *Natchez Democrat*, 5 July 1964, 1; "Rights 'Fact Finders' Dissatisfied with Receptions in Some Areas of State," AP, *Vicksburg Evening Post*, 7 July 1964, 1; "Rights Group Testing Law of Land," AP, *Laurel Leader-Call*, 4 July 1964, 1; "Rights Leaders Ask for Talks," UPI, Columbus *Commercial Dispatch*, 6 July 1964, 1; "Rights Leaders Continue Trips," UPI, Columbus *Commercial Dispatch*, 7 July 1964, 1; "Rights Leaders Planning Tour of 'Hot' Spots," UPI, Greenville *Delta Democrat-Times*, 6 July 1964, 1.

79. "Negroes Turned Back at Hotels, Motels, Theaters," *Clarksdale Press Register*, 7 July 1964, 1.

80. "NAACP Leaders Continue Tour of Mississippi," UPI, *Clarksdale Press Register*, 7 July 1964, 1.

81. "Holiday Inns to Integrate," UPI, Pascagoula *Chronicle*, 7 July 1964, 3; "Holiday Inns Told to Obey New Civil Rights Law," UPI, Corinth *Daily Corinthian*, 7 July 1964, 1.

82. "NAACP Finds Mississippi Police State," UPI, Jackson *Daily News*, 9 July 1964, 1; "NAACP Group Pledges Greater Effort to Breach State's Segregation Laws," UPI, *Clarksdale Press Register*, 9 July 1964, 1.

83. "Chicago Negroes Want All Troops Sent to Mississippi," UPI, West Point *Times-Herald*, 30 June 1964, 1; "Governor of Mississippi Target of NAACP," UPI, Pascagoula *Chronicle*, 26 June 1964, 2; "NAACP Committee Labels State 'Hell,' " AP, *Hattiesburg American*, 10 July 1964, 4; "NAACP Criticizes Mississippi," UPI, *Clarksdale Press Register*, 26 June 1964, 1; "NAACP Head Makes Report to Kennedy," AP, Gulfport *Daily Herald*, 24 July 1964, 13; "NAACP Leaders Ask Federal Invasion of Mississippi," UPI, Columbus *Commercial Dispatch*, 10 July 1964, 1; "NAACP Leaders Make Request," AP, *Laurel Leader-Call*, 10 July 1964, 1; "NAACP Leaders Urge Mississippi Takeover," AP, McComb *Enterprise-Journal*, 29 June 1964, 3; "NAACP 'Legalizes' Takeover of State's Affairs," AP, Jackson *Daily News*, 29 June 1964, 1; "NAACP Plans to Stampede in Nation's Capital," UPI, Columbus *Commercial Dispatch*, 24 June 1964, 1; "NAACP Tells of Visit to State," AP, Gulfport *Daily Herald*, 10 July 1964, 1; "NAACP 'Tourists' Urge Barry to Visit State, Complain Negroes Are Scared," AP, McComb *Enterprise-Journal*, 7 July 1964, 1; "NAACP Urges Government to 'Take Over' Mississippi," UPI, Tupelo *Daily Journal*, 27–28 June 1964, 1; "Negroes Urge U.S. Invasion of State by Black Soldiers," UPI, Jackson *Daily News*, 29 June 1964, 1; "Racial Barriers Remain Strong," AP, *Laurel Leader-Call*, 10 July 1964, 1; "Urge U.S. Takeover of State," AP, *Greenwood Commonwealth*, 10 July 1964, 1; "Violence Forecast as NAACP Concludes Tour," UPI, *Clarksdale Press Register*, 11 July 1964, 1.

84. "Governor Refuses to Meet NAACP," AP, *Natchez Democrat*, 15 July 1964, 12; "Integration Leaders Seek Parley with Gov. Johnson," UPI, Corinth *Daily Corinthian*, 8 July 1964, 5; "Integrationists Seek Audience with Governor," UPI, Pascagoula *Chronicle*, 8 July 1964, 2; "Johnson Declines Talks with Civil Rights Relations Team," Jackson *Clarion-Ledger*, 8 July 1964, 1; "NAACP Officials Hope to Meet with Governor," AP, *Hattiesburg American*, 8 July 1964, 1; "NAACP Is Seeking Conference with Governor," AP, Gulfport *Daily Herald*, 29 June 1964, 1; "Paul Stands Tall," AP, *Natchez Democrat*, 8 July 1964, 1; "Rights Leaders Ask for Talks," UPI, Columbus *Commercial Dispatch*, 6 July 1964, 1; "Touring Inte-

grationists Fail to Gain Meeting with Governor," UPI, Tupelo *Daily Journal*, 9 July 1964, 4.

85. Jack Lotto, "Commies Demand Troops Invade State," Jackson *Daily News*, 4 July 1964, 4.

86. W. David Brown, "A Better Idea," Pascagoula *Chronicle*, 29 June 1964, 4.

87. "Not the Answer," from the *Ft. Worth Telegram*, in the Jackson *Clarion-Ledger*, 4 July 1964, 4.

88. Joseph Ellis, Jr., "Patience, Patience, Patience. Summer Almost Over," *Clarksdale Press Register*, 8 July 1964, 4.

89. "Atlanta Café Owner Defies Court," AP, Jackson *Clarion-Ledger*, 12 August 1964, 1; "Balky Restaurateur Faces Court Action," AP, Jackson *Daily News*, 10 July 1964, 5; "Civil Rights Law Faces First Test," UPI, West Point *Times-Leader*, 17 July 1964, 1; "Civil Rights Law Gets First Test in Federal Court," UPI, Pascagoula *Chronicle*, 12 July 1964, 3; "Color Barriers Fall, But Not All," UPI, Greenville *Delta Democrat-Times*, 5 July 1964, 7; "Federal Court Rules Civil Rights Section Is Legal," AP, Jackson *Clarion-Ledger*, 29 July 1964, 1; "Federal Muscle Flexed in Civil Rights Test," UPI, Columbus *Commercial Dispatch*, 10 July 1964, 1; "Federal Panel Ponders Decision in Civil Rights Test," AP, *Hattiesburg American*, 22 July 1964, 1; "Feds Facing First Tests of Civil Rights Act," AP, *Meridian Star*, 11 July 1964, 1; "First Rights Bill Court Test," UPI, Corinth *Daily Corinthian*, 17 July 1964, 1; "Judges Ponder First Civil Rights Test," AP, *Laurel Leader-Call*, 22 July 1964, 1; "Legal Test of Civil Rights Bill in Atlanta," AP, *Natchez Democrat*, 11 July 1964, 1; "Lester Maddox Does Serio-Comic Opera," UPI, Greenville *Delta Democrat-Times*, 12 August 1964, 1; "Lester Maddox, Jail before Integration," UPI, Columbus *Commercial Dispatch*, 8 July 1964, 1; "Maddox Doing Better Selling Ax Handles," UPI, Jackson *Clarion-Ledger*, 16 August 1964, 1; "Maddox Doing Better Selling Ax Handles," UPI, Jackson *Daily News*, 16 August 1964, 16; "Maddox Expected to Reveal Why He Defied Civil Rights Statute," UPI, Corinth *Daily Corinthian*, 20 July 1964, 1; "Maddox Says He Received Support," AP, McComb *Enterprise-Journal*, 9 July 1964, 7. "Maddox Straps on Six Shooter, Keeps Restaurant Segregated," UPI, Corinth *Daily Corinthian*, 12 August 1964, 1; "Motel and Restaurant Owners Plan Appeal of Civil Rights Bill," AP, *Greenwood Commonwealth*, 23 July 1964, 1; "Ordered to Integrate," UPI, Columbus *Commercial Dispatch*, 28 July 1964, 1; "Pistol, Ax Handles Drive Negroes from Restaurant," AP, Jackson *Daily News*, 4 July 1964, 1; "Restaurant Owner Helped in Rights Case," AP, Gulfport *Daily Herald*, 9 July 1964, 1; "Rights Act Upheld in Early Case," AP, McComb *Enterprise-Journal*, 23 July 1964, 3; "Ruling on First Test Case of Civil Rights Law May Come Today," UPI, Tupelo *Daily Journal*, 22 July 1964, 1; "Test of Rights Law," AP, Gulfport *Daily Herald*, 21 July 1964, 19; "U.S. Court Rules Civil Rights Law Is Unconstitutional," AP, *Starkville Daily News*, 23 July 1964, 1; "Whites Stand by Battling Owner," AP, Jackson *Daily News*, 8 July 1964, 5.

90. "Atlanta Man Keeps Word," UPI, Grenada *Sentinel-Star*, 11 August 1964, 1; "Atlanta Restaurateur Bars Negroes despite Court," UPI, Tupelo *Daily Journal*, 12 August 1964, 1; "Judges Back New Civil Rights Act," AP, Jackson *Clarion-Ledger*, 23 July 1964, 1; "Lester Maddox Closes Up," UPI, Greenville *Delta Democrat-Times*, 14 August 1964, 1; "Maddox Changes His Line to Ax Handles," AP, *Meridian Star*, 16 August 1964, 1; "Maddox Closes to Avoid Mix," UPI,

Corinth *Daily Corinthian*, 14 August 1964, 1; "Maddox Closes for Good," AP, *Meridian Star*, 14 August 1964, 1; "Maddox Defies Court, Turns Negroes Down," UPI, Pascagoula *Chronicle*, 12 August 1964, 6; "Maddox Prepares to Close after Losing Civil Rights Plea," AP, Jackson *Daily News*, 11 August 1964, 1; "Militant Maddox Closes Café," AP, Jackson *Daily News*, 14 August 1964, 1; "Owner Plans for Decision Repeal," AP, *Laurel Leader-Call*, 23 July 1964, 1; "Pickrick in Atlanta Closed," UPI, Tupelo *Daily Journal*, 14 August 1964, 1; "Restaurant Owner Will Not Integrate," AP, *Hattiesburg American*, 11 August 1964, 1; "Restaurant Owner to Stand by Vow," UPI, West Point *Times-Leader*, 11 August 1964, 1; "Restaurant Shuts Down Permanently, Rights Law Upheld in Court Test," AP, Gulfport *Daily Herald*, 23 July 1964, 1.

91. "Negroes Idled by U.S. Order to Close Café," AP, *Vicksburg Evening Post*, 15 August 1964, 1; "Restaurant Shuts Down Permanently in Atlanta," AP, *Hattiesburg American*, 14 August 1964, 1.

92. "Charges Face Café Owners," Jackson *Clarion-Ledger*, 25 July 1964, 1; "Delay Is Granted in Café Mix Suits," UPI, Corinth *Daily Corinthian*, 16 July 1964, 1; "NAACP Files 'Rights' Suit," AP, *Meridian Star*, 25 July 1964, 1; "NAACP Sues to Mix Jackson Restaurant," UPI, Tupelo *Daily Journal*, 25–26 June 1964, 1; "Primos Accused of Civil Rights Violation, Negroes Say Barred by Armed Guards," Jackson *Daily News*, 24 July 1964, 1.

93. "Jackson Hotel, Cafes, Go Private," UPI, Greenville *Delta Democrat-Times*, 10 July 1964, 1; "Now 'Private,' Two Jackson Restaurants, the Belmont Café and the Rotisserie," UPI, Corinth *Daily Corinthian*, 10 July 1964, 1; "Restaurants Adopt Private Club Approach," AP, Gulfport *Daily Herald*, 4 July 1964, 23; "Restaurants Join Clubs," AP, *Laurel Leader-Call*, 4 July 1964, 1.

94. "House Praises Jackson Hotel," UPI, Grenada *Sentinel-Star*, 8 July 1964, 1.

95. "Hotel Closes Rather than Mix," Jackson *Daily News*, 6 July 1964, 1; "Jackson Hotel Closes Doors to Protest Civil Rights Law," UPI, Greenville *Delta Democrat-Times*, 6 July 1964, 1; "Jackson Hotel Closes Due to Rights Statute," AP, *Vicksburg Evening Post*, 6 July 1964, 2; "Jackson Hotel Closes Rather Than Admit Negroes," AP, *Hattiesburg American*, 6 July 1964, 1; "Jackson Hotel Closes Rather Than Integrate," UPI, Columbus *Commercial Dispatch*, 6 July 1964, 1; "Jackson Hotel Closes, Won't Bow to Civil Rights," UPI, Pascagoula *Chronicle*, 7 July 1964, 1; "Jackson Hotel Won't Surrender," UPI, Greenville *Delta Democrat-Times*, 7 July 1964, 1; "Robert E. Lee Closed," UPI, West Point *Times-Leader*, 6 July 1964, 1; "Robert E. Lee Closed Rather Than Integrate," UPI, Corinth *Daily Corinthian*, 6 July 1964, 1; "Robert E. Lee Closes Doors to Public," AP, *Greenwood Commonwealth*, 6 July 1964, 1; "Robert E. Lee Hotel Closes Doors," UPI, Grenada *Sentinel-Star*, 6 July 1964, 1; "Robert E. Lee Closes Doors," AP, *Laurel Leader-Call*, 6 July 1964, 1; Jerry Delaughter, "Robert E. Lee Shut, Civil Rights Act Blamed," Jackson *Clarion-Ledger*, 7 July 1964, 1; "Robert E. Lee Shuts Doors Rather Than Yield," AP, *Meridian Star*, 6 July 1964, 1.

96. "Closed Hotel Offers Solons Free Housing," UPI, Tupelo *Daily Journal*, 8 July 1964, 1; "Hotel Closed, Hosting Solons," UPI, Pascagoula *Chronicle*, 8 July 1964, 2; "Hotel Reopens, but Lawmakers Only Guests," UPI, Corinth *Daily Corinthian*, 8 July 1964, 1; "Legislators Move Free into Robert E. Lee," Jackson *Daily News*, 8 July 1964, 1; "Legislators Move to Robert E. Lee," UPI, *Meridian Star*, 8

July 1964, 1; "Lodging at Robert E. Lee Offered to State Legislators," Jackson *Daily News*, 7 July 1964, 1; "Robert E. Lee Converts to Private Club," Jackson *Daily News*, 8 July 1964, 1; "Robert E. Lee Will Operate as Private Club," AP, *Meridian Star*, 9 July 1964, 1; "State's Solons Get Free Rooms at Robert E. Lee," UPI, Columbus *Commercial Dispatch*, 8 July 1964, 1.

97. "Private Club Raided Here," Jackson *Daily News*, 16 August 1964, 16; "Whiskey Nabbed at Lee Hotel," UPI, West Point *Times-Leader*, 17 August 1964, 1.

98. "Jackson Hotels Yield to Civil Rights Law," UPI, West Point *Times-Leader*, 6 July 1964, 1; "Jackson Motel Drops Segregation Policy, Negro Served," UPI, Greenville *Delta Democrat-Times*, 5 July 1964, 1; "Mixing at Facilities in State," AP, Gulfport *Daily Herald*, 6 July 1964, 1; "Race Barriers Fall in Some Dixie Areas," UPI, Jackson *Clarion-Ledger*, 4 July 1964, 1; "Several Places Mixed in Jackson," AP, McComb *Enterprise-Journal*, 6 July 1964, 1; "Some Mix, Some Balk on Civil Rights Law," UPI, Jackson *Daily News*, 3 July 1964, 1; "Test Civil Rights Bill in State," UPI, Pascagoula *Chronicle*, 5 July 1964, 2; "Three Hotels in Jackson Lower Racial Barriers but Laurel Mixing Try Sparks Rioting," UPI, Corinth *Daily Corinthian*, 6 July 1964, 1; "Three Jackson Hotels Lower Racial Barriers, Admit Negroes Quietly, Treat with Courtesy," UPI, Tupelo *Daily Journal*, 6 July 1964, 1.

99. "Innkeepers Won't Test Civil Section," Jackson *Daily News*, 8 July 1964, 3; "Mississippi Innkeepers Association Believes Accommodations Clause Unconstitutional," UPI, Grenada *Sentinel-Star*, 8 July 1964, 1.

100. "Jackson Mayor Asks Compliance with Rights Act," UPI, Pascagoula *Chronicle*, 10 July 1964, 2; "Jackson Mayor Backs Chamber, Opposes Tall Paul," UPI, Grenada *Sentinel-Star*, 10 July 1964, 1; "Jackson Mayor Now Announces Civil Rights Compliance Until Changed," UPI, Tupelo *Daily Journal*, 10 July 1964, 1; "Jackson Mayor in Anti-PBJ Reaction," AP, *Starkville Daily News*, 10 July 1964, 1; "Jackson Mayor Urges Civil Rights Law Compliance," UPI, Corinth *Daily Corinthian*, 10 July 1964, 1; "Jackson Mayor Urges Full Compliance with Rights Act," AP, *Hattiesburg American*, 9 July 1964, 1; "Mayor Asks Compliance," Jackson *Clarion-Ledger*, 10 July 1964, 1; "Mayor Supports Law and Order," Jackson *Daily News*, 9 July 1964, 1; "Thompson Urges Civil Rights Compliance," AP, *Greenwood Commonwealth*, 9 July 1964, 1; "Thompson Urging Compliance," AP, *Laurel Leader-Call*, 9 July 1964, 1.

101. "Maintain Law, Order—Stennis," AP, Jackson *Clarion-Ledger*, 21 July 1964, 1; "Southern Senators Urge Compliance," AP, Jackson *Daily News*, 16 July 1964, 8; "Stennis Calls for Compliance," AP, Gulfport *Daily Herald*, 21 July 1964, 2; "Stennis: Comply for Time Being," AP, McComb *Enterprise-Journal*, 21 July 1964, 1; "Stennis Says Civil Rights Bill Must Be Obeyed," AP, *Hattiesburg American*, 21 July 1964, 1; "Stennis Urges Civil Rights Compliance," *Laurel Leader-Call*, 21 July 1964, 6; "Stennis Urges Compliance to Civil Rights Bill Until Courts Rule," AP, *Greenwood Commonwealth*, 21 July 1964, 1; "Stennis Urges Maintaining Law and Order," AP, *Starkville Daily News*, 23 July 1964, 4.

102. "House Blasts Jackson Chamber of Commerce Stand on Law," UPI, Tupelo *Daily Journal*, 9 July 1964, 1; "Lawmakers Condemn Jackson Chamber of Commerce," UPI, Grenada *Sentinel-Star*, 9 July 1964, 1; "Legislators Hit Jackson Chamber of Commerce," AP, *Vicksburg Evening Post*, 9 July 1964, 1; "Legislature

Disagrees with Chamber of Commerce," AP, *Natchez Democrat*, 16 July 1964, 2; "Mississippians Differ on New Law, Some Urge Compliance," UPI, Tupelo *Daily Journal*, 6 July 1964, 1; "Pending Civil Rights Bill Testing, Chamber Asks Compliance," Jackson *Clarion-Ledger*, 4 July 1964, 1; "Resolution Censures Chamber," AP, Gulfport *Daily Herald*, 9 July 1964, 1; "Rules Committee Checks Measure," AP, *Laurel Leader-Call*, 10 July 1964, 1; "Senate Slows Down Chamber of Commerce Censure Move," AP, Jackson *Daily News*, 10 July 1964, 1.

103. Hodding Carter III, "Changes in Mississippi," Greenville *Delta Democrat-Times*, 21 July 1964, 4.

104. "Citizens' Council Planning Private School System," Jackson *Daily News*, 24 August 1964, 6; "Citizens' Councils Plan Private Schools," UPI, Corinth *Daily Corinthian*, 24 August 1964, 1; "Citizens' Council Urges Resistance to Civil Rights Bill," *Greenwood Commonwealth*, 10 July 1964, 1; "Council Maps School Plan," Jackson *Daily News*, 12 August 1964, 1; "Council Plans to Establish Private Schools," AP, *Meridian Star*, 24 August 1964, 1; "Council Raps Appeal for Public Schools," UPI, Tupelo *Daily Journal*, 22 July 1964, 1; "Don't Eat or Sleep at Integrated Places, Mississippi Urged," AP, *Meridian Star*, 7 July 1964, 1; "Jackson Citizens' Council Gives Integration Protest," Jackson *Clarion-Ledger*, 7 July 1964, 1; "Jackson Citizens' Council Plans System of Schools," Jackson *Clarion-Ledger*, 24 August 1964, 1; McMillen, *The Citizens' Council*, 299; "Resistance Is Urged by Lawful Means," Columbus *Commercial Dispatch*, 23 July 1964, 1; "See Need for Private Schools," AP, Gulfport *Daily Herald*, 12 August 1964, 1.

105. "State's Solons Ask People to Resist Civil Rights," Jackson *Daily News*, 16 July 1964, 8.

106. "All Four Negro Candidates Are Soundly Beaten in Primaries," UPI, Tupelo *Daily Journal*, 3 June 1964, 1; "All Negro Candidates Trounced," UPI, *Meridian Star*, 3 June 1964, 1; "County's Voters Turn Out to Back Two Incumbents," *Clarksdale Press Register*, 3 June 1964, 1; "Negro Candidates Soundly Defeated," UPI, Tupelo *Daily Journal*, 3 June 1964, 1.

107. "Election Holds No Surprises, Mississippians Vote as Expected," UPI, *Clarksdale Press Register*, 3 June 1964, 1.

108. United States Commission on Civil Rights, *Voting in Mississippi* (Washington, D.C.: Government Printing Office, 1965), 61.

109. "Integrationists Announce Challenge Plans," UPI, Columbus *Commercial Dispatch*, 20 July 1964, 1.

110. James Loewen and Charles Sallis, eds., *Mississippi: Conflict and Change* (New York: Pantheon Books, 1974), 276–278.

111. "All-Negro Group of Delegates Caucus-Bound," UPI, Pascagoula *Chronicle*, 2 August 1964, 2; "Freedom Democrat Controversy Rages," UPI, Corinth *Daily Corinthian*, 24 August 1964, 1; "Freedom Democrat Party Formed," AP, *Starkville Daily News*, 21 July 1964, 1; "Freedom Democrat Party Has No Basis," AP, *Meridian Star*, 13 August 1964, 1; "Freedom Democrat Party Hits Convention," UPI, Greenville *Delta Democrat-Times*, 21 August 1964, 1; "Freedom Democrat Party Leaders Are Enjoined, State Fights Name Use," AP, Jackson *Clarion-Ledger*, 13 August 1964, 1; "Freedom Democrat Party Picks Candidates for Atlantic City," UPI, Tupelo *Daily Journal*, 7 August 1964, 1; "Freedom Democratic Party Announces Plans," AP, *Greenwood Commonwealth*, 20 July 1964, 1; "Freedom Democratic Party Will Fight for Seats," AP, *Greenwood Common-*

wealth, 7 August 1964, 1; "Freedom Democrats Aim for Seats at Convention," UPI, Corinth *Daily Corinthian*, 20 July 1964, 1; "Freedom Democrats Don't Like Actions of State Party," UPI, Columbus *Commercial Dispatch*, 29 July 1964, 1; "Freedom Democrats Making Big Plans," UPI, Grenada *Sentinel-Star*, 7 August 1964, 1; "Freedom Democrats Might Be Seated," UPI, Corinth *Daily Corinthian*, 18 August 1964, 1; "Freedom Democrats Pick Delegates," UPI, Corinth *Daily Corinthian*, 7 August 1964, 1; "Freedom Democrats Reveal Plans," AP, McComb *Enterprise-Journal*, 20 July 1964, 1; "Freedom Democrats Vow Strong Effort," AP, McComb *Enterprise-Journal*, 7 August 1964, 3; "Freedom Party Plans to Keep Seeking Seating," AP, *Starkville Daily News*, 14 August 1964, 2; "Freedom Party to Send Group to Convention," UPI, Greenville *Delta Democrat-Times*, 20 July 1964, 1; "Mississippi Democrats Hope to Avoid Open Fight," UPI, Grenada *Sentinel-Star*, 28 July 1964, 1; "Mississippi Freedom Democrats Make Claim," UPI, Grenada *Sentinel-Star*, 18 August 1964, 1; "Negroes from Political Party to Challenge State Democrats," AP, Jackson *Daily News*, 20 July 1964, 1; "Negroes Seek Democratic Party Shake-Up," UPI, Corinth *Daily Corinthian*, 29 June 1964, 1; "New Party Plans Big Effort," *Laurel Leader-Call*, 7 August 1964, 1; "Rights Backers Announce Plans for Freedom Democratic Party," AP, *Hattiesburg American*, 20 July 1964, 1; "Victory Predicted by Freedom Party," AP, *Vicksburg Evening Post*, 18 August 1964, 1.

112. Sherrill Nash, "Thanks, Aaron," *Starkville Daily News*, 27 August 1964, 4.

113. "Chancellor Bans Use of 'Democrat' in Freedom Party Title," AP, *Starkville Daily News*, 13 August 1964, 1; "Federal Democrat Party Probes Injunction," AP, *Hattiesburg American*, 13 August 1964, 1; "Freedom Democratic Party Ordered to Quit Politics," UPI, Tupelo *Daily Journal*, 13 August 1964, 1; "Freedom Democratic Party under Orders to Halt Plans," UPI, West Point *Times-Leader*, 13 August 1964, 1; "Freedom Democrats Fight to Keep Label," Jackson *Daily News*, 13 August 1964, 1; "Freedom Democrats Ready to Defy Court," UPI, Pascagoula *Chronicle*, 19 August 1964, 2; "Group Is Barred by Injunction," AP, Gulfport *Daily Herald*, 13 August 1964, 1; "State's Bi-racial Political Group Told to Halt All Activities," UPI, *Meridian Star*, 13 August 1964, 1.

114. "Commies Tied to Freedom Democrat Group," UPI, Jackson *Daily News*, 22 August 1964, 1; "Freedom Democrat Party Link with Reds Charged," AP, *Hattiesburg American*, 22 August 1964, 1; "Freedom Democrats Tied to Reds," AP, Gulfport *Daily Herald*, 22 August 1964, 1; "Freedom Group Linked to Communist Front," AP, Jackson *Clarion-Ledger*, 22 August 1964, 1; "Patterson Charging Freedom Party," AP, *Laurel Leader-Call*, 22 August 1964, 1; "Patterson Says Freedom Democratic Party Has Many Reds in Group," AP, *Meridian Star*, 22 August 1964, 1; "Patterson Says Freedom Party Red-Led," AP, *Starkville Daily News*, 22 August 1964, 1; "Reds Linked to Freedom Party," AP, *Vicksburg Evening Post*, 22 August 1964, 1.

115. Gary Holland, "Picketing the Democrats," Pascagoula *Chronicle*, 20 August 1964, 4.

116. W.H. Harris, "Pencil Shavings," *Starkville Daily News*, 21 August 1964, 1.

117. "They Want to Represent Mississippi," photograph, Jackson *Daily News*, 21 August 1964, 1.

118. J.O. Emmerich, "Heatwave or Tempest, Sunshine or Showers," McComb *Enterprise-Journal*, 15 June 1964, 2.

119. "Freedom Democrats," Jackson *Clarion-Ledger*, 28 July 1964, 5.

120. "Compromise Civil Rights Plank Rejected by Negroes," UPI, West Point *Times-Leader*, 21 August 1964, 1; "Mississippi Delegation Scorns Credentials Group Compromise," AP, *Starkville Daily News*, 26 August 1964, 1; "Mississippi Regulars May Balk at Compromise," AP, McComb *Enterprise-Journal*, 25 August 1964, 1; "Negro Democrats Reject Compromise Proposal," UPI, Pascagoula *Chronicle*, 21 August 1964, 1; "Negro Group Rejects Compromise," AP, Jackson *Daily News*, 21 August 1964, 1.

121. "Alabamans Give In, Mississippi Firm on Loyalty Oaths," UPI, Greenville *Delta Democrat Times*, 25 August 1964, 1; "Convention Boycotted, All but Three Mississippi Delegates Come Home," AP, *Meridian Star*, 26 August 1964, 1; "Lonesome Three Worried about Returning Home," UPI, *Meridian Star*, 27 August 1964, 1; "Mississippi Delegates, Three Signed Loyalty Oath and Were Seated," AP, *Greenwood Commonwealth*, 28 August 1964, 1; "Old Line Dixie Democrats Will Be among Those Missing Convention," AP, *Natchez Democrat*, 2 August 1964, 1; "Regular Democrats Walked Away," AP, *Vicksburg Evening Post*, 26 August 1964, 1; "Remaining State Delegates Are Unhappy," UPI, West Point *Times-Leader*, 27 August 1964, 1; "State Democrats Who Stayed Okay Ticket," AP, *Starkville Daily News*, 29 August 1964, 1; "Three Who Stayed," UPI, Pascagoula *Chronicle*, 26 August 1964, 1.

122. "Angry Mississippi Walks Away," AP, *Hattiesburg American*, 26 August 1964, 1; "Floor Fight Looming on Alabama and Mississippi," AP, *Greenwood Commonwealth*, 25 August 1964, 1; "Gov. Johnson Calls Mississippi Group Home," UPI, Corinth *Daily Corinthian*, 26 August 1964, 1; "Gov. Johnson Orders Mississippi Delegation to Leave Convention," UPI, Tupelo *Daily Journal*, 26 August 1964, 1; "Mississippi Fight at Democratic Convention," AP, Gulfport *Daily Herald*, 24 August 1964, 1; "Loyalty Disputes Tackled by Democrats," UPI, Pascagoula *Chronicle*, 23 August 1964, 1; "Loyalty Pledge Rejected," AP, *Vicksburg Evening Post*, 26 August 1964, 1; "Mississippi Delegates Boycott Hearings," UPI, Pascagoula *Chronicle*, 18 August 1964, 1; "Mississippi Democrats Leave Convention," UPI, Greenville *Delta Democrat-Times*, 26 August 1964, 1; "Mississippi Group Boycotts Session," AP, Gulfport *Daily Herald*, 26 August 1964, 1; "Mississippi Ready to Denounce Freedom Democratic Party," UPI, *Clarksdale Press Register*, 22 August 1964, 1; "More State Democrats Bolt," Jackson *Daily News*, 27 August 1964, 1; "Paul Backs Regular Democrats on Refusal to Sign Oath," AP, *Starkville Daily News*, 26 August 1964, 1; "Paul Lauds Stand of State Group," UPI, West Point *Times-Leader*, 26 August 1964, 1; "Some Alabama Delegates Sign Loyalty Oath," AP, *Hattiesburg American*, 24 August 1964, 1; "State Delegates Boycott Democratic Convention," Jackson *Clarion-Ledger*, 25 August 1964, 1; "State Group Out," UPI, West Point *Times-Leader*, 26 August 1964, 1; "State Group Votes 53–3 for Boycott," Jackson *Clarion-Ledger*, 26 August 1964, 1; "Walkout Strategy Described," AP, Gulfport *Daily Herald*, 28 August 1964, 1; "Where Do Mississippi Democrats Go from Here?" McComb *Enterprise-Journal*, 27 August 1964, 1; Howard Zinn, *SNCC: The New Abolitionists* (Boston: Beacon Press, 1964), 251–256.

123. Hodding Carter III, "Three Who Didn't Leave," Greenville *Delta Democrat-Times*, 27 August 1964, 4.

124. James Lambert, "Needed to Walk," *Natchez Democrat*, 27 August 1964, 4.

125. Ibid.

126. J.O. Emmerich, "Why Were We Asked to Take Loyalty Oath?" McComb *Enterprise-Journal*, 28 August 1964, 2.

127. Harry Rutherford, "The Seats Are Ours, Let's Sit in Them," Tupelo *Daily Journal*, 14 August 1964, 13.

128. "Delegates Agree, Democratic Party Dead in Mississippi," UPI, Corinth *Daily Corinthian*, 27 August 1964, 1; "Democratic Loyalty Dead for 100 Years," AP, Gulfport *Daily Herald*, 27 August 1964, 1; "Democratic Riff Won't Heal," Jackson *Clarion-Ledger*, 26 August 1964, 1; "Democrats Not with Mississippi Anymore," Corinth *Daily Corinthian*, 28 July 1964, 1; "Democrats Say Party Dead for 100 Years," AP, *Vicksburg Evening Post*, 27 August 1964, 1; "Negro Party, Brady Says of Democrats," UPI, *Meridian Star*, 28 August 1964, 1; "Party Killed, Some Say," UPI, Pascagoula *Chronicle*, 27 August 1964, 1; "State Leaders Blast Democrats," UPI, Tupelo *Daily Journal*, 27 August 1964, 1; "State's Ties to Party Believed Broken," AP, McComb *Enterprise-Journal*, 26 August 1964, 7; "Walkout Severs Ties with National Party," AP, *Greenwood Commonwealth*, 26 August 1964, 1.

129. James B. Skewes, "Out of Place," *Meridian Star*, 23 August 1964, 4.

130. John Perkins, "Brady Asserts Oath Was Discrimination," Jackson *Clarion-Ledger*, 27 August 1964, 1.

131. "Brady Says Mississippi Can Never Be Pressed into National Party Mold," UPI, West Point *Times-Leader*, 28 August 1964, 1; " 'Negro Party' Brady Says of Democrats," UPI, *Meridian Star*, 28 August 1964, 1.

132. John Perkins, "Brady Says Southerners Must Use Economic Boycott," Jackson *Daily News*, 8 July 1964, 6.

133. Loewen and Sallis, *Mississippi*, 253.

134. "Citizens' Council Planning Private School System," Jackson *Daily News*, 24 August 1964, 6; "Citizens' Councils Plan Private Schools," UPI, Corinth *Daily Corinthian*, 24 August 1964, 1; "Citizens' Council Urges Resistance to Civil Rights Bill," *Greenwood Commonwealth*, 10 July 1964, 1; "Council Maps School Plan," Jackson *Daily News*, 12 August 1964, 1; "Council Plans to Establish Private Schools," AP, *Meridian Star*, 24 August 1964, 1; "Council Raps Appeal for Public Schools," UPI, Tupelo *Daily Journal*, 22 July 1964, 1; "Don't Eat or Sleep at Integrated Places, Mississippi Urged," AP, *Meridian Star*, 7 July 1964, 1; "Jackson Citizens' Council Gives Integration Protest," Jackson *Clarion-Ledger*, 7 July 1964, 1; "Jackson Citizens' Council Plans System of Schools," Jackson *Clarion-Ledger*, 24 August 1964, 1; Neil R. McMillen, *The Citizens' Council: Organized Resistance to the Second Reconstruction, 1954–1964* (Urbana: University of Illinois Press, 1971), 299; "Resistance Is Urged by Lawful Means," Columbus *Commercial Dispatch*, 23 July 1964, 1; "See Need for Private Schools," AP, Gulfport *Daily Herald*, 12 August 1964, 1.

135. "Simmons Says Civil Rights Heralds Negro Revolution," Jackson *Daily News*, 30 June 1964, 7.

136. "Cleve Refused Readmission to Ole Miss," UPI, Grenada *Sentinel-Star*, 30

July 1964, 1; "College Board Says No to Negro," UPI, Greenville *Delta Democrat-Times*, 5 June 1964, 1; "Court Hears Readmission Arguments," *Meridian Star*, 20 July 1964, 1; "Dean Quizzed on Gun Rule," AP, Jackson *Clarion-Ledger*, 21 July 1964, 1; "Expelled McDowell Gains Court Say," AP, Jackson *Daily News*, 14 July 1964, 1; "Expelled Negro Granted Hearing," UPI, Corinth *Daily Corinthian*, 15 July 1964, 1; "Judge Mize to Hear McDowell's Case Soon," UPI, Jackson *Clarion-Ledger*, 15 July 1964, 1; "Judge Orders University of Mississippi to Produce Records," AP, *Hattiesburg American*, 21 July 1964, 1; "McDowell Case to be Argued Monday," AP, *Meridian Star*, 14 July 1964, 1; "McDowell Contends That Expulsion Discriminatory," UPI, West Point *Times-Leader*, 21 July 1964, 1; "McDowell Files Suit Asking Readmission to Ole Miss," AP, *Greenwood Commonwealth*, 25 June 1964, 1; "McDowell Flunks Test in Court," UPI, Pascagoula *Chronicle*, 30 July 1964, 1; "McDowell Loses Suit to Re-enter Ole Miss," UPI, Tupelo *Daily Journal*, 31 July 1964, 12; "McDowell Says Pistol in Pocket Accidentally," UPI, Tupelo *Daily Journal*, 21 July 1964, 7; "McDowell Says Whites with Pistols Stay," UPI, Tupelo *Daily Journal*, 26 June 1964, 8; "McDowell Seeks to Reenter Ole Miss," AP, *Hattiesburg American*, 25 June 1964, 1; "McDowell Seeks UM Admittance," UPI, Jackson *Clarion-Ledger*, 2 June 1964, 1; "McDowell Trying Ole Miss Again," AP, Jackson *Daily News*, 25 June 1964, 14; "McDowell Wants Back in Ole Miss," AP, McComb *Enterprise-Journal*, 26 June 1964, 8; "Mize Sets McDowell Hearing," AP, *Laurel Leader-Call*, 20 July 1964, 1; "Mize Studies McDowell Readmission," UPI, Corinth *Daily Corinthian*, 22 July 1964, 1; "Negro Asks Reentry to Ole Miss," AP, Gulfport *Daily Herald*, 14 July 1964, 2; "Negro Given Hearing on Ole Miss," UPI, Greenville *Delta Democrat-Times*, 15 July 1964, 1; "Negro Loses Bid to Secure UM Records," AP, McComb *Enterprise-Journal*, 30 July 196, 9; "Negro Ousted at Ole Miss Granted Court Hearing," UPI, *Clarksdale Press Register*, 15 July 1964, 1; "Negro Seeks Re-entrance to Ole Miss," AP, *Laurel Leader-Call*, 27 June 1964, 1; "Ole Miss Dean Says Expulsion Was Routine," AP, *Starkville Daily News*, 22 July 1964, 1.

137. "Attorneys Ask Court to Let Negro Register," UPI, *Greenwood Commonwealth*, 9 June 1964, 1; "Attorneys Seeking Restraining Order," AP, Jackson *Daily News*, 9 June 1964, 16; "Affidavits to Be Filed," UPI, Grenada *Sentinel-Star*, 9 June 1964, 1; "Board Eyes Mixing Bid," Jackson *Daily News*, 4 June 1964, 1; "College Board May Act Soon on Negro Bid," UPI, *Meridian Star*, 4 June 1964, 1; "College Board Mum on Negro Student," UPI, Tupelo *Daily Journal*, 5 June 1964, 1; "College Board Studies Negro Issue," UPI, Greenville *Delta Democrat-Times*, 4 June 1964, 1; "Court Asked to Open Way for Negro," UPI, Pascagoula *Chronicle*, 7 June 1964, 1; "Court Is Asked to Force Entry to Ole Miss," UPI, Greenville *Delta Democrat-Times*, 7 June 1964, 1; "Court Ruling Expected Today on Ole Miss Integration Try," UPI, Corinth *Daily Corinthian*, 9 June 1964, 1; "Cox Rules Negro Must Be Enrolled," AP, McComb *Enterprise-Journal*, 10 June 1964, 1; "Discuss Ole Miss Negro Applicant," UPI, Pascagoula *Chronicle*, 4 June 1964, 1; "Donald Asked Not to Appear at Ole Miss," UPI, Grenada *Sentinel-Star*, 8 June 1964, 5; "Donald Hearing Is Asked," AP, Jackson *Clarion-Ledger*, 5 June 1964, 1; "Donald Seems Headed for Ole Miss," UPI, *Meridian Star*, 10 June 1964, 1; "Federal Court to Ensure UM's Mix," Jackson *Daily News*, 7 June 1964, 1; "Federal Judge Orders Admission," UPI, Grenada *Sentinel-Star*, 10 June 1964, 1; "Hearing Asked on Mix Suit," AP, *Vicksburg Evening Post*, 5 June 1964, 1; "Judge

Clears Negro's Way at Ole Miss," AP, Jackson *Clarion-Ledger*, 11 June 1964, 1; "Judge Orders Negro Admitted to Ole Miss," UPI, Greenville *Delta Democrat-Times*, 10 June 1964, 1; "Judge Orders Ole Miss to Enroll Negro," AP, *Greenwood Commonwealth*, 10 June 1964, 1; "Judge Orders Negro to Enroll," AP, *Hattiesburg American*, 10 June 1964, 1; "Judge Orders UM to Admit Negro," AP, Jackson *Daily News*, 10 June 1964, 1; "Federal Judge's Ruling Waited at Ole Miss," UPI, Greenville *Delta Democrat-Times*, 9 June 1964, 1; "Judge Refuses to Act in Negro's Admission," AP, *Hattiesburg American*, 6 June 1964, 1; "Judge Will Order Ole Miss to Enroll Negro," UPI, Pascagoula *Chronicle*, 10 June 1964, 1; "NAACP Asks Court Order," AP, *Greenwood Commonwealth*, 6 June 1964, 1; "NAACP Asks Federal Court to Admit Negro," AP, *Natchez Democrat*, 7 June 1964, 1; "Ole Miss to Defer Issuing Entrance Permit," UPI, West Point *Times-Leader*, 5 June 1964, 1; "Orders Negro to Ole Miss," AP, Gulfport *Daily Herald*, 10 June 1964, 1; "Showdown Draws Near at Ole Miss," AP, McComb *Enterprise-Journal*, 9 June 1964, 1; "State College Board Asks Hearing on Entry," UPI, *Starkville Daily News*, 5 June 1964, 1; "State College Board Asks Hearing on Negro," AP, *Hattiesburg American*, 5 June 1964, 1; "State College Board Considers Negro's Bid to Enter Ole Miss," UPI, *Clarksdale Press Register*, 4 June 1964, 1; "Student Waits Board Action," UPI, Grenada *Sentinel-Star*, 4 June 1964, 1; "Third Negro Admitted to Ole Miss," UPI, *Starkville Daily News*, 12 June 1964, 1; "Suit Proposes Forcing Ole Miss to Admit Negro," AP, *Vicksburg Evening Post*, 25 June 1964, 1; "Third Negro Registers for Class," AP, *Laurel Leader-Call*, 11 June 1964, 1; "University Instructed to Hold Up on Entrance Certification of Negro," UPI, *Meridian Star*, 5 June 1964, 1; "University of Mississippi Plans to Admit Negro in Summer School," UPI, *Starkville Daily News*, 10 June 1964, 1; "Young Negro Hopes to Enroll at Ole Miss," AP, *Hattiesburg American*, 9 June 1964, 1.

138. "Ole Miss Prof Backs Donald's Claim That Delay Hurts His Career," UPI, Tupelo *Daily Journal*, 9 June 1964, 1; "Ole Miss Professor Claims Delay Would Harm Negro Seeking Admission," UPI, *Clarksdale Press Register*, 8 June 1964, 1; "Ole Miss Professor Favors Summer Admission for Negro," UPI, Greenville *Delta Democrat-Times*, 8 June 1964, 1; "Ole Miss Professor Says Donald Would 'Suffer,' " UPI, *Meridian Star*, 8 June 1964, 1; "University of Mississippi Professor Supports Negro in Court Plea," AP, Jackson *Clarion-Ledger*, 9 June 1964, 1.

139. "Campus Okay, School Opens for Summer," UPI, Grenada *Sentinel-Star*, 11 June 1964, 1; "Donald Admitted to Ole Miss, Third Negro Student Ignored by Whites," UPI, Corinth *Daily Corinthian*, 11 June 1964, 1; "Donald Enrolls at University, Tells Newsmen to Return in Three or Four Years," UPI, *Clarksdale Press Register*, 11 June 1964, 1; "Donald Enters Ole Miss, No Incidents," UPI, Tupelo *Daily Journal*, 12 June 1964, 1; "Donald Is in Class Today," UPI, *Meridian Star*, 12 June 1964, 1; "Donald Now at Ole Miss," AP, Gulfport *Daily Herald*, 11 June 1964, 1; "Donald Will Enroll at Ole Miss Today," UPI, Tupelo *Daily Journal*, 11 June 1964, 1; "Everything Quiet at Ole Miss," AP, McComb *Enterprise-Journal*, 12 June 1964, 7; "Negro's Enrollment Quiet at University," AP, Jackson *Clarion-Ledger*, 12 June 1964, 1; "Negro Enrolls at Ole Miss," UPI, Greenville *Delta Democrat-Times*, 11 June 1964, 1; "Negro Enters Ole Miss Quietly Today," UPI, *Meridian Star*, 11 June 1964, 1; "Negro Goes to Classes," UPI, Greenville *Delta Democrat-Times*, 12 June 1964, 1; "Negro Quietly Enrolls at Ole Miss," AP, *Hattiesburg American*, 11 June 1964, 1; "Negro Quietly Registers at Ole Miss," AP,

Jackson *Daily News*, 11 June 1964, 1; "Negro Quietly Enrolls as Student at Ole Miss," AP, McComb *Enterprise-Journal*, 11 June 1964, 1; "Negro Registers at Ole Miss Today," AP, *Greenwood Commonwealth*, 11 June 1964, 1; "Ole Miss Enrolls Negro," AP, *Vicksburg Evening Post*, 11 June 1964, 1; "Ole Miss Quiet to Negro Entry," UPI, West Point *Times-Leader*, 12 June 1964, 1; "Third Negro Enters Ole Miss, No Fanfare," UPI, Pascagoula *Chronicle*, 11 June 1964, 1; "Third Negro Is Enrolled at Ole Miss," UPI, West Point *Times-Leader*, 11 June 1964, 1; "University Is Integrated for Third Time," UPI, Columbus *Commercial Dispatch*, 11 June 1964, 1.

140. "Negro Student Barred by Court Order from Civil Rights Activities," UPI, Tupelo *Daily Journal*, 11 June 1964, 1.

141. "Controversial Ole Miss Professor Leaving Campus," UPI, *Meridian Star*, 19 June 1964, 1; "Dr. Silver Given Leave to Teach at Notre Dame," UPI, Tupelo *Daily Journal*, 20–21 June 1964, 1; "Ole Miss Critic Fears Dismissal," AP, *Vicksburg Evening Post*, 19 June 1964, 1; "Prof. Silver Granted Leave," UPI, Corinth *Daily Corinthian*, 19 June 1964, 1; "Silver Gets Year to Teach Away from Ole Miss," UPI, Pascagoula *Chronicle*, 19 June 1964, 2; "Silver Given Year's Leave," Jackson *Daily News*, 19 June 1964, 1.

142. "Silver Says White Man Not Free," AP, *Greenwood Commonwealth*, 19 June 1964, 1.

143. "Dr. Silver Writes Book, Expects to Lose Job," AP, McComb *Enterprise-Journal*, 19 June 1964, 1.

144. "Bites Hand Again, Silver Slashes Mississippi," AP, Jackson *Daily News*, 19 June 1964, 7.

145. J.O. Emmerich, "Silver's *Mississippi: The Closed Society*," McComb *Enterprise-Journal*, 22 June 1964, 2.

146. "College Is Ordered to Admit Negro," AP, Gulfport *Daily Herald*, 6 June 1964, Sec. 2, 1; "LSU Admits Negro," UPI, *Clarksdale Press Register*, 9 June 1964, 1; "LSU Admits Negro under Court Directive," AP, *Laurel Leader-Call*, 10 June 1964, 5; "Negroes Seek Admission to LSU," AP, Gulfport *Daily Herald*, 5 June 1964, 6.

147. "Integration at Colleges on Increase," AP, Gulfport *Daily Herald*, 17 June 1964, 20.

148. "Johnson Signs New School Bill," UPI, Greenville *Delta Democrat-Times*, 16 July 1964, 1.

149. "Committee to Resume School Work," UPI, Grenada *Sentinel-Star*, 15 June 1964, 1; "Lawmakers Bide Time on Schools," Jackson *Daily News*, 5 June 1964, 1; "Lawmakers Divided on School Proposal," AP, *Laurel Leader-Call*, 4 June 1964, 1; "Lawmakers Split on Private School Plan," AP, Gulfport *Daily Herald*, 4 June 1964, 1; "Lawmakers Split Over School System," UPI, Grenada *Sentinel-Star*, 30 June 1964, 1; "Legislators Fight School Mixing,' UPI, Grenada *Sentinel-Star*, 5 June 1964, 1; "Lt. Gov. Gartin Presiding, Special Committee to Deal with Mississippi School Problem," UPI, Grenada *Sentinel-Star*, 11 June 1964, 3; "Private School Action Asked of Legislature," AP, Jackson *Clarion-Ledger*, 4 June 1964, 1; "Private School Bill Causes Sharp Split," UPI, *Greenwood Commonwealth*, 4 June 1964, 1; "Private School Bill Considered," UPI, *Starkville Daily News*, 4 June 1964, 1; "Private School Plan Debated, Anti-Integration Effort Seen," UPI, *Clarksdale Press Register*, 4 June 1964, 1; "Private School Plan Studied," UPI, Greenville *Delta*

Democrat-Times, 4 June 1964, 1; "School Bill Goes behind Closed Doors," UPI, Grenada *Sentinel-Star*, 4 June 1964, 1; "School Bill Still Deadlocked," UPI, Corinth *Daily Corinthian*, 10 July 1964, 1; "School Committee Meets," AP, McComb *Enterprise-Journal*, 10 June 1964, 1; "Senate Asks Committee for Student Funds for Private Schools," UPI, *Meridian Star*, 4 June 1964, 1; "Senate Takes Action to Organize School Study Group," UPI, West Point *Times-Leader*, 4 June 1964, 1; "Showdown Looms on Private School Plans," AP, *Vicksburg Evening Post*, 26 June 1964, 1; "Solons Debate When to Tackle School Plan," AP, *Hattiesburg American*, 4 June 1964, 1; "Solons Study Ways to Prevent School Mix," UPI, Pascagoula *Chronicle*, 8 June 1964, 1; "Special Legislative Session Looms on Private School Plan," AP, *Vicksburg Evening Post*, 4 June 1964, 1; "Special Session June 17," UPI, West Point *Times-Leader*, 12 June 1964, 1; "Special Session Set for June 17," AP, Gulfport *Daily Herald*, 6 June 1964, 1; "State Moves to Cope with Legal Thrust of Mixers," AP, *Natchez Democrat*, 15 June 1964, 1; "State Pay for Private School Plan," UPI, Greenville *Delta Democrat-Times*, 18 June 1964, 1.

150. "Altered School Bill Passes House," AP Gulfport *Daily Herald*, 1 July 1964, 1; "Battle in Legislature Looms over Schools," UPI, Pascagoula *Chronicle*, 26 June 1964, 1; "Battle Looms on Church Schools," UPI, West Point *Times-Leader*, 26 June 1964, 1; "Church-related Schools Excluded," AP, *Vicksburg Evening Post*, 1 July 1964, 1; "Differing School Bills Pass," AP, *Natchez Democrat*, 26 June 1964, 1; "House Key to Final School Bill Action," UPI, Tupelo *Daily Journal*, 30 June 1964, 1; "House, Senate, Stage War of Nerves," AP, *Laurel Leader-Call*, 30 June 1964, 1; "Lawmakers Split on Church School Tuition," UPI, Pascagoula *Chronicle*, 30 June 1964, 1; "Legislators Adopt Last Ditch Plan," Jackson *Daily News*, 16 July 1964, 1; "Legislature School Try Bogs Down," AP, *Starkville Daily News*, 11 July 1964, 1; "Nonsectarian Private School Bill Approved," AP, McComb *Enterprise-Journal*, 16 July 1964, 1; "Parochial Schools Are Football for State Legislature," AP, *Starkville Daily News*, 2 July 1964, 1; "Private Schools Grants Passed by Senate," UPI, Greenville *Delta Democrat-Times*, 1 July 1964, 1; "Private School Plan Up in Air," Jackson *Clarion-Ledger*, 11 July 1964, 1; "Reaction Mixed on Proposed School Tuition," UPI, Pascagoula *Chronicle*, 25 June 1964, 1; "School Aid Questioned by Churches," AP, *Starkville Daily News*, 25 June 1964, 1; "School Plan Reaction Is Mixed," AP, *Meridian Star*, 24 June 1964, 1; "Senate Alters Bill, Church Schools Out," AP, *Laurel Leader-Call*, 1 July 1964, 1; "Senate Is Not Expected to Budge on School Bill," AP, McComb *Enterprise-Journal*, 14 July 1964, 1; "Senate Stands Pat on Decision to Aid Only Nonsectarian Schools," AP, *Hattiesburg American*, 1 July 1964, 1; "Solons Seesaw toward School Plan Decision," AP, McComb *Enterprise-Journal*, 30 June 1964, 1; "Solons Try Again for Tuition Grants Accord," UPI, Tupelo *Daily Journal*, 14 July 1964, 1.

151. "A Sharp Blow for Mississippi in Surry Ruling," UPI, *Meridian Star*, 19 June 1964, 1; "County Ordered to Raise Money to Reopen Schools Closed Five Years," UPI, West Point *Times-Leader*, 18 June 1964, 1; "Federal Court Crushes Private School Tuition Plan," UPI, Corinth *Daily Corinthian*, 19 June 1964, 1; "Federal Judge Issues Injunction," UPI, Grenada *Sentinel-Star*, 19 June 1964, 1; "Federal Judge Throws Out Tax Paid Tuition," AP, Jackson *Daily News*, 19 June 1964, 1; "Legislature Adopts Tuition Bill despite Claims It Can't Stand Court Challenge," UPI, Corinth *Daily Corinthian*, 16 July 1964, 1; "Mississippi Will Wait and See," UPI, Greenville *Delta Democrat-Times*, 19 June 1964, 1; "Must Open

Schools, Board Told," AP, Gulfport *Daily Herald*, 18 June 1964, 1; "Prince Edward County Must Levy New Taxes," UPI, Tupelo *Daily Journal*, 18 June 1964, 1; "Prince Edward Has Week to Raise Funds," AP, *Hattiesburg American*, 18 June 1964, 1; "Prince Edward Seeks Way to Obey Law," AP, Jackson *Daily News*, 23 June 1964, 1; "Private School Plan Squashed," UPI, Greenville *Delta Democrat-Times*, 19 June 1964, 1; "State Solons Watch Surry County Case," UPI, Tupelo *Daily Journal*, 15 June 1964, 8; "Tax Levy Ruled in Prince Edward," AP, Jackson *Clarion-Ledger*, 18 June 1964, 1; "Virginia Decision Is Blow to State School Plan," UPI, Tupelo *Daily Journal*, 20–21 June 1964, 1; "U.S. Judge Again Declares Tuition Grants Unlawful," AP, Jackson *Daily News*, 22 July 1964, 1; "Virginia Judge Refuses to Block Segregation Plan," UPI, West Point *Times-Leader*, 9 July 1964, 1; "Virginia Schools Issue," AP, *Natchez Democrat*, 18 June 1964, 1.

152. "Dual Public-Private School Proposal Ready for Legislature's Consideration," AP, *Meridian Star*, 18 June 1964, 1; "Dual School System Awaits Legislation by Special Session," UPI, Grenada *Sentinel-Star*, 18 June 1964, 1; "Dual School System Plan Nearly Ready," UPI, Greenville *Delta Democrat-Times*, 17 June 1964, 1; "Governor Favors School Proposal," AP, Gulfport *Daily Herald*, 23 June 1964, 1; "Governor to Call Special Session," UPI, Pascagoula *Chronicle*, 7 June 1964, 1; "Johnson to Call Special Session," AP, *Laurel Leader-Call*, 5 June 1964, 1; "Johnson to Outline Private School Bid," AP, *Laurel Leader-Call*, 23 June 1964, 1; "Lawmakers Plot Course If State Schools Mix," UPI, Tupelo *Daily Journal*, 4 June 1964, 1; "Legislators Order Study of Schools, Private System Urged by Some in Jackson," UPI, *Clarksdale Press Register*, 5 June 1964, 1; "Paul B. Joins 'School Mix' Work Group," UPI, *Meridian Star*, 11 June 1964, 1; "Paul Urges Fast School Decision," Jackson *Daily News*, 23 June 1964, 1; "PBJ Planning Special Session," AP, *Vicksburg Evening Post*, 11 June 1964, 1; "PBJ Vows Private School Plan Will Stand U.S. Court Tests," AP, *Vicksburg Evening Post*, 23 June 1964, 1; "School Session to Open Tuesday," AP, McComb *Enterprise-Journal*, 22 June 1964, 1; "Special Session on Private Schools Convened Today," AP, *Starkville Daily News*, 23 June 1964, 1; "State Legislature Meets Tuesday to Consider Tuition Grants," AP, *Natchez Democrat*, 22 June 1964, 1; "Tall Paul Signs New School Act," UPI, Grenada *Sentinel-Star*, 16 July 1964, 1; "Urgency Surrounds School Plan as Court Orders Mix," UPI, Corinth *Daily Corinthian*, 8 July 1964, 1.

153. "Governor Gives Views on Civil Rights Law," AP, Gulfport *Daily Herald*, 13 August 1964, 1; "Integration like Prohibition—Paul," AP, Jackson *Daily News*, 13 August 1964, 2; "PBJ Attacks Civil Rights Attempts," Jackson *Clarion-Ledger*, 13 August 1964, 1; "PBJ Says Mississippi Has No Obligation," AP, *Laurel Leader-Call*, 13 August 1964, 2; "State to Shun Enforcement of Rights Statute," AP, *Vicksburg Evening Post*, AP, 13 August 1964, 1; "Talk of Town," Corinth *Daily Corinthian*, 14 August 1964, 1.

154. "Appeal in School Case Won't Stop Integration," Jackson *Clarion-Ledger*, 8 July 1964, 1; "Boards Ready Plans to Integrate Schools," Jackson *Clarion-Ledger*, 14 July 1964, 1; "Court Orders Schools to Begin Mixing," UPI, Columbus *Commercial Dispatch*, 30 July 1964, 1; "Desegregation Injunctions Now Permanent," UPI, Columbus *Commercial Dispatch*, 7 July 1964, 1; "Desegregation Order Given Permanent Status," AP, McComb *Enterprise-Journal*, 7 July 1964, 1; "Federal Judge Makes Mix Order for State Permanent," AP, *Greenwood Commonwealth*, 7 July 1964, 1; "Gives Orders for Schools," AP, *Laurel Leader-Call*, 7 July

1964, 1; "Jackson Announces Plans for School Integration," AP, *Greenwood Commonwealth*, 6 August 1964, 1; "Jackson, Biloxi File Plans for Integration," UPI, Greenville *Delta Democrat-Times*, 15 July 1964, 1; "Jackson Defends Integration Plan," Jackson *Daily News*, 29 July 1964, 1; "Jackson Schools Open First Grade to Negroes," AP, *Greenwood Commonwealth*, 3 August 1964, 1; "Judge Mize Orders School Mix in Jackson, Biloxi, Leake County," UPI, Tupelo *Daily Journal*, 8 July 1964, 1; "Judge Okays Plan for School Mix," AP, *Laurel Leader-Call*, 30 July 1964, 1; "Judge Orders State Schools to Take Negroes This Fall," UPI, Greenville *Delta Democrat-Times*, 7 July 1964, 1; "Mixing Orders to Stand," AP, *Vicksburg Evening Post*, 7 July 1964, 1; "Mize Okays Desegregation Plans," AP, McComb *Enterprise-Journal*, 30 July 1964, 1; "Mize Orders Three Cities to Mix Schools by This Fall," UPI, West Point *Times-Leader*, 7 July 1964, 1; "Mize Issues Mix Decrees for Three Districts," UPI, Corinth *Daily Corinthian*, 7 July 1964, 1; "Mize Orders Three Schools Mixed," AP, *Starkville Daily News*, 8 July 1964, 1; "Negro Suits Seeking September Desegregation in Public Schools in Jackson, Biloxi and Leake Co.," UPI, *Clarksdale Press Register*, 4 June 1964, 1; "Orders Given to Integrate Three State Schools," UPI, Pascagoula *Chronicle*, 7 July 1964, 3; "School Areas Plan to Appeal Court Decision," UPI, *Meridian Star*, 8 July 1964, 1; "School Desegregation Order Made Permanent," AP, *Hattiesburg American*, 7 July 1964, 1; "School Boards Submit Plans," AP, *Laurel Leader-Call*, 15 July 1964, 1; "School Officials Submit Plans," UPI, Grenada *Sentinel-Star*, 15 July 1964, 1; "Stairstep Plan Proposed for Jackson Schools," UPI, Tupelo *Daily Journal*, 15 July 1964, 1; "Three School Boards File Appeal Notices," AP, *Greenwood Commonwealth*, 3 August 1964, 1; "Three School Systems Will Desegregate," AP, Gulfport *Daily Herald*, 16 July 1964, 8; "Two Boards Submit School Mixing Plans," AP, *Greenwood Commonwealth*, 15 July 1964, 1.

155. "Grade-a-Year Objection Set before Mize," UPI, Pascagoula *Chronicle*, 29 July 1964, 3; "NAACP Objects to Mixing Plans," Jackson *Daily News*, 16 July 1964, 1; "Negroes Ask Faster Mix," AP, *Starkville Daily News*, 17 July 1964, 1; "Negroes Charge Stairstep Mix Plan Is Too Slow," UPI, Tupelo *Daily Journal*, 17 July 1964, 15; "Negroes Contesting Desegregation Plan," Jackson *Clarion-Ledger*, 17 July 1964, 1.

156. "Court Gives Tentative Approval to Mix Plan," Jackson *Clarion-Ledger*, 30 July 1964, 1; "Court Orders Mix for School Plan," Jackson *Clarion-Ledger*, 15 July 1964, 1; "Impending School Crisis Viewed in Jackson," UPI, *Clarksdale Press Register*, 6 June 1964, 1; "Judge Mize Orders School Mix Move at One Grade a Year," AP, *Starkville Daily News*, 30 July 1964, 1; "School Mix Order Made Permanent," AP, Gulfport *Daily Herald*, 7 July 1964, 1; "School Mixing Plans Okay," UPI, Corinth *Daily Corinthian*, 30 July 1964, 1; "Three School Systems File First Grade Stair Step Plans," Jackson *Clarion-Ledger*, 16 July 1964, 1; "Two School Boards Submit Mixing Plans," AP, *Hattiesburg American*, 15 July 1964, 1.

157. "Desegregation Plans Presented," *Clarksdale Press Register*, 28 July 1964, 1; "Judge Orders Class Mixed," *Clarksdale Press Register*, 20 August 1964, 1; "Judge Orders Integration Plan Crafted, Clarksdale Public Schools," *Clarksdale Press Register*, 27 June 1964, 1; "Negroes Want Desegregation Plan Revised," *Clarksdale Press Register*, 31 July 1964, 1.

158. "City School Registration Produces No Mixed Classes," *Clarksdale Press Register*, 25 August 1964, 1.

159. "Group Supporting Public Schools Opens Statewide," UPI, Tupelo *Daily Journal*, 20 July 1964, 1; McMillen, *The Citizen's Council*, 263; "Mississippians for Public Education Organize Here," UPI, Tupelo *Daily Journal*, 2 July 1964, 1; "Oxford Group Warns about Private Set Up," Jackson *Daily News*, 9 July 1964, 4; "Public School Support Gaining," UPI, Tupelo *Daily Journal*, 1–2 August, 1964, 1; "Public School Supporters Organize," Greenville *Delta Democrat-Times*, 23 July 1964, 1; "School Plan Getting More Controversial," UPI, Grenada *Sentinel-Star*, 21 July 1964, 1; "Urges Parents to Keep Sending Children to Public Schools," Jackson *Daily News*, 25 August 1964, 5.

160. "League of Women Voters Oppose Dual School System," UPI, West Point *Times-Leader*, 19 June 1964, 1; "Opposed to School Proposal," AP, Gulfport *Daily Herald*, 19 June 1964, 1; "Women Voters Oppose Bill for Tuition," UPI, Pascagoula *Chronicle*, 19 June 1964, 1.

161. "Educators, Clerics Assail Dual School System," UPI, Tupelo *Daily Journal*, 25 June 1964, 1.

162. Hodding Carter III, "Experimenting with Failure," Greenville *Delta Democrat-Times*, 11 June 1964, 4.

163. Ibid.

164. Hodding Carter III, "Schools and Taxes," Greenville *Delta Democrat-Times*, 1 July 1964, 4; Hodding Carter III, "Risky Adventure," Greenville *Delta Democrat-Times*, 17 July 1964, 4.

165. Hodding Carter III, "Let's Face the Truth," Greenville *Delta Democrat-Times*, 22 June 1964, 2.

166. J.O. Emmerich, "Can Tax Money Pay for Private Schools?" McComb *Enterprise-Journal*, 16 June 1964, 2.

167. Leonard Lowrey, "Wise Course," *Hattiesburg American*, 5 June 1964, 10.

168. Leonard Lowrey, "Covering the News," *Hattiesburg American*, 10 August 1964, 10.

169. Harry Rutherford, "Court Saves Our State from Legislature," Tupelo *Daily Journal*, 19 June 1964, 14; Harry Rutherford, "Experiments in Ignorance Are Too Costly," Tupelo *Daily Journal*, 4 June 1964, 3; Harry Rutherford, "Keep Public Schools," Tupelo *Daily Journal*, 26 August 1964, 16; Harry Rutherford, "State's White Schools in Serious Danger," Tupelo *Daily Journal*, 9 June 1964, 11; Harry Rutherford, "Virginia Example," Tupelo *Daily Journal*, 10 June 1964, 11.

170. Harry Rutherford, "Experience of Other States Can Guide Us," Tupelo *Daily Journal*, 23 June 1964, 11.

171. Harry Rutherford, "Unbelievable Offense," Tupelo *Daily Journal*, 29 June 1964, 12.

172. Harry Rutherford, "Handing State to Extremists on Platter," Tupelo *Daily Journal*, 6 July 1964, 15.

173. James "Jimmy" Ward, "Desegregation in Jackson," Jackson *Daily News*, 21 August 1964, 10.

174. "Bishop Orders Catholic Schools to Integrate," UPI, *Meridian Star*, 10 August 1964, 1; "Bishop Urges Catholics to Accept Law," Jackson *Daily News*, 3 July 1964, 1; "Catholic Bishop Orders Schools to Integrate," AP, *Greenwood Commonwealth*, 10 August 1964, 1; "Catholics to Integrate Pupils in First Grade," Jackson *Clarion-Ledger*, 10 August 1964, 1; "Catholics Prepare for Integration of Beginning Students," Jackson *Daily News*, 10 August 1964, 1; "Catholic Schools

Will Desegregate," AP, Greenville *Delta Democrat-Times*, AP, 10 August 1964, 1; "Catholics Will Mix Mississippi Schools," UPI, Corinth *Daily Corinthian*, 10 August 1964, 1; "Mississippi Catholic Schools to Mix in Fall," UPI, Tupelo *Daily Journal*, 10 August 1964, 1; "Pascagoula Catholics Face Mixing," UPI, Pascagoula *Chronicle*, 10 August 1964, 1; "Plans to Mix Catholic Schools Announced," UPI, West Point *Times-Leader*, 10 August 1964, 1; "Protests in Mixing Parochial Schools," AP, Gulfport *Daily Herald*, 12 August 1964, 1; "Saint Peter's Plans to Drop Racial Bars This Year," Pascagoula *Chronicle*, 11 August 1964, 2; "State Catholics Plan Integration," AP, *Vicksburg Evening Post*, 10 August 1964, 1; "State's Catholic Schools Told to Mix," AP, McComb *Enterprise-Journal*, 10 August 1964, 1.

175. "Alphonsus to Remain Segregated," McComb *Enterprise-Journal*, 17 August 1964, 1; "No Mixing at McComb Parochials," AP, Gulfport *Daily Herald*, 19 August 1964, 1.

176. "No Catholic School Integration Here This Year," *Hattiesburg American*, 10 August 1964, 1.

177. Hodding Carter III, "A Lie Exposed Again," Greenville *Delta Democrat-Times*, 17 August 1964, 4.

178. Leonard Lowrey, "The Best Way," *Hattiesburg American*, 4 June 1964, 14.

179. "Membership Grows, Klan Claims Whites Resent Civil Rights," AP, Gulfport *Daily Herald*, 17 July 1964, 4.

180. "APWR President Says His Group Is Not Violent," AP, McComb *Enterprise-Journal*, 6 July 1964, 11; "APWR Head States Group's Future Plans," AP, *Laurel Leader-Call*, 6 July 1964, 1; "APWR Leader Refutes Charges," Jackson *Clarion-Ledger*, 21 June 1964, 3; "APWR Refutes Charges," Jackson *Daily News*, 21 June 1964, 3; "New Organization Preserves White Race," AP, Gulfport *Daily Herald*, 6 July 1964, 1.

181. Hodding Carter III, "The True Image," Greenville *Delta Democrat-Times*, 10 August 1964, 4.

182. "Accommodations Section Will Not Be Tested," AP, Jackson *Daily News*, 2 July 1964, 3; "Don't Plan to Test Civil Rights Bill, Say College Students," AP, *Greenwood Commonwealth*, 1 July 1964, 1.

183. "Agitators Classes Taught at Small Ohio College," AP, Jackson *Daily News*, 19 June 1964, 1; "More Civil Rights Workers Head South," UPI, *Clarksdale Press Register*, 27 June 1964, 1; "Rededicate Selves, Integrators Urged," AP, Jackson *Clarion-Ledger*, 26 June 1964, 1; "Train for Invasion of State," AP, Gulfport *Daily Herald*, 16 June 1964, 1.

184. Sally Belfrage, *Freedom Summer* (New York: Viking Press, 1965), introduction; Seth Cagin and Philip Dray, *We Are Not Afraid: The Story of Goodman, Schwerner and Chaney and the Civil Rights Campaign for Mississippi* (New York: Bantam Books, 1991), 29–32; Thomas Clark and Albert D. Kirwan, eds., *The South since Appomattox: A Century of Regional Change* (New York: Oxford University Press, 1967), 371; Harry Holloway, *The Politics of the Southern Negro* (New York: Random House, 1969), 50; Len Holt, *The Summer That Didn't End* (New York: William Morrow, 1965), 31–42; Walter Lord, *The Past That Would Not Die* (New York: Harper and Row, 1965), 246; Doug McAdam, *Freedom Summer* (New York: Oxford University Press, 1988), introduction; Anne Moody, *Coming of Age in*

Mississippi (New York: Dial Press, 1968), 330–348; Juan Williams, *Eyes on the Prize: America's Civil Rights Years, 1954–1965* (New York: Viking Press, 1987), 239.

185. Charles M. Payne, *I've Got the Light of Freedom* (Berkeley: University of California Press, 1995), 301–306.

186. John Dittmer, *Local People: The Struggle for Civil Rights in Mississippi* (Urbana: University of Illinois Press, 1994), 259.

187. "Civil Rights Director Says Workers to Shun Area," AP, *Natchez Democrat*, 1 July 1964, 1; "Civil Rights Recruiting for State Closed, Area Restricted," AP, Jackson *Clarion-Ledger*, 1 July 1964, 1; "Northern Students Won't Be Sent to Area Soon," AP, McComb *Enterprise-Journal*, 1 July 1964, 1; "Project Workers Plan to Move Cautiously in Areas of Tension," UPI, Tupelo *Daily Journal*, 1 July 1964, 1; "Rights Leader Vows to Send Professional People," UPI, Columbus *Commercial Dispatch*, 1 July 1964, 1.

188. Dittmer, *Local People*, 251; Clark and Kirwan, *The South since Appomattox*, 371; Lord, *The Past That Would Not Die*, 237; Elizabeth Sutherland, ed., *Letters from Mississippi* (New York: McGraw-Hill, 1965), 73.

189. Carlton Mabee, "Evolution of Non-Violence," *The Nation*, 21 August 1961, 78–81.

190. C. Vann Woodward, *The Strange Career of Jim Crow* (New York: Oxford University Press, 1966), 170.

191. Martin Oppenheimer, "The Genesis of the Southern Negro Movement: A Study in Contemporary Negro Protest" (Ph.D. diss., University of Pennsylvania, 1963), 63–64.

192. William Lang Baradell, "An Analysis of the Coverage Given by Five North Carolina Newspapers of Three Events in the Civil Rights Movement in the State" (Master's thesis, University of North Carolina at Chapel Hill, 1990), 5.

193. Fitz McCoy, "McCoy's Column," *Hattiesburg American*, 13 June 1964, 10.

194. Oppenheimer, "The Genesis of the Southern Negro Student Movement," 63–64.

195. "Florida Strike Continues, Integration Leader Reports Life Threatened," UPI, *Clarksdale Press Register*, 5 June 1964, 1; "Grand Jury Refuses King's Truce Terms," AP, *Hattiesburg American*, 19 June 1964, 1; "Integrationist King Is Arrested," UPI, Pascagoula *Chronicle*, 11 June 1964, 1; "King Jailed as Vowed in St. Augustine," AP, *Meridian Star*, 11 June 1964, 1; "King Issues New Threats," UPI, West Point *Times-Leader*, 2 July 1964, 5; "King Jailed in Florida," AP, *Starkville Daily News*, 12 June 1964, 1; "King May Cause Trouble Again in Florida," UPI, Greenville *Delta Democrat-Times*, 17 June 1964, 1; "King Opens All-Out Mixing in St. Augustine," UPI, Corinth *Daily Corinthian*, 10 June 1964, 1; "King Says No Let Up," AP, *Laurel Leader-Call*, 25 June 1964, 1; "Martin Luther King Arraigned in Court," AP, *Hattiesburg American*, 12 June 1964, 1; "Martin Luther King Jailed for Sit-In," AP, *Hattiesburg American*, 11 June 1964, 1; "Martin Luther King Jailed in St. Augustine," UPI, Jackson *Daily News*, 11 June 1964, 1; "Martin Luther King Plans Massive Tests of Civil Rights," UPI, Jackson *Daily News*, 11 June 1964, 1; "Martin Luther King Pleads Innocent, Held under Bond," UPI, *Clarksdale Press Register*, 12 June 1964, 1; "Martin Luther King Takes Florida Spotlight," AP, McComb *Enterprise-Journal*, 11 June 1964, 3.

196. "Civil Rights Leader Plans Boost to Negro Democratic Party," UPI, West Point *Times-Leader*, 21 July 1964, 2; "King Asks Nonviolence and Pushes New Party," *Meridian Star*, 25 July 1964, 1; "King Plans to Boost New Democrat Party," AP, *Laurel Leader-Call*, 21 July 1964, 1; "King Tells Plan for New Party," AP, Gulfport *Daily Herald*, 22 July 1964, 1; "King Urges Plan to Unseat Party," AP, *Laurel Leader-Call*, 22 July 1964, 1; "Martin Luther King Comes to State to Boost Freedom Democrats," AP, *Hattiesburg American*, 21 July 1964, 1; "Negro Leader Touring State for Freedom Democrats," UPI, *Clarksdale Press Register*, 21 July 1964, 1; "New Party Forming, Martin Luther King to Aid," UPI, Columbus *Commercial Dispatch*, 21 July 1964, 1.

197. Jane Biggers, "Small Crowd Greets King at Greenwood," AP, Jackson *Clarion-Ledger*, 22 July 1964, 1; "King Exhorts Greenwood Negroes to Register, Vote," UPI, Tupelo *Daily Journal*, 22 July 1964, 4; "King in Mississippi to Help Organize 'Freedom Democrats,' " UPI, Tupelo *Daily Journal*, 22 July 1964, 1; "King Is Due in State to Help Movement," AP, Gulfport *Daily Herald*, 21 July 1964, 1; "King Sparks Voter Drive," UPI, Corinth *Daily Corinthian*, 22 July 1964, 1; "King to Speak at Rally Here," AP, *Greenwood Commonwealth*, 22 July 1964, 1; "King Recruits Voters, Slaps at FBI," AP, Jackson *Daily News*, 22 July 1964, 1; "Martin Luther King's Oratory Pushes Registration," UPI, Columbus *Commercial Dispatch*, 22 July 1964, 1; "Registration Effort Due in Greenwood," UPI, *Clarksdale Press Register*, 22 July 1964, 1; "Rev. King Is Slated to Pay Visit to Delta Area Today," Greenville *Delta Democrat-Times*, 21 July 1964, 1.

198. "King Denies Red Charges," AP, Jackson *Daily News*, 23 July 1964, 1; "King Denies Reds Infiltrate Racial Struggle," UPI, Corinth *Daily Corinthian*, 25 July 1964, 1; "Leader Denies Reds in Civil Rights Movement," UPI, Greenville *Delta Democrat-Times*, 24 July 1964, 1; "Martin Luther King Denies Red Action in Civil Rights Movement," UPI, *Clarksdale Press Register*, 23 July 1964, 12; "Martin Luther King Tired of Commie Label," AP, McComb *Enterprise-Journal*, 23 July 1964, 1; "Negro King Denies Red Infiltration of 'Righters,' " UPI, West Point *Times-Leader*, 23 July 1964, 1.

199. "King Agrees Missing Trio Probably Dead," UPI, Tupelo *Daily Journal*, 25, 26 July 1964, 9; "King Tells Pool Hall Crowd Trio Now Dead," UPI, Jackson *Clarion-Ledger*, 25 July 1964, 1; Ken Tolliver, "King Launches Attack on FBI," Greenville *Delta Democrat-Times*, 22 July 1964, 1.

200. "King Finds North More Explosive," AP, Jackson *Daily News*, 1 August 1964, 1; "King Says North Race Relations Worse Than South," AP, *Hattiesburg American*, 1 August 1964, 1; "Race Relations in North Bad, King Declares," AP, Gulfport *Daily Herald*, 1 August 1964, 1.

201. Birney Imes, Jr., "Economic Blackmail," Columbus *Commercial Dispatch*, 5 July 1964, 4.

202. James Lambert, "Unwanted Outsiders," *Natchez Democrat*, 11 July 1964, 4.

203. Unsigned letter to the editor, *Greenwood Commonwealth*, 8 July 1964, 8.

204. James B. Skewes, "We Make Poor Slaves," *Meridian Star*, 12 June 1964, 4.

205. James "Jimmy" Ward, "Plate Passing Philosophy," Jackson *Daily News*, 22 July 1964, 6.

206. Harry Rutherford, "False Leaders Can Turn Progress to Loss," Tupelo *Daily Journal*, 12 June 1964, 16.

207. Loewen and Sallis, *Mississippi*, 268.

208. "Governor Raps Council Effort," UPI, *Clarksdale Press Register*, 3 July 1964, 1; "Johnson Hits Council," UPI, West Point *Times-Leader*, 3 July 1964, 1; "National Council of Churches Plans State Strategy," UPI, Greenville *Delta Democrat-Times*, 11 June 1964, 1; "NCC Blasted by Governor," UPI, *Meridian Star*, 3 July 1964, 1; "NCC Tells Mississippi to Change Thinking," UPI, Greenville *Delta Democrat-Times*, 14 June 1964, 3; "NCC Abandons Pulpit," Jackson *Daily News*, 14 June 1964, B1; "Paul Lashes Rights Drive in Mississippi," UPI, Corinth *Daily Corinthian*, 10 June 1964, 1; "Paul Blasts Church Aid to Project," UPI, Greenville *Delta Democrat-Times*, 3 July 1964, 1.

209. Leonard Lowrey, "NCC Cranks Up," *Hattiesburg American*, 13 June 1964, 2.

210. Leonard Lowrey, "The Mission of the Church," *Hattiesburg American*, 25 July 1964, 2.

211. Leonard Lowrey, "The Church Errs," *Hattiesburg American*, 29 August 1964, 2.

212. T.M. Hederman, Jr., "NCC Abandons the Pulpit?" Jackson *Clarion-Ledger*, 14 June 1964, 20.

213. W. David Brown, "NCC Aids Insurrectionists," Pascagoula *Chronicle*, 10 July 1964, 4.

214. "City Methodists Ask Council of Churches to Change Policies on Civil Rights," *Clarksdale Press Register*, 8 July 1964, 1; "Clarksdale Methodists Blast NCC," Jackson *Daily News*, 9 July 1964, 8.

215. "Galloway Group Holds NCC Funds," UPI, Grenada *Sentinel-Star*, 11 August 1964, 1; "Methodists Withhold FCC Funds," AP, Gulfport *Daily Herald*, 11 August 1964, 1.

216. "City Methodists Ask Council of Churches to Change Policies on Civil Rights," *Clarksdale Press Register*, 8 July 1964, 1.

217. "Mississippi Methodists Ask Clergymen to Avoid Racial Demonstrations," UPI, *Clarksdale Press Register*, 5 June 1964, 1.

218. Ed Williams, "Lowman Raps NCC, Warns of Leftists," Jackson *Daily News*, 17 June 1964, 11; "Lowman Says Invasion Goal Is to Bring in Troops," *Vicksburg Evening Post*, 25 June 1964, 1; "Lowman to Speak Here on NCC's Delta Project," *Clarksdale Press Register*, 17 June 1964, 1.

219. "Asks NCC to Withdraw from Civil Rights Movement," AP, *Natchez Democrat*, 28 June 1964, 1; "Lowman, Church Leaders Disclose Plan for Mix Campaign," Jackson *Daily News*, 13 June 1964, 1; Stanley Dearman, "Methodist Church Attacked in Speech by Circuit Rider," *Meridian Star*, 19 June 1964, 1; "Methodists Told Not to Sit on Sidelines," AP, *Greenwood Commonwealth*, 4 June 1964, 2; "NCC Soundly Hit by Speaker Here," Jackson *Clarion-Ledger*, 17 June 1964, 1; "Red Activity in Racial Stir to Be Discussed," *Greenwood Commonwealth*, 19 June 1964, 1; "Role of Church Lowman's Topic," Jackson *Daily News*, 16 June 1964, 4.

220. "Presbyterians Decline Strong NCC Criticism," Jackson *Clarion-Ledger*, 5 June 1964, 3; "Presbyterians Reject Move to Slap NCC," Jackson *Daily News*, 4

June 1964, 1; "Tennessee Presbyterian Synod Urges Churches to Admit Negroes," UPI, Tupelo *Daily Journal*, 17 June 1964, 1.

221. "550 Civil Rights Workers Now in State," AP, *Natchez Democrat*, 2 July 1964, 1; "Another Group Comes to Mississippi," AP, McComb *Enterprise-Journal*, 29 June 1964, 3; "Mixers Arrive in State," AP, *Natchez Democrat*, 29 June 1964, 1; "More Rightists Reach State," UPI, *Clarksdale Press Register*, 29 June 1964, 1; "More Workers Still Plan to Come South," AP, *Hattiesburg American*, 24 June 1964, 1; "New Volunteers Flood State," UPI, Greenville *Delta Democrat-Times*, 29 June 1964, 1; "New Wave of Right Groups Due," AP, Gulfport *Daily Herald*, 27 June 1964, 1; "Second Contingent of 'Mississippi Project' Workers Arrive in State," UPI, Tupelo *Daily Journal*, 29 June 1964, 1; "Second Wave of Summer Volunteers Head South," AP, *Greenwood Commonwealth*, 27 June 1964, 1.

222. "Southern Foes Kill State Line Amendment," AP, *Laurel Leader-Call*, 13 June 1964, 1; "Stennis Beaten on Anti-Rider Amendment," UPI, Jackson *Daily News*, 12 June 1964, 12; "Senate Defeats Stennis' Freedom Rider Amendment," AP, *Hattiesburg American*, 12 June 1964, 1; "Stennis Appeals for Federal Aid against Riders," AP, *Vicksburg Evening Post*, 18 June 1964, 1; "Stennis Appeals to LBJ, RFK, in Halting Invasion," AP, *Laurel Leader-Call*, 19 June 1964, 14; "Stennis Asks Johnson to Halt Invasion," UPI, Pascagoula *Chronicle*, 25 June 1964, 2; "Stennis Asks President to Halt Invasion," Jackson *Daily News*, 24 June 1964, 1; "Stennis Calls for Halt to 'Invasion,' " UPI, *Meridian Star*, 24 June 1964, 1; "Stennis Calls on LBJ to Stop Invasion," AP, Gulfport *Daily Herald*, 27 June 1964, 2; "Stennis Calls on President, Attorney General to Halt Invasion of Mississippi," UPI, West Point *Times-Leader*, 24 June 1964, 1; "Stennis Deplores Mass Invasion by Outsiders," AP, Jackson *Clarion-Ledger*, 25 June 1964, 1B; "Stennis Urges Invasion Be Called Off," AP, *Starkville Daily News*, 25 June 1964, 7; "Stennis Urges LBJ Advise Civil Rights Invaders to Stay Home," UPI, Tupelo *Daily Journal*, 23 June 1964, 1; "Stop Invasion, Stennis Asks in Capital," UPI, *Clarksdale Press Register*, 24 June 1964, 1.

223. Thatcher Walt, "Tries Again," *Greenwood Commonwealth*, 23 June 1964, 4.

224. Sherrill Nash, "Too Late, Senator," *Starkville Daily News*, 24 June 1964, 4.

225. "Court Dismisses Suit Attacking Picket Law," UPI, West Point *Times-Leader*, 16 July 1964, 1; "Court Rules in Picket Law," UPI, Grenada *Sentinel-Star*, 17 July 1964, 1; "Court Upholds Anti-Picket Law in State," UPI, *Clarksdale Press Register*, 17 July 1964, 1; "Cox Rejects NAACP," UPI, *Greenwood Commonwealth*, 4 June 1964, 1; "Demonstrators and NAACP Hit Cox Ruling," AP, *Meridian Star*, 4 June 1964, 1; "Federal Court Dismisses Anti-Picket Suit," AP, *Natchez Democrat*, 17 July 1964, 1; "Judge Refuses Negro's Request for Injunction," Jackson *Daily News*, 4 June 1964, 1; "Law Passed to Deal with Demonstrators," UPI, Pascagoula *Chronicle*, 5 June 1964, 1; "New Ordinance Gives Police Assistance," AP, *Starkville Daily News*, 1 July 1964, 1; "New Techniques Aimed at Mixers," McComb *Enterprise-Journal*, 24 June 1964, 2; "Race Bills Get Okay by Senate," AP, *Starkville Daily News*, 6 June 1964, 1; "Solons Clear Bills to Quell Racial Troubles," AP, *Vicksburg Evening Post*, 7 June 1964, 3; "State Anti-Picket Law Upheld by Judges," AP, Jackson *Clarion-Ledger*, 17 July 1964, 5; "U.S. Court Panel Says Anti-Picket Law Valid," UPI, Tupelo *Daily Journal*, 17 July 1964, 1.

226. "Bill Aimed at Civil Rights Freedom Schools," AP, Jackson *Daily News*, 5 June 1964, 3; "Freedom Schools Target of Bill Today," AP, Pascagoula *Chronicle*, 5 June 1964, 1; "House Seeks to Impose Curbs on Planned Freedom Schools," UPI, *Clarksdale Press Register*, 5 June 1964, 1; "Senate Bill Is Aimed at Racial Schools," UPI, *Meridian Star*, 5 June 1964, 1.

227. "Asks That Agitators Depart," AP, Gulfport *Daily Herald*, 21 July 1964, 1.

228. "Civil Rights Volunteers Urged to Register with Local Police," UPI, Grenada *Sentinel-Star*, 1 July 1964, 1; "Group to Discuss Civil Rights," UPI, Columbus *Commercial Dispatch*, 30 June 1964, 1; "Mayors Consult on Race Strife," UPI, *Clarksdale Press Register*, 30 June 1964, 1; "Mayors Discuss Rights Invasion of Mississippi," UPI, Pascagoula *Chronicle*, 1 July 1964, 1; "Mayors Discuss State Race Image," AP, McComb *Enterprise-Journal*, 30 June 1964, 7; "Mayors Meet Here on Racial Situation," Jackson *Daily News*, 26 June 1964, 1; "Mayors Request Registration of Rights Workers," UPI, Pascagoula *Chronicle*, 1 July 1964, 1; "Mayors Urge COFO Workers to Register," UPI, Tupelo *Daily Journal*, 1 July 1964, 1; "MMA Executives Meet to Discuss Racial Issues," AP, *Hattiesburg American*, 30 June 1964, 1; "MMA Urges State's 'Visitors' to Register with Local Police," AP, *Starkville Daily News*, 1 July 1964, 1; "Municipal Group Urges Civil Rights Workers to Register," AP, *Greenwood Commonwealth*, 1 July 1964, 1; "Rights Workers Urged to Register with Police," AP, McComb *Enterprise-Journal*, 1 July 1964, 1; William Chaze, "State Mayors Urge Civil Rights Squads Register," Jackson *Clarion-Ledger*, 1 July 1964, 1; "Urge Civil Rights Workers to Register," AP, *Natchez Democrat*, 1 July 1964, 2; "Volunteers Urged to Be Registered," UPI, Columbus *Commercial Dispatch*, 1 July 1964, 1.

229. "Civil Rights Heads Try to Void Law," UPI, Grenada *Sentinel-Star*, 31 July 1964, 1; "Civil Rights Leaders File Suit to Avoid Lawyer Law," UPI, West Point *Times-Leader*, 31 July 1964, 1; "Civil Rights Workers File Suit in Effort to Void State Laws," UPI, Greenville *Delta Democrat-Times*, 31 July 1964, 1; "COFO Attacks Law Qualifying Attorneys," UPI, Tupelo *Daily Journal*, 31 July 1964, 1; "COFO Attacks Law Regulating Attorneys," AP, *Laurel Leader-Call*, 31 July 1964, 1; "COFO Suit Attacks Restricting Civil Rights Attorneys," AP, Jackson *Daily News*, 31 July 1964, 3; "Court to Consider Lawyers' Case," UPI, *Clarksdale Press Register*, 1 August 1964, 1; "Curb on Lawyers Attacked," AP, Gulfport *Daily Herald*, 31 July 1964, 1; "File Answer to Suit by Mix Group on Attorneys," AP, *Natchez Democrat*, 20 August 1964, 4; "Mississippi Lawyers Deny Charges," UPI, Grenada *Sentinel-Star*, 14 August 1964, 1; "Negro Leaders Defy Ban," UPI, Corinth *Daily Corinthian*, 31 July 1964, 1; "Negroes' Attorneys Sidelined in Columbia," AP, McComb *Enterprise-Journal*, 30 June 1964; "Out-of-State Lawyers Included in Entourage Following Rights Workers," UPI, *Clarksdale Press Register*, 23 July 1964, 1; "Out-of-State Lawyers' Restrictions Attacked," UPI, Columbus *Commercial Dispatch*, 31 July 1964, 2; "Restrictions on Lawyers Contested by COFO," UPI, *Meridian Star*, 31 July 1964, 1; "State Lawyers File Reply to COFO Suit," AP, *Starkville Daily News*, 20 August 1964, 1; "Task Force of Lawyers to Tackle Dixie," UPI, Greenville *Delta Democrat-Times*, 7 June 1964, 1.

230. "Clueless Trail Is Left by Interracial Trio," UPI, *Meridian Star*, 23 June 1964, 1; "COFO Claims FBI Shirking," AP, Jackson *Clarion-Ledger*, 23 June 1964, 1; "COFO, CORE Say Three 'Righters' Lost in State," AP, McComb *Enterprise-*

Journal, 22 June 1964, 1; "COFO Workers Vanish, Fail to Return to Meridian," UPI, Tupelo *Daily Journal*, 23 June 1964, 1; "FBI Hunting Rights Trio," UPI, Greenville *Delta Democrat-Times*, 23 June 1964, 1; "FBI Hunting Three Civil Rights Workers Missing in State," UPI, Corinth *Daily Corinthian*, 23 June 1964, 1; "FBI Seeks Three Missing Civil Rights Workers in State," UPI, Pascagoula *Chronicle*, 23 June 1964, 1; "FBI Seeks Trio Missing in State," UPI, *Clarksdale Press Register*, 23 June 1964, 1; "Hunt for Workers Is Pressed," AP, Gulfport *Daily Herald*, 23 June 1964, 1; "LBJ Asks FBI to Spare No Effort," UPI, Grenada *Sentinel-Star*, 24 June 1964, 1; "LBJ Sparks Search for Missing Trio," Jackson *Daily News*, 23 June 1964, 1; "Massive Federal, State Probe Fails to Yield Lost 'Righters,' " AP, *Vicksburg Evening Post*, 24 June 1964, 1; "Search Begins for Missing Trio," UPI, Columbus *Commercial Dispatch*, 24 June 1964, 1; "Rights Workers Still Missing," AP, *Laurel Leader-Call*, 23 June 1964, 1; "Spare No Effort in Case Orders President," UPI, Columbus *Commercial Dispatch*, 23 June 1964, 1; "Three Civil Rights Workers Jailed but Released," UPI, Columbus *Commercial Dispatch*, 22 June 1964, 1; "Three Civil Rights Workers Reported Missing by COFO," AP, *Hattiesburg American*, 22 June 1964, 1; "Three Civil Rights Workers Said Missing," AP, *Starkville Daily News*, 23 June 1964, 1; "Three Rights Workers Reported Missing," UPI, West Point *Times-Leader*, 23 June 1964, 1; "Three Summer Workers Said Missing in Neshoba," AP, *Greenwood Commonwealth*, 22 June 1964, 1.

231. "Attack on Mississippi," from the *Manchester* (N.H.) *Union Leader* in the *Clarksdale Press Register*, 18 July 1964, 4; "Attack on Mississippi," from the *Manchester* (N.H.) *Union Leader* in the *Starkville Daily News*, 22 July 1964, 4; "Attack on Mississippi," from the *Manchester* (N.H.) *Union Leader* in the West Point *Times-Leader*, 21 July 1964, 4; "Let the South Alone," from the *Manchester* (N.H.) *Union Leader* in the Pascagoula *Chronicle* 2 July 1964, 4.

232. Hodding Carter III, "Time for Prayer in Mississippi," Greenville *Delta Democrat-Times*, 24 June 1964, 4.

233. Hodding Carter III, "Help Needed," Greenville *Delta Democrat-Times*, 30 June 1964, 4.

234. Hodding Carter III, "Bitter Lesson," Greenville *Delta Democrat-Times*, 29 June 1964, 4.

235. W. David Brown, "Inexcusable Action," Pascagoula *Chronicle*, 24 June 1964, 4.

236. W.H. Harris, "Pencil Shavings," *Starkville Daily News*, 2 July 1964, 2.

237. "Agents Comb Swamps in Search of Mix Trio," AP, *Laurel Leader-Call*, 24 June 1964, 1; "FBI Expands Search for Missing Trio," AP, *Starkville Daily News*, 30 June 1964, 1; "Lawmen Comb Swamps, Hills, for Missing 'Righters,' " AP, McComb *Enterprise-Journal*, 24 June 1964, 1; "LBJ Orders Intensive FBI Efforts," UPI, Clarksdale *Press Register*, 23 June 1964, 1; "LBJ Pleads for Justice, Sends More Federal Agents to Mississippi," UPI, Greenville *Delta Democrat-Times*, 28 June 1964, 1; "More FBI Agents Ordered into State," UPI, Jackson *Daily News*, 28 June 1964, 1; "President Sends More FBI Agents to State," UPI, Pascagoula *Chronicle*, 28 June 1964, 2; "Reinforcements Ordered for FBI Search," UPI, Columbus *Commercial Dispatch*, 28 June 1964, 1; "Search Continues for Missing Rights Workers," AP, *Hattiesburg American*, 24 June 1964, 1; "Send More FBI to State," AP, Gulfport *Daily Herald*, 26 June 1964, 1.

238. "50 FBI Agents Being Placed in State," AP, *Hattiesburg American*, 10 July 1964, 1; "50 FBI Officers Remain in State," AP, *Laurel Leader-Call*, 10 July 1964, 1; "50 New FBI Agents Coming," AP, *Starkville Daily News*, 11 July 1964, 6; "Director of FBI Coming to City," Jackson *Clarion-Ledger*, 10 July 1964, 1; "FBI Director Hoover Sees Governor Today," UPI, Tupelo *Daily Journal*, 10 July 1964, 1; "FBI Director in Jackson," AP, *Greenwood Commonwealth*, 10 July 1964, 1; "FBI Pledges All Out Effort," UPI, Clarksdale *Press Register*, 11 July 1964, 1; "FBI Strengthens Forces in State," AP, *Vicksburg Evening Post*, 11 July 1964, 1; "FBI Top Man in Mississippi," UPI, Grenada *Sentinel-Star*, 10 July 1964, 1; "FBI's Hoover Flies to State, Sees PBJ," UPI, Pascagoula *Chronicle*, 10 July 1964, 1; "Hoover Arrives Today," *Meridian Star*, 10 July 1964, 1; "Hoover in State," UPI, West Point *Times-Leader*, 10 July 1964, 1; "Hoover in Town to Beef Up FBI," Jackson *Daily News*, 10 July 1964, 1; "Hoover in State to Increase Agents," AP, Gulfport *Daily Herald*, 10 July 1964, 1; "J. Edgar Hoover Arrives in State," AP, *Hattiesburg American*, 10 June 1964, 1; "J. Edgar Hoover Beefs Up State FBI on Crash Basis, 50 Agents in State," AP, *Natchez Democrat*, 11 July 1964, 1; "Jackson FBI Office," AP, *Meridian Star*, 11 July 1964, 1; "LBJ to Station 50 FBI Agents in State," AP, McComb *Enterprise-Journal*, 10 July 1964, 1.

239. Charles Hills, "Affairs of State," Jackson *Clarion-Ledger*, 12 July 1964, 2F.

240. W. David Brown, "Inexcusable Action," Pascagoula *Chronicle*, 24 June 1964, 4.

241. "Hoover Says Events of Dixie Over-played," Jackson *Clarion-Ledger*, 13 July 1964, 1; "Lawlessness," *Hattiesburg American*, 15 July 1964, 4; "Mr. Hoover's Remarks," *Vicksburg Evening Post*, 13 July 1964, 3; " 'North, Too' Says Hoover of Lawlessness," UPI, *Meridian Star*, 12 July 1964, 1; "Overemphasis on Situation in Mississippi, Hoover Says," AP, *Natchez Democrat*, 12 July 1964, 1.

242. "Gov. Johnson Satisfied with Search," UPI, Clarksdale *Press Register*, 23 June 1964, 1.

243. "Futile Search in Philadelphia Continuing," UPI, Clarksdale *Press Register*, 29 June 1964, 1; "Fruitless Search Enters Tenth Day," UPI, Greenville *Delta Democrat-Times*, 1 July 1964, 1.

244. "Officials Fear Missing Trio Met with Foul Play," UPI, Clarksdale *Press Register*, 24 June 1964, 1.

245. "SNCC Leader Thinks Missing Men Dead," AP, Jackson *Daily News*, 29 June 1964, 1.

246. "FBI Chief Hoover in State, Thinks Civil Rights Workers Dead," AP, *Starkville Daily News*, 11 July 1964, 1; "Hoover Believes Trio Dead," AP, *Meridian Star*, 11 July 1964, 1; "Hoover Says Vanished Trio Probably Dead," UPI, Tupelo *Daily Journal*, 11–12 July 1964, 1.

247. "200 Marines Entered in Search," UPI, West Point *Times-Leader*, 25 June 1964, 1; "200 Marines to Aid in Search for Missing Civil Rights Trio," AP, *Vicksburg Evening Post*, 24 June 1964, 1; "Johnson Sends Marines to Aid in Search," UPI, Greenville *Delta Democrat-Times*, 25 June 1964, 1; "Marines Help in Search for Missing Trio," UPI, Clarksdale *Press Register*, 25 June 1964, 1; "Marines Join Feds, State Officers in Search for Rights Trio," AP, *Hattiesburg American*, 25 June 1964, 1; "Marines Join Vast Search in Swamp for Missing Trio," AP, McComb *Enterprise-Journal*, 25 June 1964, 1; "Marines Ordered into Search," UPI, Colum-

bus *Commercial Dispatch*, 25 June 1964, 1; 'Marines to State," UPI, Pascagoula *Chronicle*, 25 June 1964, 1; "Orders Marines to State Search," AP, *Laurel Leader-Call*, 25 June 1964, 1; "President Orders Marines to State," AP, *Greenwood Commonwealth*, 25 June 1964, 1; "Search Teams Scouring Ten Square Mile Area," UPI, Corinth *Daily Corinthian*, 26 June 1964, 1.

248. "200 U.S. Sailors Assist in Searching for Missing Three," AP, *Natchez Democrat*, 26 June 1964, 1; "300 More Navy Men Join Hunt in Philadelphia," AP, *Natchez Democrat*, 1 July 1964, 1; "400 Sailors Search," AP, *Greenwood Commonwealth*, 1 July 1964, 1; "Doubles Navy Search," UPI, Corinth *Daily Corinthian*, 30 June 1964, 1; "Johnson Orders 400 More Troops," AP, *Laurel Leader-Call*, 30 June 1964, 1; "Navy Sends 400 Sailors to Join in Search for Rights Workers," AP, *Hattiesburg American*, 30 June 1964, 1; "Sailors Comb Bogue Chitto Swamp," UPI, Tupelo *Daily Journal*, 26 June 1964, 1; "Sailors, FBI, Continue Searching for Missing Trio," UPI, Pascagoula *Chronicle*, 26 June 1964, 1; "Sailors Join in Hope of Finding Men," UPI, Columbus *Commercial Dispatch*, 26 June 1964, 1; "Sailors Join Search," AP, *Starkville Daily News*, 26 June 1964, 1; "Sailors Ordered into Search for Missing Trio," UPI, *Meridian Star*, 25 June 1964, 1; "Sailors Ordered to Join Search," Jackson *Daily News*, 25 June 1964, 1; "Sailors Resume Search for Three Civil Rights Workers," UPI, Greenville *Delta Democrat-Times*, 29 June 1964, 1; "Search Gets Confusing for Unequipped Sailors," AP, McComb *Enterprise-Journal*, 26 June 1964, 1; "White House Ordered to Add Sailors to Hunt," AP, Gulfport *Daily Herald*, 30 June 1964, 1.

249. "Governor Not Told in Advance of Federal Order," AP, *Natchez Democrat*, 26 June 1964, 1; "Governor Surprised by Marines," AP, *Vicksburg Evening Post*, 25 June 1964, 1; "Gov. Surprised by LBJ's Orders," AP, *Hattiesburg American*, 25 June 1964, 1; "Marine Order Is Surprise to PBJ," UPI, Pascagoula *Chronicle*, 26 June 1964, 1; "Paul's Offer Not Accepted," UPI, West Point *Times-Leader*, 25 June 1964, 1.

250. Birney Imes, Jr., "Mississippi Pays," Columbus *Commercial Dispatch*, 5 July 1964, 4.

251. Bill Simpson, "Talk of Town," Corinth *Daily Corinthian*, 24 June 1964, 1.

252. Ibid.

253. Leonard Lowrey, "Political Move," *Hattiesburg American*, 26 June 1964, 12.

254. W.H. Harris, "Pencil Shavings," *Starkville Daily News*, 24 June 1964, 4.

255. James "Jimmy" Ward, "Troops for New York," Jackson *Daily News*, 25 July 1964, 6.

256. Bill Simpson, "Talk of Town," Corinth *Daily Corinthian*, 24 June 1964, 1.

257. W.H. Harris, "Pencil Shavings," West Point *Times-Leader*, 2 June 1964, 1.

258. "Marines Help in Search for Missing Trio," UPI, Clarksdale *Press Register*, 25 June 1964, 1.

259. "FBI Offers Cash about Lost Trio," AP, *Vicksburg Evening Post*, 3 August 1964, 1; "FBI Offers Cash for Data on Missing Trio," AP, McComb *Enterprise-Journal*, 3 August 1964, 1; "FBI Reportedly Willing to Buy Info," AP, *Meridian*

Star, 3 August 1964, 1; "Money Talks, or Makes People Talk," *Vicksburg Evening Post*, 7 August 1964, 4.

260. "Investigators Optimistic," UPI, Columbus *Commercial Dispatch*, 2 July 1964, 1; "Investigators Cite Progress in Hunt," UPI, Greenville *Delta Democrat-Times*, 2 July 1964, 1; "Officials Pleased with Search," UPI, Corinth *Daily Corinthian*, 2 July 1964, 1; "Searchers for Trio Pleased by Progress," UPI, Pascagoula *Chronicle*, 2 July 1964, 2.

261. "Bus Rider Looks like One of Missing Trio," UPI, Tupelo *Daily Journal*, 1 July 1964, 1; "Corinth Police Chief Saw Man like Schwerner," AP, *Hattiesburg American*, 30 June 1964, 1; "Murphy Saw Civil Rights Worker Here Sunday," Corinth *Daily Corinthian*, 30 June 1964, 1; "One of Missing Trio Believed Sighted in Corinth," AP, *Vicksburg Evening Post*, 30 June 1964, 1; "Reports of Sightings Complicate Search," Jackson *Clarion-Ledger*, 6 July 1964, 6; "Schwerner on Bus? Driver, Police Chief Think So," AP, *Meridian Star*, 30 June 1964, 1; "Three Report Seeing Man like Missing Civil Rights Worker," AP, Jackson *Clarion-Ledger*, 1 July 1964, 1.

262. "Man Who Looks like Worker Is Reported Seen," AP, Jackson *Daily News*, 26 June 1964, 1; "Missing Worker Seen in Baton Rouge," AP, *Hattiesburg American*, 26 June 1964, 2.

263. L.P. Cashman, Jr., "An Idea for Real Speculation," *Vicksburg Evening Post*, 30 June 1964, 4.

264. "Dead Horse Is Found in Hunt for Civil Rights Workers," AP, *Natchez Democrat*, 10 July 1964, 1; "Find Grave of Horse, Not Workers," AP, Gulfport *Daily Herald*, 9 July 1964, 1; "Grave Probed in Trio Search," AP, McComb *Enterprise-Journal*, 9 July 1964, 1; "Latest Lead in Trio's Search Is Washed Out," AP, *Hattiesburg American*, 9 July 1964, 1; "Patrol Probes Horse Grave," AP, *Greenwood Commonwealth*, 9 July 1964, 1; " 'Righterless' Horse Is Found in Grave," AP, *Meridian Star*, 10 July 1964, 3.

265. " 'Righterless' Horse Is Found in Grave," AP, *Meridian Star*, 10 July 1964, 3.

266. "Angler Finds Body in Mississippi River," UPI, Tupelo *Daily Journal*, 13 July 1964, 1; "Body Identified, Not Civil Rights Worker," Jackson *Daily News*, 13 July 1964, 1; "Body Not One of Missing Civil Rights Workers," AP, *Greenwood Commonwealth*, 13 July 1964, 1; "Corpse in Mississippi River May Be Missing Worker," UPI, Corinth *Daily Corinthian*, 13 July 1964, 1; "Half Body Found in River Not 'Civil Rights' Worker," UPI, West Point *Times-Leader*, 13 July 1964, 1; "Navy Divers Probe Mississippi River," AP, *Vicksburg Evening Post*, 15 July 1964, 1; "Says Body in River Is Not Missing Civil Rights Workers," UPI, Pascagoula *Chronicle*, 13 July 1964, 2; "Water Yields Part of Body," AP, McComb *Enterprise-Journal*, 13 July 1964, 1.

267. "Civil Rights Push in State Gets Aid of Red Supporters, Eastland Cites Ties," AP, Jackson *Clarion-Ledger*, 23 July 1964, 1; "Eastland Brands Invaders Pro-Red," UPI, Jackson *Daily News*, 22 July 1964, 1; "Eastland Calls Trio's Disappearance a Hoax," UPI, Greenville *Delta Democrat-Times*, 22 July 1964, 1; "Eastland Says Many Feel Trio Voluntarily Missing," AP, McComb *Enterprise-Journal*, 23 July 1964, 1; "Eastland Says Missing Workers Can Be Hoax," AP, *Starkville Daily News*, 23 July 1964, 6; "Eastland Suggests Civil Rights Hoax," UPI, Pascagoula *Chronicle*, 23 July 1964, 2; "Eastland Suggests Philadelphia Inci-

dent May Be Deliberate Hoax," UPI, Tupelo *Daily Journal*, 23 July 1964, 1; "Sen. Eastland Suggests Missing Three May Be Hoax," UPI, Grenada *Sentinel-Star*, 23 July 1964, 1; "May be Hoax," UPI, *Meridian Star*, 25 June 1964, 1; "Missing Workers May Be Red Plot, Eastland Claims," AP, *Greenwood Commonwealth*, 22 July 1964, 1.

268. W.H. Harris, "Good for Jim!" *Starkville Daily News*, 24 July 1964, 4; W.H. Harris, "Good for Jim!" West Point *Times-Leader*, 23 July 1964, 4.

269. "KKK Head Says Trio Story Is Hoax," AP, *Laurel Leader-Call*, 26 June 1964, 1; "KKK Wizard Charges Hoax," AP, McComb *Enterprise-Journal*, 26 June 1964, 1; "KKK Wizard Thinks Incident a Hoax," AP, Gulfport *Daily Herald*, 26 June 1964, 1; "Klan Leader Sees Missing Three as Hoax," AP, *Natchez Democrat*, 27 June 1964, 10.

270. "Winstead Says May Be Hoax," UPI, Jackson *Daily News*, 25 June 1964, 1.

271. "$3 Million Spent, FBI and Sailors Still Search for Three Civil Rights Workers," AP, *Greenwood Commonwealth*, 2 August 1964, 1.

272. "$30,000 Reward Led FBI to Graves of Three," AP, *Natchez Democrat*, 6 August 1964, 1; "All Three Bodies Now Identified, Neshoba Grave Finally Found," *Meridian Star*, 5 August 1964, 1; "Bodies Found near Philadelphia Identified as Rights Workers," UPI, Clarksdale *Press Register*, 5 August 1964, 1; "Bodies Found near Philadelphia May Be Civil Rights Trio," UPI, Tupelo *Daily Journal*, 5 August 1964, 1; "Bodies Identified as Missing Civil Rights Workers," UPI, West Point *Times-Leader*, 5 August 1964, 1; "Bullets Recovered from Bodies Identified as Missing Civil Rights Workers," AP, *Hattiesburg American*, 5 August 1964, 1; "Cash Figures in Body Find," AP, McComb *Enterprise-Journal*, 5 August 1964, 1; "COFO Trio Died of Gunshot Wounds, Bodies Identified," Jackson *Daily News*, 5 August 1964, 1; "FBI Find Three Bodies near Site Civil Rights Workers Disappeared," AP, *Natchez Democrat*, 5 August 1964, 1; "FBI Led to Graves of 'Workers' by Informer," UPI, Grenada *Sentinel-Star*, 5 August 1964, 1; "FBI Men Find Three Bodies, Civil Rights Trio," Jackson *Clarion-Ledger*, 5 August 1964, 1; "Find Bodies of Mix Trio," AP, *Laurel Leader-Call*, 5 August 1964, 1; "Find Three Bodies near Philadelphia," AP, Gulfport *Daily Herald*, 5 August 1964, 1; "Informer May Have Been Paid $25,000 in Triple Murder Probe," UPI, Tupelo *Daily Journal*, 6 August 1964, 1; "Missing Trio Found," UPI, Greenville *Delta Democrat-Times*, 5 August 1964, 1; "Records Identify Three Bodies," UPI, Pascagoula *Chronicle*, 5 August 1964, 1; "Three Bodies Found near Philadelphia," AP, *Starkville Daily News*, 5 August 1964, 1; "Three Civil Rights Workers Found Dead in Philadelphia," UPI, Corinth *Daily Corinthian*, 5 August 1964, 1; "Three Corpses Identified as Lost Righters," AP, *Vicksburg Evening Post*, 5 August 1964, 1.

273. "Civil Rights: Fantasy's End," *Newsweek*, 17 August 1964, 28–29.

274. James B. Skewes, "Cause for Optimism," *Meridian Star*, 6 August 1964, 4.

275. James "Jimmy" Ward, "Crossroads," Jackson *Daily News*, 30 August 1964, 1.

276. "Comedian Says Letter Told Location of Bodies," UPI, Pascagoula *Chronicle*, 6 August 1964, 3; "Dick Gregory Says He Told Location of Bodies," AP, McComb *Enterprise-Journal*, 6 August 1964, 1; "FBI Weaving Tight Case in Philadelphia," UPI, Clarksdale *Press Register*, 7 August 1964, 1; "Informer Pinpointed

Trio's Burial Place," UPI, Corinth *Daily Corinthian*, 6 August 1964, 1; "Informer Was Scared, Negro Comedian Says," UPI, Greenville *Delta Democrat-Times*, 6 August 1964, 1; "State Troopers Guard Graves in Neshoba," UPI, *Clarksdale Press Register*, 5 August 1964, 1.

277. "Always Find Someone Who Will Talk, FBI Says," UPI, *Meridian Star*, 6 July 1964, 1; "FBI Weaving Tight Case in Philadelphia," UPI, Clarksdale *Press Register*, 7 August 1964, 1; "Gregory Claim Disproved," AP, *Laurel Leader-Call*, 6 August 1964, 1; "Gregory Tipoff Note Said Worthless," UPI, Tupelo *Daily Journal*, 7 August 1964, 1; "Probers Discount Comedian's Tip," Jackson *Daily News*, 6 August 1964, 1; "Sources Deny Gregory's Letter Helped Find Missing Civil Rights Trio," AP, *Greenwood Commonwealth*, 6 August 1964, 1; "Tip Off Claim by Negro Dick Gregory Branded 'Worthless,' " AP, *Meridian Star*, 6 August 1964, 1.

278. "Tip Off Claim by Negro Dick Gregory Branded 'Worthless,' " AP, *Meridian Star*, 6 August 1964, 1.

279. "Probers Discount Comedian's Tip," Jackson *Daily News*, 6 August 1964, 1.

280. James "Jimmy" Ward, "Crossroads," Jackson *Daily News*, 8 August 1964, 1.

281. "Autopsy on Three Slain Civil Rights Workers Expected Today," UPI, Tupelo *Daily Journal*, 10 August 1964, 1; "Autopsy Shows Three Civil Rights Workers Shot to Death," AP, *Greenwood Commonwealth*, 4 August 1964, 1; "Coroner's Jury Report," AP, *Meridian Star*, 26 August 1964, 1; "Coroner Reports on Three Workers," AP, Gulfport *Daily Herald*, 26 August 1964, 1; "Official Autopsy May Come Today," AP, *Meridian Star*, 10 August 1964, 1; "Second Autopsy Sparks Controversy," UPI, Clarksdale *Press Register*, 8 August 1964, 1.

282. "Autopsy on Chaney Stirs Controversy," Jackson *Daily News*, 8 August 1964, 1; "Claim Beating," Jackson *Clarion-Ledger*, 9 August 1964, 1; "Mother Releases Report on Body," Jackson *Daily News*, 9 August 1964, 1; "Physician Says Rights Worker Brutally Beaten," UPI, Pascagoula *Chronicle*, 9 August 1964, 1.

283. "Mississippi Governor Defends State, Killings Deplored," UPI, Clarksdale *Press Register*, 13 August 1964, 1.

284. Hodding Carter III, "Who's to Blame?" Greenville *Delta Democrat-Times*, 14 August 1964, 4.

285. Hodding Carter III, "Justice Must Prevail," Greenville *Delta Democrat-Times*, 9 August 1964, 4.

286. L.P. Cashman, Jr., "Our Purpose Must Be Clear," *Vicksburg Evening Post*, 6 August 1964, 4.

287. W.H. Harris, "Pencil Shavings," West Point *Times-Leader*, 5 August 1964, 1.

288. Harry Rutherford, "Faulkner Comes to Life, Our State Suffers," Tupelo *Daily Journal*, 7 August 1964, 14.

289. "Another Mississippi Tragedy," from the New Orleans *Times-Picayune*, in the Gulfport *Daily Herald*, 29 June 1964, 4.

290. "Mississippi," from the Dallas *Morning Star*, in the Gulfport *Daily Herald*, 11 July 1964, 4.

291. "Meet Summer Project with Dignity, Patience," UPI, *Clarksdale Press Register*, 18 June 1964, 1.

292. Joseph Ellis, Jr., "Mississippi Is Prepared," *Clarksdale Press Register*, 22 June 1964, 4.

293. Joseph Ellis, Jr., "City and County in Readiness," *Clarksdale Press Register*, 23 June 1964, 3.

294. Joseph Ellis, Jr., "With Dignity and Restraint," *Clarksdale Press Register*, 20 June 1964, 1.

295. Joseph Ellis, Jr., "The People and the Intruders," *Clarksdale Press Register*, 24 June 1964, 4.

296. *Clarksdale Press Register*, photograph, 27 June 1964, 1.

297. B.J. Skelton, "Civil Rights Worker Tells Why He's Here," *Clarksdale Press Register*, 27 June 1964, 1.

298. McAdam, *Freedom Summer*, 257.

299. "Civil Rights Group Plans Activity Here," *Clarksdale Press Register*, 23 June 1964, 1.

300. McAdam, *Freedom Summer*, 257.

301. "New Yorkers to Defend Negro in Traffic Case," *Clarksdale Press Register*, 30 June 1964, 1.

302. "Lawyers Fail to Meet Mississippi Requirements," *Clarksdale Press Register*, 3 July 1964, 1.

303. McAdam, *Freedom Summer*, 262.

304. Ibid., 263.

305. "Lawyer Arrested in Aftermath of Integration Efforts in City," *Clarksdale Press Register*, 11 July 1964, 1.

306. "Girls Fined $100 Each on Trespassing Charge," *Clarksdale Press Register*, 23 July 1964, 1.

307. "Negroes Go to Church, Fail to Gain Admittance," *Clarksdale Press Register*, 20 July 1964, 1.

308. "Freedom Rally Held in City," *Clarksdale Press Register*, 9 July 1964, 1.

309. "Negro Leader Touring State for Freedom Democrats," UPI, *Clarksdale Press Register*, 21 July 1964, 1.

310. "Martin Luther King Denies Reds' Action in Civil Rights Movement," UPI, *Clarksdale Press Register*, 23 July 1964, 12.

311. McAdam, *Freedom Summer*, 260–261.

312. Ibid., 261–262.

313. Ibid., 264.

314. Ibid.

315. Ibid., 278, 281.

316. "Clarksdale Police Chief Denies Brutality Charge," AP, Columbus *Commercial Dispatch*, 10 July 1964, 3.

317. "Negroes Turned Back at Hotels, Motels, Theaters," *Clarksdale Press Register*, 7 July 1964, 1.

318. "Integrationists Probe for Breakthrough Here," *Clarksdale Press Register*, 8 July 1964, 1.

319. "Pranksters Break Window, Strew Garbage," *Clarksdale Press Register*, 25 July 1964, 1.

320. "111 Jailed in Greenwood March," UPI, *Clarksdale Press Register*, 17 July 1964, 1; "FBI Agents Charge Three in Greenwood," UPI, *Clarksdale Press Register*, 23 July 1964, 1; "Integration of Greenwood Theater Sparks Strife," UPI, *Clarksdale*

Press Register, 26 July 1964, 1; "Negroes Seek to Move Case to U.S. Court," UPI, *Clarksdale Press Register*, 16 July 1964, 1; "Move SNCC Headquarters from Atlanta to Greenwood," UPI, *Clarksdale Press Register*, 13 June 1964, 8; "Negro Attacked in Greenwood," UPI, *Clarksdale Press Register*, 12 August 1964, 1; "Registration Effort Due in Greenwood," UPI, *Clarksdale Press Register*, 22 July 1964, 1; "Self-Appointed Groups Warned in Greenville," UPI, *Clarksdale Press Register*, 1 July 1964, 1; "Three Jailed in Greenwood Attack," UPI, *Clarksdale Press Register*, 4 August 1964, 1.

321. "Northerners Say They Were Assaulted in Southern Mississippi," UPI, *Clarksdale Press Register*, 9 June 1964, 1; "Two Hurt in Blast in McComb Earlier Today," UPI, *Clarksdale Press Register*, 8 July 1964, 8.

322. "Summer Project Continues on Limited Scale," *Clarksdale Press Register*, 24 August 1964, 1.

323. "Summer Project Called Eminently Successful," UPI, *Clarksdale Press Register*, 20 August 1964, 1.

324. Birney Imes, Jr., "What about Reverse Riders?" Columbus *Commercial Dispatch*, 26 June 1997, 4.

325. McAdam, *Freedom Summer*, 258.

326. Ibid., 259.

327. Ibid., 261.

328. Ibid., 276.

329. "Claim Negro Beaten," UPI, Columbus *Commercial Dispatch*, 27 July 1964, 2; "Clarksdale Police Chief Denies Brutality Charge," UPI, Columbus *Commercial Dispatch*, 10 July 1964, 3; "Greenwood Police Halt Three Demonstrations," UPI, Columbus *Commercial Dispatch*, 17 July 1964, 2; "Rights Worker Hurt in Blast in McComb," UPI, Columbus *Commercial Dispatch*, 8 July 1964, 1; "Trio Arrested in Greenwood for Rights Violation," UPI, Columbus *Commercial Dispatch*, 24 July 1964, 1.

330. "Negroes Claim Beat by Police, Commie Type Propaganda Found in Car Says Sheriff," Columbus *Commercial Dispatch*, 10 June 1964, 1.

331. "Iowa Opinion," from the Oelwein (Iowa) *Daily Register*, in the *Hattiesburg American*, 7 July 1964, 2; "Mississippi: Yankee, Go Home," from the Oelwein (Iowa) *Daily Register*, in the Grenada *Sentinel-Star*, 6 July 1964, 3; "Stick Together," from the Oelwein (Iowa) Daily Register, in the *Starkville Daily News*, 8 July 1964, 4; "Yankee, Go Home," from the Oelwein (Iowa) *Daily Register*, in the Corinth *Daily Corinthian*, 25 June 1964, 4; "Yankee, Go Home," from the Oelwein (Iowa) *Daily Register*, in the Greenville *Delta Democrat-Times*, 25 July 1964, 4; "Yankee, Go Home," from the Oelwein (Iowa) *Daily Register*, in the *Meridian Star*, 9 July 1964, 4.

332. "Explosion Rips McComb Civil Rights Worker's Home," UPI, Corinth *Daily Corinthian*, 8 July 1964, 8; "FBI, McComb Police Probe Bombing of Civil Rights Worker's Home," UPI, Corinth *Daily Corinthian*, 9 July 1964, 1; "McComb Blast," UPI, Corinth *Daily Corinthian*, 23 June 1964, 5.

333. "111 Pickets Go to Jail (in Greenwood)," UPI, Corinth *Daily Corinthian*, 17 July 1964, 1; "Moss Point Negroes Shot at Newsman," UPI, Corinth *Daily Corinthian*, 7 July 1964, 1; "Negroes Charge They Were Beaten (in Columbus)," UPI, Corinth *Daily Corinthian*, 10 June 1964, 10; "Negroes Seeking Democratic Party Shakeup," UPI, Corinth *Daily Corinthian*, 29 June 1964, 1; "Three Towns

Face Threat of Pickets (Greenville, Greenwood, Cleveland)," UPI, Corinth *Daily Corinthian*, 16 July 1964, 1.

334. McAdam, *Freedom Summer*, 257–281.

335. Bill Simpson, "Lawyers Advise Citizens of Rights," Corinth *Daily Corinthian*, 4 August 1964, 6.

336. Thatcher Walt, "A Challenge for Leflore County," Greenwood *Commonwealth*, 22 June 1964, 1.

337. "Mississippi," from the *Dallas Morning News*, in the Columbus *Commercial Dispatch*, 8 July 1964, 6; "Mississippi," from the *Dallas Morning News*, in the *Greenwood Commonwealth*, 7 July 1964, 8; "Mississippi," from the *Dallas Morning News*, in the *Starkville Daily News*, 3 July 1964, 4; "Mississippi Invasion," from the *Dallas Morning News*, in the Gulfport *Daily Herald*, 11 July 1964, 4.

338. "Statement Issued by Greenwood City Council," *Greenwood Commonwealth*, 14 July 1964, 1.

339. "77 Civil Rights Workers Held (Pascagoula)," AP, *Greenwood Commonwealth*, 4 August 1964, 7; "Bomb Blast Rocks McComb," AP, *Greenwood Commonwealth*, 16 August 1964, 1; "Church Fired, Canton," AP, *Greenwood Commonwealth*, 27 June 1964, 1; "Explosion Rocks Negro Church in Canton," AP, *Greenwood Commonwealth*, 12 June 1964, 1; "FBI Arrests Three Itta Bena Men under Civil Rights Act," AP, *Greenwood Commonwealth*, 27 June 1964, 1; "Fire Destroys Church in Itta Bena," AP, *Greenwood Commonwealth*, 22 August 1964, 1; "Hattiesburg Library Closed," *Greenwood Commonwealth*, 18 August 1964, 1; Natchez Church Burned," AP, *Greenwood Commonwealth*, 16 August 1964, 1; "Separate Blasts Shake Three McComb Houses," AP, *Greenwood Commonwealth*, 23 June 1964, 1; "Three Blasts Rock McComb Negro Center," AP, *Greenwood Commonwealth*, 8 July 1964, 1; "White Writers Beaten in McComb," AP, *Greenwood Commonwealth*, 9 June 1964, 1.

340. "SNCC Says Headquarters Coming Here," AP, *Greenwood Commonwealth*, 15 June 1964, 1.

341. "Pickets Gain Stay of Trial," *Greenwood Commonwealth*, 24 June 1964, 1.

342. "Don't Plan to Test Civil Rights Bill, Say College Students," *Greenwood Commonwealth*, 1 July 1964, 1.

343. McAdam, *Freedom Summer*, 258–263.

344. "Citizens' Council Urges Resistance to Civil Rights Bill," *Greenwood Commonwealth*, 10 July 1964, 1.

345. "Church East of City Razed by Fire," *Greenwood Commonwealth*, 11 July 1964, 1.

346. "Negro Groups Call 'Freedom Day' in City," *Greenwood Commonwealth*, 15 July 1964, 1.

347. McAdam, *Freedom Summer*, 265.

348. Ibid., 264; "Negroes Leave Movies as Angry Crowd Gathers," *Greenwood Commonwealth*, 16 July 1964, 1.

349. "Pickets Move Case into U.S. Court," AP, *Greenwood Commonwealth*, 18 July 1964, 1.

350. "Civil Rights Workers Given Trial in City Police Court Yesterday," *Greenwood Commonwealth*, 21 July 1964, 1.

351. "Parents Committee Raises Bail for Civil Rights Workers," AP, *Greenwood Commonwealth*, 18 July 1964, 1.

352. "Known Red Group Helps Local Pickets," *Greenwood Commonwealth*, 22 July 1964, 1.

353. "Agents Arrest Three Men Here under Civil Rights Bill," AP, *Greenwood Commonwealth*, 23 July 1964, 1; McAdam, *Freedom Summer*, 268.

354. McAdam, *Freedom Summer*, 277–279.

355. "Negro to Face Court Martial for Civil Rights Work," *Greenwood Commonwealth*, 18 August 1964, 1.

356. "Bond Forfeited in Assault Case," *Greenwood Commonwealth*, 22 August 1964, 1; "Warrant Issued for Negro Who Slapped Officer," *Greenwood Commonwealth*, 19 August 1964, 1.

357. "King to Speak at Rally Here," AP, *Greenwood Commonwealth*, 21 July 1964, 1.

358. "Martin Luther King's Oratory Pushes Registration," UPI, Columbus *Commercial Dispatch*, 22 July 1964, 1.

359. "KKK Leaflets Dropped in King's Audience," UPI, Tupelo *Daily Journal*, 23 July 1964, 4; "LBJ and MLK Dish Out Strong Propaganda," AP, *Natchez Democrat*, 22 June 1964, 1.

360. "NAACP Hits Beckwith Sale," AP, *Starkville Daily News*, 1 August 1964, 1; "NAACP Raps Beckwith Homestead Purchase," UPI, Tupelo *Daily Journal*, 1–2 August 1964, 8.

361. "Belafonte Gives $70,000 to Civil Rights Workers Here," *Greenwood Commonwealth*, 11 August 1964, 1.

362. McAdam, *Freedom Summer*, 276.

363. "Shots Disperse Negro Pickets," *Greenwood Commonwealth*, 16 August 1964, 1.

364. "Pickets Gather at Grocery," *Greenwood Commonwealth*, 17 August 1964, 1.

365. Hodding Carter III, "Warning—or Precedent?" Greenville *Delta Democrat-Times*, 3 June 1964, 4.

366. Hodding Carter III, "Long Hot Summer," Greenville *Delta Democrat-Times*, 13 July 1964, 4.

367. Hodding Carter III, "Invasion Imminent," Greenville *Delta Democrat-Times*, 17 June 1964, 4.

368. "Yankee, Go Home," from the Oelwein (Iowa) *Daily Register*, in the Greenville *Delta Democrat-Times*, 5 July 1964, 4.

369. "Bid of Greenwood Civil Rights Workers Is Rejected by Federal Court," UPI, Greenville *Delta Democrat-Times*, 22 June 1964, 1; "Civil Rights Workers Appeal to Federal Court," UPI, Greenville *Delta Democrat-Times*, 4 August 1964, 1; "Civil Rights Workers Want Move to U.S. Court," UPI, Greenville Delta *Democrat-Times*, 5 August 1964, 1; "Flames Ruin Negro Church in Greenwood," UPI, Greenville *Delta Democrat-Times*, 12 July 1964, 1; "Greenwood Demonstrators Ask U.S. Court Hearing," UPI, Greenville *Delta Democrat-Times*, 19 July 1964, 1; "Greenwood Voter March Broken Up," UPI, Greenville *Delta Democrat-Times*, 17 July 1964, 1; "Negro Star Delivers $70,000 to Civil Rights Group," UPI, Greenville *Delta Democrat-Times*, 11 August 1964, 2; "Rev. King Is Slated to Pay Visit to Delta Area Today," UPI, Greenville *Delta Democrat-Times*, 21 July 1964,

1; "Shot Negro's Mother Sought by Police," UPI, Greenville *Delta Democrat-Times*, 19 August 1964, 1; "Tension Runs High in Greenwood," UPI, Greenville *Delta Democrat-Times*, 17 August 1964, 1.

370. "Blast Hits Civil Rights House in McComb," UPI, Greenville *Delta Democrat-Times*, 8 July 1964, 1; "Brutality Is Charged in Delta (Clarksdale)," UPI, Greenville *Delta Democrat-Times*, 9 July 1964, 1; "Civil Rights Trial Postponed (Columbus)," UPI, Greenville *Delta Democrat-Times*, 30 June 1964, 1; "Cleveland Target for Pickets," UPI, Greenville *Delta Democrat-Times*, 16 July 1964, 1; "Cross Burned at Mayor's House (Ruleville)," UPI, Greenville *Delta Democrat-Times*, 21 August 1964, 1; "Freedom House Bombed in Canton, No One Hurt," UPI, Greenville *Delta Democrat-Times*, 8 June 1964, 1; "McComb Dynamiters Blast Negro House," UPI, Greenville *Delta Democrat-Times*, 27 July 1964, 1; "Pike County Church Burned," UPI Greenville *Delta Democrat-Times*, UPI, 22 July 1964, 2; "Police Find Dynamite in Negro's Yard (McComb)," UPI, Greenville *Delta Democrat-Times*, 23 June 1964, 1; "Rabbi Feels Sorrow for State (Hattiesburg)," UPI, Greenville *Delta Democrat-Times*, 12 July 1964, 1; "Students Say Brass Knuckles Used in Attack (McComb)," UPI, Greenville *Delta Democrat-Times*, 9 June 1964, 1; "Tension Runs High in Greenwood," UPI, Greenville *Delta Democrat-Times*, 17 August 1964, 1; "Three Righters Beaten by Pair in Hattiesburg," UPI, Greenville *Delta Democrat-Times*, 10 July 1964, 1; "Two Negro Churches Burned near Natchez," UPI, Greenville *Delta Democrat-Times*, 13 July 1964, 1.

371. "County Democratic Convention Runs Smoothly, COFO Attends," Greenville *Delta Democrat-Times*, 23 July 1964, 1; "Freedom Democrat Party to Hold Nine Precinct Meetings Here Tonight," Greenville *Delta Democrat-Times*, 29 July 1964, 2; "Freedom Democrats Plan Convention July 23," Greenville *Delta Democrat-Times*, 10 July 1964, 1; "Little COFO Work at Democratic Precincts," Greenville *Delta Democrat-Times*, 16 June 1964, 1; "Negroes Attend Democratic Precinct Meeting Here," Greenville *Delta Democrat-Times*, 15 June 1964, 1; "Precinct Elections Planned by Civil Rights Democrats," Greenville *Delta Democrat-Times*, 23 July 1964, 2.

372. "Voter Registration Drive Set Thursday, COFO," Greenville *Delta Democrat-Times*, 14 July 1964, 2.

373. "Summer Campaign Registers 30," Greenville *Delta Democrat-Times*, 14 July 1964, 1.

374. Hodding Carter III, "Questions Summer Project," Greenville *Delta Democrat-Times*, 26 June 1964, 4.

375. Hodding Carter III, "Check for Facts," Greenville *Delta Democrat-Times*, 6 July 1964, 1.

376. John Childs, "COFO Says Greenville to Be Pushed to Limit," Greenville *Delta Democrat-Times*, 24 June 1964, 1.

377. "City Police Thoroughly Prepared," Greenville *Delta Democrat-Times*, 24 June 1964, 1.

378. "Mayor Says Obedience to Law Is Lifeblood," Greenville *Delta Democrat-Times*, 25 June 1964, 1.

379. "Mayor Issues Second Word of Caution on Racial Issue," Greenville *Delta Democrat-Times*, 1 July 1964, 2.

380. "No Testing Planned in Greenville," Greenville *Delta Democrat-Times*, 3 July 1964, 1.

381. "Negro Is Served in Motel Here, No Incident," Greenville *Delta Democrat-Times*, 8 July 1964, 1.

382. "First Negro Group Applies for Registration Here," Greenville *Delta Democrat-Times*, 8 July 1964, 1.

383. Robert Hooker, "Race and the News Media in Mississippi, 1962–1964" (Master's thesis, Vanderbilt University, 1971), 194.

384. "Racial Employment Gap Cited at Greenville COFO Meeting," Greenville *Delta Democrat-Times*, 26 June 1964, 1.

385. John Childs, "Race Problems More Apparent in South than in North," Greenville *Delta Democrat-Times*, 12 July 1964, 6.

386. McAdam, *Freedom Summer*, 265.

387. Foster Davis, "COFO Leaders Cheer Following Vote Drive," Greenville *Delta Democrat-Times*, 17 July 1964, 1.

388. Ken Tolliver, "Freedom Day Has Surprises for Civil Rights Units," Greenville *Delta Democrat-Times*, 17 July 1964, 1.

389. Hodding Carter III, "Remarkable Trial," Greenville *Delta Democrat-Times*, 5 July 1964, 2.

390. "Three Whites Knife Negro Handyman," Greenville *Delta Democrat-Times*, 3 August 1964, 1.

391. Hodding Carter III, "Answer to Aberraton," Greenville *Delta Democrat-Times*, 5 August 1964, 1.

392. "Already Tried, Lawyer Claims," Greenville *Delta Democrat-Times*, 12 August 1964, 1.

393. Hodding Carter III, "Burden on Negro Leadership," Greenville *Delta Democrat-Times*, 26 July 1964, 2; "Battle Joined," Greenville *Delta Democrat-Times*, 31 July 1964, 4.

394. Hodding Carter III, "Professionalism at Its Best," Greenville *Delta Democrat-Times*, 12 August 1964, 4.

395. Hodding Carter III, "No Compromise," Greenville *Delta Democrat-Times*, 13 August 1964, 4.

396. Hodding Carter III, "What of Tomorrow?" Greenville *Delta Democrat-Times*, 3 August 1964, 4.

397. Hodding Carter III, "Arson in the House of God," Greenville *Delta Democrat-Times*, 2 August 1964, 2.

398. "Yankee, Go Home," from the Oelwein (Iowa) *Daily Register*, in the Grenada *Sentinel-Star*, 25 June 1964, 4.

399. "Highway 55 Opened," Grenada *Sentinel-Star*, 23 June 1964, 1.

400. McAdam, *Freedom Summer*, 267.

401. "Clarksale Hotel Closes Doors," UPI, Grenada *Sentinel-Star*, 9 July 1964, 1; "FBI Investigating Weekend Incidents," UPI, Grenada *Sentinel-Star*, 27 July 1964, 1; "Greenwood Civil Rights Workers Fined $100, Sentenced," UPI, Grenada *Sentinel-Star*, 21 July 1964, 1; "Greenwood Has First Civil Rights Arrest," UPI, Grenada *Sentinel-Star*, 24 July 1964, 1.

402. "Exaggerates Story," UPI, Grenada *Sentinel-Star*, 29 June 1964, 1.

403. "Greenville Officials Warn Group," UPI, Grenada *Sentinel-Star*, 1 July 1964, 1.

404. E.P. Wilkes, "Civil Rights Crusaders," Gulfport *Daily Herald*, 27 June 1964, 4.

405. "Burning of Church Probed (McComb)," AP, Gulfport *Daily Herald*, 7 August 1964, 18; "Civil Rights Case Taken on Affidavits (Hattiesburg)," AP, Gulfport *Daily Herald*, 30 June 1964, 1; "Civil Rights Quarters Hit by Explosive (Canton)," AP, Gulfport *Daily Herald*, 8 June 1964, 14; "Demonstrators Arrested in Greenwood," AP, Gulfport *Daily Herald*, 16 July 1964, 1; "Explosion at Negro Home and Church (McComb)," Gulfport *Daily Herald*, 12 June 1964, 8; "Negro Church at Itta Bena Burned," AP, Gulfport *Daily Herald*, 22 August 1964, 13; "Northern White Writers Beaten near Summit," AP, Gulfport *Daily Herald*, 9 June 1964, 5; "Police Arrest 98 Agitators in Greenwood," AP, Gulfport *Daily Herald*, 17 July 1964, 1; "Remands Case of Marchers (Greenwood)," AP, Gulfport *Daily Herald*, 19 June 1964, 30; "Two Hurt in Racial Trouble (Greenwood)," AP, Gulfport *Daily Herald*, 27 July 1964, 17; "Two Men Held in Laurel Race Violence," AP, Gulfport *Daily Herald*, 4 July 1964, sec. 2, 4; "Worker Jailed at Pascagoula," Gulfport *Daily Herald*, 6 August 1964, 13.

406. "No Set Policy by Restaurants," Gulfport *Daily Herald*, 4 July 1964, 1.

407. "Coastal Facilities Are Mixed, No Incidents," Gulfport *Daily Herald*, 8 July 1964, 1.

408. Billy Ray Quave, "Jackson County Sheriff Says Let Law Handle Matters," Gulfport *Daily Herald*, 26 June 1964, 1.

409. "Freedom School at Gulfport," AP, Gulfport *Daily Herald*, 1 July 1964, 3.

410. "Freedom Schools Open Today," AP, Gulfport *Daily Herald*, 2 July 1964, 1.

411. "Let Officers Handle Situations, Leaflet Says," Gulfport *Daily Herald*, 3 July 1964, 3.

412. "Rights Workers Argue about Summer Plans," Gulfport *Daily Herald*, 3 July 1964, 8.

413. "Girl Is Wounded at Rally," Gulfport *Daily Herald*, 7 July 1964, 2; "No Arrests in Moss Point Case," Gulfport *Daily Herald*, 13 July 1964, 2.

414. "Warning Given to Civil Rights Workers by Judge," Gulfport *Daily Herald*, 16 July 1964, 1.

415. "Grand Jury Probes Vote Complaint," Gulfport *Daily Herald*, 18 July 1964, 1.

416. "Challenges Report on Workers," Gulfport *Daily Herald*, 21 July 1964, 1.

417. McAdam, *Freedom Summer*, 260–262.

418. Ibid., 270–278.

419. Ibid., 282.

420. Leonard Lowrey, "A Time for Self-Control," *Hattiesburg American*, 23 June 1964, 4.

421. Leonard Lowrey, "Problem Places," *Hattiesburg American*, 12 August 1964, 16.

422. Unsigned letter to editor, "Dissenting Voice," *Hattiesburg American*, 12 June 1964, 10.

423. Joseph Albright, "Negro Expresses Pride in His Race," letter to editor of the Jackson *Advocate*, in the *Hattiesburg American*, 30 June 1964, 4.

424. "Another Negro Church Building Burns as FBI Strengthen Force," AP, *Hat-*

tiesburg American, 11 July 1964, 1; "Another Negro Church Burns in McComb," AP, *Hattiesburg American*, 22 July 1964, 1; Blast Jars Negro Home in McComb," AP, *Hattiesburg American*, 28 August 1964, 1; "Canton Negro Church, Home, Are Damaged," AP, *Hattiesburg American*, 12 June 1964, 1; "Explosion Damages Freedom House (McComb)," AP, *Hattiesburg American*, 8 July 1964, 1; "Five Rights Workers Arrested in Greenwood," AP, *Hattiesburg American*, 2 August 1964, 1; "Greenwood Police Arrest 50 Pickets," AP, *Hattiesburg American*, 16 July 1964, 1; "McComb Explosion Touches Off Demand for Protection," AP, *Hattiesburg American*, 9 July 1964, 12; "Moss Point Negro Shot at Rights Rally," AP, *Hattiesburg American*, 7 July 1964, 1; "Separate Explosions Shake Negro Homes in McComb," AP, *Hattiesburg American*, 23 June 1964, 1; "Three Charged with Threatening Worker (Itta Bena)," AP, *Hattiesburg American*, 27 June 1964, 1; "Two Buildings in Southwestern Mississippi Damaged by Bombings (McComb)," AP, *Hattiesburg American*, 15 August 1964, 1; "Two Negroes Hit by Flying Glass," AP, *Hattiesburg American*, 27 July 1964, 1.

425. "Holes Shot in Parked Car of Two Civil Rights Workers," *Hattiesburg American*, 29 June 1964, 1; McAdam, *Freedom Summer*, 259.

426. McAdam, *Freedom Summer*, 260–262.

427. Terri Shaw, "COFO Worker Explains Summer Project," *Hattiesburg American*, 7 July 1964, 4.

428. "Three Civil Rights Workers Attacked," *Hattiesburg American*, 10 July 1964, 1.

429. "Second Man Remains in Hospital," *Hattiesburg American*, 20 July 1964, 1.

430. "Collins Man Charged with Beating of Ohio Rabbi," *Hattiesburg American*, 18 July 1964, 1; McAdam, *Freedom Summer*, 265; "Pair Fined in Beating of Rabbi," *Hattiesburg American*, 8 August 1964, 1.

431. McAdam, *Freedom Summer*, 262; "Search Continues for Attackers, Rabbi Leaves Town," *Hattiesburg American*, 12 July 1964, 1.

432. "Mayor Pittman Issues Statement," *Hattiesburg American*, 12 July 1964, 1.

433. "Police Chief Warns against Violence," *Hattiesburg American*, 11 July 1964, 1.

434. "Citizens' Council Urges Civil Rights Act Resistance," *Hattiesburg American*, 21 July 1964, 4.

435. "Local Negroes Lose Picketing Suit," AP, *Hattiesburg American*, 16 July 1964, 1.

436. "Library Closed after Integration Attempt, Mayor Says Inventory Made," *Hattiesburg American*, 14 August 1964, 1; "Public Library Closed Again," *Hattiesburg American*, 17 August 1964, 1.

437. McAdam, *Freedom Summer*, 266–278.

438. T.M. Hederman, Jr., "Summer Lark for Youth," Jackson *Clarion-Ledger*, 21 June 1964, 2.

439. "Students Go Home!" from the *Nashville Banner*, in the Jackson *Clarion-Ledger*, 21 July 1964, 2.

440. T.M. Hederman, Jr., "Latest Wave of Invaders Badly Needed in New York Area Today," Jackson *Clarion-Ledger*, 22 July 1964, 4.

441. Letter to the editor, Jackson *Clarion-Ledger*, 18 June 1964, 14.

442. Charles Hills, "Affairs of State," Jackson *Clarion-Ledger*, 22 June 1964, 6.

443. "Marshal Skeptical Klan Fired Crosses," Jackson *Clarion-Ledger*, 18 August 1964, 1.

444. McAdam, *Freedom Summer*, 257–277.

445. "Church Razed in Madison," Jackson *Clarion-Ledger*, 20 July 1964, 1; "Civil Rights Cases Returned to State (Hattiesburg)," Jackson *Clarion-Ledger*, 28 July 1964, "FBI, Police, Guard McComb Blast Site," Jackson *Clarion-Ledger*, 9 July 1964, 1; "Greenwood Has More Race Troubles," Jackson *Clarion-Ledger*, 3 August 1964, 3; "Greenwood Tense, Incidents Continue," AP, Jackson *Clarion-Ledger*, 18 August 1964, 2; "Negro Church Burned (Greenwood)," AP, Jackson *Clarion-Ledger*, 12 July 1964, 1; "Three Whites Attack Man (Greenville)," Jackson *Clarion-Ledger*, 5 August 1964, 4; "Suspect Surrenders in Assault on Rabbi," Jackson *Clarion-Ledger*, 19 July 1964, 9; "Trio Arrested in Greenwood," Jackson *Clarion-Ledger*, 24 July 1964, 1.

446. William Chaze, "Odor of Sweat, Dirt, Fill Hattiesburg COFO Office," Jackson *Clarion-Ledger*, 14 July 1964, 2.

447. "Registrar in Marshall Claims Unfair Tactics," Jackson *Clarion-Ledger*, 23 August 1964, 1.

448. "Ole Miss Students Get Lots of Civil Rights Propaganda," Jackson *Clarion-Ledger*, 21 June 1964, 4.

449. Fred Taylor, letter to the editor, Jackson *Clarion-Ledger*, 10 August 1964, 10.

450. Kate Wilkinson, letter to the editor, Jackson *Clarion-Ledger*, 10 August 1964, 4.

451. D. Stephen Holbrook, letter to the editor, Jackson *Clarion-Ledger*, 18 August 1964, 6.

452. T.M. Hederman, Jr., "Blaming Mississippi Won't Help United States," Jackson *Clarion-Ledger*, 12 August 1964, 6.

453. "What about Prejudice?" from the *Richland* (Rayville, Louisiana) *Beacon News*, in the Jackson *Clarion-Ledger*, 4 August 1964, 4.

454. William Chaze, "Mississippi Project to Conclude August 24, Workers to Abandon State," Jackson *Clarion-Ledger*, 8 August 1964, 1.

455. "Mayor Thompson, Law, Order Promised during Fall Desegregation," Jackson *Clarion-Ledger*, 7 August 1964, 3.

456. "Mayor Talks Tax Cuts, Pay Raises, Civil Rights Project," Jackson *Clarion-Ledger*, 14 August 1964, 12.

457. Tommy Herrington, "43 Negroes Apply at White Schools," Jackson *Clarion-Ledger*, 21 August 1964, 1.

458. "First Rider Wave Due on Weekend," AP, Jackson *Daily News*, 19 June 1964, 1.

459. "Agitators Getting Shakes at Kick Off," AP, Jackson *Daily News*, 19 June 1964, 2.

460. "New Yorkizing the South," Jackson *Daily News*, 4 June 1964, 6.

461. James "Jimmy" Ward, "Level Heads Are Necessary to Control Situation," Jackson *Daily News*, 23 June 1964, 10.

462. James "Jimmy" Ward, "Crossroads," Jackson *Daily News*, 15 July 1964, 1.

463. Ibid., 10 July 1964, 1.

464. "NCC Unveils Summer Agitation Plans," AP, Jackson *Daily News*, 8 June 1964, 6.

465. "CORE Regards Civil Rights Passage as New Signal for Agitation," AP, Jackson *Daily News*, 8 June 1964, 9.

466. "98 Demonstrators Held in Greenwood," AP, Jackson *Daily News*, 17 July 1964, 2; "Beating of Three Civil Rights Men Reported," AP, Jackson *Daily News*, 10 July 1964, 1; "Blast Rocks CORE House in Canton," AP, Jackson *Daily News*, 9 June 1964, 7; "Blasts Rock Negro Church near Canton," AP, Jackson *Daily News*, 12 June 1964, 2; "Cars of COFO Fired Upon, COFO Claims (Hattiesburg)," Jackson *Daily News*, 29 June 1964, 5; "COFO Says Church Hit by Firebomb (Ruleville)," Jackson *Daily News*, 25 June 1964, 10; "McComb Dynamite Damages Report," AP, Jackson *Daily News*, 23 June 1964, 7; "Negroes Plan Voter March in Meridian," AP, Jackson *Daily News*, 12 June 1964, 2; "Three Charge Beating after McComb Visit," AP, Jackson *Daily News*, 9 June 1964, 7; "Three Men Bound Over in Delta Case (Greenwood)," UPI, Jackson *Daily News*, 28 June 1964, 1; "Two Students Arrested at Moss Point," UPI, Jackson *Daily News*, 24 June 1964, 3.

467. James "Jimmy" Ward, "When Bombings Aren't News," Jackson *Daily News*, 12 August 1964, 12.

468. "Greenwood Officials Note More Commie Evidence," Jackson *Daily News*, 24 July 1964, 2.

469. W.C. Shoemaker, "Mixing Ordered in Schools Here," Jackson *Daily News*, 7 July 2964, 1.

470. James "Jimmy" Ward, "Desegregation in Jackson," Jackson *Daily News*, 21 August 1964, 10.

471. Jay West, "Laurel Publisher Refutes Lies Circulated in Anonymous Letter," *Laurel Leader-Call*, 1 June 1964, 1.

472. Jay West, "President Should Halt 'Long Hot Summer,' " *Laurel Leader-Call*, 26 June 1964, 4.

473. "Voter Registration Slows in This County," *Laurel Leader-Call*, 22 July 1964, 8.

474. "Arraignment Scheduled for Three Itta Bena Men," *Laurel Leader-Call*, 27 June 1964, 1; "Biloxi Has 18 Workers," AP, *Laurel Leader-Call*, 6 July 1964, 5; "Bullets Hit Worker's Car in Hub City (Hattiesburg)," AP, *Laurel Leader-Call*, 29 June 1964, 1; "Civil Rights Workers Claim Threats (Gulfport)," AP, *Laurel Leader-Call*, 3 July 1964, 3; "Dynamite Blasts Three Residences in McComb," AP, *Laurel Leader-Call*, 23 June 1964, 1; "Explosion Hits Church in Canton," AP, *Laurel Leader-Call*, 12 June 1964, 1; "Explosion Sets Off Mixer Safety Pleas (McComb)," AP, *Laurel Leader-Call*, 9 July 1964, 1; "FBI Arrest Three under New Rights Law (Greenwood)," *Laurel Leader-Call*, 24 July 1964, 1; "Five Rights Workers Arrested in Greenwood," AP, *Laurel Leader-Call*, 3 August 1964, 2; "Flames Destroy Church in Delta, Racial Trouble Hits Hattiesburg," AP, *Laurel Leader-Call*, 11 July 1964, 1; "Greenwood Pickets Held in Voter Demonstration," AP, *Laurel Leader-Call*, 16 July 1964, 1; "Judge Orders Civil Rights Case to High Court (Greenwood)," AP, *Laurel Leader-Call*, 18 July 1964, 1; "McComb Blast Injures Two," AP, *Laurel Leader-Call*, 8 July 1964, 1; "McComb Grocery Bombed," AP, *Laurel Leader-Call*, 15 August 1964, 1; "Men Fire Shots Wounding Girl (Moss

Point)," AP, *Laurel Leader-Call*, 7 July 1964, 1; "Racial Violence Flares over Weekend (Greenwood)," AP, *Laurel Leader-Call*, 17 August 1964, 1; "Workers Jailed (Columbus)," AP, *Laurel Leader-Call*, 27 June 1964, 2.

475. "Poise and Forbearance Urged for Local People," *Laurel Leader-Call*, 20 June 1964, 1.

476. McAdam, *Freedom Summer*, 261.

477. "Racial Violence Flows in Laurel, Arrests Follow Drive-In Clash," *Laurel Leader-Call*, 6 July 1964, 1.

478. "Civil Rights Group Touring Mississippi," UPI, *Clarksdale Press Register*, 6 July 1964, 1; "Laurel Has Race Flurry," AP, Jackson *Clarion-Ledger*, 5 July 1964, 1; "Laurel Has Race Flurry," AP, Jackson *Daily News*, 5 July 1964, 1; "Laurel Mixing Try Sparks Rioting," UPI, Corinth *Daily Corinthian*, 6 July 1964, 1; "Racial Clashes Erupt at Laurel," AP, *Meridian Star*, 12 July 1964, 1; "Two Men Held in Laurel Race Violence," AP, *Gulfport Daily Herald*, 4 July 1964, B4.

479. "Mayor Meets with Negroes," *Laurel Leader-Call*, 6 July 1964, 1.

480. "Laurel Is Likely Eating Test Site, Civil Rights Tour Stops in City," *Laurel Leader-Call*, 7 July 1964, 1.

481. "First Laurel Black Policeman," UPI, Grenada *Sentinel-Star*, 3 August 1964, 1.

482. "Laurel Beefs Up Police and Cars, Mayor to Add 13 New Policemen," *Laurel Leader-Call*, 8 July 1964, 1; "Negro Policemen Added by Laurel," *Laurel Leader-Call*, 1 August 1964, 1.

483. "Laurel Returns to Normal After Negro Group Leaves," *Laurel Leader-Call*, 8 July 1964, 2.

484. "Suspends Civil Rights Worker Sentence," *Laurel Leader-Call*, 6 July 1964, 1; McAdam, *Freedom Summer*, 261.

485. "Civil Rights Worker Appeals," *Laurel Leader-Call*, 24 July 1964, 1; "Vagrancy Case on Appeal," *Laurel Leader-Call*, 28 July 1964, 2.

486. McAdam, *Freedom Summer*, 277.

487. "Police List Complaint in COFO Attack," *Laurel Leader-Call*, 17 August 1964, 1.

488. McAdam, *Freedom Summer*, 278; "Police List Complaint in COFO Attack," *Laurel Leader-Call*, 17 August 1964, 1.

489. "Eviction Notice for COFO Group," *Laurel Leader-Call*, 27 August 1964, 1.

490. J.O. Emmerich, "This Could Be a Case of Reality, Not Prejudice," McComb *Enterprise-Journal*, 7 July 1964, 2.

491. J.O. Emmerich, "Let's Stop Repeating Wild Rumors," McComb *Enterprise-Journal*, 11 June 1964, 2.

492. J.O. Emmerich, "Insiders Could Cool Off Long Hot Summer," McComb *Enterprise-Journal*, 19 June 1964, 2.

493. "Reason Must Rule This Summer," from the Perkinston Junior College *Bulldog Barks*, in the McComb *Enterprise-Journal*, 18 June 1964, 2.

494. J.O. Emmerich, "Highlights in the Headlines," McComb *Enterprise-Journal*, 9 July 1964, 1.

495. Ibid., 4 August 1964, 1.

496. Ibid., 11 August 1964, 1.

497. "Ross Suggests Righters Bathe," AP, McComb *Enterprise-Journal*, 22 July 1964, 3.

498. "Workers Unaware," from the *Lowell* (Massachusetts) *Liberator*, in the McComb *Enterprise-Journal*, 7 August 1964, 4.

499. David R. Davies, "J. Oliver Emmerich and the McComb *Enterprise-Journal*: Slow Change in McComb, 1964," *Journal of Mississippi History* (February 1995): 1; McAdam, *Freedom Summer*, 262–281.

500. "Three Men Claim Ambush Beating in Pike County," AP, McComb *Enterprise-Journal*, 9 June 1964, 1.

501. Charles Dunagin, "Negro Tells of Being Flogged by Whites," McComb *Enterprise-Journal*, 19 June 1964, 1.

502. Charles Dunagin, "Explosion Rocks Three McComb Negro Houses," McComb *Enterprise-Journal*, 23 June 1964, 1.

503. "McComb Hires Negro Policeman," McComb *Enterprise-Journal*, 24 June 1964, 1.

504. Charles Gordon, "Law Continues Efforts to Determine If Negro Officer Was Fired Upon," McComb *Enterprise-Journal*, 10 July 1964, 1.

505. "Police Continue Probe of Local Dynamiting," McComb *Enterprise-Journal*, 26 June 1964, 1.

506. "Threatening Note Hits *Enterprise-Journal* Employes [*sic*] House," McComb *Enterprise-Journal*, 29 June 1964, 1.

507. Davies, "J. Oliver Emmerich and the McComb *Enterprise-Journal*," 10.

508. "City Restaurant Group Discusses Rights Law," McComb *Enterprise-Journal*, 10 July 1964, 7.

509. Charles Gordon, "Mayor Pledges Law and Order in McComb," McComb *Enterprise-Journal*, 14 July 1964, 1; "Mayor Appeals against Local Acts of Violence," McComb *Enterprise-Journal*, 15 July 1964, 1.

510. "Mayor Gets Backing on Statement," McComb *Enterprise-Journal*, 15 July 1964, 1.

511. Charles Dunagin, "Jaycees and Rotary Club Endorse Mayor on Stand," McComb *Enterprise-Journal*, 16 July 1964, 1.

512. "Northern Students Won't Be Sent to Area Soon," AP, McComb *Enterprise-Journal*, 1 July 1964, 1.

513. "Civil Rights Group in City," McComb *Enterprise-Journal*, 6 July 1964, 1.

514. Charles Gordon, "Blast Rips Quarters of Mixed COFO Group," McComb *Enterprise-Journal*, 8 July 1964, 1.

515. "98 Arrested at Greenwood," AP, McComb *Enterprise-Journal*, 17 July 1964, 1; "COFO Worker Attacked (Gulfport)," AP, McComb *Enterprise-Journal*, 18 August 1964, 3; "Collinsville Negro Church Hit by Flames," AP, McComb *Enterprise-Journal*, 19 August 1964, 3; "CORE Quarters Hit by Blast (Canton)," AP, McComb *Enterprise-Journal*, 9 June 1964, 1; "Explosion Rocks Negro Home, Church in Canton," AP, McComb *Enterprise-Journal*, 12 June 1964, 7; "Greenwood Police Nab Civil Rights Pickets," AP, McComb *Enterprise-Journal*, 16 July 1964, 3; "Klan Leaflets Flutter (Pascagoula)," AP, McComb *Enterprise-Journal*, 3 July 1964, 1; "Negro Chapel Hit by Bomb (Ruleville)," AP, McComb *Enterprise-Journal*, 25 June 1964, 2; "Negro Church Hit by Flames (Pearl)," AP, McComb *Enterprise-Journal*, 14 August 1964, 3; "Negro Girl Hit at Coast Rally (Moss

Point)," AP, McComb *Enterprise-Journal*, 7 July 1964, 7; "Over 70 Civil Rights Workers Arrested (Pascagoula)," AP, McComb *Enterprise-Journal*, 5 August 1964, 1; "Rights Worker Not Missing, Found in Jail in Greenwood," AP, McComb *Enterprise-Journal*, 7 July 1964, 7, "Two Whites Released, Leave Jackson County," AP, McComb *Enterprise-Journal*, 25 June 1964, 1.

516. Charles Gordon, "Blast, COFO Liquor Raid, Crosses Fracture Weekend," McComb *Enterprise-Journal*, 17 August 1964, 1.

517. McAdam, *Freedom Summer*, 262.

518. Hooker, "Race and the Mississippi Media," 196.

519. "Voter School Instructor Says White Man Hit Him," McComb *Enterprise-Journal*, 21 July 1964, 1; McAdam, *Freedom Summer*, 266.

520. Charles Gordon, "Fire Destroys Church at Quin Park," McComb *Enterprise-Journal*, 17 July 1964, 1; McAdam, *Freedom Summer*, 265.

521. "McComb Might Be Placed under Martial Law," McComb *Enterprise-Journal*, 20 July 1964, 1.

522. Charles Dunagin and Charles Gordon, "Second Park Area Negro Church Is Lost in Fire," McComb *Enterprise-Journal*, 22 July 1964, 1; McAdam, *Freedom Summer*, 266.

523. "Church Burnings No Solution," from the *Baptist Record*, in the McComb *Enterprise-Journal*, 10 August 1964, 2.

524. Charles Gordon, "Blast, COFO Liquor Raid, Crosses Fracture Weekend," McComb *Enterprise-Journal*, 17 August 1964, 1; "Two Crosses Flare Up near City Homes Today," McComb *Enterprise-Journal*, 12 August 1964, 1.

525. Paul Pittman, "The Cross Burners," from the *Tylertown Times*, in the McComb *Enterprise-Journal*, 21 August 1964, 2.

526. Charles Gordon, "Six Pike Negroes Bid for Voter Registration, No Incidents Reported at Protected Sign-Up,' McComb *Enterprise-Journal*, 18 August 1964, 1.

527. "Albert Heffner Issues Statement," McComb *Enterprise-Journal*, 22 July 1964, 1.

528. Hodding Carter, Jr., *So the Heffners Left McComb* (Garden City, N.Y.: Doubleday and Company, 1965), 60.

529. Ibid., 76–80.

530. Ibid., 105.

531. McAdam, *Freedom Summer*, 267–281.

532. Charles Gordon, "City Firebomb Story Folds Up, Rumor Spread by COFO," McComb *Enterprise-Journal*, 21 August 1964, 1.

533. Hooker, "Race and the Mississippi Media," 209.

534. David R. Davies, "J. Oliver Emmerich and the McComb *Enterprise-Journal*," 16–23.

535. James B. Skewes, "The Ultimate Result? It's Mongrelization," *Meridian Star*, 20 June 1964, 4.

536. James B. Skewes, "A Body Blow," *Meridian Star*, 12 June 1964, 4.

537. James B. Skewes, "Words to the Wise," *Meridian Star*, 7 June 1964, 4.

538. "Yankee, Go Home!" from the Oelwein (Iowa) *Register*, in the *Meridian Star*, 9 July 1964, 5.

539. James B. Skewes, "Reverse the Trend," *Meridian Star*, 4 July 1964, 4.

540. Hooker, "Race and the News Media in Mississippi," 188.

541. "Wait for Court Test, Blind Compliance Move Is Hit by Meridian Group," *Meridian Star*, 10 July 1964, 3.

542. "Clueless Trail Is Left by Interracial Trio," UPI, *Meridian Star*, 23 June 1964, 1.

543. "Could This Be a Publicity Hoax?" *Meridian Star*, 24 June 1964, 1.

544. "May Be Hoax," UPI, *Meridian Star*, 25 June 1964, 1.

545. Roy Bain, "Neshoba Citizens Dislike Invasion of Newsmen," *Meridian Star*, 26 June 1964, 1.

546. Billy Rainey, "Still No Trace of Missing Men, It's Possible They Left State," *Meridian Star*, 30 June 1964, 1.

547. "All Bodies Fully Clothed When Found," AP, *Meridian Star*, 5 August 1964, 1; Bain and Rainey, "All Three Bodies Now Identified, Neshoba Grave Finally Found," *Meridian Star*, 5 August 1964, 1; "No Idea Who Did It, Property Owner Says," UPI, *Meridian Star*, 5 August 1964, 1.

548. Roy Bain and Bill Rainey, " 'Rights' Worker Buried Here, 700 at Memorial," *Meridian Star*, 8 August 1964, 1.

549. James B. Skewes, "Cause for Optimism," *Meridian Star*, 6 August 1964, 4.

550. "Another Negro Church Destroyed by Fire (Greenwood)," AP, *Meridian Star*, 12 July 1964, 1; "Bomb Shatters Windows of 'Righters' (Canton)," UPI, *Meridian Star*, 8 June 1964, 1; "Civil Rights Worker Is Wounded in Greenville," AP, *Meridian Star*, 16 August 1964, 1; "Collins Man Charged in Hub Beating (Hattiesburg)," UPI, *Meridian Star*, 19 July 1964, 1; "Explosion Rocks Canton Negro Area," UPI, *Meridian Star*, 12 June 1964, 1; "FBI Arrest Three Men in Itta Bena," UPI, *Meridian Star*, 27 June 1964, 1; "FBI Probes Explosion in Negro Store in McComb," AP, *Meridian Star*, 16 August 1964, 1; "Invaders Arrested in Columbus," UPI, *Meridian Star*, 9 July 1964, 1; "Mixers' House Wrecked by Trio of Blasts (McComb)," AP, *Meridian Star*, 8 July 1964, 1; "Negro Church Number 13 on List, Burns to Ground (Brandon)," UPI, *Meridian Star*, 31 July 1964, 1; "Negro Grocer Claims Pressure Was Applied (Canton)," AP, *Meridian Star*, 30 July 1964, 1; "Negro Pickets Dispersed on Patrol Request (Greenwood)," UPI, *Meridian Star*, 2 August 1964, 1; "Racial Clashes Erupt at Laurel," AP, *Meridian Star*, 12 July 1964, 1; "Racial Group Wants Case in U.S. Court (Canton)," UPI, *Meridian Star*, 13 June 1964, 2; " 'Righters' Report Three State Attack Incidents," UPI, *Meridian Star*, 27 July 1964, 1; "Tension Grips Delta City of Greenwood," AP, *Meridian Star*, 17 August 1964, 1; "Three Deltans Face Hearing on Civil Rights Charges (Greenwood)," AP, *Meridian Star*, 24 July 1964, 1; "Two 'Writers' Claim Beating in Philadelphia," UPI, *Meridian Star*, 18 July 1964, 1; "White CORE Worker Claims Beating in Jail (Jackson)," UPI, *Meridian Star*, 28 June 1964, 1.

551. McAdam, *Freedom Summer*, 270–272.

552. James B. Skewes, "Carry the Fight," *Meridian Star*, 26 August 1964, 4.

553. James Lambert, "Attainment by Merit," *Natchez Democrat*, 9 June 1964, 4; James Lambert, "We Have Confidence," *Natchez Democrat*, 18 June 1964, 2.

554. James Lambert, "We Have Confidence," *Natchez Democrat*, 18 June 1964, 2.

555. James Lambert, "We Have Best Record," *Natchez Democrat*, 30 June 1962, 4.

556. Joseph Ellis, Jr., "Meet Summer Project with Dignity, Patience," AP, *Clarksdale Press Register*, 18 June 1964, 1.

557. "Elect Officers of APWR at Meeting in Ferriday," *Natchez Democrat*, 5 June 1964, 1.

558. "APWR Accuses Dulles of Smear Campaign," AP, *Natchez Democrat*, 28 June 1964, 1.

559. "Arrest 109 Picketing in Leflore County," AP, *Natchez Democrat*, 17 July 1964, 1; "Attempt to Burn Church near McComb," AP, *Natchez Democrat*, 8 August 1964, 1; "Bombard King from Plane with Leaflets (Greenwood)," AP, *Natchez Democrat*, 22 July 1964, 1; "COFO School to Open in McComb," AP, *Natchez Democrat*, 14 July 1964, 1; "KKK Urges Let Law Handle Crisis (Gulfport)," AP, *Natchez Democrat*, 4 July 1964, 6; 'Ohio Rabbi Attacked in Hattiesburg," AP, *Natchez Democrat*, 11 July 1964, 1; "Predawn Blast in McComb Rips House," UPI, *Natchez Democrat*, 9 July 1964, 1; "Sheriff Says Dynamiting 'Senseless' (Soso)," AP, *Natchez Democrat*, 4 July 1964, 6; "Two Civil Rights Trials for 102 Slated Today (Greenwood)," AP, *Natchez Democrat*, 18 July 1964, 1; "White CORE Worker Says Beaten (Jackson)," AP, *Natchez Democrat*, 28 June 1964, 1.

560. "Six Civil Rights Workers Arrive Sunday in Meridian," AP, *Natchez Democrat*, 29 June 1964, 1.

561. "Civil Rights Director Says Workers to Shun Area," AP, *Natchez Democrat*, 1 July 1964, 1.

562. McAdam, *Freedom Summer*, 263–280.

563. "Investigate Two Church Fires in County," *Natchez Democrat*, 13 July 1964, 1.

564. "Funds for Rebuilding Burned Churches Sought," *Natchez Democrat*, 14 July 1964, 1.

565. "Much Interest in Rebuilding," *Natchez Democrat*, 15 July 1964, 1.

566. "Building Funds Still Needed," *Natchez Democrat*, 19 July 1964, 1; "Church Building Fund Increased," *Natchez Democrat*, 23 July 1964, 1.

567. "Building Fund Nearing $2,500," *Natchez Democrat*, 26 July 1964, 1.

568. "Building Fund over $4,000," *Natchez Democrat*, 30 July 1964, 1.

569. "City Bank Gives Churches $1,000," *Natchez Democrat*, 2 August 1964, 1.

570. "Liberty Park Not Available for Klan Talk," *Natchez Democrat*, 19 August 1964, 1.

571. "Large Crowd Heard by Shelton," *Natchez Democrat*, 30 August 1964, 1.

572. "Gary Holland Named *Chronicle* Editor," Pascagoula *Chronicle*, 4 August 1964, 1.

573. W. David Brown, "Inexcusable Action," Pascagoula *Chronicle*, 24 June 1964, 4; W. David Brown, "Should Stay Home," Pascagoula *Chronicle*, 9 July 1964, 4.

574. W. David Brown, "Natural Confusion," Pascagoula *Chronicle*, 14 July 1964, 4.

575. Joseph Albright, "Negro Speaks Out on Race Pride," from the Jackson *Advocate*, in the Pascagoula *Chronicle*, 7 August 1964, 4.

576. "Arrest Two Whites for Setting Fire to Negro Churches as Natchez," UPI, Pascagoula *Chronicle*, 14 July 1964, 3; "Beatings Said Given Negroes (Columbus)," UPI, Pascagoula *Chronicle*, 10 June 1964, 1; "Bomb Shatters Quarters (Canton),"

UPI, Pascagoula *Chronicle*, 8 June 1964, 1; "Explosion in McComb Rips Civil Rights Worker's Home," UPI, Pascagoula *Chronicle*, 8 July 1964, 2; "Greenwood Jails Three Civil Rights Workers," UPI, Pascagoula *Chronicle*, 3 August 1964, 5; "Meridian Police Arrest Pickets," UPI, Pascagoula *Chronicle*, 14 June 1964, 1; "Over 100 Jailed after Greenwood Disturbance," UPI, Pascagoula *Chronicle*, 17 July 1964, 2; "Rabbi Says He's Sorry for Mississippi People," UPI, Pascagoula *Chronicle*, 12 July 1964, 2; "Threat to Civil Rights Men Discounted (Holly Springs)," UPI, Pascagoula *Chronicle*, 1 July 1964, 1; "Three State Men First Arrests (Greenwood)," UPI, Pascagoula *Chronicle*, 23 July 1964, 1; "Two Negro Churches Burned in Natchez," UPI, Pascagoula *Chronicle*, 13 July 1964, 2; "White Farmer Admits Beating in Hattiesburg," UPI, Pascagoula *Chronicle*, 19 July 1964, 2.

577. McAdam, *Freedom Summer*, 257; "Moss Point Police Hold COFO Workers," Pascagoula *Chronicle*, 24 June 1964, 1.

578. "Sheriff Urges Whites, Negroes to 'Stand Firm,' " Pascagoula *Chronicle*, 26 June 1964, 1.

579. "Negro against Civil Rights Activities from Meridian in Pascagoula," Pascagoula *Chronicle*, 8 July 1964, 2.

580. Bill Barton, "Negro Group Organizes Anti-COFO Unit in Moss Point," Pascagoula *Chronicle*, 9 July 1964, 1.

581. "Judge to Back Civil Rights Act If U.S. Halts Reds Here," Pascagoula *Chronicle*, 15 July 1964, 1.

582. "Judge Gives COFO Man Warning," Pascagoula *Chronicle*, 16 July 1964, 1.

583. "Two COFO Drivers from Moss Point Are Held in Biloxi," UPI, Pascagoula *Chronicle*, 15 July 1964, 2.

584. "Pascagoula Police Arrest 62 at Rally," Pascagoula *Chronicle*, 5 August 1964, 1.

585. "Charge Changed against Negroes," Pascagoula *Chronicle*, 7 August 1964, 1.

586. McAdam, *Freedom Summer*, 257–282.

587. "Half Million Negroes Added to Dixie Voters," UPI, Pascagoula *Chronicle*, 2 August 1964, 3.

588. Gary Holland, "Racial Voting Gains," Pascagoula *Chronicle*, 5 August 1964, 4.

589. W.H. Harris, "Pencil Shavings," *Starkville Daily News*, 27 June 1964, 1.

590. Ibid., 25 June 1964, 1.

591. Ibid., 15 August 1964, 1.

592. Paul Harvey, "Outsiders Cause Dark Days for Negroes," *Starkville Daily News*, 4 August 1964, 4.

593. Sherrill Nash, "Discrimination," *Starkville Daily News*, 9 July 1964, 4.

594. W.H. Harris, "Pencil Shavings," *Starkville Daily News*, 16 July 1964, 1.

595. Sherrill Nash, "Goodbye, Freedom," *Starkville Daily News*, 21 August 1964, 4.

596. W.H. Harris, "Lawyers Advise Citizens' Rights," *Starkville Daily News*, 1 August 1964, 4.

597. McAdam, *Freedom Summer*, 265.

598. "Sheriff's Auxiliary Unit Nearing Readiness Status," *Starkville Daily News*, 16 June 1964, 1.

599. "Harpole Says Civil Rights Work Is Communist Inspired," *Starkville Daily News*, 26 June 1964, 1.

600. "100 COFOs Parade in Greenville," AP, *Starkville Daily News*, 11 August 1964, 4; "Civil Rights Charge Laid to Three (Greenwood)," AP, *Starkville Daily News*, 24 July 1964, 1; "Negro Leaders Given Rebuff, No Success (Meridian)," AP, *Starkville Daily News*, 7 July 1964, 1; "Three Itta Bena Men Arrested by FBI," AP, *Starkville Daily News*, 27 June 1964, 1; "Rabbi Is Beaten in Hattiesburg," AP, *Starkville Daily News*, 11 July 1964, 1; "Tempers Flare in Greenwood as Pickets Are Picked Up," AP, *Starkville Daily News*, 17 July 1964, 1; "Three Accused of Threatening Civil Rights Workers, Post Bond," UPI, Tupelo *Daily Journal*, 29 June 1964, 8; "Three Blasts Hit House in McComb," *Starkville Daily News*, AP, 9 July 1964, 1; "Three Jailed in Threats (Itta Bena)," UPI, Tupelo *Daily Journal*, 27–28 June 1964, 1.

601. Harry Rutherford, "A Little More Patience and We Will Win," Tupelo *Daily Journal*, 27 July 1964, 15.

602. James Graham, "Doty Warns Incidents Would Play into Hands of Civil Rights Invaders," Tupelo *Daily Journal*, 26 June 1964, 1.

603. Harry Rutherford, "COFO Campaign No Substitute for School," Tupelo *Daily Journal*, 6 August 1964, 10.

604. Harry Rutherford, "So Little Done, So Great the Damage," Tupelo *Daily Journal*, 21 August 1964, 15.

605. Harry Rutherford, "Let Us Stand Tall, Not Sit Small," Tupelo *Daily Journal*, 16 July 1964, 15; Harry Rutherford, "Still Need Work, but Not for Shame," Tupelo *Daily Journal*, 28 July 1964, 10.

606. McAdam, *Freedom Summer*, 281.

607. "98 Jailed in Greenwood," UPI, Tupelo *Daily Journal*, 22 July 1964, 1; "Barred by Democrats, Negress Says," UPI, Tupelo *Daily Journal*, 24 June 1964, 1; "Beaten Pair Free on Bond (Canton)," UPI, Tupelo *Daily Journal*, 17 July 1964, 20; "Bi-racial Group Stages March in Greenville," UPI, Tupelo *Daily Journal*, 26 June 1964, 1; "Burning of Negro Churches Called Arson (Natchez)," UPI, Tupelo *Daily Journal*, 14 July 1964, 1; "Civil Rights Leaders Charge 'Freedom House' Was Bombed (Canton)," UPI, Tupelo *Daily Journal*, 9 June 1964, 1; "Columbus Trial Delayed until Lawyers Qualified," UPI, Tupelo *Daily Journal*, 1 July 1964, 8; "Fire Destroys Small Church in Greenwood," UPI, Tupelo *Daily Journal*, 13 July 1964, 4; "Greenwood Negro Mob Dispersed, Three Jailed," UPI, Tupelo *Daily Journal*, 3 August 1964, 1; "Greenwood Trio Nabbed in Beating of Negro," UPI, Tupelo *Daily News*, 24 July 1964, 1; "Two Men Beaten in Philadelphia (Journalists), Fire Levels McComb Negro Church," UPI, Tupelo *Daily Journal*, 18–19 July 1964, 1; "Greenville Will Not Tolerate Vigilantes," UPI, Tupelo *Daily Journal*, 2 July 1964, 10; "Holly Springs Police Discount Story COFO Workers Threatened," UPI, Tupelo *Daily Journal*, 2 July 1964, 9; "Negro Church Burned in McComb," UPI, Tupelo *Daily Journal*, 23 July 1964, 1; "Negro Church Burned near Madison," UPI, Tupelo *Daily Journal*, 20 July 1964, 10; "Negro Says He Was Beaten at Greenwood," UPI, Tupelo *Daily Journal*, 17 July 1964, 12; "Police Break Up Three Racial Demonstrations at Greenwood," UPI, Tupelo *Daily Journal*, 17 July 1964, 1; "Police Stymied in Holly Springs," UPI, Tupelo *Daily Journal*, 25–26 July

1964, 1; "Probe Moss Point Fire, Civil Rights Workers Released," UPI, Tupelo *Daily Journal*, 25 June 1964, 7; "Rabbi Beaten in Hattiesburg," UPI, Tupelo *Daily Journal*, 13 July 1964, 12; "Reports of Firebomb at Canton Keep FBI Busy," UPI, Tupelo *Daily Journal*, 13 July 1964, 1; "Solon Says McComb Bomb Aimed at Him," UPI, Tupelo *Daily Journal*, 9 July 1964, 1; "SNCC to Move to Greenwood," UPI, Tupelo *Daily Journal*, 13–14 June 1964, 1; "Ten Pickets Jailed in Meridian," UPI, Tupelo *Daily Journal*, 15 June 1964, 1; "Three Civil Rights Students Jailed in Columbus," UPI, Tupelo *Daily Journal*, 9 July 1964, 10.

608. L.P. Cashman, Jr., "Their Backs Turned on Responsibility," *Vicksburg Evening Post*, 14 June 1964, 4.

609. "Bigotry and Hate," UPI, *Vicksburg Evening Post*, 21 June 1964, 4.

610. "15 Negroes Register as Voters (Meridian)," AP, *Vicksburg Evening Post*, 15 July 1964, 8; "98 Workers Jailed in Leflore," AP, *Vicksburg Evening Post*, 17 July 1964, 2; "Blasts Probed at McComb, Natchez," AP, *Vicksburg Evening Post*, 15 August 1964, 2; "FBI Investigating Church Fire at Greenwood," AP, *Vicksburg Evening Post*, 12 July 1964, 1; "Freedom House at McComb Hit by Three Blasts," AP, *Vicksburg Evening Post*, 8 July 1964, 3; "Jackson Mixers Arrested," AP, *Vicksburg Evening Post*, 13 July 1964, 1; "Rights Tests Are Causes of Two Clashes in Laurel," AP, *Vicksburg Evening Post*, 12 July 1964, 1; "Three Men Arraigned at Oxford," AP, *Vicksburg Evening Post*, 28 June 1964, 12; "Two 'Righters' Released from Pascagoula Jail," AP, *Vicksburg Evening Post*, 25 June 1964, 1; "Violence Strikes Greenwood Again," AP, *Vicksburg Evening Post*, 2 August 1964, 2.

611. "Fighting Flares in Borneo," AP, *Vicksburg Evening Post*, 22 June 1964, 1.

612. "Lunch Counter Mixed Here, No Incidents," *Vicksburg Evening Post*, 6 July 1964, 1.

613. "Judy Simono of Vicksburg Miss Mississippi 1964," *Vicksburg Evening Post*, 26 July 1964, 1.

614. "Martin Luther King Plans Speaking Tour of Mississippi," AP, *Vicksburg Evening Post*, 19 July 1964, 1.

615. "King Leaves," AP, *Vicksburg Evening Post*, 26 July 1964, 2.

616. McAdam, *Freedom Summer*, 159–179.

617. "Harris Given Vice President Post," UPI, West Point *Times-Leader*, 15 June 1964, 1.

618. W.H. Harris, "Pencil Shavings," West Point *Times-Leader*, 24 June 1964, 1.

619. "Tom Abernethy Says Civil Rights Invasion Planned to Stimulate Trouble," *Starkville News*, 1 July 1964, 1.

620. W.H. Harris, "Pencil Shavings," West Point *Times-Leader*, 7 July 1964, 1.

621. W.H. Harris, "Stick Together," West Point *Times-Leader*, 9 July 1964, 4.

622. W.H. Harris, "Discrimination," West Point *Times-Leader*, 9 July 1964, 4.

623. John Stennis, "The Stennis Report," West Point *Times-Leader*, 22 July 1964, 4.

624. McAdam, *Freedom Summer*, 159–179.

625. "111 Pickets Jailed in Greenwood," UPI, West Point *Times-Leader*, 17 July 1964, 1; "98 Civil Rights Workers Convicted (Greenwood)," UPI, West Point *Times-Leader*, 21 July 1964, 1; "Fire Destroys Two Churches in Natchez," UPI, West Point *Times-Leader*, 13 July 1964, 2; "House Hit by Blast (McComb)," UPI,

West Point *Times-Leader*, 8 July 1964, 1; "McComb Blast Investigated," UPI, West Point *Times-Leader*, 9 July 1964, 2.

626. "Equal Pay for Women," Columbus *Commercial Dispatch*, 16 June 1964, 4; "Equal Pay for Women," Gulfport *Daily Herald*, 11 June 1964, 4; "Equal Pay Law Goes into Effect," AP, McComb *Enterprise-Journal*, 11 June 1964, 8; "New Law Goes into Effect to Raise Women's Wages," AP, *Laurel Leader-Call*, 11 June 1964, 1.

627. Daniel Hallin, *The "Uncensored War": The Media and Vietnam* (New York: Oxford University Press, 1986), 15.

628. "Dilemma in Dixie," *Time*, 20 February 1956, 76; "Dixie Flamethrowers," *Time*, 4 March 1966, 64; "Moderation in Dixie," *Time*, 19 March 1965, 71; Edwin W. Williams, "Dimout in Jackson," *Columbia Journalism Review* 9 (Summer 1970): 56.

629. "Belting One Down for the Road," *Nation*, 6 October 1962, 190; Charles Butts, "Mississippi: The Vacuum and the System," in *Black, White and Gray: 21 Points of View on the Race Question*, ed. Bradford Daniel (New York: Sheed and Ward, 1964), 104; "Dilemma in Dixie," 76; "Dixie Flamethrowers," 64; "Moderation in Dixie"; Ted Poston, "The American Negro and Newspaper Myths," in *Race and the News Media*, ed. Paul Fisher and Ralph Lowenstein (New York: Praeger, 1967), 63; Pat Watters and Reese Cleghorn, *Climbing Jacob's Ladder: The Arrival of Negroes in Southern Politics* (New York: Harcourt, Brace and World, 1967), 73; Simeon Booker, *Black Man's America* (Englewood Cliffs, NJ: Prentice-Hall, 1964), 15; Roger Williams, "Newspapers in the South," *Columbia Journalism Review* 6 (Summer 1967): 27; James Boylan, "Birmingham Newspapers in Crisis," *Columbia Journalism Review* 2 (Summer 1963): 30.

630. "Race Violence across Nation," UPI, Corinth *Daily Corinthian*, 10 August 1964, 1; "Racial Incidents Flare across America," UPI, Jackson *Clarion-Ledger*, 17 July 1964, 1; "Racial Strife All over Nation," UPI, *Clarksdale Press Register*, 10 August 1964, 8; "Racial Violence Jars South over Weekend," UPI, Greenville *Delta Democrat-Times*, 6 July 1964, 10; "Tense Racial Situation Described All over Country," AP, Gulfport *Daily Herald*, 21 July 1964, 9.

631. "Chicago Negroes Riot," UPI, Corinth *Daily Corinthian*, 17 August 1964, 1; "Chicago Race Problems," UPI, Columbus *Commercial Dispatch*, 18 June 1964, 1; "Chicago Race Riots, 1,000 Negroes Erupt," UPI, Greenville *Delta Democrat-Times*, 17 August 1964, 1; "Chicago Riots," AP, Gulfport *Daily Herald*, 18 August 1964, 1; "Chicago Riots," AP, *Hattiesburg American*, 17 August 1964, 1; "Chicago Riots," AP, Jackson *Clarion-Ledger*, 17 August 1964, 1; "Race Riots in Chicago," UPI, *Clarksdale Press Register*, 17 August 1964, 1; "Race Riots in Chicago," AP, *Natchez Democrat*, 18, 19 August 1964, 1; "Race Riots in Chicago," UPI, Pascagoula *Chronicle*, 17, 18 August 1964, 5; "Race Riots in Chicago," AP, *Starkville Daily News*, 18, 19 August 1964, 1; "Race Riots in Chicago," UPI, Tupelo *Daily Journal*, 18, 19 August 1964, 1; "Race Riots in Chicago," UPI, West Point *Times-Leader*, 17, 18 August 1964, 1.

632. "$5 Million Pledged, New York to Add Police as Racial Strife Mounts," UPI, *Clarksdale Press Register*, 3 June 1964, 8; "Civil Rights Leaders Demand Arrest of Police," UPI, Columbus *Commercial Dispatch*, 20 July 1964, 1; "Many Hurt in New York Race Riot," UPI, *Clarksdale Press Register*, 20 July 1964, 1; "Negro Bands Terrorize New York," AP, *Meridian Star*, 1 June 1964, 1; "Negro

Mobs," AP, *Laurel Leader-Call*, 20 July 1964, 1; "Negro Rioting Spreading in New York," UPI, Columbus *Commercial Dispatch*, 22 July 1964, 1; "Negro Terrorist Attacks," AP, McComb *Enterprise-Journal*, 2 June 1964, 1; "New York Race Riots," AP, *Hattiesburg American*, 20, 22, 23, 25, 27 July 1964, 1; "New York Riots, Commies Blamed," AP, Jackson *Daily News*, 22, 23, 24, 25, 28, 30 July 1964, 1; "New York Riots," UPI, Corinth *Daily Corinthian*, 22, 26, 27, 31 July 1964, 1; "New York Riots," UPI, Greenville *Delta Democrat-Times*, 15 June 1964, 2; "New York Riots," UPI, *Greenwood Commonwealth*, 17, 27, 28 July 1964, 1; "New York Riots," UPI, Grenada *Sentinel-Star*, 21, 24, 27, 28 July 1964, 1; "New York Riots," AP, Gulfport *Daily Herald*, 18, 23, 25, 27 July 1964, 2; "New York Riots," AP, Jackson *Clarion-Ledger*, 6 June 1964, 1; 'New York Riots," UPI, Jackson *Daily News*, 2, 6, 15 June 1964, 1; "New York Riots," AP, *Laurel Leader-Call*, 22, 23, 25, 27, 28, 29 July 1964, 1; "New York Riots," AP, McComb *Enterprise-Journal*, 20, 21, 23, 27 July 1964, 1; "New York Riots," AP, *Meridian Star*, 20, 23, 25, 26, 27 July 1964, 1; "New York Riots," AP, *Natchez Democrat*, 17, 20, 21, 22, 23, 24, 25, 26, 27, 28 July 1964, 1; "New York Riots," UPI, Pascagoula *Chronicle*, 23 June 1964, 1; "New York Riots," AP, *Starkville Daily News*, 2 June 1964, 1; "New York Riots," UPI, Tupelo *Daily Journal*, 6, 7 June 1964, 1; "New York Riots," AP, *Vicksburg Evening Post*, 20, 21, 22, 23, 24, 25, 26 July 1965, 1; "New York Riots," UPI, West Point *Times-Leader*, 4 June 1964, 1; "Street Fights Continue, New York Officials Grapple with Race Strife," UPI, *Clarksdale Press Register*, 2, 5 June 1964, 8; "Terror in New York," AP, Pascagoula *Chronicle*, 3, 4 June 1964, 3; "Violence Continues, New Policemen Poised to Nip Racial Strife," UPI, *Clarksdale Press Register*, 6 June 1964, 8.

633. "Bloody Race War," UPI, Corinth *Daily Corinthian*, 20 July 1964, 1; "Communists Get Blame for Rioting in Harlem," AP, McComb *Enterprise-Journal*, 22 July 1964, 1; "Harlem Box Score," UPI, Grenada *Sentinel-Star*, 23 July 1964, 1; "Harlem Riots," UPI, *Clarksdale Press Register*, 21 July 1964, 1; "Harlem Riots," AP, Gulfport *Daily Herald*, 20, 21 July 1964, 1; "Harlem Riots," AP, *Hattiesburg American*, 24 July 1964, 1; "Harlem Riots," AP, Jackson *Clarion-Ledger*, 21, 25, 26, 27, 28, 29, 31 July 1964, 1; "Harlem Riots," AP, *Natchez Democrat*, 2 August 1964, 1; "Harlem Riots," UPI, Tupelo *Daily Journal*, 18 June 1964, 1; "Harlem Riots," UPI, West Point *Times-Leader*, 20 July 1964, 1; "Seek Ways to Halt Harlem Tension," UPI, Greenville *Delta Democrat-Times*, 20 July 1964, 1; "Troubled Harlem," UPI, *Clarksdale Press Register*, 24 July 1964, 1.

634. "Negroes Rampage in Brooklyn," UPI, Columbus *Commercial Dispatch*, 23 July 1964, 1.

635. "Dallas Faces Racial Strife," UPI, *Clarksdale Press Register*, 31 July 1964, 1; "White Youth Dies in Race Violence," UPI, Jackson *Clarion-Ledger*, 10 August 1964, 1.

636. "Guardsmen in Rochester Fray," UPI, *Clarksdale Press Register*, 26 July 1964, 1; "Race Riots Rack [*sic*] Rochester," UPI, *Clarksdale Press Register*, 25 July 1964, 1; "Rochester Negroes Use Shotguns," UPI, Columbus *Commercial Dispatch*, 26 July 1964, 1.

637. "Florida War May Be Over," AP, *Laurel Leader-Call*, 29 June 1964, 1; "Integrationists Plan New Assaults on Beaches at St. Augustine," UPI, *Clarksdale Press Register*, 23 June 1964, 1; "Nation's Oldest Cities Have Common Race Problem," UPI, *Clarksdale Press Register*, 4 June 1964, 8; "Race War Stops in St. Au-

gustine," AP, *Laurel Leader-Call*, 1 July 1964, 1; "Riots in St. Augustine," UPI, *Greenwood Commonwealth*, 13, 18, 25, 27 June 1964, 1; "Riots in St. Augustine," AP, *Meridian Star*, 12, 14, 18, 20, 22, 29 June 1964, 1; "St. Augustine Businessmen Say They Will Abide," AP, *Laurel Leader-Call*, 2 July 1964, 1; "St. Augustine Florida Motel Pool Site of Wild Clash," UPI, *Clarksdale Press Register*, 18 June 1964, 1; "St. Augustine Riots," UPI, Corinth *Daily Corinthian*, 15, 16, 18, 23 June 1964, 1; "St. Augustine Still Wracked by Violence," UPI, *Clarksdale Press Register*, 24 June 1964, 1; "St. Augustine Riots," AP, Jackson *Clarion-Ledger*, 13, 14, 19, 21, 26 June 1964, 1; "St. Augustine Riots," AP, Jackson *Daily News*, 3, 12, 13, 14, 18, 21, 22, 23, 26, 27 June 1964, 3; "St. Augustine Riots," AP, *Laurel Leader-Call*, 10, 11, 12, 13, 15, 18, 19, 23, 26, 27 June 1964, 1; "St. Augustine Trouble," AP, Gulfport *Daily Herald*, 12, 15 June 1964, 20; "St. Augustine Riot," AP, *Hattiesburg American*, 10, 18, 22, 26, 27, 30 June 1964, 1; "St. Augustine Violence," UPI, *Clarksdale Press Register*, 11 July 1964, 1; "St. Augustine Violence," UPI, Columbus *Commercial Dispatch*, 14, 16, 17, 19 June 1964, 1; "St. Augustine Violence," AP, McComb *Enterprise-Journal*, 12, 15, 18, 22, 23, 25, 26, 30 June 1964, 7; "St. Augustine Violence," AP, *Natchez Democrat*, 15 June 1964, 1; "Violence Hits St. Augustine," UPI, Greenville *Delta Democrat-Times*, 11, 15, June 1964, 2; "St. Augustine Violence," AP, Pascagoula *Chronicle*, 10, 17, 19, 21, 22, 23, 26 June 1964, 1; "Violence in St. Augustine," AP, *Starkville Daily News*, 13, 19, 24, 30 June 1964, 1; "Violence in St. Augustine," AP, Tupelo *Daily Journal*, 2, 12, 13, 14, 15, 18, 19, 22, 27, 28, 29, 30 June 1964, 1; "Violence in St. Augustine," AP, *Vicksburg Evening Post*, 1, 2, 22 June 1964, 1; "Violence in St. Augustine," "Whites March through Negro Neighborhood in St. Augustine," AP, *Hattiesburg American*, 13 June 1964, 1.

638. "Massachusetts Racial Violence," UPI, Columbus *Commercial Dispatch*, 29 July 1964, 1; "Massachusetts Riot," UPI, Corinth *Daily Corinthian*, 29 July 1964, 1; "Negroes, Whites Clash in Massachusetts," UPI, *Clarksdale Press Register*, 29 July 1964, 1.

639. "500 Screaming Negroes Battle Police in Riot at Jersey City," UPI, Corinth *Daily Corinthian*, 3, 4, 6 August 1964, 1; "New Jersey Riots," UPI, Greenville *Delta Democrat-Times*, 3 August 1964, 1; "New Jersey Riots," AP, Gulfport *Daily Herald*, 3 August 1964, 3; "New Jersey Riots," AP, *Hattiesburg American*, 3, 12, 13 August 1964, 1; "New Jersey Riots," AP, Jackson *Clarion-Ledger*, 3, 4, 14, 15 August 1964, 1; "New Jersey Riots," AP, *Laurel Leader-Call*, 3, 4, 14 August 1964, 1; "New Jersey Riots," AP, *Meridian Star*, 3, 4, 12, 13, 14 August 1964, 1; "New Jersey Riots," AP, McComb *Enterprise-Journal*, 3, 12 August 1964, 1; "New Jersey Riots," AP, *Natchez Democrat*, 4, 13 August 1964, 1; "Riots in New Jersey," UPI, *Clarksdale Press Register*, 3, 4, 12, 13 August 1964, 1; "Riots in New Jersey," UPI, Pascagoula *Chronicle*, 3, 4, 12, 13 August 1964, 1; "Riots in New Jersey," AP, *Starkville Daily News*, 4 August 1964, 1; "Riots in New Jersey," AP, Tupelo *Daily Journal*, 4, 6, 12 August 1964, 1; "Riots in New Jersey," AP, *Vicksburg Evening Post*, 4, 13 August 1964, 1; "Riots in New Jersey," UPI, West Point *Times-Leader*, 3, 5, 12, 14 August 1964, 1.

640. "St. Augustine Racial Strife Continues," AP, *Hattiesburg American*, 18 July 1964, 1.

641. Hodding Carter III, "Time to Wait," Greenville *Delta Democrat-Times*, 19 July 1964, 4.

642. "Half Million Negroes Added to Dixie Voters," UPI, Pascagoula *Chronicle*, 2 August 1964, 3; "Sponsor Claims Negro Drive for Registration Paying Off," UPI, Jackson *Clarion-Ledger*, 3 August 1964, 2.

643. "Civil Rights Being Applied on Military," AP, *Meridian Star*, 17 July 1964, 1; "Commanders Urged to Push Civil Rights near Bases," UPI, Corinth *Daily Corinthian*, 14 July 1964, 1; "Military Removing Color Designation," AP, Jackson *Daily News*, 23 June 1964, 3; "National Guard Mixing Studied," UPI, Corinth *Daily Corinthian*, 17 July 1964, 1; "Pentagon Eyes Guard, ROTC Racial Status," UPI, Jackson *Daily News*, 17 July 1964, 4; "Pentagon Opens Campaign to End Race Discrimination in Service," UPI, Tupelo *Daily Journal*, 17 July 1964, 1; "Racial Designations Removed from Defense Dept. Forms," AP, *Hattiesburg American*, 22 June 1964, 13; "Robert McNamara Wants Civil Rights Used in Military," UPI, Columbus *Commercial Dispatch*, 14 July 1964, 1.

644. Holloway, *Politics of the Southern Negro*, 36.

Chapter 6

1968: The Death of Martin Luther King, Jr., and the Mississippi Daily Press

A Southern black Christian minister, Martin Luther King, Jr. (1929–1968), was a civil rights activist who espoused non-violent protest.[1] Awarded a Nobel Peace Prize in 1964,[2] King was a founder of the Southern Christian Leadership Conference and helped organize the successful Alabama bus boycott in Montgomery in 1955,[3] a yearlong strike that resulted in the 1956 U.S. Supreme Court decision to ban segregation on public buses. Many streets in Mississippi are named in his honor, and his birthday, 18 January, was proclaimed a national holiday and first celebrated in 1986.[4] The notion of Martin Luther King, Jr. Day was proposed nearly twenty years earlier by Senator Ed Brooks (R-Mass.), the only black member of the U.S. Senate when King was assassinated in 1968.[5] Interestingly, and conveniently for staunch Southern traditionalists and others who opposed King and what he stood for, that same day is celebrated in Mississippi as the birthday of Confederate General Robert E. Lee.[6]

King was the married father of four young children when he was assassinated in Memphis, Tennessee, on 4 April 1968. James Earl Ray, a white Southerner, pleaded guilty to the murder in 1968 but recanted soon after he was given a ninety-nine-year prison term without a trial. Ray died in 1998, still in prison and continuing to declare his innocence.

King and his civil rights activities were the focus of news and editorials in the Mississippi daily press many times before his death. Most of the opinion was oppositional, and some of the objection was from the black community. Percy Greene, editor of the black weekly Jackson *Advocate*, took an editorial swipe at King during the Freedom Rider movement to desegregate bus lines in the early 1960s. "Greene asserted that Dr. King preached civil disobedience but refused to accept consequences personally,"

Erle Johnston, a former editor of the *Scott County Times* in Forest, Mississippi, recalled. "Instead of joining Freedom Riders in jail, Greene wrote, 'the generalissimo of the boycott of the Montgomery Jim Crow bus line is making speeches and taking bows in the relative safety of northern environments.' "[7]

During the desegregation of Ole Miss in 1962, King expressed his support for James Meredith at an NAACP meeting in New York. He told the crowd that Meredith "must be okayed for entrance."[8] King also urged President John Kennedy to consider sending the Peace Corps to "help" Mississippi desegregate and referred to the state as an "underdeveloped land of the world."[9] His comments failed to win him many friends among the editors of the Mississippi daily press.

King went to Mississippi for the 1963 funeral of civil rights leader Medgar Evers, who was shot to death in the driveway of his home in Jackson. Soon after the funeral procession in downtown Jackson, King left the state. "His aides, fearing for his life, took him to the airport," Johnston wrote.[10] During Freedom Summer in 1964, King returned to Mississippi and spoke at voter registration rallies,[11] including those held in Greenwood and Vicksburg. "We need Negro representation in Congress from Mississippi," he said. "At the present pace of registration, it will take 135 years for half the Negro population to become registered voters."[12] Two years later, the number of registered black voters in Mississippi had grown dramatically, from 30,000, to 170,000.[13]

While in Mississippi during Freedom Summer, King toured briefly to promote the Mississippi Freedom Democrat Party (MFDP).[14] In Meridian, King spoke to the mother of missing civil rights worker James Chaney, advocated non-violence in seeking compliance with the newly passed Civil Rights Act, and offered his support to the local MFDP, a group denigrated by the *Meridian Star*.[15] King made front-page news in the Mississippi daily press during Freedom Summer for asserting that race relations were just as bad in the North as they were in the South.[16] None of the Mississippi daily press editors offered words of support for King during his visits to the state. Most had nothing at all to say about him.

In the early days of April 1968, significant news to most Mississippians dealt with the war in Vietnam[17] and President Lyndon Johnson's announcement that he would not seek another term in office, a revelation that "flabbergasted Dixie."[18] Even more "shocking" to many Southerners was that Johnson's decision placed Robert Kennedy, despised by many for his advocacy of civil rights, in the front-runner position for the Democratic nomination.[19] Staggered by a full-blown war in Indochina that was being protested by Americans from all walks of life and Johnson's decision that he no longer desired the responsibilities of the presidency, the civil rights movement was just another of the many issues boiling beneath the surface of a tense and angry nation in April 1968.

King, who was also involved in the anti-war movement, had gone to Memphis in early April for the funeral of a youth killed by police.[20] While there, he lent his support to striking Memphis sanitation workers who were asking for better pay, better working conditions, enhanced worker safety and promotions without racial discrimination.[21] King's arrival in Memphis provoked verbal attacks from several Mississippi daily newspapers. He was accused of "trying to overthrow order" by the Columbus *Commercial Dispatch*[22] and of "taking trouble into the streets" by the Jackson *Daily News*.[23] The Greenville *Delta Democrat-Times* noted with prophetic accuracy, "What Martin Luther King proposes for Memphis is certain to trigger bloody confrontation."[24]

At 6:01 P.M. on 4 April 1968, King was killed by one bullet to his head as he stood alone on the balcony of the Lorraine Hotel in Memphis, a location to which he and his entourage had been moved at the last minute.[25] Ralph Abernathy was in King's motel room when he heard the shot and said it sounded like "a firecracker."[26] An arrest for King's murder was not made until 8 June, and while there was only one gun, and one bullet fired, evidence suggests that the assassination of King was not the work of one man.[27]

James Earl Ray arrived in Memphis the day before King's murder and checked into Bessie Brower's boardinghouse across the street from the Lorraine. He used the name John Willard to rent the room, but he usually used the alias Eric Galt.[28] No witnesses claimed to see Ray shoot King.[29] According to police, Ray committed the murder from a bathroom window and then ran outside the boardinghouse and threw down a bundle containing a rifle and several other items covered with his fingerprints.[30] Included with the possessions that Ray allegedly dropped at the scene of the crime was a portable radio engraved with his identification number from the Missouri State Penitentiary, from which he had escaped almost a year before.[31]

For more than thirty years, a debate has raged over who killed King. Suspects have included Ray, the Central Intelligence Agency (CIA), the FBI, militant blacks, and King's inner circle. Ten years after his death, the *Washington Post* did not subscribe to a conspiracy theory. "In 1977, prompted by a disclosure of Hoover's war on King, the Carter Justice Department released and endorsed a review of the FBI's investigation of the assassination and of its possible complicity in the murder," the *Post* reported. "The probe found no evidence of a conspiracy: James Earl Ray had acted alone and now sits in a prison cell, busy creating a fictional tale to baffle and titillate a world so conditioned to its own violence that it was prepared to accept the fantasies he served up to it."[32]

Regardless of who was responsible for the assassination, the nation was stunned. An AP report by Barry Scheid, published two days after King's death, described King as a man who meant many different things to many different people. "To the guilt-ridden, he was a bedeviling reminder that at this late stage of human development, the Negro still rides steerage," Scheid wrote. "To the well-meaning, but anxious, he was the potential spark that might someday ignite a racial explosion in this country, one that could be set off as much by a man speaking non-violence as by the most militant blood-and-guts thunder. But perhaps, most of all, King looked like a last chance."[33]

On 5 April, the day after King's death, most of Mississippi "remained calm," although "Negro areas were tense."[34] National SNCC leader and militant Stokely Carmichael called for all blacks to arm themselves,[35] and H. Rap Brown, another black power advocate, was jailed for inciting a riot in Virginia.[36] Mississippi Governor John Bell Williams (1968–1972) urged composure during a statewide telecast. He also advised the state that the Mississippi National Guard was on alert and would be deployed if necessary.[37]

In Greenville, the community was urged by the Greenville *Delta Democrat-Times* to consider "restraint and prayers."[38] Two days later, more than 200 people gathered at a "peaceful memorial" for King.[39] "We're in business for butter, not guns," a black leader at the memorial told a Greenville *Delta Democrat-Times* reporter.[40] That same night, several arson fires were reported to Greenville police.[41]

In neighboring Greenwood, more than forty cases of "glass breaking" were reported,[42] and a peace walk was held from Greenwood to Itta Bena,[43] where the president of historically black Mississippi Valley State University asked the Highway Patrol to leave the 1,000 marchers alone during their procession. Two marchers were later shot and wounded by patrolmen.[44] According to an AP report, "The religious emphasis of the event was offset by the jeering and laughter of young marchers."[45]

Local memorial services for King were announced in Mississippi daily newspapers in Grenada,[46] Clarksdale,[47] Natchez,[48] McComb,[49] Corinth[50] and Pascagoula.[51] In Hattiesburg, the NAACP gathered at Mt. Zion Baptist Church to pray for King and to urge non-violence.[52] A two-hour work stoppage every day for a week by Hattiesburg blacks to honor King affected the University of Southern Mississippi cafeteria, where workers observed the boycott.[53] The *Vicksburg Evening Post* announced a local memorial for King.[54] The *Meridian Star* interviewed a local black businessman the day after King's death. Charles Young told the newspaper, "King's death makes it hard for leaders who advocate working it out within the system to say 'follow me' when they are shot down."[55] In Pascagoula, a parade permit allowed mourners to march through the city.[56]

In the state capital, a weeklong black boycott of all white-owned businesses and public schools was threatened through a statement issued to the news media by Lawrence Guyot, chair of the Mississippi Freedom Democrats. "White racist America has murdered the Reverend Dr. Martin Luther

King," he said. "Words are not enough."[57] A white-owned market in a black Jackson neighborhood was bombed, though no one was injured.[58] Civil rights activist Charles Evers was instrumental in averting riots at Jackson State College,[59] although two white news reporters were attacked while on the campus,[60] and Jackson Police stood nervous watch[61] before deciding to disperse the angry, milling crowd with tear gas.[62] More than 1,000 National Guardsmen were called to duty in the city,[63] and fifteen arrests were made.[64] Evers later went on statewide television to call for "racial harmony."[65] "It's a terrible thing to hate," he said during the fifteen-minute broadcast. "Please, I appeal to you on the eve of the funeral of our great leader, don't discredit the things he and Medgar died for."[66]

The Mississippi Economic Council (MEC) issued a statement, but it was not published in the Mississippi daily press. "We deeply regret the assassination of Dr. Martin Luther King, Jr.," the MEC said. "We extend our sympathy to his family at this time of sorrow."[67]

Mississippi did not order flags to half-staff at state facilities to mourn King's death. The federal government, however, did.[68]

King's chosen successor, Ralph Abernathy, said he would keep King's dreams alive and blamed King's death on "a racist and sick nation."[69] Abernathy continued negotiations on behalf of the Memphis sanitation workers,[70] and the strike was successfully settled.[71]

MISSISSIPPI DAILY PRESS RESPONSE TO KING'S ASSASSINATION

The wire service reports on King's murder were front-page news and focused primarily on the police search for the assassin.[72] Several of the Mississippi daily newspapers concentrated on the rioting that broke out around the nation.[73] At the Jackson *Daily News*, local riots were described in stories with headlines such as, "Jackson Negroes Rumble."[74] President Johnson called a meeting with black leaders and pleaded for peace in the nation's cities, where riots were erupting into a chaos of looting, arson and random acts of racial violence.[75]

For the week following King's death, the National Guard was placed on alert around the country.[76] Sixteen people died as a result of rioting within twenty-four hours of the assassination.[77] Three days later, that number had grown to twenty-nine.[78] Most of the dead were black, and most were under the age of twenty.[79] In Ohio, a white schoolteacher was dragged from his car and fatally stabbed.[80] By the final count, nineteen of the thirty-nine-dead were reported killed while looting or starting fires.[81] Eleven people died in Chicago, seven in Washington, D.C., six in Baltimore, six in Kansas City, two in Cincinnati, two in Detroit and one each in Memphis, Minneapolis, Tallahassee, Jacksonville and Atlantic City.[82] Riots broke out in eighty-five American towns and cities,[83] to which over 60,000 National

Guardsmen were deployed.[84] Millions of dollars of damage was done,[85] which included over $45 million in insurance claims.[86] Thousands of arrests were made.[87] In mid-April, two Chicago gangs, the Blackstone Rangers and the East Side Disciples, joined in a temporary alliance to urge a halt to violence and looting in that city.[88] A few days later, Chicago Mayor Richard Daley gave police a "shoot to kill" order for looters and arsonists.[89] The mandate was not obeyed, much to Daley's chagrin.[90]

An interesting aspect of the sudden importance of the National Guard was a story reported in the Jackson *Daily News* in early April. "Only a few short months ago, the Secretary of Defense, Robert S. McNamara, was threatening to dissolve the National Guard as an effective force in the event of domestic violence," the report stated. "Our entire congressional delegation sprang into action and helped to stall and prevent the Pentagon's orders from being executed. The need for the National Guard has never been displayed more dramatically than in recent hours."[91]

The National Guard, prior to King's assassination, was being considered an expendable and expensive branch of the military and targeted for elimination. That termination never occurred, of course. Within a few months of the "threatened" dissolution of the National Guard, riots in eighty-five American cities had over 60,000 National Guardsmen proving their importance to national security. A conspiracy enthusiast could easily discern a possible motive within this information. No death, other than King's, could have driven the black inner-city communities to such a degree of unleashed fury and destruction in 1968.

King was buried in Atlanta a few days after his murder.[92] His casket was drawn in a wagon pulled by a mule team, as he requested, four miles through the streets of Atlanta.[93] An estimated 150,000 mourners lined the route to pay their last respects.[94] King then delivered his own pre-recorded eulogy, and the opening words sounded self-aggrandizing to critics. "To whoever speaks my eulogy, tell him not to mention that I have a Nobel Prize, that isn't important," King said. "Tell him not to mention that I have 300 or 400 other awards, that's not important."[95]

The search for King's assassin was headline news in the Mississippi daily press.[96] In late April, when fingerprints on the weapon found at the scene were finally traced, the accused assassin was James Earl Ray, "[a] drifter, loner, avid dancer and prison escapee."[97] Ray had been in trouble with the law since his youth. In 1959, he was convicted of stealing a car and committing a robbery in Missouri, where he was sentenced to twenty years in the state penitentiary. In April 1967, Ray escaped from the Missouri prison in the back of a bread truck and remained on the loose until he was arrested for King's murder a year later.[98] A cellmate of Ray's in the Missouri State Penitentiary told the news media that Ray often talked about a $1 million bounty placed on King by a Ku Klux Klan businessman's associate.[99] The

KKK was ruled out almost immediately by the FBI as a possible perpetrator of the crime.[100]

A conspiracy to murder King became apparent within days of his death, at least to the wire services,[101] a theory that was initially supported by the U.S. Justice Department but later reversed.[102] Faked radio dispatches that interfered with the police investigation were reported,[103] and a Cuban conspiracy was proposed by syndicated columnist David Lawrence.[104]

In response to King's murder, civil rights legislation being considered by Congress was quickly rushed to passage by a vote of 250 to 171.[105] The 1968 Civil Rights Act prohibited racial discrimination in "eighty percent" of all rental and sales of housing and was signed into law a week after King's death.[106] President Johnson was behind the push,[107] and most Southern congressmen were in opposition.[108] Representative William Colmer (D-Miss.), who was also the House Rules Committee chair in 1968, protested the quick action, which was "spurred on," he said, by the death of King.[109] Senator Mike Mansfield (D-Mont.) agreed with Colmer.[110] The West Point *Times-Leader* referred to King's death as "a civil rights passkey."[111] Black leaders skeptical about civil rights legislation complained, "There are hundreds of such laws already on the books but none is being enforced."[112]

Syndicated columnist Drew Pearson discussed the growing dissension among civil rights activists on the issue of non-violence, which had become more evident in the days following King's murder.[113] The burgeoning Black Power movement of the 1960s proclaimed "black supremacy" and advocated militancy to obtain civil rights, rather than the non-violent protest and "racial equality" sanctioned by King and the NAACP. Many people, especially the younger generation, were beginning to refer to themselves as "black," rather than Negro.[114] Stokely Carmichael and SNCC supported black power, as did CORE. King, however, shortly before his death, had said, "Black supremacy or aggressive black violence is as invested with evil as white supremacy or violence."[115] Roy Wilkins, executive director of the NAACP, agreed. "The term black power means anti-white power," he said. "We of the NAACP will have none of this. We seek, as we have sought before, the inclusion of Negro Americans in the nation's life, not their exclusion."[116]

In the Mississippi daily press, editorial response to King's death was varied. At the *Clarksdale Press Register*, Joseph Ellis, Jr., continued as editor. In early April, prior to King's death, Ellis responded positively to President Johnson's decision not to seek re-election and noted that Mississippi Governor Williams did not support either Johnson or Robert Kennedy.[117] Ellis made no comment in April 1968 regarding the murder of King, but a syndicated column by Drew Pearson in the *Clarksdale Press Register* placed the blame for the ensuing race riots on the television coverage of looting and arson.[118]

At the Columbus *Commercial Dispatch*, editor Birney Imes, Jr., made no mention of King's death except for the riots that followed King's assassination. In his only editorial regarding King during April, "What Now?" Imes wrote, "The only real solution can be based on fairness to all regardless of skin color, religion or economic station."[119] King's commitment to non-violence was questioned by the Columbus *Commercial Dispatch* in a syndicated column by Thurman Sensing, who said that King did not "truly" advocate non-violence because "civil disobedience is an incitement to riot."[120] A syndicated column by David Lawrence agreed with Sensing and questioned King's true intentions as a prophet of non-violence.[121] Two other columns by Lawrence attempted to analyze the riots that tore the nation apart the week following King's murder and wondered how the looters and arsonists could justify their actions as a protest to the assassination of a man who publicly advocated just the opposite.[122] Lawrence believed that King's death was the result of a covert conspiracy by parties unknown.[123]

At the Corinth *Daily Corinthian*, Warren Sanders had taken the helm as editor. The only editorial related to King's assassination in the Corinth *Daily Corinthian* in April 1968 was a syndicated column from the UPI, "King Assassination Motivates Passage of Civil Rights Bill."[124]

At the Greenville *Delta Democrat-Times*, editor Hodding Carter III continued his support of the struggle for civil rights, but he thought that King's work sometimes instigated violence. On 3 April, the day before King was assassinated, Carter wrote, "It will take very little this year to initiate racial violence and further polarization and hatred."[125] Two days after King was killed, Carter voiced his concerns for a society that would commit murder for racial reasons. He expressed his desire that all Americans work for "the eradication of the racism that has sickened our country to the point of death."[126] By the middle of April, Carter was beginning to believe that King's death was the result of a conspiracy rather than a lone assassin, that it might have been "a well-planned, coldly-executed plot."[127]

Blacks in Greenville held a memorial march for King on 7 April, reported by the *Delta Democrat-Times* as "peaceful."[128] That day, Carter penned an editorial, "Greenville Comes Close," in which he praised the community for keeping the peace with no "gun play or looting" and noted, "We need to create a truly better society for all our people."[129] A letter to the editor of the *Delta Democrat-Times* from Josh Bogan, a student of law at Ole Miss, called for an end to racism and expressed his "feelings of anger, guilt and shame" at the death of King. "We must work toward one nation with liberty and justice for all," he wrote.[130] In response to negative remarks made about Charles Evers when he called for peace and non-violence,[131] Carter defended Evers as "no Uncle Tom" in an editorial, "Evers Rises to Occasion."[132] That same day and for several more, syndicated columnists analyzed King, both positively and negatively, on the editorial pages of the Greenville *Delta Democrat-Times*. Jack Anderson compared King to Gandhi and linked the two assassinated advocates of non-violent protest as "kindred spirits."[133] Cartoonist Bill Mauldin created a drawing of Gandhi and King in heaven, with Gandhi saying, "The odd thing about assassination, Dr. King, is they think they've killed us."[134] William F. Buckley remarked on "Dr. King's flouting of the law" and said, "perhaps the shooter had heard King's talks about individual conscience."[135] Rowland Evans and Robert Novak commented that Stokely Carmichael might be the person to take over for King because he "fits the ghetto mood."[136] In response to the looting and arson terrorizing the nation's cities, Tom Wicker cautioned, "Mob violence delays King's dream rather than achieving it,"[137] and Jack Anderson warned that a resurgence of racial violence in the country might lead to a rekindling of "the hard-line right."[138]

Carter was not one to make excuses, not for himself and not for anyone else. Two weeks after King's assassination, Carter told his readers, "It's time for all our responsible citizens, white and Negro, to call a halt to the prophesying of doom."[139] Carter was no racist, and he had no tolerance for anyone who voiced racism, black or white. Carter, like his Pulitzer Prize-winning father before him, held particular disdain for elected officials who flaunted their racial prejudice and preached the "happy Negro" theme. In response to the comments of several state officials regarding King's death, Carter wrote, "Any politician who seeks to ignore the problems, or the racial crisis which underlies them, or seeks to exacerbate that crisis by racist pronouncements or actions, does not deserve public office."[140]

Carter was not a defender of King, but he endorsed the concept of equal rights. A week after King's death, a group of black youths brought to the Greenville *Delta Democrat-Times* a list of complaints they had compiled against the Greenville Police Department. Staff writer Bob Boyd was given the assignment, and a front-page story resulted.[141] No other Mississippi daily newspaper in April 1968 reported a story from this perspective. The *Delta Democrat-Times* also covered a black protest of the Greenville Housing Authority.[142]

A photo spread of NAACP bumper stickers covered the entire top half of the Greenville *Delta Democrat-Times* on 11 April. Carter's willingness to print the photos and his determination to keep peace in his community are clearly evident in the messages displayed on the stickers: "Rumors Feed Riots, Check All Rumors," "Alive You Can Fight, Dead You're Dead," "Hot Head, Hot Lead, Cold Dead," "Over No Dead Bodies" and "No Young Blood on the Pavement, Prevent Riots."[143] A front-page headline later in the month expressed the Greenville *Delta Democrat-Time*'s commitment to a fair and just society in a report on Hubert Humphrey's presidential campaign, "Bi-Racial Delegation Urged for Mississippi."[144]

At the *Greenwood Commonwealth*, Edmund Noel was editor. SNCC headquarters returned to Atlanta after Freedom Summer in 1964, but black activism was alive and well in this Delta town. The day after King was assassinated, the police "allowed" mourners to take a "peace walk" in his memory.[145] When a group of black ministers staged their own march, the *Greenwood Commonwealth* proclaimed it as "not official."[146] Five days after King's death, five arrests were made for acts of vandalism said to be protests of the assassination,[147] and forty windows were reported broken in businesses and homes.[148] Only two editorials related to King's death were published in the *Greenwood Commonwealth* in April 1968, and none were by Noel. A King Syndicate cartoon showed a tombstone towering over Washington, D.C., with the engraving, "Civil Rights Bill,"[149] and the other was an editorial reprinted from the *Chicago Tribune*, "Day of Mourning," which described King's funeral.[150]

At the Grenada *Sentinel-Star*, Joseph Lee remained as editor. Similar to his editorial leadership during the desegregation of Ole Miss in 1962 and Freedom Summer, Lee had nothing to say in April 1968 regarding the assassination of Martin Luther King, Jr.

At the Gulfport *Daily Herald*, editor E.P. Wilkes published two opinion columns regarding King's assassination in April 1968. The first one, two days after the murder, was a tribute to King by United Nations Secretary Ralphe Bunche. Both men were identified in the column as having won Nobel Peace Prizes "for work on the betterment of humanity."[151] Bunche received the award in 1950 for helping achieve an Arab–Israeli agreement. The other editorial in the Gulfport *Daily Herald* in April 1968 regarding King's death was Thurman Sensing's "Outbreak of Savagery," in which Sensing wrote, "The death of Dr. King brought to the surface the savage instincts that lie just below the surface of many of our cities."[152]

At the *Hattiesburg American*, Leonard Lowrey continued as editor. The day before King's murder, Lowrey published an editorial expressing his fear that when "Negro militants" said that they were out to "burn America down," the authorities "refused to take it seriously."[153] The day after King's death, Lowrey published a lengthy editorial about the assassination:

> We often disagreed with Dr. King's tactics in applying his principle of non-violence, and to pretend otherwise on the occasion of his death would be highly improper. We felt strongly that he should not have become involved with massive demonstrations in the tense Memphis labor situation, since this could not lead to a solution but only to more trouble. But we totally and emphatically reject the mad act of the assassin who hid in the darkness and took his life and we believe all thoughtful people should feel saddened and sickened because of this act. Violence and turmoil and disorder have gone far enough.[154]

In the middle of April, Lowrey published an editorial every day for three days that addressed an issue related to the murder. In the first, Lowrey could not contain his feelings that the assassination, though despicable to him, was the primary motivating factor behind passage of the 1968 Civil

Rights Act. "Among other things, the slaying of Dr. Martin Luther King in Memphis has resulted in the rapid passage by Congress of civil rights legislation," he wrote. "It might be said in passing that the slaying, aside from the fact that it was brutal, ugly and in direct contradiction to God's law, could not have been more helpful to 'the movement.' "[155] In the second editorial, Lowrey disagreed with the President's Commission on Civil Disorders that "white racism" was responsible for "Negro rioting."[156] Instead, Lowrey cast blame on professional agitators intent on causing turmoil for the sake of rebellion. In the third editorial, Lowrey continued to declare his disgust at the excuses made for the riots, "the orgy of burning and looting 'supposedly' in reaction to the death of King."[157] Lowrey concluded in his last editorial in April 1968 related to King's death that the "result of Civil Disobedience" is rioting and chaos.[158]

At the Jackson *Clarion-Ledger*, the day before the assassination, editor T.M. Hederman, Jr., questioned King's actual commitment to non-violence. "Doesn't he really advocate violence by his repeated warning that violence will be the result of officials' failure to bow to whatever demands are at issue?" Hederman wrote. "The unvarnished truth is that King, by his foggy notions on civil disobedience which came through to the untaught as simple law-breaking and pillage, is the devil's advocate behind the continuing wave of rebellions."[159]

The day after King's death, the editorial voice at the Jackson *Clarion-Ledger* softened a bit but found it ironic that a "disciple of non-violence" would die violently and that "some of his people" would become violent criminals to protest his death. The newspaper also expressed chagrin that "history will have to assign a place" to King. Hederman wrote:

> Every person in America who feels or thinks deeply has profound regrets at the assassination in Memphis of one of the nation's most controversial figures. A professed and proclaimed disciple of non-violence, it was ironic that violence seemed to follow in his train whenever and wherever he went. And violence, senseless, criminal and tragic, ended his life. He was and is a hero to the vast majority of his race, which makes it more unfortunate that some of his people broke out into demonstrations of violence as their way of protesting the death of the disciple of non-violence.[160]

In response to rioting across the nation, a letter to the editor of the Jackson *Clarion-Ledger* from George Kopp in Pennsylvania said, "Maybe if the government gave blacks less and told them to earn their bread by the sweat of their brow, they would be just like me, too damned tired to protest."[161] Toward the end of April, an unsigned letter to the editor of the newspaper referred to King as "a power drunk demagogue" whose assassination "stampeded" the passage of civil rights legislation, just as John Kennedy had been a "power drunk demagogue" whose death resulted in the same action.[162]

Two days after President Johnson signed the 1968 Civil Rights Act, syndicated columnist Paul Harvey expressed his displeasure with the law. In "Jungle Drums Prod Primitive Passions," he addressed the reason that the legislature "rushed" to passage:

> The White House, at the point of a gun, demands of Congress "civil rights" legislation. This recent ferment which devastated sections of forty cities was not a conclusive plea for additional legal "rights," most of it was illegal thievery of other people's property. Let none pretend that this was anybody's way of honoring a dead man. Let none contend that this was righteous wrath directed by all black men at all white men. This was nothing more or less than lawless grand larceny.[163]

Jackson *Clarion-Ledger* headlines relating to King in April 1968 often portrayed him as the cause of the nation's violence, such as "King Prime Mover of Social Upheaval," which captioned three photos of the rioting.[164] In news reports and editorial columns, the Jackson *Clarion-Ledger* denigrated and denounced King before and after his death in April 1968.

Across town at the Jackson *Daily News*, editor James "Jimmy" Ward's attitude toward King was similar to that at the Jackson *Clarion-Ledger*. Identical photos and headline, on the same day and on the same page of the Jackson *Daily News*, proclaimed, "King Prime Mover of Social Upheaval."[165] Two days after King's death, a Jackson *Daily News* editorial described him as a leader who had been "fading from prominence" and who had gone to Memphis to stir racial unrest:

> The man who pulled the trigger in Memphis certainly did no favor to a nation that was already torn with civil strife. Rather than solve any problems, the killer has magnified national difficulties, the extent of which we do not claim to foresee. It is sickening that Dr. King went to Memphis to fan the flames of racial discord. All responsible voices had warned that his presence would lead to trouble, as it so often has.[166]

A week after King's death, as the riots began to subside, Ward returned to praise Mississippi for "orderly" discipline. "Mississippians of all races today have every reason to stand just a little taller in quiet pride over their conduct during the past few days of national turmoil," he wrote. "Mississippi, which has been held to ridicule in the eyes of the world as perpetuating the worst of racial relations, deliberately accused of everything from starvation of its citizens to oppression of every despicable description, has, with few exceptions, maintained a calm and orderly discipline."[167]

When the 1968 Civil Rights Act was passed just a few days after King's death, a Jackson *Daily News* editorial voiced outrage. Ward wrote:

> An otherwise unacceptable Civil Rights Act, going farther afield and deeper into invasion of private property rights than anything heretofore imagined, has received

approval for presidential signature. Additional millions and millions of dollars for every conceivable kind of federal giveaway program, directed to militants who now have an intimidating upper hand right into the White House, will be demanded by Congress. Sadly, much of this appeasement (blackmail?) money will be voted in the name of shame, grief and atonement for all the things claimed to cause rioting, looting, arson and frustration.[168]

Two days later, an editorial, "What Is Next, Please?" chided the legislators. "Will Uncle Sam be told that if every Negro doesn't get a paid three-week vacation to Bimini that Washington will be burned?"[169] Participants in the Poor Peoples' March on Washington were referred to as "professional troublemakers."[170] Similar to the Jackson *Clarion-Ledger*, in news reports and editorial columns, the Jackson *Daily News* deprecated and condemned King before and after his death.

At the *Laurel Leader-Call*, editor J.W. "Jay" West was more quiet regarding the assassination of King than he had been during Freedom Summer in 1964 and the desegregation of Ole Miss in 1962. His only editorial concern in April 1968 was to wonder who was behind the assassination. In "King's Killer Hides, Who's Helping Him?" West remarked, "The answer, when and if ascertained, may be rather revealing."[171]

At the McComb *Enterprise-Journal*, editor J.O. "Oliver" Emmerich was never one to avoid issues of social and political importance. He responded to King's death with an editorial:

Like Gandhi, he advocated nonviolence, a policy accompanied by riots he deplored, and like Gandhi, he suffered death at the hands of an assassin. Gandhi's power increased after his death. And the nationwide memorial occasion across America bore evidence that Dr. King, like Mahatma Gandhi, would become even more powerful after life. The person who fired that fatal bullet into the body of Dr. King not only committed a dastardly murder, but he rendered a tremendous disservice to our American nation. There is no way of knowing how many people will be killed because of that assassin's bullet.[172]

Emmerich published the editorial cartoon by Mauldin of Gandhi and King in heaven,[173] and when the 1968 Civil Rights Act was passed, Emmerich responded in his last editorial regarding King in April 1968. "Such is the political reaction to the violence of an extremist in Memphis," he wrote. "Unquestionably, the party responsible for the assassination was opposed to the civil rights legislation then pending in Washington. But his extremist action did the reverse of what he sought. It is a dangerous thing for Congress to move from the pressure of emotionalism rather than from the results of debate and deliberations."[174]

At the *Meridian Star*, the blatant racism and conservative Southern traditionalism of editor James B. Skewes were tempered by the murder of King. "The *Meridian Star* certainly was never a follower of Martin Luther

King," he wrote. "Nevertheless, we deplore the murder of any man, no matter who. We hope in the ensuing days, that the American people will rededicate themselves to a determination that no further acts of lawlessness or violence will be tolerated, regardless of race."[175]

When black boycotts of schools and white-owned businesses were called in the state in response to King's murder, Skewes was outraged:

> Anyone who calls for school or economic boycotts by Negroes is speaking against, not for, the best interest of the race. Why? (1) Education is the surest road to progress. Therefore, anyone who advises Negroes to stay away from school only hurts the Negro. (2) Business boycotts hurt our economy. Anything that hurts our economy hurts all our people, black as well as white. We advise the Negroes not to participate in such schemes, for their own good.[176]

The *Meridian Star* responded negatively to the 1968 Civil Rights Act, just as it had responded negatively to the Civil Rights Act of 1964. "The newest so-called 'civil rights' bill is an example of what the liberal establishment can accomplish given the opportune moment," Skewes wrote.[177]

At the *Natchez Democrat*, editor James Lambert was no supporter of civil rights legislation, but he also deplored violence. Two days after King was murdered, he wrote, "Most Dastardly of Acts," a front-page editorial in which he referred to the assassination as "one of the most heinous and regrettable crimes" in many years. "No effort must be spared to find and properly punish the person or persons who are responsible for, or connected with, the shooting death of Dr. King," he wrote. "It must be pointed out, however, that additional lawlessness such as rioting and wanton destruction of property cannot and must not be tolerated on any level, as it can only ultimately lead to more death and bloodshed."[178]

Syndicated columnist Drew Pearson's column, "Martin Luther King, Jr.," in which Pearson stated, "King's death, in the eyes of Negroes, culminates a long history of Southern violence in which they have been on the receiving end," was printed in the *Natchez Democrat*.[179] Lambert also published Pearson's column "Looting in DC," in which Pearson noted that cities with integrated police forces, such as Atlanta, had less violence following King's death.[180]

King's alleged ties to the Communist Party were addressed by the *Natchez Democrat* following his assassination. Syndicated columnist and conservative Tom Anderson said he was not certain that King had been a Communist but that he "was surrounded by Communists and was carrying out the Communist program more effectively than any other known American Communist."[181] No further explanation was offered and, a week later, another Anderson column tied King to the Communists. "Yes, Martin Luther King had a 'dream,' and it was substantially the same dream that Karl Marx had," he wrote. "More guilty than the Negroes and Communists who brought us to the brink of civil war, however, are the Roosevelts,

Stevensons, Kennedys, Warrens, Goldbergs and Johnsons who encouraged, pacified, appeased and rewarded them."[182] King's assassination was also linked to the Communist Party by the *Natchez Democrat.* Syndicated columnist David Lawrence suggested that the Communists had hired the killer because they knew King's murder would cause civil upheaval.[183]

At the Pascagoula *Mississippi Press*, formerly the Pascagoula *Chronicle*, Gary Holland remained as editor. The day after King's murder, a story in the *Mississippi Press* headlined, "King Reached Point of No Return in Montgomery," referring to the 1956 bus boycott that was King's first major civil rights activity.[184] Three days into the riots following King's death, Circuit Judge Darwin Maples of Pascagoula commented in a front-page story, "It's a disgrace that the police have been ordered to shoot only in self-defense when these hoodlums run wild, loot, steal, burn, kill and murder."[185]

Three days after King's death, Holland addressed the assassination in an editorial in which he termed King's murder a tragedy:

> The *Mississippi Press*, although it does not endorse King's philosophy, abhors this act of violence and joins with the nation in mourning his death, because in essence, no man is an island and the deprivation of this man's freedom affects us all. The fact that our nation has a few paranoids who would commit such an act is no reason to justify racial war. The majority of our people are still law-abiding citizens who reject such actions. The Negro should remember the majority and not inflict his wrath on them because of the dastardly act of an apparent crackpot.[186]

A letter to the editor of the Pascagoula *Mississippi Press* by Tom Roper of Moss Point accused the assassin of a "coward's slaying."[187] Another letter to the editor of the Pascagoula *Mississippi Press* by attorney Douglass Baker of Pascagoula, who referred to himself as a "disciple" of King, stated, "All men, irrespective of any incidence of color, must take a giant step, perhaps those of Dr. Martin Luther King, Jr."[188]

At the *Starkville Daily News*, editor Sherrill Nash published two editorials about King during April 1968, and neither was written by him. The first, reprinted from the weekly *Picayune* (Mississippi) *Item*, questioned the "good" that King had accomplished with his life and blamed politicians who courted the black vote for the passage of the 1968 Civil Rights Act. "It is hard to imagine how it would have been without television coverage and the plaudits of the pundits," the editorial stated. "It is also hard to imagine now what lasting good King has accomplished, and if it will be outdone by the disorder and damage that followed his near-deification by the politicos who sought the Negro vote."[189] The other editorial concerning King during April 1968 in the *Starkville Daily News* was Anderson's syndicated column that alleged Communists ties with the assassination.[190]

At the Tupelo *Daily Journal*, publisher George McLean was back at the editorial helm. The death of King was never mentioned in editorials in the

Tupelo *Daily Journal* in April 1968, nor was the Civil Rights Act of 1968. Two opinion columns by McLean did, however, address civil rights issues. Five days after King's murder, McLean wrote that Americans should strive to "create national unity out of racial diversity."[191] In response to the Poor Peoples' March on Washington, McLean observed that economic progress by the indigent required the efforts of three groups to succeed, "government, business and the poor."[192]

At the *Vicksburg Evening Post*, L.P. Cashman, Jr., remained as editor. King was the topic of three editorials in the *Vicksburg Evening Post* in April 1968. The first, three days after King's death, remarked, "The nation's reaction was one of shock and shame, anger and violence."[193] A week after King's death, an editorial addressed the murder and laid blame on King for the riots that ensued without ever mentioning his name. "The past week has been one of the most shameful in our history, and yet the call is for more federal laws to cover almost every phase of our national life, under the guise of civil rights," he wrote. "The rioters of Washington, Chicago, Detroit and Baltimore and the dozens of other cities have obviously secured rights to riot and to plunder and to burn. Non-violence, what crimes have occurred in your name."[194]

Cashman was a staunch supporter of Chicago Mayor Daley's "shoot to kill" decree against arsonists and looters.[195] Syndicated columnist David Lawrence agreed and thought that Daley's directive was the only way to maintain law and order in most of the inner cities torn by riots after King's death.[196] In his last editorial pertaining to King in April 1968, "The Big Manhunt," Cashman commented, "We join with all the people of this nation in the hope that this man, who brought martyrdom to King, will eventually pay the proper penalty for his deed."[197] The uncertainty here, regarding Cashman's remark, is whether the "proper penalty for his deed" refers to the murder of King or the creation of King as a martyr.

At the West Point *Times-Leader*, editor W.H. Harris continued to berate civil rights and racial equality in his front-page "Pencil Shavings" column. "If a white civil rights leader was killed by a Negro, does anyone believe that white citizens of the nation would take to the streets, looting, burning?" he wrote. "The rioters and looters are not mourning the death of Dr. King. They are not revenging his death. They are making a mockery of everything he believed."[198]

The West Point *Times-Leader* published Paul Harvey's syndicated column, "Wallowing in the Mud with Minorities."[199] The newspaper also published Tom Anderson's "Straight Talk" column, which suggested that King "was carrying out the Communist program more effectively than any other known American Communist,"[200] and Anderson's "Martin Luther King" column, which suggested that King shared "a dream" with Karl Marx.[201] Harris had no intention of encouraging martyr status for the slain civil rights leader.

SUMMARY OF COVERAGE

As evidenced by the majority of the editors of the Mississippi daily press, the issues of concern addressed following the assassination of Martin Luther King, Jr., were the same as those addressed during Freedom Summer 1964, the desegregation of Ole Miss in 1962, the *Brown v. Board of Education* decision in 1954 to desegregate public schools and the Dixiecrat walkout of the Democratic National Convention in 1948: (1) Mississippians were not ready for the reality of a desegregated society, as advocated by King, and (2) national civil rights laws not only supplanted states' and individual rights but had become a way to court "Negro" votes. According to most Mississippi daily press editorials following King's assassination, the notion that blacks and whites were equal as races of people was a concept that remained unacceptable.

The propensity toward reporting civil rights issues in Mississippi daily newspapers following King's assassination was daily news coverage of either the investigation of the murder, the ensuing riots around the nation or the Civil Rights Act of 1968. The majority of the news stories regarding King's death in the Mississippi daily press came from the wire services, AP and UPI, and most of the nineteen Mississippi daily newspapers published at least one editorial pertaining to the assassination. Most of the editorials focused on King's alleged involvement with the Communist Party or the motivating effect that his death had on passage of the Civil Rights Act of 1968 or questioned his true commitment to non-violence. King's assassination was undoubtedly a top news story on the front pages of the Mississippi daily press during April 1968.

Contrary to what media critics have noted about the promotion of violent suppression of civil rights activity in a small sampling of Southern newspapers,[202] the Mississippi daily press did not encourage the assassination of King or condone it. Not once was this found in any of the nineteen newspapers. However, the Mississippi daily press, as an entirety, did not mourn King.

In their news coverage of civil rights issues during April 1968, preceding and following King's death, the two most widely circulated Mississippi daily newspapers, the Jackson *Clarion-Ledger* and the Jackson *Daily News*, were not representative of the Mississippi daily press. The editorials in the Jackson *Daily News* and the Jackson *Clarion-Ledger* were deserving of their reputation for proliferating the expanding polarization of blacks and whites in the state, intensifying the opposition of Mississippi whites to desegregation and condescension toward blacks.[203] Their combined criticism of King in April 1968 was the most derogatory of all the Mississippi daily newspapers, and although this deprecatory position was true of most other editors of the Mississippi daily press regarding King in April 1968, it was to a much lesser degree than in the two Jackson newspapers.

The editorial consensus regarding King's death was the "us against them" theme proposed during the 1948 Dixiecrat protest, the 1954 *Brown v. Board of Education* decision, the desegregation of Ole Miss in 1962 and Freedom Summer in 1964. In the case of King's assassination, the "us" were white conservative Mississippi, and "they" were the black power advocates rioting in the nation's cities, "liberal" whites who supported equal rights and the U.S. Congress that passed the Civil Rights Act of 1968.

Two pieces of state legislation that impacted Mississippi society, possibly even more than the aftermath of King's assassination, were basically ignored by the Mississippi daily press in April 1968. An 1892 law that outlawed segregation in Mississippi jail cells was repealed, becoming "the first desegregation bill approved by the Mississippi Legislature in modern times."[204] The vote was 63–37.[205] The second piece of legislation made jury duty for women a legal obligation for the first time in Mississippi.[206]

NOTES

1. James Loewen and Charles Sallis, eds., *Mississippi: Conflict and Change* (New York: Pantheon Books, 1974), 280.
2. *The World Almanac and Book of Facts*, 125th ed. (New York: St. Martin's Press, 1992), 310.
3. Martin Oppenheimer, "The Genesis of the Southern Negro Movement: A Study in Contemporary Negro Protest" (Ph.D. diss., University of Pennsylvania, 1963), 63–64.
4. *The World Almanac and Book of Facts*, 125th ed, 527.
5. "Asks January 15 for King Day," AP, Gulfport *Daily Herald*, 9 April 1968, 19.
6. Earle Johnston, *Mississippi's Defiant Years, 1953–1973: An Interpretive Documentary with Personal Experiences* (Forest, Miss.: Lake Harbor Publishers, 1990), 402.
7. Ibid., 132.
8. "King Says Negro Must Be Okayed for Entrance," UPI, Columbus *Commercial Dispatch*, 21 September 1962, 1; "Meredith Must Be Admitted, King Says," UPI, Corinth *Daily Corinthian* 21 September, 1962, 1; "Meredith 'Must' Win, Negro Minister Says," UPI, *Clarksdale Press Register*, 21 September, 1962, 12.
9. "King Urges JFK to Nix Segregation," AP, *Greenwood Commonwealth*, 20 September 1962, 1; "King Suggests Kennedy Send Peace Corps to Mississippi," UPI, Corinth *Daily Corinthian*, 20 September 1962, 5.
10. Johnston, *Mississippi's Defiant Years*, 180–181.
11. "King Exhorts Greenwood Negroes to Register, Vote," UPI, Tupelo *Daily Journal*, 22 July 1964, 4; "King in Mississippi to Help Organize 'Freedom Democrats,' " UPI, Tupelo *Daily Journal*, 22 July 1964, 1; "King Is Due in State to Help Movement," AP, Gulfport *Daily Herald*, 21 July 1964, 1; "King Sparks Voter Drive," UPI, Corinth *Daily Corinthian*, 22 July 1964, 1; "King to Speak at Rally Here," AP, *Greenwood Commonwealth*, 22 July 1964, 1; "King Recruits Voters, Slaps at FBI," AP, Jackson *Daily News*, 22 July 1964, 1; "Martin Luther King's

Oratory Pushes Registration," UPI, Columbus *Commercial Dispatch*, 22 July 1964, 1; "Registration Effort Due in Greenwood," UPI, *Clarksdale Press Register*, 22 July 1964, 1; "Rev. King Is Slated to Pay Visit to Delta Area Today," Greenville *Delta Democrat-Times*, 21 July 1964, 1; "Small Crowd Greets King at Greenwood," AP, Jackson *Clarion-Ledger*, 22 July 1964, 1.

12. Johnston, *Mississippi's Defiant Years*, 266.

13. Ibid., 325.

14. "Civil Rights Leader Plans Boost to Negro Democratic Party," UPI, West Point *Times-Leader*, 21 July 1964, 2; "King Asks Nonviolence and Pushes New Party," *Meridian Star*, 25 July 1964, 1; "King Plans to Boost New Democrat Party," AP, *Laurel Leader-Call*, 21 July 1964, 1; "King Tells Plan for New Party," AP, Gulfport *Daily Herald*, 22 July 1964, 1; "King Urges Plan to Unseat Party," AP, *Laurel Leader-Call*, 22 July 1964, 1; "Martin Luther King Comes to State to Boost Freedom Democrats," AP, *Hattiesburg American*, 21 July 1964, 1; "Negro Leader Touring State for Freedom Democrats," UPI, *Clarksdale Press Register*, 21 July 1964, 1; "New Party Forming, Martin Luther King to Aid," UPI, Columbus *Commercial Dispatch*, 21 July 1964, 1.

15. "King Asks Nonviolence and Pushes New 'Party,' " *Meridian Star*, 25 July 1964, 1.

16. "King Finds North More Explosive," AP, Jackson *Daily News*, 1 August 1964, 1; "King Says North Race Relations Worse Than South," AP, *Hattiesburg American*, 1 August 1964, 1; "Race Relations in North Bad, King Declares," AP, Gulfport *Daily Herald*, 1 August 1964, 1.

17. Gabriel Kolko, *Anatomy of a War: Vietnam, the United States, and the Modern Historical Experience* (New York: Pantheon Books, 1985), 303; "U.S. Bombers Curb Action, Most of Vietnam Spared," AP, *Clarksdale Press Register*, 1 April 1968, 1.

18. "I Will Not Seek and I Will Not Accept Party's Nomination," AP, *Meridian Star*, 1 April 1968, 1; "Johnson Steps Out of Race," AP, Jackson *Clarion-Ledger*, 1 April 1968, 1; "LBJ Calls Decision Totally Irrevocable," AP, McComb *Enterprise-Journal*, 1 April 1968, 1; "LBJ Shocker," AP, Gulfport *Daily Herald*, 1 April 1968, 1; "LBJ's Action Stuns Nation," UPI, *Laurel Leader-Call*, 1 April 1968, 1; "President Johnson Not to Seek Re-Election," AP, Columbus *Commercial Dispatch*, 1 April 1968, 1; "President Stuns Nation, World by Announcing He Will Not Run," UPI, Greenville *Delta Democrat-Times*, 1 April 1968, 1.

19. "Bobby Kennedy Front Runner after Johnson's Decision," AP, *Clarksdale Press Register*, 1 April 1968, 1.

20. "King Returns, Funeral Rites Are Watched," UPI, Corinth *Daily Corinthian*, 2 April 1968, 1; "Memphis Is Jittery," UPI, Greenville *Delta Democrat-Times*, 1 April 1968, 3.

21. "Dr. King Fights Ban on Marching," UPI, Greenville *Delta Democrat-Times*, 4 April 1968, 1; "King Defies March Ban," AP, Tupelo *Daily Journal*, 4 April 1968, 1; "King Moves to Overthrow Injunction," UPI, Grenada *Sentinel-Star*, 3 April 1968, 1; "King Set to March in Memphis," UPI, Corinth *Daily Corinthian*, 3 April 1968, 1; "King Supporters Fight Injunction," UPI, Corinth *Daily Corinthian*, 3 April 1968, 1; "Legal Action Eyed against Dr. King," UPI, Greenville *Delta Democrat-Times*, 3 April 1968, 3; "Memphis March Expected," AP, Gulfport *Daily Herald*, 3 April 1968, 30.

22. "Martin Luther King Trying to Overthrow Order," UPI, Columbus *Commercial Dispatch*, 4 April 1968, 1.

23. "King to Ignore Injunction, Take Trouble into Streets," AP, Jackson *Daily News*, 4 April 1968, 1.

24. Hodding Carter III, "Triggers Bloody Confrontation," Greenville *Delta Democrat-Times*, 3 April 1968, 4.

25. William F. Pepper, *Orders to Kill: The Truth behind the Murder of Martin Luther King* (New York: Carroll and Graf Publishers, 1995), 269.

26. Philip H. Melanson, *The Murkin Conspiracy: An Investigation into the Assassination of Dr. Martin Luther King, Jr.* (New York: Praeger, 1989), 3.

27. Ibid., 5.

28. Ibid., 7.

29. Ibid., 92.

30. Select Committee on Assassinations, U.S. House of Representatives, *The Final Assassination Report* (New York: Bantam Books, 1979), 183.

31. Melanson, *The Murkin Conspiracy*, 109.

32. "Probe by Justice Concludes James Earl Ray Acted Alone," *Washington Post*, 2 February 1977, 3.

33. "Picture of Calm Uneasy Posture," AP, Jackson *Daily News*, 6 April 1968, 4.

34. Johnston, *Mississippi's Defiant Years*, 356.

35. "Carmichael Says Slaying Sparks New Negro Unity," AP, *Vicksburg Evening Post*, 13 April 1968, 6; "Carmichael Urges Arms for Negroes," AP, Jackson *Daily News*, 5 April 1968, 1.

36. "Black Power Head Charged with Inciting to Riot," UPI, Columbus *Commercial Dispatch*, 16 April 1968, 3; "Rap Stays in Jail," UPI, Greenville *Delta Democrat-Times*, 9 April 1968, 1.

37. "Gov. to Speak on TV at 4 O'Clock," *Hattiesburg American*, 5 April 1968, 1; "Guard on Standby, Williams Pledges to Keep Order in State," UPI, Tupelo *Daily Journal*, 6–7 April 1968, 1; "John Bell Calls Guard, Governor Acts Quickly to Enforce Law, Order," UPI, *Meridian Star*, 6 April 1968, 1; "State Citizens Urged to Ignore All Demagogues," AP, *Vicksburg Evening Post*, 6 April 1968, 1; "State Guard Alerted," AP, *Natchez Democrat*, 6 April 1968, 1; "State Protected, Guard at Ready," Jackson *Daily News*, 6 April 1968, 1.

38. "Community Leaders Here Call for Restraint, Prayers," Greenville *Delta Democrat-Times*, 5 April 1968, 1.

39. "Negroes Here Stage March," Greenville *Delta Democrat-Times*, 8 April 1968, 1.

40. "Memorial Service Held Here, We're in Business for Butter, Not Guns, Says Negro Leader," Greenville *Delta Democrat-Times*, 9 April 1968, 1.

41. "Two Arrests, Rash of Fires, Marks Night in Greenville," Greenville *Delta Democrat-Times*, 8 April 1968, 1.

42. "Police Count 43 Cases of Glass Breaking Here," *Greenwood Commonwealth*, 8 April 1968, 1.

43. "Greenwood Negroes in Peaceful March," AP, Jackson *Clarion-Ledger*, 6 April 1968, 1; "Negroes Allowed to Demonstrate Here, Agreement Calls for Peace Walk," *Greenwood Commonwealth*, 5 April 1968, 1.

44. "Dr. White Issues Statement," *Greenwood Commonwealth*, 5 April 1968, 1; "Two Students Wounded," AP, *Vicksburg Evening Post*, 5 April 1968, 1.

45. "1,000 Negroes Stage March in Greenwood," AP, *Meridian Star*, 7 April 1968, 8.

46. "Memorial Services Held in Mississippi for Martin Luther," Grenada *Sentinel-Star*, 5 April 1968, 1.

47. "Slain Negro Leader Honored, About 1,500 Pay Tribute to Dr. King at Memorial Service Here," *Clarksdale Press Register*, 8 April 1968, 1.

48. "Memorial Service for King Today," *Natchez Democrat*, 7 April 1968, 2.

49. "Memorial Held Here for King," McComb *Enterprise-Journal*, 9 April 1968, 1.

50. "King Memorial Held at Eason (High School)," Corinth *Daily Corinthian*, 9 April 1968, 1.

51. "Memorial Rites Here for Martin Luther King," Pascagoula *Mississippi Press*, 7 April 1968, 2.

52. "Local NAACP Calls Meeting to Cut Chances of Violence," *Hattiesburg American*, 5 April 1968, 1.

53. "1500 March Here in Tribute to King, Negro Work Stoppage and Boycott Begin," *Hattiesburg American*, 8 April 1968, 1.

54. "Memorial for Dr. King Planned Here," *Vicksburg Evening Post*, 5 April 1968, 8.

55. "Negro Community Upset, Charles Young Hopes People Will Remain Calm," *Meridian Star*, 5 April 1968, 1.

56. "150 Pascagoula Negroes March," Pascagoula *Mississippi Press*, 10 April 1968, 12.

57. "Civil Rights Forces Pushing for Boycotts," UPI, Greenville *Delta Democrat-Times*, 7 April 1968, 1; "Guyot and Other Leaders Ask Boycotts in Jackson," UPI, *Meridian Star*, 5 April 1968, 1; "Jackson Threatened with Boycott," *Greenwood Commonwealth*, 5 April 1968, 1; "Negroes Call for Boycott of Jackson Schools, Businesses," AP, *Hattiesburg American*, 5 April 1968, 1; "Negroes Planning Boycott," AP, *Starkville Daily News*, 6 April 1968, 1; "Negroes Urge State Boycott," AP, *Meridian Star*, 6 April 1968, 1.

58. "Jackson Market Bombed," AP, West Point *Times-Leader*, 5 April 1968, 1.

59. "Charles Evers in Jackson after Stopping Student Riots at Jackson State College," Gulfport *Daily Herald*, 5 April 1968, 1; "Pleader for Nonviolence," *Hattiesburg American*, 5 April 1968, 1.

60. "Negroes Riot in Jackson, Itta Bena, Looters Get Busy in East," UPI, *Meridian Star*, 5 April 1968, 1; "Newsmen Attacked at Jackson State," Jackson *Clarion-Ledger*, 5 April 1968, 1.

61. "Police Stand Guard," Jackson *Clarion-Ledger*, 5 April 1968, 1.

62. Gary Barnett, "Tear Gas Launched by Jackson Police," Jackson *Daily News*, 5 April 1968, 1.

63. "1,400 Guardsmen Gear to Quell Disorders," UPI, Tupelo *Daily Journal*, 6–7 April 1968, 1; "Guardsmen Force Peace at Jackson," AP, *Vicksburg Evening Post*, 5 April 1968, 1; "Police, Guardsmen Halt Jackson Uprising," UPI, *Meridian Star*, 8 April 1968, 1; "Stern Guardsmen Curb Agitators," AP, *Vicksburg Evening Post*, 8 April 1968, 1.

64. "Police Reveal Arrests in Jackson Disorders," Jackson *Clarion-Ledger*, 8 April 1968, 1.

65. "Evers Asks Harmony between Races," AP, *Starkville Daily News*, 7 April 1968, 1; "Evers Asks Harmony between Races," AP, West Point *Times-Leader*, 9 April 1968, 5.

66. "Evers Calls for Halt of Racial Violence," UPI, Tupelo *Daily Journal*, 9 April 1968, 4; "Evers Urges Restraint," McComb *Enterprise-Journal*, 9 April 1968, 3.

67. Johnston, *Mississippi's Defiant Years*, 356.

68. "Flags at Half Mast, LBJ Asks Day of Mourning," AP, *Meridian Star*, 5 April 1968, 1; "Half-Staff Flag Ordered," AP, Jackson *Daily News*, 5 April 1968, 1; "Johnson Declares Sunday Day of Mourning," AP, *Natchez Democrat*, 6 April 1968, 1; Johnston, *Mississippi's Defiant Years*, 356.

69. "Abernathy to Carry on King's Plans," AP, Jackson *Clarion-Ledger*, 11 April 1968, 20; "King's Successor Promises Negro 'Dream Come True,' " UPI, Columbus *Commercial Dispatch*, 16 April 1968, 1; "To Push King's Drive to Help Poor," UPI, Tupelo *Daily Journal*, 11 April 1968, 10.

70. "Memphis Strike Negotiations Continuing, Abernathy Speaks," UPI, Corinth *Daily Corinthian*, 16 April 1968, 1.

71. "Garbage Strikers Agree to End Memphis Walkout," AP, *Starkville Daily News*, 17 April 1968, 1; "Settlement Ends Memphis Strike," UPI, Corinth *Daily Corinthian*, 17 April 1968, 1.

72. "Best Known Civil Rights Leader," UPI, *Laurel Leader-Call*, 5 April 1968, 1; "Broad Dragnet Is Pressed for Gunman at Memphis," AP, *Vicksburg Evening Post*, 5 April 1968, 1; "Clark Thinks Dr. King's Killer Will Be Captured, Rights Leader Slain by Memphis Sniper," UPI, Greenville *Delta Democrat-Times*, 5 April 1968, 1; "Dr. Martin Luther King Is Dead," UPI, *Laurel Leader-Call*, 5 April 1968, 1; "Hint Arrest Near in King Slaying," UPI, *Laurel Leader-Call*, 5 April 1968, 1; "King Dead, Johnson Delays Hawaii Trip," AP, Gulfport *Daily News*, 5 April 1968, 1; "King's Followers Plan to Finish His Work," AP, *Clarksdale Press Register*, 5 April 1968, 1; "King Shot by Lone Assassin," AP, Gulfport *Daily Herald*, 5 April 1968, 1; "Law Hunts White Man Who May Have Wielded Rifle," AP, McComb *Enterprise-Journal*, 5 April 1968, 1; "Martin Luther King Dies in Memphis," UPI, Grenada *Sentinel-Star*, 5 April 1968, 1; "Police Hunting Killer," AP, Gulfport *Daily Herald*, 5 April 1968, 1; "Police Seek King's Killer," AP, *Greenwood Commonwealth*, 5 April 1968, 1; "Slaying Blamed on White Man, Unidentified," AP, *Meridian Star*, 5 April 1968, 1; "Slaying of King Shadows Politics," AP, *Vicksburg Evening Post*, 5 April 1968, 1; "Sniper Arrest Seen Near, Probe Links Lone Suspect," UPI, Pascagoula *Mississippi Press*, 5 April 1968, 1.

73. "Angry Mobs Stage Riots around Nation," UPI, Greenville *Delta Democrat-Times*, 5 April 1968, 1; "Curb Memphis Violence," AP, *Vicksburg Evening Post*, 5 April 1968, 1; "Have Some Leads in King's Murder, Assassination of Civil Rights Leader Spurs Riots, Looting across Country," AP, *Hattiesburg American*, 5 April 1968, 1; "King Slaying Starts Rash of Riots," AP, Tupelo *Daily Journal*, 5 April 1968, 1; "Martin Luther King Killed While Standing on Balcony, Order 4,000 National Guard to Memphis," AP, *Natchez Democrat*, 5 April 1968, 1; "Memphis Fears Violence," AP, *Starkville Daily News*, 5 April 1968, 1; "Nation's Reaction to Slaying of King Is Violent in Some Places," AP, McComb *Enterprise-*

Journal, 5 April 1968, 1; "Negro Violence Rocks U.S. Cities, Search Continues for King's Killer," AP, *Meridian Star*, 5 April 1968, 1; "Students Restless after Fiery Night across U.S.," AP, Jackson *Daily News*, 5 April 1968, 1; "Tight Security Imposed after Slaying of King," AP, Jackson *Clarion-Ledger*, 5 April 1968, 1; "Violence, Looting, around U.S.," AP, Jackson *Clarion-Ledger*, 5 April 1968, 1; "Violent Reaction in Places," AP, Gulfport *Daily News*, 5 April 1968, 1.

74. James Watts, "Jackson Negroes Rumble," Jackson *Daily News*, 5 April 1968, 1.

75. "Don't Let Violence Be Victor," AP, Gulfport *Daily News*, 5 April 1968, 1; "Johnson Calls Negro Leaders for Meeting," UPI, Columbus *Commercial Dispatch*, 5 April 1968, 1; "LBJ Asks Nation to Deny Violence, Says Law to Prevail," UPI, *Laurel Leader-Call*, 5 April 1968, 1; "LBJ Meets Negroes, Deplores 'Bullet Rules,' " UPI, Greenville *Delta Democrat-Times*, 5 April 1968, 1; "LBJ Meets with Leaders of Civil Rights Movement," AP, *Hattiesburg American*, 5 April 1968, 1; "LBJ Pleads against Violence, Substantial Lead in Case," AP, Jackson *Daily News*, 5 April 1968, 1; "LBJ Tries to Avert Violence," UPI, Corinth *Daily Corinthian*, 5 April 1968, 1; "LBJ Won't Be Ruled by Bullet," UPI, Pascagoula *Mississippi Press*, 5 April 1968, 1; "Lyndon Begs for Calm following King's Death," AP, West Point *Times-Leader*, 5 April 1968, 1; "President Appeals for End to Violence," AP, *Greenwood Commonwealth*, 5 April 1968, 1.

76. "41,000 Troops Are Guarding U.S. Cities," AP, Jackson *Daily News*, 7 April 1968, 1; "Guard Out as Violence Flares across Country," AP, *Meridian Star*, 7 April 1968, 2; "Guards Ordered against Rioters," AP, *Vicksburg Evening Post*, 11 April 1968, 12; "Riots and Threats Bring Guard Out," AP, *Starkville Daily News*, 9 April 1968, 1; "Violence Continues around Country, Troops Added," AP, *Meridian Star*, 7 April 1968, 1.

77. "13 Deaths Counted as Riots Rip Northern Cities," UPI, Tupelo *Daily Journal*, 6–7 April 1968, 1; "16 Killed in Violence over Nation," AP, *Clarksdale Press Register*, 6 April 1968, 1; "Arrests Mount, Thousands Hurt, Damage Fantastic in Race Riots," UPI, Tupelo *Daily Journal*, 8 April 1968, 1; "Sixteen Known Dead as Fire Burns Nearly Two Blocks," AP, *Natchez Democrat*, 7 April 1968, 1; "New Violence Flares," UPI, Columbus *Commercial Dispatch*, 7 April 1968, 1; "Racial Strife Ravages Cities," UPI, *Laurel Leader-Call*, 8 April 1968, 1; "Rioting Goes Unabated in Many Big Cities of U.S.," AP, *Starkville Daily News*, 7 April 1968, 1; "Riots Shake Big Cities," AP, *Meridian Star*, 6 April 1968, 1; "Violence, Looting Rises in Nation's Major Cities," AP, *Greenwood Commonwealth*, 6 April 1968, 1.

78. "24 Deaths Are Counted in North and East," AP, *Meridian Star*, 8 April 1968, 1; "85 U.S. Cities Visited by Violence, 29 Dead," UPI, Greenville *Delta Democrat-Times*, 8 April 1968, 1.

79. "All but Five Riot Deaths Are Negroes, Most Shot," AP, *Greenwood Commonwealth*, 12 April 1968, 1; "Death Toll, Property Damage Mount in Nation's Violence," AP, *Vicksburg Evening Post*, 6 April 1968, 1; "Death Toll Rises in Rioters' Paths," AP, *Vicksburg Evening Post*, 10 April 1968, 1; "Deaths in Racial Violence Number 34," AP, *Hattiesburg American*, 10 April 1968, 1; "New Racial Outbreaks Bring Toll to 33 Dead," AP, Jackson *Clarion-Ledger*, 10 April 1968, 1; "Riot Toll Mounting," UPI, *Laurel Leader-Call*, 9 April 1968, 1; "Violence Cooling, Toll 34," AP, Gulfport *Daily Herald*, 10 April 1968, 12.

80. "White Teacher Dragged from Car and Stabbed to Death," AP, *Meridian Star*, 9 April 1968, 1.

81. "A Rundown on Deaths from Riots," AP, Gulfport *Daily Herald*, 12 April 1968, 23; "19 of 39 Killed Are Arsonists or Looters," AP, *Vicksburg Evening Post*, 13 April 1968, 2.

82. "A Rundown on Deaths from Riots," 23; "Racial Violence Subsides as Death Toll at 34," UPI, *Natchez Democrat*, 11 April 1968, 15; "Rioting Death Toll: 34 Negro, 5 White," AP, Jackson *Clarion-Ledger*, 13 April 1968, 1.

83. "85 U.S. Cities Visited by Violence," UPI, Greenville *Delta Democrat-Times*, 8 April 1968, 1; "Race Violence Hits Four Major Cities," UPI, *Natchez Democrat*, 7 April 1968, 1; "Violence Racks [*sic*] Cities," UPI, Pascagoula *Mississippi Press*, 8 April 1968, 1.

84. "61,000 Guards in Strife-Torn Cities," AP, *Vicksburg Evening Post*, 9 April 1968, 1; "61,000 Troops on Duty in Cities across U.S.," AP, West Point *Times-Leader*, 9 April 1968, 8; "61,000 Troops Used in Riot Torn Cities," AP, *Meridian Star*, 9 April 1968, 1; "More Troops Battle Riots," AP, Jackson *Clarion-Ledger*, 9 April 1968, 1; "Trouble Boils, 61,000 Troops Protect Nation's Aching Cities," AP, Jackson *Daily News*, 9 April 1968, 1; "Violence Ebbs, 61,000 Troops Keep Watch over Troubled Cities," AP, *Clarksdale Press Register*, 9 April 1968, 1.

85. "Damage from Riots in Millions," AP, *Greenwood Commonwealth*, 12 April 1968, 1; "Damage in Riots Runs to Millions," AP, West Point *Times-Leader*, 12 April 1968, 1; "Riot Damage Claims Eclipse 30 Million Dollars," UPI, Corinth *Daily Corinthian*, 11 April 1968, 1; "Riot Damage Estimated in Millions," AP, *Clarksdale Press Register*, 12 April 1968, 1; "Riot Damage May Exceed $30 Million," AP, *Hattiesburg American*, 12 April 1968, 1; "Rioting Damage Set in Millions," AP, *Vicksburg Evening Post*, 13 April 1968, 10.

86. "Insurance Losses from Civil 'Riots' Pass $45 Million," UPI, Columbus *Commercial Dispatch*, 12 April 1968, 1; "Nation's Riot Damage $45 Million," AP, Gulfport *Daily Herald*, 12 April 1968, 1; "Riot Damages Estimated in Millions," AP, McComb *Enterprise-Journal*, 12 April 1968, 1; "Rioting Losses around Nation $45 Million," UPI, Greenville *Delta Democrat-Times*, 12 April 1968, 1.

87. "Courts Processing Riot Arrest Cases," AP, *Hattiesburg American*, 15 April 1968, 1; "Riot Charges Engage Courts," AP, *Greenwood Commonwealth*, 15 April 1968, 1; "Thousands in Courts from Riots, Looting," AP, West Point *Times-Leader*, 15 April 1968, 1.

88. "Cool It, Baby,' Gangs Try to Stop Looting, Arson in Chicago," UPI, Tupelo *Daily Journal*, 15 April 1968, 11; "Gang Leaders Oppose Riots in Big Cities," AP, *Vicksburg Evening Post*, 9 April 1968, 1.

89. "Chicago Mayor Repeats Order to Shoot Arsonists," AP, *Vicksburg Evening Post*, 18 April 1968, 8; "Daley's Shoot to Kill Orders Win Support, Condemnation," UPI, Tupelo *Daily Journal*, 18 April 1968, 10; "Shoot to Kill," UPI, Pascagoula *Mississippi Press*, 16 April 1968, 1; "Shoot to Kill Orders Issued by Mayor Daley," UPI, *Meridian Star*, 16 April 1968, 1.

90. "Mayor Daley Mad Arsonists Not Shot," AP, *Starkville Daily News*, 16 April 1968, 1; "Mayor Daley Mad Arsonists Not Shot," AP, West Point *Times-Leader*, 16 April 1968, 1.

91. "Guard Availability Vital," Jackson *Daily News*, 10 April 1968, 14.

92. "50,000 at Service, Dignitaries Include Humphrey, Mrs. JFK," AP, Mc-

Comb *Enterprise-Journal*, 9 April 1968, 1; "Atlanta Crowded for King Funeral," AP, West Point *Times-Leader*, 8 April 1968, 2; "Atlanta Crowded for King Funeral," AP, *Starkville Daily News*, 7 April 1968, 2; "Atlanta Prepares for King Funeral," AP, Jackson *Clarion-Ledger*, 9 April 1968, 1; "Friends, Mourners, Pay Last Respects to King," UPI, *Laurel Leader-Call*, 10 April 1968, 1; "King Eulogized, Riots Continue in Some Areas," AP, *Vicksburg Evening Post*, 9 April 1968, 1; "King Funeral Draws 50,000," UPI, *Laurel Leader-Call*, 9 April 1968, 1; "King Funeral Held Tuesday in Atlanta," AP, *Natchez Democrat*, 10 April 1968, 7; "King's Funeral Under Way in Atlanta," AP, *Meridian Star*, 9 April 1968, 1; "King Laid to Rest in Day Long Tribute," AP, Jackson *Clarion-Ledger*, 10 April 1968, 1; "Last Rites Held for King," UPI, Corinth *Daily Corinthian*, 9 April 1968, 1; "Nation's Leaders Attend Final Rites, 50,000 Pack Streets near Atlanta Church," UPI, Greenville *Delta Democrat-Times*, 9 April 1968, 1; "Thousands Throng to King's Funeral," AP, *Starkville Daily News*, 9 April 1968, 8; "Services Held in Atlanta for Martin King," UPI, Grenada *Sentinel-Star*, 9 April 1968, 1; "Thousands Mourn Slain Dr. King," AP, Tupelo *Daily Journal*, 8 April 1968, 1; "Throngs on Hand for King's Rites," AP, West Point *Times-Leader*, 9 April 1968, 2; "Throng Pays Respects to Dr. King," AP, *Clarksdale Press Register*, 9 April 1968, 1; "Throngs Attend Negro Leader's Funeral," AP, Gulfport *Daily Herald*, 9 April 1968, 1.

93. "Mules Draw King Casket to Graveside," AP, *Greenwood Commonwealth*, 9 April 1968, 1; "The Wagon," photo, Jackson *Daily News*, 10 April 1968, 1.

94. "150,000 Attend Final Rites for Dr. King," UPI, Tupelo *Daily Journal*, 10 April 1968, 1; "Guards Are Placed Where 150,000 Attended Funeral March," photo, AP, McComb *Enterprise-Journal*, 10 April 1968, 1.

95. "Recorded Voice Enables King to Give Eulogy," UPI, Pascagoula *Mississippi Press*, 9 April 1968, 1; "Speaks Own Last Eulogy," UPI, Tupelo *Daily Journal*, 10 April 1968, 13; "Spoke His Own Funeral Rites by Recording," AP, Jackson *Daily News*, 9 April 1968, 1.

96. "Assassin's Arrest Is Quite Close," UPI, Corinth *Daily Corinthian*, 8 April 1968, 1; "Broad Dragnet Is Pressed for Gunman at Memphis," AP, *Vicksburg Evening Post*, 5 April 1968, 1; "FBI, Local Officials Merge Forces, 'Substantial Leads' Grow in Search for Assassin," AP, *Clarksdale Press Register*, 6 April 1968, 1; "Have Clues in Search for Sniper," AP, Gulfport *Daily Herald*, 6 April 1968, 1; "Have Some Leads in King's Murder," AP, *Hattiesburg American*, 5 April 1968, 1; "Hint Arrest Near in King Slaying," UPI, *Laurel Leader-Call*, 5 April 1968, 1; "Hunt for King's Killer Settles into Grim Routine," AP, McComb *Enterprise-Journal*, 10 April 1968, 1; "Hunt One Man in Crime," AP, *Natchez Democrat*, 8 April 1968, 1; "Killer's Dragnet Spreads," AP, *Vicksburg Evening Post*, 6 April 1968, 1; "Landlady Says Sniper Has 'Silly' Smile," UPI, Tupelo *Daily Journal*, 6–7 April 1968, 1; "Lawmen Indicate They're on the Trail of Martin Luther King's Killer," UPI, Greenville *Delta Democrat-Times*, 7 April 1968, 1; "Manhunt Continues," UPI, Pascagoula *Mississippi Press*, 7 April 1968, 1; "Massive Hunt Spreads for King's Killer," UPI, Columbus *Commercial Dispatch*, 7 April 1968, 1; "No Lead on Killer," AP, *Starkville Daily News*, 10 April 1968, 1; "Officials Claim They Are Getting Close to Slayer," UPI, Grenada *Sentinel-Star*, 5 April 1968, 1; "Search Continues for King's Killer," AP, *Meridian Star*, 5 April 1968, 1; "Search Widens for King's Killer," AP, *Greenwood Commonwealth*, 6 April 1968, 1; "Sec-

ond Night of Riots, Hunt for Killer Spreads," AP, Jackson *Daily News*, 6 April 1968, 1; "Suspected Assassin Described," AP, Jackson *Clarion-Ledger*, 6 April 1968, 1; "This Crime Will Be Solved, U.S. Attorney General Says He Is Confident Killer Will Be Caught," UPI, Corinth *Daily Corinthian*, 5 April 1968, 1.

97. "Bulletin: Galt Is Ray," AP, Jackson *Daily News*, 19 April 1968, 1; "Escaped Ex-Con Ray Identified as Galt," AP, Jackson *Clarion-Ledger*, 20 April 1968, 1; "FBI Identifies Galt as Fugitive Named James Earl Ray," UPI, Tupelo *Daily Journal*, 20–21 April 1968, 1; "FBI Identifies Suspect as Pen Escapee," UPI, *Laurel Leader-Call*, 20 April 1968, 1; "FBI Makes Charges in King Murder (Ray)," UPI, Grenada *Sentinel-Star*, 18 April 1968, 1; "FBI Names Galt, Says He's Escapee (Ray)," AP, *Greenwood Commonwealth*, 19 April 1968, 1; "FBI Puts Ray on Most Wanted List," AP, *Hattiesburg American*, 20 April 1968, 1; "Galt Is Identified, James Earl Ray," AP, *Hattiesburg American*, 19 April 1968, 1; "Galt Known as Ray as FBI Checks," AP, *Starkville Daily News*, 20 April 1968, 1; "Galt or Ray? Loner or Swinging Mixer," AP, *Greenwood Commonwealth*, 20 April 1968, 1; "Habitual Criminal Gets Finger in King's Death," UPI, Columbus *Commercial Dispatch*, 21 April 1968, 1; "Hunt for Galt Is Stopped," AP, McComb *Enterprise-Journal*, 21 April 1968, 1; "James Earl Ray Object of Nationwide Search," AP, *Meridian Star*, 19 April 1968, 1; "King's Slayer Is Sought," AP, *Clarksdale Press Register*, 20 April 1968, 1; "Martin Luther King Killer (Ray)," UPI, Greenville *Delta Democrat-Times*, 15 April 1968, 1; "Press Manhunt for Ray," AP, *Natchez Democrat*, 21 April 1968, 1; "Ray FBI's Most Wanted," AP, Pascagoula *Mississippi Press*, 21 April 1968, 1; "Ray Is No. 11 of 10 Most Wanted," UPI, Greenville *Delta Democrat-Times*, 21 April 1968, 1; "Sniper Described as Loner, Dancer," AP, *Vicksburg Evening Post*, 20 April 1968, 6.

98. "Identify Ex-Con as King Slayer," AP, Gulfport *Daily Herald*, 20 April 1968, 1.

99. "A Million Dollar Price Tag for Murder of King," UPI, Columbus *Commercial Appeal*, 21 April 1968, 2; "Convict Says Ray Hoped to Earn King's Bounty," UPI, *Laurel Leader-Call*, 24 April 1968, 1; "James Earl Ray Once Bragged He Would Collect on King, Georgia Convict Claims," UPI, *Meridian Star*, 24 April 1968, 1; "Million Dollar Bounty Mentioned," UPI, Corinth *Daily Corinthian*, 24 April 1968, 1; "Ray Sought King Bounty," UPI, Pascagoula *Mississippi Press*, 24 April 1968, 1; "Ray Talked about Bounty," AP, Jackson *Clarion-Ledger*, 24 April 1968, 1; "Ray Talked about Bounty," AP, Jackson *Daily News*, 24 April 1968, 1; "Ray Quoted as Okaying Pay Killing," AP, West Point *Times-Leader*, 24 April 1968, 1.

100. "FBI Rules Out White Knights in King Slaying," UPI, Tupelo *Daily Journal*, 12 April 1968, 12; "Klan Not Suspect in King Death," UPI, Pascagoula *Mississippi Press*, 14 April 1968, 8; "White Knights Counted Out of King's Death," UPI, *Meridian Star*, 14 April 1968, 1; "White Knights Ruled Out in Assassination of King," UPI, Columbus *Commercial Dispatch*, 14 April 1968, 1.

101. "Conspiracy Eyed in King's Death," AP, *Meridian Star*, 14 April 1968, 1; "Conspiracy in King's Death Brought Out," UPI, Grenada *Sentinel-Star*, 10 April 1968, 1; "Descriptions Held at Odds in Big Hunt," AP, West Point *Times-Leader*, 22 April 1968, 1; "Hint Slaying Is Conspiracy," UPI, *Laurel Leader-Call*, 10 April 1968, 1; "Many Discrepancies in Galt/Ray Manhunt," AP, McComb *Enterprise-Journal*, 22 April 1968, 1; "More Than One Assassin Possible in King Murder,"

AP, *Vicksburg Evening Post*, 14 April 1968, 1; "Mysterious Circumstances Surround Martin King's Death," UPI, Grenada *Sentinel-Star*, 5 April 1968, 1; "Suggests Slayer May Have Had Getaway Help," AP, Gulfport *Daily Herald*, 10 April 1968, 33.

102. "Justice Dept. Suspects More Than One in King Slaying," UPI, Tupelo *Daily Journal*, 27–28 April 1968, 1.

103. "Charge Conspiracy in King Slaying," AP, *Natchez Democrat*, 18 April 1968, 1; "Fake Radio Calls May Have Aided Killer's Flight," AP, Corinth *Daily Corinthian*, 10 April 1968, 1; "Fingerprints Conflict on King Killer," UPI, Pascagoula *Mississippi Press*, 26 April 1968, 2; "Hint Slaying Is Conspiracy," UPI, *Laurel Leader-Call*, 10 April 1968, 1; "Slaying Probers Puzzled," AP, *Vicksburg Evening Post*, 22 April 1968, 1.

104. "Cuban Conspiracy Hinted At," AP, *Vicksburg Evening Post*, 26 April 1968, 4.

105. "Civil Rights Action in House," AP, *Clarksdale Press Register*, 9 April 1968, 1; "Civil Rights Bill Awaits LBJ's Signature," UPI, Grenada *Sentinel-Star*, 11 April 1968, 1; "Civil Rights Bill Due for Railroading," AP, *Starkville Daily News*, 10 April 1968, 1; "Congress Expects to Pass Historic Civil Rights Bill," UPI, Greenville *Delta Democrat-Times*, 10 April 1968, 1; "House Backers Push Action to Enact 'Rights' Legislation," AP, Jackson *Clarion-Ledger*, 1 April 1968, 1; "House Passes Civil Rights Measure," UPI, *Laurel Leader-Call*, 11 April 1968, 1; "House Votes Rights Bill," UPI, Pascagoula *Mississippi Press*, 11 April 1968, 1.

106. "Johnson Signs Open Housing Law, Deplores King's Murder," UPI, Tupelo *Daily Journal*, 12 April 1968, 1; "LBJ Signs Civil Rights Legislation," AP, *Clarksdale Press Register*, 12 April 1968, 1; "Open Housing Given Final Okay by Happy LBJ," AP, *Meridian Star*, 12 April 1968, 1; "Outraged at King's Death, LBJ Signs Measure for Mixed Housing," AP, *Vicksburg Evening Post*, 13 April 1968, 1; "President Signs Civil Rights Bill," AP, Gulfport *Daily Herald*, 12 April 1968, 1; "President Signs Civil Rights Bill," AP, Jackson *Clarion-Ledger*, 12 April 1968, 1; "Souvenirs of Civil Rights Signing," UPI, Greenville *Delta Democrat-Times*, 12 April 1968, 1.

107. "LBJ Presses Congress for Rights Bill," AP, Tupelo *Daily Journal*, 8 April 1968, 1; "LBJ Urges Swift Action on Civil Rights Bill," AP, Gulfport *Daily Herald*, 8 April 1968, 12; "Shocked LBJ Has Proposals for Congress," UPI, Tupelo *Daily Journal*, 6–7 April 1968, 1; "Urge Action on Civil Rights Bill," UPI, *Laurel Leader-Call*, 8 April 1968, 1.

108. "Most Southerners Fight Civil Rights Bill," AP, McComb *Enterprise-Journal*, 11 April 1968, 6.

109. "Colmer Critical, Civil Rights Vote Linked to King's Death," AP, *Vicksburg Evening Post*, 10 April 1968, 1; "Colmer Sees Political Heads Rolling," UPI, Pascagoula *Mississippi Press*, 12 April 1968, 12; "Colmer Speaks on Legislating under the Gun," AP, Gulfport *Daily Herald*, 10 April 1968, 1; "Colmer Says Killing Spurring Rights Bill," AP, *Greenwood Commonwealth*, 9 April 1968, 1; "Gun Point Legislation, Colmer Calls Civil Rights Bill," AP, *Meridian Star*, 10 April 1968, 1.

110. "Congress Cautioned against Impetuosity," AP, West Point *Times-Leader*, 8 April 1968, 1; "Senator Raps Hasty Action on Civil Rights Measure," AP, Jackson *Daily News*, 8 April 1968, 1.

111. "King Death Called Civil Rights Pass Key," AP, West Point *Times-Leader*, 10 April 1968, 1.

112. "Negro Leaders Still Unhappy after Passage of Rights Bill," AP, *Meridian Star*, 11 April 1968, 1.

113. "King's Followers Divided on Nonviolence," *Clarksdale Press Register*, 22 April 1968, 4; "Leaders Are Seeking Nonviolent Directions," UPI, Columbus *Commercial Dispatch*, 28 April 1968, 1; "Militants Redefine King's Nonviolence," UPI, Greenville *Delta Democrat-Times*, 21 April 1968, 7.

114. Loewen and Sallis, *Mississippi*, 311.

115. Johnston, *Mississippi's Defiant Years*, 324.

116. Ibid., 324.

117. Joseph Ellis, Jr., "Johnson's Decision," *Clarksdale Press Register*, 3 April 1968, 4.

118. Drew Pearson, "Race Riots Partly Inspired by TV," *Clarksdale Press Register*, 17 April 1968, 4.

119. Birney Imes, Jr., "What Now?" Columbus *Commercial Dispatch*, 7 April 1968, 6.

120. Thurman Sensing, "Not Truly Non-Violent, Philosophy Expounded by King," Columbus *Commercial Dispatch*, 22 April 1968, 4.

121. David Lawrence, "Some Went Unreported," Columbus *Commercial Dispatch*, 10 April 1968, 4.

122. David Lawrence, "Rioting and Looting Hard to Explain to the World," Columbus *Commercial Dispatch*, 11 April 1968, 4; David Lawrence, "Country's Riots Are Puzzling," Columbus *Commercial Dispatch*, 15 April 1968, 4.

123. David Lawrence, "King's Killer, Who Hired Him for the Job?" Columbus *Commercial Dispatch*, 26 April 1968, 4.

124. "King Assassination Motivates Passage of Civil Rights Bill," UPI, Corinth *Daily Corinthian*, 18 April 1968, 2.

125. Hodding Carter III, "Triggers Bloody Confrontation," Greenville *Delta Democrat-Times*, 3 April 1968, 4.

126. Hodding Carter III, "Symbol of Sickness," Greenville *Delta Democrat-Times*, 7 April 1968, 4.

127. Hodding Carter III, "The Smell of Conspiracy," Greenville *Delta Democrat-Times*, 16 April 1968, 4.

128. "Negroes Here Stage March," Greenville *Delta Democrat-Times*, 8 April 1968, 1.

129. Hodding Carter III, "Greenville Comes Close," Greenville *Delta Democrat-Times*, 8 April 1968, 4.

130. Josh Bogan, letter to editor, Greenville *Delta Democrat-Times*, 8 April 1968, 4.

131. "Charles Evers in Jackson after Stopping Student Riots at Jackson State College," Gulfport *Daily Herald*, 5 April 1968, 1; "Evers Asks Harmony between Races," AP, *Starkville Daily News*, 7 April 1968, 1; "Evers Asks Harmony between Races," AP, West Point *Times-Leader*, 9 April 1968, 5; "Pleader for Nonviolence," *Hattiesburg American*, 5 April 1968, 1.

132. Hodding Carter III, "Evers Rises to Occasion," Greenville *Delta Democrat-Times*, 9 April 1968, 4.

133. Jack Anderson, "King, Gandhi, Kindred Spirits, Resemblance Now Even Greater," Greenville *Delta Democrat-Times*, 9 April 1968, 4.

134. Bill Mauldin, editorial cartoon, Greenville *Delta Democrat-Times*, 10 April 1968, 4.

135. William F. Buckley, "Respect for Law Is Part of Non-Violence," Greenville *Delta Democrat-Times*, 9 April 1968, 4.

136. Rowland Evans and Robert Novak, "Carmichael Fits Ghetto Mood, May Fill Void Left by King," Greenville *Delta Democrat-Times*, 9 April 1968, 4.

137. Tom Wicker, "Mob Violence Delays King's Dream," Greenville *Delta Democrat-Times*, 12 April 1968, 4.

138. Jack Anderson, "Student Riots, Negro Unrest, Could Lead to Revival of Right," Greenville *Delta Democrat-Times*, 25 April 1968, 4.

139. Hodding Carter III, "Self-Fulfilling Prophesy of Hard Work," Greenville *Delta Democrat-Times*, 18 April 1968, 4.

140. Hodding Carter III, Greenville *Delta Democrat-Times*, 24 April 1968, 4.

141. Bob Boyd, "Negro Youths Adopt List of Grievances," Greenville *Delta Democrat-Times*, 11 April 1968, 1.

142. "Negro Group Protests Greenville Housing Authority," Greenville *Delta Democrat-Times*, 17 April 1968, 1.

143. Photographs, Greenville *Delta Democrat-Times*, 11 April 1968, 1.

144. "Bi-Racial Delegation Urged for Mississippi," Greenville *Delta Democrat-Times*, 28 April 1968, 1.

145. "Negroes Allowed to Demonstrate Here, Agreement Calls for Peace Walk," *Greenwood Commonwealth*, 5 April 1968, 1.

146. "Pastors March Not Official Order," *Greenwood Commonwealth*, 8 April 1968, 1.

147. "Five Face Fines, Vandal Charge," *Greenwood Commonwealth*, 9 April 1968, 1.

148. "Police Count 43 Cases of Glass-Breaking Here," *Greenwood Commonwealth*, 8 April 1968, 1.

149. "Civil Rights Bill," editorial cartoon, King Syndicate, *Greenwood Commonwealth*, 10 April 1968, 9.

150. "Day of Mourning," editorial cartoon from the *Chicago Tribune*, in the *Greenwood Commonwealth*, 19 April 1968, 4.

151. Ralphe Bunche, "Ralphe Bunche Pays Tribute to King," Gulfport *Daily News*, 6 April 1968, 2.

152. Thurman Sensing, "Outbreak of Savagery," Gulfport *Daily News*, 15 April 1968, 3.

153. Leonard Lowrey, "Firebrands Mean What They Say," *Hattiesburg American*, 4 April 1968, 4.

154. Leonard Lowrey, "Another Foolish Act of Violence," *Hattiesburg American*, 5 April 1968, 4.

155. Leonard Lowrey, "Open Housing Law Provision," *Hattiesburg American*, 15 April 1968, 6.

156. Leonard Lowrey, "Planning behind Burning and Riots," *Hattiesburg American*, 16 April 1968, 4.

157. Leonard Lowrey, "Riot Questions Still Unanswered," *Hattiesburg American*, 17 April 1968, 4.

158. Leonard Lowrey, "Results of Civil Disobedience," *Hattiesburg American*, 20 April 1968, 2.

159. T.M. Hederman, Jr., "King's Nonviolent Riot," Jackson *Clarion-Ledger*, 3 April 1968, 4.

160. T.M. Hederman, Jr., "History Will Have to Assign Eventual Place to Dr. King," Jackson *Clarion-Ledger*, 6 April 1968, 1.

161. George Kopp, letter to the editor, Jackson *Clarion-Ledger*, 22 April 1968, 12.

162. Unsigned letter to the editor, Jackson *Clarion-Ledger*, 26 April 1968, 10.

163. Paul Harvey, "Jungle Drums Prod Primitive Passions," Jackson *Clarion-Ledger*, 14 April 1968, 4.

164. "King Prime Mover of Social Upheaval," AP, Jackson *Clarion-Ledger*, 7 April 1968, 14.

165. "King Prime Mover of Social Upheaval," AP, Jackson *Daily News*, 7 April 1968, 14; "King Prime Mover of Social Upheaval," AP, Jackson *Clarion-Ledger*, 7 April 1968, 14.

166. James "Jimmy" Ward, "The Death of Dr. King," Jackson *Daily News*, 6 April 1968, 6.

167. James "Jimmy" Ward, "State Has Done Itself Proud," Jackson *Daily News*, 9 April 1968, 8.

168. James "Jimmy" Ward, "Hysteria Swamps Solons," Jackson *Daily News*, 11 April 1968, 18.

169. James "Jimmy" Ward, "What Is Next, Please?" Jackson *Daily News*, 13 April 1968, 6.

170. James "Jimmy" Ward, " 'Poor' March Still Builds," Jackson *Daily News*, 30 April 1968, 10.

171. Jay West, "King's Killer Hides, Who's Helping Him?" *Laurel Leader-Call*, 17 April 1968, 4.

172. J.O. Emmerich, "Thoughts on Murder of Martin Luther King," McComb *Enterprise-Journal*, 6 April 1968, 2.

173. Bill Mauldin, editorial cartoon, McComb *Enterprise-Journal*, 6 April 1968, 2.

174. J.O. Emmerich, "One Bullet, One Law—Recoil of Emotionalism," McComb *Enterprise-Journal*, 12 April 1968, 2.

175. James B. Skewes, "We Deplore Murder," *Meridian Star*, 5 April 1968, 4.

176. James B. Skewes, "They Gain Nothing," *Meridian Star*, 7 April 1968, 4.

177. James B. Skewes, "An Infringement," *Meridian Star*, 14 April 1968, 4.

178. James Lambert, "Most Dastardly of Acts," *Natchez Democrat*, 6 April 1968, 1.

179. Drew Pearson, "Martin Luther King, Jr.," *Natchez Democrat*, 11 April 1968, 4.

180. Drew Pearson, "Looting in DC," *Natchez Democrat*, 14 April 1968, 4.

181. Tom Anderson, "Martin Luther King, Jr.," *Natchez Democrat*, 23 April 1968, 5.

182. Tom Anderson, "Dream of MLK," *Natchez Democrat*, 30 April 1968, 2.

183. David Lawrence, "Who Hired Assassin?" *Natchez Democrat*, 30 April 1968, 4.

184. "King Reached Point of No Return in Montgomery," UPI, Pascagoula *Mississippi Press*, 5 April 1968, 5.

185. "Judge Raps Riots," Pascagoula *Mississippi Press*, 8 April 1968, 1.

186. Gary Holland, "The Martin Luther King Tragedy," Pascagoula *Mississippi Press*, 7 April 1968, 4.

187. Tom Roper, letter to the editor, Pascagoula *Mississippi Press*, 8 April 1968, 5.

188. Douglass Baker, letter to the editor, Pascagoula *Mississippi Press*, 10 April 1968, 4.

189. Editorial from the *Picayune Item*, in the *Starkville Daily News*, 17 April 1968, 4.

190. Tom Anderson, "Straight Talk," *Starkville Daily News*, 23 April 1968, 4.

191. George McLean, "Tried and Proven Route to Unity Is Best," Tupelo *Daily Journal*, 9 April 1968, 4.

192. George McLean, "Progress by Poor Takes Three-Way Effort," Tupelo *Daily Journal*, 25 April 1968, 15.

193. L.P. Cashman, Jr., "Racial Violence, Deaths Curb Efforts for Peace," *Vicksburg Evening Post*, 6 April 1968, 4.

194. L.P. Cashman, Jr., "The Emotional Crisis," *Vicksburg Evening Post*, 11 April 1968, 4.

195. L.P. Cashman, Jr., "The Soft Approach," *Vicksburg Evening Post*, 19 April 1968, 4.

196. David Lawrence, "Shoot to Kill Order Needed to Enforce Law," *Vicksburg Evening Post*, 21 April 1968, 4.

197. L.P. Cashman, Jr., "The Big Manhunt," *Vicksburg Evening Post*, 22 April 1968, 4.

198. W.H. Harris, "Pencil Shavings," West Point *Times-Leader*, 9 April 1968, 1.

199. Paul Harvey, "Wallowing in the Mud with Minorities," West Point *Times-Leader*, 15 April 1968, 4.

200. Tom Anderson, "Straight Talk," West Point *Times-Leader*, 22 April 1968, 4.

201. Tom Anderson, "Martin Luther King," West Point *Times-Leader*, 29 April 1968, 4.

202. "Dilemma in Dixie," *Time*, 20 February 1956, 76; "Dixie Flamethrowers," *Time*, 4 March 1966, 64; "Moderation in Dixie," *Time*, 19 March 1965, 71; Edwin W. Williams, "Dimout in Jackson," *Columbia Journalism Review* 9 (Summer 1970): 56.

203. "Belting One Down for the Road," *Nation*, 6 October 1962; "Dilemma in Dixie," 76; "Moderation in Dixie"; Ted Poston, "The American Negro and Newspaper Myths," in *Race and the News Media*, ed. Paul Fisher and Ralph Lowenstein (New York: Praeger, 1967), 63; Pat Watters and Reese Cleghorn, *Climbing Jacob's Ladder: The Arrival of Negroes in Southern Politics* (New York: Harcourt, Brace and World, 1967), 73; Simeon Booker, *Black Man's America* (Englewood Cliffs, NJ: Prentice-Hall, 1964), 15; Roger Williams, "Newspapers in the South," *Columbia Journalism Review* 6 (Summer 1967): 27; James Boylan, "Birmingham Newspapers in Crisis," *Columbia Journalism Review* 2 (Summer 1963): 30.

204. "Desegregation Bill Awaits Gov. Williams' Signature," UPI, Grenada

Sentinel-Star, 25 April 1968, 1; "House Approves Integrated Jails," UPI, Grenada *Sentinel-Star*, 24 April 1968, 1; "House Okays Mix in Jail," AP, West Point *Times-Leader*, 24 April 1968, 6; "House Okays Mix in Jails," AP, *Starkville Daily News*, 24 April 1968, 1; "House Votes to End Jail Segregation," UPI, Tupelo *Daily Journal*, 24 April 1968, 1; "Jail Cell Segregation Repealed," UPI, Corinth *Daily Corinthian*, 26 April 1968, 1; "Jail Mixing Is Approved by Senators," AP, West Point *Times-Leader*, 25 April 1968, 7; "Senate Passes Bill to End Segregation in Jails," AP, Jackson *Daily News*, 25 April 1968, 1; "State Jail Segregation Bill Ready," UPI, *Laurel Leader-Call*, 26 April 1968, 1.

205. "House Votes to Repeal Ban on Jail Integration," AP, Jackson *Clarion-Ledger*, 24 April 1968, 1.

206. Loewen and Sallis, *Mississippi*, 312; "Women Win Jury Duty," UPI, *Laurel Leader-Call*, 5 April 1968, 1.

Chapter 7

Conclusion

The Mississippi daily newspapers published between 1948 and 1968 advocated white supremacy and the suppression of equal rights for blacks, who accounted for nearly half the state's population. This traditional Southern view was the norm for hundreds of years and remained intact during the Dixiecrat walkout of the Democratic National Convention in 1948, the *Brown v. Board of Education* mandate to desegregate public schools in 1954, the court-ordered desegregation of Ole Miss in 1962, the civil rights challenges of Freedom Summer in 1964, and the assassination of civil rights activist Martin Luther King, Jr., in 1968.

The Mississippi daily press between 1948 and 1968 generally failed in their local reporting and editorial responsibilities regarding civil rights and race issues during this period. The newspapers failed *all* Mississippians, not just the white power structure of which the editors and reporters were part. Any Mississippians looking to their daily newspaper for editorial guidance or local news on civil rights topics between 1948 and 1968 usually received condescending and pessimistic reports that consistently denigrated black intelligence and maligned the black community. Civil rights for blacks, according to the majority of the Mississippi daily newspapers, were an aspect of legalized equality that negatively impacted white society.

Newspapers edited by Hodding Carter, Jr., Hodding Carter III and Ira Harkey were the exceptions among the Mississippi daily press from 1948 through 1968. These men bravely challenged the traditional South by offering a voice of reason in reporting about black members of their communities with respect and fairness and by advocating equal rights and justice for all Mississippians—regardless of the color of their skin.

A COMPLEX SITUATION

Exactly what possessed editors of the Mississippi daily press from 1948 through 1968 to conduct themselves in print as they did regarding equal rights for blacks is not a simple issue. Ted Poston was wrong, however, when he wrote, "The majority of Southern editors and publishers have been cynically defending a myth they know to be untrue—white superiority."[1] On the contrary, a staunch and heartfelt belief in, and commitment to, the traditional Southern way of life were motivating factors behind Mississippi editors such as W.H. Harris of the West Point *Times-Leader*, Joseph Ellis, Jr., of the Clarksdale *Press Register*, Birney Imes, Jr., of the Columbus *Commercial-Dispatch* and James H. and James B. Skewes of the *Meridian Star*, who wrote their South-shall-rise-again editorials. White superiority was not a myth to these editors. It was a fact. Carter III, who followed in his father's footsteps at the Greenville *Delta Democrat-Times* and became known as one of the more liberal journalists of the Mississippi daily press, defended his fellow editors to some extent by offering an explanation for the manner in which racial issues were covered by the state's press. "In the South we have peculiar mores, and these have been reflected in our newspapers," he wrote in 1968. "My point is that this was not a case of an evil conspiracy of bad men, but of men totally reflecting the community in which they moved in the same way that most other newspaper publishers do."[2]

A NATIONAL PROBLEM

Many analysts in the 1960s viewed the portrayal of race in the media as one of concern throughout the country. Lerone Bennett, editor of *Ebony* magazine, considered race relations a major national crisis, not just a Southern problem. "The basic fact in race relations today is that black and white Americans do not live and act within the perspective of the same community or the same communications channel," he wrote in 1968. "Mass media in America reflect that general reality."[3] Carter III agreed with Bennett. "As the South becomes more nationalized in its approach to the race problem, we are discovering that it is a national problem, and I think we are discovering in Los Angeles as well as in Greenville, Mississippi, that what we are doing in response to the problem is very bad indeed," he wrote in 1968. "This, I say, is true not only for press coverage, but of the entire nation's approach to the problem."[4]

Historian John Howard Griffin observed the same national predicament. "Racism, discrimination based on skin color, has grown strong, hard and bitter throughout the length and breadth of America," he wrote in 1964. "We are now a deeply concerned people, but we are not well informed."[5] Beverlee Bruce, a black high school teacher, concurred. "The problem with the American press is that it is hamstrung by the society in which we live," she wrote in 1968. "I am convinced, along with a number of other black people in this country, that we do live in a racist society. These are harsh words, but I feel they reflect reality."[6] More than a decade later, H. Eugene Goodwin, a professor of journalism at Pennsylvania State University, thought the problem remained one of national scope.[7]

Criticism of the Southern press was viewed as its own form of prejudice in 1963 at a UPI-sponsored conference of editors and publishers. "We've had open season on the South now for some time," Turner Catledge of the *New York Times* said. "There seems to be a disposition, especially on our editorial pages, to demand that the Southerners accept some sort of an emotional change in this matter, which they're not going to do. Integration is coming to the South. It's coming very slowly, but it's not wanted. Is it wanted any more in Minnesota or in New York? I think this is the question our readers are entitled to have us explore."[8]

THE AMERICAN PRESS: WHITE OWNERSHIP, WHITE BIAS

The Mississippi daily press between 1948 and 1968 presented a clear illustration of what a 1968 study, the President's National Advisory Commission on Civil Disorders, known as the Kerner Commission, called "the 'white press,' a press that repeatedly, if unconsciously, reflects the biases, the paternalism and the indifference of white America."[9] The commission also noted, "If what the white American reads in the newspaper or sees on television conditions his expectations of what is ordinary and normal in the larger society, he will neither understand nor accept the black American."[10]

In 1968, the year King was assassinated, the American public was becoming more aware of the news media's role in racial understanding and the reasons behind the media's deficiency in that regard. "The media still are almost exclusively shaped for the taste, some would say the prejudices, of the white audience," wrote Charles Daly, director of the Center for Policy Study. "Almost all media in the United States is owned by whites. Since the nation is largely white, one might say there is no great problem. But there is a problem."[11]

Most news media administrators in the 1960s knew that the problem existed. "Executives believe that coverage and understanding of the Negro are generally inadequate, but that the mass media are beginning to provide better communication between blacks and whites," a 1967 survey sponsored by the *Columbia Journalism Review* and the Anti-Defamation League of B'nai B'rith reported. "Like so many other professions, journalism is beginning to recognize its responsibility in the quest for better race relations in America."[12]

SOCIALLY RESPONSIBLE—OR NOT

Whether the Mississippi daily newspapers from 1948 through 1968 adequately addressed the precepts of the 1947 Commission on Freedom of the Press is a difficult judgment to make. It could easily be said that they failed "to provide a truthful, comprehensive, and intelligent account of the day's events in a context which gives them meaning"; that they failed "to provide a forum for the exchange of comment and criticism"; that they failed "to project a representative picture of the constituent groups in society"; that they failed "to present and clarify the goals and values of the society"; and that they failed "to provide a full access to the day's intelligence."[13] This would be the conclusion based on the fact that blacks were considered a separate and inferior community within the state and judged unworthy of comprehensive news coverage by most editors of the Mississippi daily press. This would be the conclusion based on the fact that any Mississippian, black or white, looking to the daily press for guidance regarding race relations and federally mandated desegregation received white supremacist and "happy Negro" rhetoric.

On the other hand, the Mississippi daily press could have opted to completely ignore civil rights issues, but it did not. Michael Novak raised an interesting point in this regard. "Suppose the media had chosen *not* to report the civil rights struggle," he wrote. "The civil rights 'movement' might not have been a movement at all."[14] From this standpoint, the Mississippi daily press could be seen as having conducted itself in a socially responsible manner, for it did cover the 1948 Dixiecrat protest, the 1954 *Brown v. Board of Education* decision, the 1962 desegregation of Ole Miss, Freedom Summer in 1964 and the assassination of King in 1968. The issues were not silenced in the Mississippi daily press, and, for the most part, they were not ignored. The five events may not have been reported and editorialized in the manner in which a Mississippi editor would cover them in 1980 or in 2000, but they were recorded from the viewpoint of white editors whose family stories still included firsthand accounts of the Civil War and the emancipation of the family's black slaves when the South was defeated less than a century earlier.

It could also be said that the Mississippi daily newspapers did adequately address the precepts of the 1947 Commission on Freedom of the Press; that they did "provide a truthful, comprehensive, and intelligent account of the day's events in a context which gives them meaning"; that they did "provide a forum for the exchange of comment and criticism"; that they did "project a representative picture of the constituent groups in society"; that they did "present and clarify the goals and values of the society"; and that they did "provide a full access to the day's intelligence."[15] This would be the conclusion based on the assessment that the white editors and reporters of the Mississippi daily press from 1948 through 1968 were writing primarily for a white audience and for a white community that generally supported and desired a traditional South. Socially responsible editorship of the Mississippi daily press during the years 1948 through 1968 might have seemed, to civil rights advocates and most blacks, an editorship that would have endorsed equal rights for all people, not just for whites. But to the white editors of the Mississippi daily press and to most white Mississippians, socially responsible editorship during those years meant the maintenance of Mississippi society as they knew it—racially segregated with blacks in subservient roles as second-class citizens.

SUMMARY OF COVERAGE

Rejection of Equal Rights and Integration

Since newspapers are a fundamental mode by which racial stereotypes and attitudes are perpetuated or eliminated, an analysis of the coverage of civil rights issues by the Mississippi daily press could be one of condemnation, for those newspapers generally condescended toward blacks and rejected equal rights for blacks in their coverage from 1948 through 1968. Hodding Carter, Jr., of the Greenville *Delta Democrat-Times*, thought a dramatic change in the Southern racial climate was imminent in 1963. "Will the contradictions and conflicts in the South last forever?" he wrote. "Some Southerners, a diminishing number, would probably answer yes. I differ. There are today fewer areas of justifiable democratic challenge to unjustifiable and undemocratic contradictions. The Southern Negro is catching up. So is the Southern white."[16]

As evidenced by most coverage in the Mississippi daily press from 1948 through 1968, the issues of concern following the assassination of King were the same as those during Freedom Summer, the desegregation of Ole Miss, *Brown v. Board of Education* and the Dixiecrat protest. First and foremost, Mississippians, black and white, were not ready for the reality of a racially integrated society. Second, national civil rights laws not only supplanted states' and individual rights but had become a way to "court" black votes. According to the vast majority of editorials examined in the Mississippi daily press from 1948 through 1968, the notion that blacks and whites were equal as races of people was a concept that remained unacceptable and inconceivable.

The propensity toward reporting civil rights issues in Mississippi daily newspapers was the same following the assassination of King in 1968, and during Freedom Summer in 1964, the desegregation of Ole Miss in 1962, the *Brown v. Board of Education* decision in 1954 and the Dixiecrat walkout from the Democratic National Convention in 1948. Coverage ranged from at least one news report a day, which was the norm, to virtual silence, which was rare. The majority of the news reports regarding civil rights activities printed in the Mississippi daily press came from the wire services—AP, INS, UP and UPI. Most of the newspapers published at least one editorial a week pertaining to some aspect of the civil rights movement, but the issue was unquestionably a top news story on the front pages of the Mississippi daily press.

"Us against Them"

The consensus among the editors of the Mississippi daily press regarding civil rights was the "us against them" theme. "We" in 1948 were white Mississippi Democrats, and "they" were the national Democrats led by Truman. In 1954, "we" were the traditional white power structure in Mississippi, and "they" were the U.S. Supreme Court and the federal government. In 1962, "we" were the traditional white political and power structure in Mississippi, and "they" were the federal authorities who mandated that Ole Miss enroll a black student. In 1964 during Freedom Summer, "we" were the traditional white politicians and white society in Mississippi, and "they" were the civil rights workers, the black activists and any person who advocated equal rights. In the case of King's assassination, "we" were the traditional Southern society, and "they" were any person who supported civil rights, as well as the black power advocates rioting in the nation's cities following King's death.

Did Not Condone Violence

The Mississippi daily press from 1948 through 1968 endorsed segregation and maintained the white power structure by denigrating the black struggle for equal rights. But contrary to what media critics have noted about the promotion of violence to suppress civil rights activity in a sampling of Southern newspapers,[17] the Mississippi daily press did not encourage or condone violence during the Dixiecrat protest of the Democratic National Convention in July 1948, the *Brown v. Board of Education* Supreme Court mandate to desegregate public schools in May 1954, the desegregation of Ole Miss in September 1962, Freedom Summer in 1964 or the assassination of King in April 1968. Not once was advocacy or support of violence encountered in any of the Mississippi daily newspapers examined. This finding did not surprise Carter III of the Greenville *Delta Democrat-Times*. "The real obligation throughout was not so much to be silent about violence, but to condemn it strongly at a time when it would have been meaningful," he wrote in 1999. "Here the record is neither distinguished nor commendable."[18]

Jackson *Clarion-Ledger* and *Daily News:* Sometimes Representative, Sometimes Not

The two most widely circulated daily newspapers in the state, the Jackson *Clarion-Ledger* and the Jackson *Daily News*, were usually representative of the other daily Mississippi newspapers in their coverage of the civil rights movement from 1948 through 1968, although to varying degrees. The Jackson *Clarion-Ledger* and the Jackson *Daily News* were representative, for the most part, of the Mississippi daily press during the 1948 Dixiecrat protest and, to some extent, during Freedom Summer in 1964. All the Mississippi daily newspapers subscribed to at least one of the three major wire services available at the time, and they usually published the copy without revision, except for the sometimes lowercased word "Negro."[19] The widely varied headlines of these wire service articles did not misrepresent the stories, although editorial bias was often evident in them. The staff-written stories in the Jackson *Clarion-Ledger* and the Jackson *Daily News* were usually more racially hostile than staff-written stories in the other Mississippi daily newspapers, and the editorials of James "Jimmy" Ward at the Jackson *Daily News* and Charles M. Hills at the Jackson *Clarion-Ledger* were laden with more condescension toward blacks than editorials at most of the other newspapers, except for the West Point *Times-Leader*, the *Meridian Star* and the *Natchez Democrat*. While not advocating support for the Civil Rights Act of 1964 or offering encouragement to the efforts of the COFO volunteers during Freedom Summer, most editors of the Mississippi daily press were not as venomous in their approach to the issue as those at the Jackson *Clarion-Ledger* and the Jackson *Daily News*. Despite the greater intensity of their racial hostility, the two newspapers were fairly representative of the daily press in the state only during the Dixiecrat protest in 1948 and Freedom Summer in 1964.

In their coverage of *Brown v. Board of Education* in 1954, the desegregation of Ole Miss in 1962 and the assassination of King in 1968, the Jackson *Clarion-Ledger* and the Jackson *Daily News* were not as representative of the Mississippi daily press as they had been during the Dixiecrat protest and Freedom Summer. The editorials of Fred Sullens at the Jackson *Daily News* and Hills at the Jackson *Clarion-Ledger* in 1954, 1962 and 1968 certainly earned their reputation for engendering racial angst and intensifying the opposition of Mississippi whites to integration,[20] but except for W.H. Harris of the West Point *Times-Leader*, Bill Simpson at the Corinth *Daily Corinthian* and the Skeweses at the *Meridian Star*, this blatant, fire-breathing racism was not generally true of the other editors of the Mississippi daily press from 1948 through 1968. At the Jackson *Clarion-Ledger* and the Jackson *Daily News*, combined criticism of King in April 1968 was the most derogatory of all the Mississippi daily newspapers, and although this deprecatory position was true of the other editors of the

Mississippi daily press regarding King in April 1968, it was to a much lesser degree than in the two Jackson newspapers.

Localized Coverage

Another issue explored by this book was whether the Mississippi daily press localized the civil rights struggle or focused on the issue as a concern for other areas of the state and nation. During the time periods examined, Southern newspapers were often accused of failing to investigate, or of completely ignoring, local incidents pertaining to civil rights and race relations.[21] One problem, according to Carter III at the Greenville *Delta Democrat-Times*, was limited staffing due to finances.[22]

Similar to daily newspapers nationwide, most Mississippi daily newspapers relied on wire copy to fill their pages and thus were subject to whatever stories were available. *Time* magazine reported that many Southern editors used wire copy when doubtful about how to cover stories related to race, and the wire stories were likely to do "an evenhanded job of straight reporting."[23] There is another positive aspect of this extensive use of wire copy. The readers of the Mississippi daily press received a more national view of the civil rights struggle without the biases that often pervaded staff-written copy.[24] Most of the daily newspapers in Mississippi from 1948 through 1968 made slight effort to use staff reporters on civil rights stories, relying primarily on the wire services, and if local coverage was available through the wire services, they often published it.

A SLOW, BUT STEADY, TRANSFORMATION

By the end of 1968, significant changes were apparent in Mississippi despite press coverage by the state's daily newspapers. More than a quarter million blacks were registered to vote, which accounted for sixty percent of those eligible.[25]

Thirty years later, the number of black students at Ole Miss had risen to more than a 1,000, or nearly twelve percent of the student body, including graduate and law students.[26] Mississippi's elected officials included a black Supreme Court justice, a black public service commissioner, a black U.S. congressman, a black circuit judge, more than 300 black city and county officials, several black mayors and a host of black state legislators. The state that had demonstrated the greatest reticence in proffering equal rights to blacks, Mississippi suddenly had more black elected officials than any other state.[27] Civil rights were becoming a reality for people of all races in Mississippi, whether the state's daily press endorsed the concept or not.

NOTES

1. Ted Poston, "The American Negro and Newspaper Myths," in *Race and the News Media*, ed. Paul Fisher and Ralph Lowenstein (New York: Praeger, 1967), 63.

2. Hodding Carter III, "Comment on the Coverage in the Domestic Press," in *The Black American and the Press*, ed. Jack Lyle (Los Angeles: W. Ritchie Press, 1968), 39.

3. Lerone Bennett, Jr., "The White Media," in *The Media and the Cities*, ed. Charles Daly (Chicago: University of Chicago Press, 1968), 7.

4. Hodding Carter III, "Comment on the Coverage in the Domestic Press," 41.

5. John Howard Griffin, "Racist Sins of Christians," in *Black, White and Gray*, ed. Bradford Daniel (New York: Sheed and Ward, 1964), 430.

6. Beverlee Bruce, "Comment on Negro Reaction to the Press," in *The Black American and the Press*, 70.

7. H. Eugene Goodwin, *Groping for Ethics in Journalism* (Ames: Iowa State University Press, 1983), 63.

8. George P. Hunt, "Racial Crisis and the News Media," in *Race and the News Media*, ed. Paul Fisher and Ralph Lowenstein (New York: Praeger, 1967), 15.

9. Kerner Commission, *Report of the National Advisory Commission on Civil Disorders* (New York: Bantam, 1968), 203.

10. Ibid., 204.

11. Charles Daly, *The Media and the Cities* (Chicago: University of Chicago Press, 1968), foreword.

12. Woody Klein, "News Media and Race Relations: A Self-Portrait," *Columbia Journalism Review* (Summer 1968): 49.

13. Commission on Freedom of the Press, *A Free and Responsible Press—A General Report on Mass Communication: Newspapers, Radio, Motion Pictures, Magazines and Books* (Chicago: University of Chicago Press, 1947), xi.

14. Michael Novak, "Why the Working Man Hates the Press," in *Ethics and the Press*, ed. John Merrill and Ralph Barney (New York: Hastings House, 1975), 112.

15. Commission on Freedom of the Press, *A Free and Responsible Press—A General Report on Mass Communication: Newspapers, Radio, Motion Pictures, Magazines and Books*, xi.

16. Hodding Carter, Jr., *First Person Rural* (Garden City, N.Y.: Doubleday and Company, 1963), 70.

17. "Dilemma in Dixie," *Time*, 20 February 1956, 76; "Dixie Flamethrowers," *Time*, 4 March 1966, 64; "Moderation in Dixie," *Time*, 19 March 1965, 71; Edwin W. Williams, "Dimout in Jackson," *Columbia Journalism Review* 9 (Summer 1970): 56.

18. Hodding Carter III, e-mail interview with Susan Weill, 4 October 1999.

19. "President's Machinery Being Oiled," AP, *Clarksdale Press Register*, 8 July 1948, 1; "Gerald K. Smith for Southerners," AP, *Greenwood Commonwealth*, 19 July 1948, 1; "Grant Bus Permit to Jackson Negro," AP, Gulfport *Daily Herald*, 9 July 1948, 1; "Highlights in the Headlines," McComb *Enterprise-Journal*, 28 July 1948, 1.

20. "Belting One Down for the Road," 190; Charles Butts, "Mississippi: The Vacuum and the System," in *Black, White and Gray*, ed. by Bradford Daniel (New York: Sheed and Ward, 1964), 104; "Dilemma in Dixie," 76; "Dixie Flamethrowers"; "Moderation in Dixie"; Poston, "The American Negro and Newspaper Myths," 63; Pat Watters and Reese Cleghorn, *Climbing Jacob's Ladder: The Arrival of Negroes in Southern Politics* (New York: Harcourt, Brace and World, 1967), 73; Simeon Booker, *Black Man's America* (Englewood Cliffs; N.J.: Prentice-Hall, 1964), 15; Williams, "Newspapers in the South," 27; Boylan, "Birmingham Newspapers in Crisis," 30.

21. "Dilemma in Dixie," 76.

22. Hodding Carter III, "Comment on the Coverage in the Domestic Press," 39.

23. "Dilemma in Dixie," 76.

24. Donald Matthews and James Protho, *Negroes and the New Southern Politics* (New York: Harcourt, Brace and World, 1966), 238.

25. John Dittmer, *Local People: The Struggle for Civil Rights in Mississippi* (Urbana: University of Illinois Press, 1994), 425.

26. "Black Enrollment at Ole Miss," Jackson *Clarion-Ledger*, 20 September 1997, 13A.

27. Erle Johnston, *Mississippi's Defiant Years, 1953–1973: An Interpretive Documentary with Personal Experiences* (Forest, Miss.: Lake Harbor Publishers, 1990), 403–404.

Appendix 1

Mississippi Daily Press Editors

	1948	1954	1962	1964	1968
Clarksdale Press Register	Joseph Ellis, Jr.	Joseph Ellis, Jr.	Joseph Ellis, Jr.	Joseph Ellis, Jr.	Joseph Ellis, Jr.
Columbus *Commercial Dispatch*	Birney Imes, Jr.	Birney Imes, Jr.	Birney Imes, Jr.	Birney Imes, Jr.	Birney Imes, Jr.
Corinth *Daily Corinthian*	C.B. McAbee	Jack Waldon	Bill Simpson	Bill Simpson	Warren Sanders
Greenville *Delta Democrat-Times*	Hodding Carter, Jr.	Hodding Carter, Jr.	Hodding Carter III	Hodding Carter III	Hodding Carter III
Greenwood Commonwealth	Tom Shepherd	Tom Shepherd	Thatcher Walt	Thatcher Walt	Edmund Noel
Greenwood *Morning Star*	James Alsop	Virgil Adams	defunct	defunct	defunct
Grenada *Sentinel-Star*	Frank Jones, Sr.	M.M. Grimes	Joseph Lee	Joseph Lee	Joseph Lee
Gulfport *Daily Herald*	G.P. Money	E.P. Wilkes	E.P. Wilkes	E.P. Wilkes	E.P. Wilkes
Hattiesburg American	Andrews Harmon	Andrews Harmon	Leonard Lowrey	Leonard Lowrey	Leonard Lowrey
Jackson *Clarion-Ledger*	T.M. Hederman, Jr.	T.M Hederman, Jr.	T.M. Hederman, Jr.	T.M. Hederman, Jr.	T.M. Hederman, Jr.
Jackson *Daily News*	Fred Sullens	Fred Sullens	James Ward	James Ward	James Ward
Laurel Leader-Call	Harriet Gibbons	Harriet Gibbons	J.W. West	J.W. West	J.W. West
McComb *Enterprise-Journal*	J.O. Emmerich	J.O. Emmerich	J.O. Emmerich	J.O. Emmerich	J.O. Emmerich
Meridian Star	J.H. Skewes	J.H. Skewes	James B. Skewes	James B. Skewes	James B. Skewes
Natchez Democrat	Elliott Trimble	Elliott Trimble	James Lambert	James Lambert	James Lambert
Natchez Times	not extant	Herman Moore	defunct	defunct	defunct
Pascagoula *Chronicle*	weekly	weekly	Ira Harkey	W. David Brown/ Gary Holland	merged*
Pascagoula *Mississippi Press*	weekly	weekly	weekly	weekly	Gary Holland
Starkville Daily News	not extant	not extant	Sherrill Nash	Sherrill Nash	Sherrill Nash
Tupelo *Daily Journal*	George McLean	George McLean	H. Rutherford	H. Rutherford	George McLean
Vicksburg Evening Post	L.P. Cashman	L.P. Cashman	L.P. Cashman, Jr.	L.P. Cashman, Jr.	L.P. Cashman, Jr.
Vicksburg Herald	L.P. Cashman	L.P. Cashman	defunct	defunct	defunct
West Point *Times-Leader*	Edgar Harris	W.H. Harris	W.H. Harris	W.H. Harris	W.H. Harris

*merged with Pascagoula *Mississippi Press* in 1966.

Appendix 2

Mississippi Daily Press Circulation

	1948	1954	1962	1964	1968
Clarksdale Press Register	4,774	5,101	4,753	5,506	6,018
Columbus *Commercial Dispatch*	7,218	8,911	9,032	9,083	9,180
Corinth *Daily Corinthian*	5,563	5,121	4,600	5,580	6,442
Greenville *Delta Democrat-Times*	11,489	11,250	13,828	13,314	13,086
Greenwood Commonwealth	3,590	3,923	4,918	5,613	6,041
Greenwood *Morning Star*	3,000	3,082	defunct	defunct	defunct
Grenada *Sentinel-Star*	2,300	2,425	2,589	2,830	2,830
Gulfport *Daily Herald*	18,906	23,861	28,682	30,666	34,836
Hattiesburg American	12,594	13,759	15,958	16,950	16,404
Jackson *Clarion-Ledger*	46,765	49,458	51,349	58,910	55,208
Jackson *Daily News*	37,796	43,415	40,980	53,694	46,975
Laurel Leader-Call	11,155	11,554	12,202	12,362	11,415
McComb *Enterprise-Journal*	4,800	5,108	6,122	6,084	6,440
Meridian Star	20,853	20,404	21,250	22,564	22,414
Natchez Democrat	4,750	5,836	6,859	9,168	9,747
Natchez Times	not extant	5,438	defunct	defunct	defunct
Pascagoula *Chronicle*	weekly	weekly	8,557	8,700	merged*
Pascagoula *Mississippi Press*	weekly	weekly	weekly	weekly	11,683
Starkville Daily News	not extant	not extant	2,475	3,900	4,040
Tupelo *Daily Journal*	9,303	11,617	16,546	17,667	20,909
Vickburg Evening Post	8,552	8,868	10,353	11,400	12,400
Vicksburg Herald	3,245	3,245	defunct	defunct	defunct
West Point *Times-Leader*	4,711	4,682	4,874	4,400	4,644
Total Mississippi daily press	221,364	247,058	265,927	298,391	300,712
Total Mississippi press	391,145	437,314	461,946	499,014	494,164
Daily press percentage of total Mississippi newspapers in circulation	56.60%	56.49%	57.57%	59.80%	60.85%

*merged with Pascagoula *Mississippi Press* in 1966.

Appendix 3

Population Statistics of Mississippi Counties with Daily Newspapers, 1948–1968

Adams County Natchez (1940 population 15,296; 1970 population 19,704):

	1940	1950	1960	1970
Blacks and others*	16,894	16,103	18,695	17,927
Whites	10,344	16,153	19,035	19,366
Total	27,238	32,256	37,730	37,293
Percent Blacks and others	62.0%	49.9%	49.5%	48.1%

Alcorn County Corinth (1940 population 7,818; 1970 population 11,581):

	1940	1950	1960	1970
Blacks and others	4,723	3,904	3,333	3,228
Whites	22,246	23,254	21,949	23,951
Total	26,969	27,158	25,282	27,179
Percent Blacks and others	17.5%	14.4%	13.2%	11.9%

Clay County West Point (1940 population 5,627; 1970 population 8,714):

	1940	1950	1960	1970
Blacks and others	11,534	10,097	9,719	9,323
Whites	7,496	7,660	9,214	9,517
Total	19,030	17,757	18,933	18,840
Percent Blacks and others	60.6%	56.9%	51.3%	49.5%

Coahoma County Clarksdale (1940 population 12,168; 1970 population 21,673):

	1940	1950	1960	1970
Blacks and others	37,342	35,659	31,582	26,215
Whites	10,991	13,702	14,630	14,232
Total	48,333	49,361	46,212	40,447
Percent Blacks and others	77.3%	72.2%	68.3%	64.8%

*others: Asians, Hispanics, etc.

Forrest County Hattiesburg (1940 population 21,026; 1970 population, 38,277):

	1940	1950	1960	1970
Blacks and others	10,938	12,965	14,752	14,325
Whites	23,963	32,090	37,970	43,524
Total	34,901	45,055	52,722	57,849
Percent Blacks and others	31.3%	28.8%	28.0%	24.8%

Grenada County Grenada (1940 population 5,831; 1970 population 9,944):

	1940	1950	1960	1970
Blacks and others	11,118	9,829	9,057	8,700
Whites	7,934	9,001	9,352	11,154
Total	19,052	18,830	18,409	19,854
Percent Blacks and others	58.4%	52.2%	49.2%	43.8%

Hinds County Jackson (1940 population 62,107; 1970 population 153,968):

	1940	1950	1960	1970
Blacks and others	55,447	63,917	74,840	84,381
Whites	51,826	78,247	112,205	130,592
Total	107,273	142,164	187,045	214,973
Percent Blacks and others	51.7%	45.0%	40.0%	39.3%

Jackson County Pascagoula (1940 population 5,900; 1970 population 27,264):

	1940	1950	1960	1970
Blacks and others	4,387	6,737	10,864	14,428
Whites	16,214	24,664	44,658	73,447
Total	20,601	31,401	55,522	87,875
Percent Blacks and others	21.3%	21.5%	19.6%	16.4%

Jones County Laurel (1940 population 20,598; 1970 population 24,145):

	1940	1950	1960	1970
Blacks and others	14,166	15,028	15,447	13,954
Whites	35,061	42,207	44,095	42,403
Total	49,227	57,235	59,542	56,357
Percent Blacks and others	28.8%	26.3%	25.9%	24.8%

Lauderdale County Meridian (1940 population 35,481; 1970 population 45,083):

	1940	1950	1960	1970
Blacks and others	22,812	23,376	23,484	20,901
Whites	35,435	40,795	67,119	67,087
Total	58,247	64,171	90,603	87,988
Percent Blacks and others	39.2%	36.4%	25.9%	23.8%

Lee County Tupelo (1940 population 8,212; 1970 population 20,471):

	1940	1950	1960	1970
Blacks and others	12,216	10,659	10,289	9,577
Whites	26,622	27,578	30,300	36,571
Total	38,838	38,237	40,589	46,148
Percent Blacks and others	31.5%	27.9%	25.3%	20.8%

Leflore County Greenwood (1940 population 14,767; 1970 population 22,400):

	1940	1950	1960	1970
Blacks and others	39,012	35,331	30,443	24,561
Whites	14,394	16,482	16,699	17,550
Total	53,406	51,813	47,142	42,111
Percent Blacks and others	73.0%	68.2%	64.6%	58.3%

Lowndes County Columbus (1940 population 13,645; 1970 population 25,795):

	1940	1950	1960	1970
Blacks and others	19,683	18,410	17,768	16,364
Whites	15,562	19,442	28,871	33,336
Total	35,245	37,852	46,639	49,700
Percent Blacks and others	55.8%	48.6%	38.1%	32.9%

Oktibbeha County Starkville (1940 population 4,900; 1970 population 11,369):

	1940	1950	1960	1970
Blacks and others	13,088	11,751	11,448	10,183
Whites	9,063	12,818	14,727	18,569
Total	22,151	24,569	26,175	28,752
Percent Blacks and others	59.1%	47.8%	43.7%	35.4%

Pike County McComb (1940 population 9,898; 1970 population 11,969):

	1940	1950	1960	1970
Blacks and others	15,711	15,709	15,408	13,868
Whites	19,291	19,428	19,655	17,945
Total	35,002	35,137	35,063	31,813
Percent Blacks and others	44.9%	44.7%	43.9%	43.6%

Warren County Vicksburg (1940 population 24,460; 1970 population 25,478):

	1940	1950	1960	1970
Blacks and others	22,285	20,092	19,759	18,507
Whites	17,310	19,524	22,447	26,474
Total	39,595	39,616	42,206	44,981
Percent Blacks and others	56.3%	50.7%	46.8%	41.1%

Washington County Greenville (1940 population 20,892; 1970 population 39,648):

	1940	1950	1960	1970
Blacks and others	49,008	47,068	43,399	38,778
Whites	18,568	23,436	35,239	31,803
Total	67,576	70,504	78,638	70,581
Percent Blacks and others	72.5%	66.8%	55.2%	54.9%

State of Mississippi

	Total Population	Whites	Blacks and Others	Percentage Black and Others
1940	2,183,796	1,106,327	1,077,469	49.3%
1950	2,178,914	1,188,632	990,282	45.4%
1960	2,178,141	1,257,546	920,595	42.3%
1970	2,216,994	1,393,339	823,655	37.2%

Bibliography

"Appreciation Day." *Newsweek*, 13 December 1965, 70.

Ayer, N.W. and Son, eds. *N.W. Ayer and Son's Directory [of] Newspapers and Periodicals*, 80th ed. Philadelphia: N.W. Ayer and Son, 1948.

———. *N.W. Ayer and Son's Directory [of] Newspapers and Periodicals*, 86th ed. Philadelphia: N.W. Ayer and Son, 1954.

———. *N.W. Ayer and Son's Directory [of] Newspapers and Periodicals*, 94th ed. Philadelphia: N.W. Ayer and Son, 1962.

———. *N.W. Ayer and Son's Directory [of] Newspapers and Periodicals*, 96th ed. Philadelphia: N.W. Ayer and Son, 1964.

———. *N.W. Ayer and Son's Directory [of] Newspapers and Periodicals*, 100th ed. Philadelphia: N.W. Ayer and Son, 1968.

Bagdikian, Ben H. "Editorial Responsibility in Times of Urban Disorder." In *The Media and the Cities*, ed. Charles Daly, 13–24. Chicago: University of Chicago Press, 1968.

Baradell, William Lang. "An Analysis of the Coverage Given by Five North Carolina Newspapers of Three Events in the Civil Rights Movement in the State." Master's thesis, University of North Carolina at Chapel Hill, 1990.

Baran, Stanley J., and Dennis K. Davis. *Mass Communication Theory: Foundations, Ferment and Future*. Belmont, Calif.: Wadsworth, 1995.

Barrett, Russell. *Integration at Ole Miss*. Chicago: Quadrangle Books, 1965.

Belfrage, Sally. *Freedom Summer*. New York: Viking Press, 1965.

"Belting Down One for the Road." *Nation*, 6 October 1962, 190.

Bennett, Lerone, Jr. "The White Media." In *The Media and the Cities*, ed. Charles Daly, 7–12. Chicago: University of Chicago Press, 1968.

Booker, Simeon. *Black Man's America*. Englewood Cliffs, N.J.: Prentice-Hall, 1964.

Boylan, James. "Birmingham Newspapers in Crisis." *Columbia Journalism Review* 2 (Summer 1963): 30–42.

Bramlett, Sharon A. "Southern vs. Northern Newspaper Coverage of a Race

Crisis—The Lunch Counter Sit-In Movement, 1960–1964: An Assessment of Press Social Responsibility." Ph.D. diss., Indiana University, 1987.

Braswell, Janet. "*American* Dates Back to 1800s." In *Mississippi Press Association 125th Anniversary Report*, 41. Jackson: Mississippi Press Association, 1991.

Breed, Warren. "Social Control in the Newsroom: A Functional Analysis." *Social Forces* (May 1955): 326–335.

Bruce, Beverlee. "Comment on Negro Reaction to Press Coverage." In *The Black American and the Press*, ed. Jack Lyle, 70–74. Los Angeles: Ward and Ritchie, 1968.

Butts, Charles. "Mississippi: The Vacuum and the System." In *Black, White and Gray: 21 Points of View on the Race Question*, ed. Bradford Daniel, 103–114. New York: Sheed and Ward, 1964.

Cagin, Seth, and Philip Dray. *We Are Not Afraid: The Story of Goodman, Schwerner and Chaney, and the Civil Rights Campaign for Mississippi*. New York: Bantam Books, 1991.

Carter, Hodding, Jr. *Lower Mississippi*. New York and London: Farrar and Rinehart, 1942.

———. *Southern Legacy*. Baton Rouge: Louisiana State University Press, 1950.

———. *Where Main Street Meets the River*. New York: Rinehart, 1953.

———. *First Person Rural*. Garden City, N.Y.: Doubleday and Company, 1963.

———. *So the Heffners Left McComb*. Garden City, N.Y.: Doubleday and Company, 1965.

Carter, Hodding, III. *The South Strikes Back*. Garden City, N.Y.: Doubleday and Company, 1959.

———. "The Wave beneath the Froth." In *Race and the News Media*, ed. Paul Fisher and Ralph Lowenstein, 1–10. New York: Praeger, 1967.

———. "Comment on the Coverage in the Domestic Press." In *The Black American and the Press*, ed. Jack Lyle, 38–41. Los Angeles: W. Ritchie Press, 1968.

———. Interview via e-mail with Susan Weill, 1999.

Carter, Roy E., Jr. "Segregation and the News: A Regional Content Study." *Journalism Quarterly* 34 (Winter 1957): 3–18.

———. "Racial Identification Effects upon the News Story Writer." *Journalism Quarterly* 36 (Summer 1959): 284–290.

Clark, Thomas D. *The Emerging South*, 2nd ed. New York: Oxford University Press, 1968.

———, and Albert D. Kirwan. *The South since Appomattox: A Century of Regional Change*. New York: Oxford University Press, 1967.

Clarksdale Press Register. July 1948; May and August 1954; September 1962; June, July and August 1964; April 1968.

"The *Clarksdale Press Register*." In *Mississippi Press Association 125th Anniversary Report*, 30. Jackson: Mississippi Press Association, 1991.

Colle, Royal D. "Negro Image in the Mass Media: A Case Study in Social Change." *Journalism Quarterly* 45 (Spring 1968): 55–60.

Columbus *Commercial Dispatch*. July 1948; May and August 1954; 15 September 1962; June, July and August 1964; April 1968.

Commission on Freedom of the Press. *A Free and Responsible Press—A General Report on Mass Communication: Newspapers, Radio, Motion Pictures, Magazines and Books*. Chicago: University of Chicago Press, 1947.

Conn, William Lance. "Crisis in Black and White: The McComb *Enterprise-Journal*'s Coverage of Racial News, 1961–1964." Master's thesis, University of Mississippi, 1991.

Corinth *Daily Corinthian*. July 1948; May and August 1954; September 1962; June, July and August 1964; April 1968.

Daly, Charles, ed. *The Media and the Cities*. Chicago: University of Chicago Press, 1968.

Daniel, Bradford, ed. *Black, White and Gray: Twenty-One Points of View on the Race Question*. New York: Sheed and Ward, 1964.

Davies, David R. "J. Oliver Emmerich and the McComb *Enterprise-Journal*: Slow Change in McComb, 1964." *Journal of Mississippi History* (February 1995): 1–24.

Davis, Dan. "State-wide Newspaper's Historic Commitment Spans 154 Years." In *Mississippi Press Association 125th Anniversary Report*, 47. Jackson: Mississippi Press Association, 1991.

"Dilemma in Dixie." *Time*, 20 February 1956, 76–81.

Dittmer, John. *Local People: The Struggle for Civil Rights in Mississippi*. Urbana: University of Illinois Press, 1994.

"Dixie Flamethrowers." *Time*, 4 March 1966, 64.

Doherty, Tim. "Red, White and Blue since 1917." In *Mississippi Press Association 125th Anniversary Report*, 41. Jackson: Mississippi Press Association, 1991.

"Edgar Harris Founded *Times-Leader* in 1928." In *Mississippi Press Association 125th Anniversary Report*, 81. Jackson: Mississippi Press Association, 1991.

Fisher, Paul L., and Ralph L. Lowenstein, eds. *Race and the News Media*. New York: Praeger, 1967.

Gandy, Joan. "Democrat Reports Natchez History 126 Years." In *Mississippi Press Association 125th Anniversary Report*, 61. Jackson: Mississippi Press Association, 1991.

Ghiglione, Loren. "Small-Town Journalism Has Some Big Ethical Headaches." In *Questioning Media Ethics*, ed. Bernard Rubin, 171–179. New York: Praeger, 1978.

Gilmore, Gene, and Robert Root. "Ethics for Newsmen." In *Ethics and the Press*, ed. John Merrill and Ralph Barney, 25–36. New York: Hastings House, 1975.

Gist, Noel P. "The Negro in the Daily Press." *Social Forces* 10 (March 1932): 405–411.

"Good-bye, Hambone." *Newsweek*, 22 July 1968, 56.

Goodwin, Doris Kearns. *Lyndon Johnson and the American Dream*. New York: St. Martin's Press, 1976.

Goodwin, H. Eugene. *Groping for Ethics in Journalism*. Ames: Iowa State University Press, 1983.

Graham, Hugh Davis. *Crisis in Print: Desegregation and the Press in Tennessee*. Nashville: Vanderbilt University Press, 1967.

Greenville *Delta Democrat-Times*. July 1948; May and August 1954; September 1962; June, July and August 1964; April 1968.

Greenwood Commonwealth. July 1948; May and August 1954; September 1962; June, July and August 1964; April 1968.

Greenwood *Morning Star*. July 1948; May and August 1954.

Grenada *Sentinel-Star*. July 1948; May and August 1954; 15 September–15 October 1962; June, July and August 1964; April 1968.

Griffin, John Howard. "Racist Sins of Christians." In *Black, White and Gray: 21 Points of View on the Race Question*, ed. Bradford Daniel, 430–432. New York: Sheed and Ward, 1964.

Gulfport *Daily Herald*. July 1948; May and August 1954; September 1962; June, July and August 1964; April 1968.

Hallin, Daniel. *The "Uncensored War": The Media and Vietnam*. New York: Oxford University Press, 1986.

Harkey, Ira B., Jr. *The Smell of Burning Crosses: An Autobiography of a Mississippi Newspaperman*. Jacksonville, Ill.: Harris-Wolfe, 1967.

Hattiesburg American. July 1948; May and August 1954; 15 September–15 October 1962; June, July and August 1964; April 1968.

Herbers, John. "Communique from Mississippi." *New York Times Magazine*, 8 November 1964, 34, 126–128.

"A History of Growth and Progress." In *Mississippi Press Association 125th Anniversary Report*, 75. Jackson: Mississippi Press Association, 1991.

Holloway, Harry. *The Politics of the Southern Negro*. New York: Random House, 1969.

Holt, Len. *The Summer That Didn't End*. New York: William Morrow, 1965.

Hooker, Robert W. "Race and the News Media in Mississippi: 1962–64." Master's thesis, Vanderbilt University, 1971.

Howell, Jesse, Jr. Unpublished telephone interview by Susan Weill, 1 July 1997.

Huey, Gary Lynn. "P.D. East: Southern Liberalism and the Civil Rights Movement, 1953–1971." Wilmington, Del.: Scholarly Resources, 1985.

Hulteng, John L. *The Messenger's Motive: Ethical Problems of the New Media*. Englewood Cliffs, N.J.: Prentice-Hall, 1976.

Hunt, George P. "The Racial Crisis and the News Media: An Overview." In *Race and the News Media*, ed. Paul Fisher and Ralph Lowenstein, 11–20. New York: Praeger, 1967.

Jackson *Clarion-Ledger*. July 1948; May and August 1954; 15 September–15 October 1962; June, July and August 1964; April 1968.

Jackson *Clarion-Ledger-News*. [Sunday combined] May and August 1954; 15 September–15 October 1962; June, July and August 1964; April 1968.

Jackson *Daily News*. July 1948; May and August 1954; 15 September–15 October 1962; June, July and August 1964; April 1968.

Johnston, Erle. *Mississippi's Defiant Years, 1953–1973: An Interpretive Documentary with Personal Experiences*. Forest, Miss.: Lake Harbor Publishers, 1990.

Kaul, Arthur J. "The Unraveling of America." In *The Press in Times of Crisis*, ed. Lloyd Chiasson, 169–187. Westport, Conn.: Greenwood Press, 1995.

———. "Hazel Brannon Smith." In *The Dictionary of Literary Biography*, vol. 127, ed. Perry Ashley, 291–301. Detroit: Gale Research, 1993.

Kerner Commission. *Report of the National Advisory Commission on Civil Disorders*. New York: Bantam, 1968.

Key, V.O., Jr. *Public Opinion and American Democracy*. New York: Alfred A. Knopf, 1961.

Klein, Woody. "News Media and Race Relations: A Self-Portrait." *Columbia Journalism Review* 7 (Fall 1968): 42–49.

Kolko, Gabriel. *Anatomy of a War: Vietnam, the United States, and the Modern Historical Experience*. New York: Pantheon Books, 1985.

Laurel Leader-Call. July 1948; May and August 1954; September 1962; June, July and August 1964; April 1968.

Lester, Paul Martin. "African-American Photo Coverage in Four U.S. Newspapers, 1937–1990." *Journalism Quarterly* 71 (Summer 1994): 380–394.

Lippmann, Walter. *Public Opinion*. New York: Harcourt, Brace, 1922.

Lively, Earl, Jr. *The Invasion of Mississippi*. Belmont, Mass.: American Opinion, 1963.

Loewen, James, and Charles Sallis, eds. *Mississippi: Conflict and Change*. New York: Pantheon Books, 1974.

Lord, Walter. *The Past That Would Not Die*. New York: Harper and Row, 1965.

Lyle, Jack, ed. *The Black American and the Press*. Los Angeles: W. Ritchie Press, 1968.

Mabee, Carlton. "Evolution of Non-Violence." *The Nation*, 21 August 1961, 78–81.

Marsh, Harry D. "Hodding Carter's Newspaper on School Desegregation, 1954–1955." *Journalism Monographs* 92 (May 1985).

Martindale, Carolyn. *The White Press and Black America*. Westport, Conn.: Greenwood Press, 1986.

McAdam, Doug. *Freedom Summer*. New York: Oxford University Press, 1988.

McComb *Enterprise Journal*. July 1948; May and August 1954; September 1962; June, July and August 1964; April 1968.

McMillen, Neil R. *The Citizens' Council: Organized Resistance to the Second Reconstruction, 1954–1964*. Urbana: University of Illinois Press, 1971.

———. *Dark Journey: Black Mississippians in the Age of Jim Crow*. Urbana: University of Illinois Press, 1990.

Melanson, Philip H. *The Murkin Conspiracy: An Investigation into the Assassination of Dr. Martin Luther King, Jr*. New York: Praeger, 1989.

Meridian Star. July 1948; May and August 1954; September 1962; June, July and August 1964; April 1968.

"The *Meridian Star*." In *Mississippi Press Association 125th Anniversary Report*, 58. Jackson: Mississippi Press Association, 1991.

Merrill, John C., and Ralph D. Barney, eds. *Ethics and the Press*. New York: Hastings House, 1975.

Methvin, Eugene H. "Objectivity and the Tactics of Terrorists." In *Ethics and the Press*, ed. John Merrill and Ralph Barney, 199–205. New York: Hastings House, 1975.

Mississippi Power and Light Company Economic Research Department. *Mississippi Statistical Summary of Population 1800–1980*. Jackson: Mississippi Power and Light Company, 1983.

Mississippi Press Association 125th Anniversary Report. Jackson: Mississippi Press Association, 1991.

"Moderation in Dixie." *Time*, 19 March 1965, 71.

Montgomery, Susan. "The Commonwealth: A 95-Year View." In *Mississippi Press*

Association 125th Anniversary Report, 40. Jackson: Mississippi Press Association, 1991.

Moody, Ann. *Coming of Age in Mississippi.* New York: Dial Press, 1968.

Natchez Democrat. July 1948; May and August 1954; September 1962; June, July and August 1964; April 1968.

Natchez *Times.* May and August 1954; September 1962.

Novak, Michael. "Why the Working Man Hates the Press." In *Ethics and the Press*, ed. John Merrill and Ralph Barney, 108–117. New York: Hastings House, 1975.

Oppenheimer, Martin. "The Genesis of the Southern Negro Movement: A Study in Contemporary Negro Protest." Ph.D. diss., University of Pennsylvania, 1963.

Paletz, David, and Robert Dunn. "Press Coverage of Civil Disorders: A Case Study of Winston-Salem, 1967." *Public Opinion Quarterly* 33 (Fall 1969): 328–335.

Pascagoula *Chronicle.* June, July and August 1964.

Pascagoula *Mississippi Press.* June, July and August 1964; April 1968.

Payne, Charles M. *I've Got the Light of Freedom.* Berkeley: University of California Press, 1995.

Pepper, William F. *Orders to Kill: The Truth behind the Murder of Martin Luther King.* New York: Carroll and Graf Publishers, 1995.

Pepper, William F. *The Truth behind the Murder of Martin Luther King.* New York: Carroll and Graf Publishers, 1995.

Peters, William. *The Southern Temper.* Garden City, N.Y.: Doubleday and Company, 1959.

Poston, Ted. "The American Negro and Newspaper Myths." In *Race and the News Media*, ed. Paul Fisher and Ralph Lowenstein, 63–72. New York: Praeger, 1967.

"Revolt in Mississippi." *Time*, 8 November 1954, 60.

Rubin, Bernard, ed. *Questioning Media Ethics.* New York: Praeger, 1978.

Sarratt, Reed. *The Ordeal of Desegregation: The First Decade.* New York: Harper and Row, 1966.

Schlesinger, Arthur M., Jr. *A Thousand Days: John F. Kennedy in the White House.* Greenwich, Conn.: Fawcett Publications, 1967.

Schwartz, Bernard, ed. *Statutory History of the United States: Civil Rights Part I.* New York: McGraw-Hill, 1970.

Select Committee on Assassinations, U.S. House of Representatives. *The Final Assassination Report.* New York: Bantam Books, 1979.

Sellers, James T. "A History of the Jackson State Times: An Agent of Change in a Closed Society." Ph.D. diss., University of Southern Mississippi, 1992.

Sentman, Mary Alice. "Black and White: Disparity in Coverage by *Life Magazine* from 1937 to 1972." *Journalism Quarterly* 60 (Fall 1983): 501–508.

Silver, James W. *Mississippi: The Closed Society.* New York: Harcourt, Brace and World, 1966.

Skates, John Ray, Jr. "A Southern Editor Views the National Scene: Frederick Sullens and the Jackson, Mississippi *Daily News.*" Ph.D. diss., Mississippi State University, 1965.

Smith, Frank E. *Congressman from Mississippi.* New York: Pantheon Books, 1964.
Starkville Daily News. September 1962; June, July and August 1964; April 1968.
Stempel, Guido H., III. "Visibility of Blacks in News and News-Picture Magazines." *Journalism Quarterly* 48 (Summer 1971): 337–339.
Sutherland, Elizabeth, ed. *Letters from Mississippi.* New York: McGraw-Hill, 1965.
Trimble, Mrs. Elliot. Unpublished telephone interview by Susan Weill, 7 September 1997.
Tupelo *Daily Journal.* July 1948; May and August 1954; September 1962; June, July and August 1964; April 1968.
U.S. Commission on Civil Rights. *Voting in Mississippi.* Washington, D.C.: Government Printing Office, 1965.
U.S. Department of Commerce, Bureau of the Census. *U.S. Census of Population: 1960.* Vol. 1, *Characteristics of the Population.* Part 26, *Mississippi.* Washington, D.C.: Government Printing Office, 1963.
Vicksburg Evening Post. July 1948; May and August 1954; September 1962; June, July and August 1964; April 1968.
Vicksburg Herald. July 1948; May and August 1954.
Vicksburg Post-Herald. [Sunday combined] July 1948; May and August 1954.
Watters, Pat, and Reese Cleghorn. *Climbing Jacob's Ladder: The Arrival of Negroes in Southern Politics.* New York: Harcourt, Brace and World, 1967.
Weill, Susan M. "African Americans and the White-Owned Mississippi Press: An Analysis of Coverage from 1944 to 1984." Master's thesis, Jackson State University, 1993.
West Point *Times Leader.* July 1948; May and August 1954; September 1962; June, July and August 1964; April 1968.
Williams, Edwin N. "Dimout in Jackson." *Columbia Journalism Review* 9 (Summer 1970): 56–58.
Williams, Juan. *Eyes on the Prize: America's Civil Rights Years, 1954–1965.* New York: Viking Press, 1987.
Williams, Roger M. "Newspapers in the South." *Columbia Journalism Review* 6 (Summer 1967): 26–35.
Woodward, C. Vann. *The Strange Career of Jim Crow.* New York: Oxford University Press, 1966.
The World Alamanac and Book of Facts, 125th ed. New York: St. Martin's Press, 1992.

Index

About the Author

SUSAN WEILL was a senior in a white high school in rural Mississippi when it merged with the local black high school in 1971, almost two decades after *Brown v. Board of Education* mandated the desegregation of the nation's public schools. Her experiences that year had a profound impact on her, and initiated three decades of research on race relations and the media. She is currently an Assistant Professor in the Communication Studies Department at the University of Alabama at Birmingham.